Inner Cleansing Cures

By Frank K. Wood and
The Editors of FC&A Medical Publishing

Notice:

This book is for information only. It does not constitute medical advice and should not be construed as such. We cannot guarantee the safety or effectiveness of any drug, treatment or advice mentioned. Some of these tips may not be effective for everyone.

A good doctor is the best judge of what medical treatment may be needed for certain conditions and diseases. We recommend in all cases that you contact your personal doctor or health care provider before taking or discontinuing any medications, or before treating yourself in any way.

Be kind and compassionate to one another, forgiving each other, just as in Christ, God forgave you.

Ephesians 4:32

My soul finds rest in God alone; my salvation comes from Him.

Psalm 62:1

FC&A Medical Publishing
103 Clover Green
Peachtree City, GA 30269

Produced by the staff of FC&A

Distributed to the trade by National Book Network

ISBN 1-932470-02-6

Contents

Introduction

Your doctor went to school for years. He put in his time as an intern and a resident. He keeps up with most of the headline-making medical news.

Thank goodness we have educated doctors to treat us when we have cancer, cataracts and health problems that we can't take care of alone.

Doctors are good at blood tests, surgery and prescription medicines.

They aren't so good at telling you how to avoid getting cancer or cataracts in the first place. And they often don't take the time to help you improve your arthritis and allergies with simple remedies you can do at home.

You're wasting your money when you go see your doctor when you don't need to. You're wasting your money *and* your time when your doctor isn't able to figure out why your head or your back or your stomach hurts all the time.

Now you have a book to fill in the holes in your health care. You possess a whole volume of *Inner Cleansing Cures.*

When you don't want to be prescribed another pill and you don't need surgery, count on the book to tell you what your doctor won't — like how to prevent hearing loss or get a better night's sleep.

You'll find out how you may be able to cut your breast cancer risk by changing the way you wear your bra. You'll discover vitamins to help calm your stress and anxiety and home remedies to get rid of hay-fever sniffles.

You'll find spicy, natural sinus relievers and tips to get rid of fatigue. You'll discover how to supercharge your memory, how to cure a headache, and how to treat an ankle sprain or a painful elbow.

And that's just the beginning.

We hope this book helps you as much as our books have helped customers like John Ciccarelli from Mississauga, Ontario. He says:

"I find it very informative and easy to read and understand. In the past month my blood pressure has lowered from 180/110 to 150/90 and is still on a downward trend, due mainly to information in that book."

Congratulations, John! You've got a lifetime of natural good health ahead of you, and we're glad to be part of it.

We don't let your doctor's education go to waste, though. If we think your fatigue, forgetfulness and irritability may be caused by an overactive thyroid, we send you to your doctor to get it checked.

We tell you to rush to your doctor at the first sign of shingles. You might need drugs to head off what can be permanent nerve damage. And we tell you when your sinus problems signal an infection that needs to be treated with prescription antibiotics.

Use our health tips along with your doctor's advice. Check with your doctor before you make a major change in your diet or lifestyle, and never quit taking prescription drugs without your doctor's approval.

With that warning said, we now welcome you to the world of *Inner Cleansing Cures.*

Good Health and God Bless!
The Editors of FC&A

Acne

Fighting acne flare-ups

If you think your days of fighting acne are over simply because you're beyond the teen-age years — guess again! Although acne usually shows up on boys and girls during puberty, those irritating whiteheads, pimples and cysts can plague you when you're an adult too.

Acne begins under the skin in the oil-producing "sebaceous glands." These glands are usually small and inactive until puberty, when hormone changes cause them to enlarge and secrete an oily substance known as sebum. The sebum builds up, plugs the hair follicles in the skin, the follicles swell, and you have acne. If bacteria grow in the oily sebum, the acne can become irritated, causing more swelling and inflammation.

So what can you do to prevent whiteheads and pimples from popping up on your face? Benzoyl peroxide is one effective remedy. Benzoyl peroxide is sold over the counter in gel, lotion, cream or pad forms. Using it once or twice a day can help unplug the blocked follicles. Your skin may appear red and dry at first. If the benzoyl peroxide continues to irritate your skin, however, this treatment may not be for you.

For more serious acne, you can take antibiotics, like tetracycline. Of course, antibiotics require a prescription. For severe acne, your doctor may prescribe isotretinoin (Accutane). Besides creams, antibiotics and medicines, you can fight acne with a few lifestyle changes.

Eat a healthy diet, but chocolate is OK! You probably have heard that you should avoid eating chocolate because it causes "zits." But clinical studies have shown no scientific evidence linking certain foods and acne. It is important to eat a well-balanced diet. You'll not only feel healthier, but your skin will look healthier as well.

Clean your face gently. Getting acne is not related to dirt. In fact, excessive scrubbing with harsh abrasives can actually make the condition worse. Wash oily skin with water and a mild, unscented soap like Dial, Ivory or Lever-2000. Don't use deodorant soaps.

Keep your hands off your face. Squeezing and picking at your pimples can lead to more redness and swelling.

Be aware of your environment. Avoid polluted and humid conditions whenever possible. Heavy sweating can aggravate your acne.

Make sure your makeup is water-based. Oil-based products will aggravate your skin condition. Also, watch out for suntan oils, hair gels and sprays.

If you make these simple changes in your skin care, you should see the results within two months. Don't give up too soon.

American Family Physician (50,1:89)

Altitude Sickness

Up, up and away without altitude sickness

Planning a vacation in the mountains? Dreaming about swooshing down the slopes or blazing new trails in the woods? If this is your first trip thousands of feet above sea level, you may want to keep some things in mind. Altitude sickness affects millions of people each year and turns many dream vacations into illness nightmares.

Many people tend to overlook altitude sickness as the reason for their ailments, as the symptoms are similar to those of the flu or the common cold. The low oxygen levels in the higher altitudes force your body to work harder to maintain the level of oxygen it needs. Shortness of breath, headaches, nausea, appetite loss and insomnia are symptoms to watch for when you first arrive at your mountain destination.

To avoid these ill feelings altogether, take a few simple precautions before you hit the slopes:

Don't try to conquer the master runs on your first day of vacation. Cutting your activities to just a half day on the first day will allow your body to adjust to the new altitude.

Drink more liquids than usual. Mountain air does not contain as much moisture as the air at sea level, so you lose moisture when you breathe. Drink enough extra water and juices so that your urine stays clear. Too much tea, coffee and alcohol can dehydrate your body, and alcohol will affect your coordination more quickly at higher altitudes.

Don't let yourself get too hungry. You want to make sure you get enough calories. A well-nourished body adjusts to changes better than a hungry one.

Don't smoke. Smoking decreases the amount of oxygen getting to your body and could harm you more the higher above sea level you go.

Some doctors will prescribe a drug called acetazolamide to prevent altitude sickness. Side effects of this drug include increased urination and tingling or numbness in the toes and fingers. Skiers, in particular, should be sure to wear a sunscreen of at least Sun Protection Factor 15 while taking acetazolamide. The drug makes you more sensitive to the sun's rays.

If you do start feeling sick, don't put off seeing a doctor. If you can't get to a doctor, descend several thousand feet, if possible, to see if the symptoms go away. Continue to drink plenty of liquids and get lots of rest. If you do not feel better in a couple of days, especially if you're coughing constantly; vomiting; or feeling confused, dizzy and short of breath, get medical care quickly. You can get fluid buildup in your lungs or brain if you do not seek help.

The Physician and Sportsmedicine (23,2:87)

Alzheimer's Disease

Researchers shed new light on zinc's link to Alzheimer's

Just a few years ago, researchers believed that low levels of zinc in the body might contribute to the development of Alzheimer's. However, when scientists at the University of Melbourne in Australia tested the zinc theory, they got disastrous and totally unexpected results.

A handful of people diagnosed with Alzheimer's were given a daily dose of 100 milligrams of zinc, approximately seven times the Recommended Daily Allowance (RDA). After only two days, the mental condition of all the study participants had deteriorated considerably. To avoid doing further damage, the scientists immediately stopped the study.

Test tubes reveal you should take it easy on the zinc. Recently, Harvard investigators took up the zinc question again, this time using test tubes instead of human subjects to answer their questions. The results support the startling findings of the Australian study, and researchers now recommend that if you have Alzheimer's or are at risk for the disease, you should take it easy on the zinc.

Of 26 dietary trace minerals tested on human blood, only large amounts of zinc caused proteins to clump together and form amyloid proteins, cell-destroying substances found in the brains of people with Alzheimer's.

Even aluminum, a longtime Alzheimer's suspect, had no effect on the amyloid proteins. These sticky proteins are believed to attach themselves to and destroy brain cells, causing characteristic signs of Alzheimer's, such as memory loss and loss of muscle control.

Don't avoid normal amounts of zinc. Researchers believe that normal amounts of zinc found in foods, or the amounts contained in daily supplements, don't appear to pose any threat.

But people who already have Alzheimer's or have a history of the disease in their families shouldn't overdo their zinc intake. Of course, if your doctor has prescribed extra zinc, follow his orders. In fact, researchers say you shouldn't avoid zinc in your diet or in supplements because it's necessary to sustain a healthy body.

Zinc works with red blood cells to remove carbon dioxide from your body; aids in healing of wounds; promotes cell repair and cell growth; helps maintain a normal level of vitamin A in the blood; and maintains normal senses of taste and smell. So don't avoid zinc in your diet or as a part of supplements; it's too important to your overall health. Just avoid taking extra zinc-only supplements.

Natural sources of zinc include egg yolks, fish, milk, black strap molasses, soybeans, whole-grain products, wheat germ, turkey and sunflower seeds.

You should be able to easily meet the 8 to 11 mg RDA by eating a well-rounded diet.

American Health (14,1:79)
Complete Guide to Vitamins, Minerals and Supplements, Fisher Books, Tucson, Ariz.
Science (265,5177:1365)

Aluminum in common foods and drinks may cause Alzheimer's

Everyone dreads Alzheimer's disease, or senile dementia, and for good reason. It affects about one out of every three people by the time they reach their 80s. The mind-robbing disease usually strikes between the ages of 40 and 60, progressing over a period of months or years to the point where you can't recall the names of your children or how to brush your teeth.

If you knew anything you could do to prevent it from happening to you, you would try it. That's one reason everyone jumped on the bandwagon when researchers discovered large amounts of aluminum in the brain tissues of Alzheimer's victims.

Does the slow accumulation of aluminum in the brain cause Alzheimer's disease? Should we avoid aluminum soft-drink cans, aluminum cookware and even our tap water if its aluminum content is higher than it should be?

After 30 years of research, the jury is still out. While some researchers found excessive aluminum in the brain tissues of Alzheimer's sufferers, other scientists said the aluminum came from chemical agents the researchers used to analyze the brain tissue.

Studies show a weak link. Other studies do seem to point to a weak link between Alzheimer's and aluminum:

➤ Population studies have shown that people were more likely to have Alzheimer's if they had been drinking from public water treated with aluminum sulfates to make the water clearer.

➤ Animal studies seem to show an aluminum/Alzheimer's link. When researchers injected aluminum into the brains of rabbits and cats, changes in their behavior and their brain mimicked changes in Alzheimer's victims.

➤ People with kidney failure who have undergone dialysis have shown a loss of intellectual function similar to Alzheimer's when the dialysis fluid is made from water containing large amounts of aluminum. This condition is called dialysis dementia.

➤ An experimental drug that draws aluminum out of the body seems to slow down the progression of Alzheimer's disease.

Researchers seem to agree that there's no doubt that aluminum is poisonous to our bodies and our brains if it gets into our nervous system. It's just that aluminum is present everywhere on the earth, and our bodies are expert at keeping the harmful metal out. We get rid of aluminum through our urine and

Has your doctor told you ...

Aspirin therapy may prevent Alzheimer's disease

You may have heard that taking an aspirin every day can ward off stroke and heart disease, but now there may be another unexpected benefit.

Some Alzheimer's experts believe that aspirin, ibuprofen, naproxen and other nonsteroidal anti-inflammatory drugs (NSAIDs) commonly recommended for arthritis can prevent Alzheimer's disease.

That's the finding of a recent study of 50 pairs of elderly twins. Only one of each set of twins had used NSAIDs. That twin was less likely to develop Alzheimer's disease or developed it years later than the other twin.

You need to talk to your doctor before you begin taking an aspirin a day, though. NSAIDs can cause ulcers and bleeding in your stomach, so you have to weigh your individual risk of heart disease, stroke and Alzheimer's against your risk of stomach problems and bleeding.

Archives of Internal Medicine (154,1:42)
Medical Abstracts Newsletter (14,11:6)
U.S. Pharmacist (15,5:62)

feces, and our brains have a mechanism called the "blood-brain barrier" that is supposed to prevent certain substances like aluminum from entering.

Most scientists believe that our brains couldn't possibly absorb enough aluminum to cause Alzheimer's, but some scientists are still holding on to the aluminum/Alzheimer's link.

Watch for big aluminum sources. If you want to be on the safe side and avoid taking in large amounts of aluminum, concern yourself with the big sources of aluminum:

➤ Some antacids contain 200 times more aluminum than we would normally consume in one day. Watch out for these.

➤ Don't take buffered aspirin with orange juice. The combination gives you a substance called aluminum citrate. This form of aluminum is absorbed by your body at five times the rate of normal aluminum.

➤ Avoid aerosol antiperspirants. The aluminum in aerosol form may be more readily absorbed into the brain through the nose.

Other, smaller sources of aluminum:

➤ Canned, noncola soft drinks contain almost six times the aluminum as bottled, noncola soft drinks. Canned cola drinks contain three times the aluminum of bottled cola drinks. Canned beer doesn't have a high aluminum content.

➤ Aluminum pots and pans can leach a good deal of aluminum into acidic foods. When boiling water or baking fish or a cake, little aluminum travels from the pan to the food. Acidic foods such as rhubarb and black currants take in a lot more aluminum from cookware.

➤ Some public water sources contain more than the recommended amount of aluminum. The World Health Organization and the European Economic Community recommend a maximum aluminum concentration of 7.4 mcM/L in drinking water. You can take care of this aluminum source by drinking pure well or bottled spring water.

➤ Small amounts of aluminum can be found in scores of other products: cosmetics, paper products, foil and prepackaged foods, to name a few. You may lose your mind more quickly by trying to avoid all these products than by ingesting the aluminum they contain.

Canadian Journal of Public Health (83,2:97)
Food Safety Notebook (3,12:111)
Medical Tribune (33,22:6 and 33,14,17)
Medical World News (33,12:12)
Taber's Cyclopedic Medical Dictionary, F.A. Davis Co., Philadelphia
The Johns Hopkins Medical Letter: Health After 50 (5,1:8)
The Lancet (343,8904:993)
University of California at Berkeley Wellness Letter (9,7:1)

Angina

Angina: Easing the ache

You had a stressful day at the office. Then you came home and ate a huge dinner. You decided the extra helping of dessert was OK because you were going to finish off the evening by mowing the lawn. Now you've barely gotten the lawn mower cranked when that tight and heavy feeling grips your chest and you know you're having an angina attack. It feels like a heart attack, but your doctor has told you not to worry — that the pain usually goes away with rest and angina doesn't permanently damage your heart. But even if it's not a medical emergency, angina is a warning sign that your heart isn't getting enough oxygen, and you could have a heart attack someday soon if you don't take care of yourself.

Stress, a heavy meal or suddenly exercising an out-of-shape body can all trigger an angina attack. When you've been diagnosed with angina, you need to make a few lifestyle changes to control your condition. Sometimes these changes can make the difference between getting rid of angina completely or having to undergo surgery. Here's what to do:

Schedule regular 30-minute walks. Although angina is sometimes triggered by overexertion, all exercise won't hurt you. Start gradually and increase to a level that you feel comfortable with. Even a small amount of exercise — walking at a moderate pace for 30 minutes, two to three days a week — can make a big difference in your health. If you exercise in extremely hot or cold weather, dress appropriately and limit the amount of time spent outdoors.

Give your heart a break: Stop smoking! Smoking makes it harder for the heart to do its work — namely, to pump blood throughout your body.

Get a handle on stress. Try to avoid tight deadlines and overcrowded schedules. Ask for help instead of trying to do everything yourself. If you can't get rid of your stressors, learn stress management. Try these two exercises:

➤ Relax all your muscles for 20 minutes twice a day.
➤ Breathe deeply and concentrate on a pleasant thought when something stressful comes your way.

Control your blood pressure. Take the blood-pressure medicine your doctor has prescribed you. Avoid over-the-counter drugs that may raise your heart rate and blood pressure, such as diet pills and decongestants. Look to see if the medicine you buy lists high blood pressure as a side effect. You can also lower your blood pressure with a low-fat, high-fiber, low-salt diet.

Eat small meals. Large meals make your digestive system and your heart work harder. Eat several smaller meals rather than three big meals a day. Take it easy after eating and try not to overdo it.

Shed pounds and you may shed your angina too. If you've always wanted to, now is the time to lose weight. A good weight-loss program should also limit your fat intake, which is doubly good for your heart. Sometimes losing weight can make angina go away altogether.

If you're going to drink alcohol, do so in moderation. Too much alcohol raises your heart rate, a definite no-no for angina sufferers.

Always carry your nitroglycerin with you. If you think that a particular activity, such as sex, may trigger angina, take nitroglycerin before you begin. As always, carefully follow your doctor's instructions about medicines prescribed for your angina. With these few simple steps you can put yourself back on the mend and get a healthful boost in the bargain.

Ischemic Heart Disease: Angina Pectoris, Scientific American Medicine, New York
Understanding Angina, American Heart Association, 7272 Greenville Ave., Dallas, Texas 75231

Has your doctor told you ...

Angina suit offers relief for chest pains

Is your angina pain so severe that you've been considering surgery? Don't go under the knife yet. Another option may be available — a pulsating body suit. The suit isn't likely to win you any fashion contests. In fact, you probably would never leave the house in it. But it seems to be a safe and effective way to treat angina pain.

The "suit" actually consists of cuffs that wrap around your arms, legs and buttocks. When your heart expands, the cuffs fill with air and squeeze extra blood to your heart — which is just what your heart needs if you have angina. When your heart contracts, the cuffs deflate. That helps the heart do its job of pumping blood back to the rest of your body.

The suit has been approved by the FDA and is marketed by Future Medical Products Inc. of Hauppauge, N.Y. Its cost is about one-sixth that of surgery and about a third of angioplasty. Ask your doctor for more information on the pulsating body suit. The new treatment may suit you to a T.

Medical Tribune for the Family Physician (35,9:22)

Ankle Sprain

How to relieve the pain of a sprain

Carla Lackey and her husband spotted the perfect Memorial Day adventure in their local newspaper — a trip down a nearby river with a community group of canoeists.

When the Lackey's rented canoe turned over in some rapids, leaving Carla scraped and bruised, she began to feel a little less adventuresome. By the time she limped back to the car that night, she wished they'd stayed home and played Monopoly.

Carla's scrapes quickly began to heal, but the pain in her lower leg wouldn't go away. And the big swollen bruise below her ankle worried her. Finally, she visited her doctor.

He diagnosed her condition right away. When Carla fell out of the canoe, her foot was stuck for just a moment — long enough to sprain her ankle.

He gave her a list of exercises, and she was back to normal in a couple of weeks — almost, but not quite, ready for another holiday adventure.

If you sprain your ankle, whether you fall off a curb or out of a canoe, here's what you should do.

For the first two days, stay off your feet. If you have to walk, use a cane or a crutch on the side that's not injured. That way, you can lean away and take weight off the hurt foot.

Ice it. Put an ice pack on your ankle for about 20 minutes three or four times a day.

Do a figure-eight wrap. Wrap your ankle in an elastic bandage to control swelling and to support and protect it, especially if you must walk around.

Start wrapping at your toes, make a figure eight at the ankle, and continue wrapping loosely about six inches up the leg. Don't wrap so tightly that your toes go numb or turn red. Wear the bandage as long as your ankle hurts when you try to walk.

Put your ankle above your heart. You need to keep your swollen ankle propped above the level of your heart if you can. Stretch out on your sofa with your foot on a pillow.

Take a "contrast bath." If your ankle is still swollen after a few days, try a contrast bath twice a day. Put your foot in a tub of cold water for one minute, then move to a tub of warm water for two minutes. Do this for 15 minutes, gently moving your foot up and down in the water all the while.

12

Give it support. Since you risk another sprain as long as your ankle is weak, continue to support it with sturdy shoes or boots even after the pain is gone. Wear a bandage or brace when you plan to walk or exercise vigorously.

Roll your foot five to 10 times a day. This exercise will strengthen the muscles that support your ankle. First, remove any bandage or brace and let your leg hang freely off a bench, sturdy table or tall chair. Roll your foot in a circle at least three or four times. Make both clockwise and counterclockwise circles.

Rock the night away. When your ankle begins to feel stronger, improve your strength, flexibility and balance with a "rockerboard":

➤ Cut a croquet ball (or other round, hard ball) in half and glue it to a small board.

➤ Find a short platform — the same height as the rockerboard. Stand with your uninjured foot on the platform and your injured foot on the flat part of the rockerboard. Evenly distribute your weight between both feet.

➤ Moving very slowly, rock your sprained ankle to the front and back and from side to side several times.

Stand like a stork. Put all your weight on the sore leg, keeping your other foot raised slightly above the floor. Maintain this position for a few minutes.

A good time to do this exercise is when you brush your teeth in the morning and evening. Repeat this exercise for seven to 10 days, then practice the same exercise with your eyes closed. Continue the exercises until you can easily maintain your balance on your injured leg.

Take the stairs — backward. You'll notice that pointing your toes toward your head can be painful for weeks after a sprain. To regain flexibility, try to climb three flights of stairs a day, backward. Keep doing this until you're completely painfree.

Don't push so hard. Some people spend half their lives in an ankle brace because they sprain it again and again. If you have a chronic ankle sprain, you may be pushing too hard and too long when you exercise.

If you walk or work out until you're exhausted or suddenly start to run faster than you normally do, you're putting yourself at risk for a sprain.

The muscles that support the ankle are particularly vulnerable to fatigue.

Postgraduate Medicine (94,2:091)
The American Journal of Sports Medicine (21,6:805)
The Physician and Sportsmedicine (21,11:43 and 22,5:40)

Arthritis

Beat arthritis with B vitamins

If you're tired of spending big bucks on doctors and drugs to relieve your arthritis pain, we've got great news for you. Vitamin B supplements offer all the pain relief of traditional prescription arthritis medicines at a fraction of the cost. The best news of all — there are no side effects.

Dr. Margaret Flynn, a certified medical nutritionist in the department of family and community medicine at the University of Missouri in Columbia, has found that taking a daily supplement of folic acid and cobalamin (two common B vitamins) can relieve the pain and tenderness of osteoarthritis.

Wear-and-tear arthritis needs new remedy. Often called wear-and-tear arthritis, osteoarthritis occurs when cartilage (the elastic tissue that lines joints) deteriorates.

When you move a joint that doesn't have this protective cartilage, the bones rub directly together and cause pain. Osteoarthritic bones also grow thicker and develop lumps, making joints stiff and difficult to move. Commonly affected joints include the hands, hips, knees and spine.

Doctors may prescribe nonsteroidal anti-inflammatory drugs (NSAIDs), corticosteroid injections and even surgery to relieve the pain and swelling of osteoarthritis. While these treatments may or may not work, their side effects can be dangerous and long-lasting.Intrigued by earlier studies linking arthritis and diet, Dr. Flynn and her associates requested and received funding from the Wallace Genetic Foundation to study the effect of B vitamins on people with osteoarthritis in their hands.

B vitamins worked better than drugs. After two months, the researchers found that people who received a daily supplement containing 6,400 micrograms (mcg) of folic acid (B9) and 20 mcg of cobalamin (B12) had as much gripping power in their hands as people who used NSAIDs.

And people who used the supplements had fewer tender joints than people who used NSAIDs. However, the pain did not disappear immediately. The researchers recommended that the participants use acetaminophen (Tylenol) when necessary. Although this study only examined how the supplements affected osteoarthritis of the hands, a previous study indicates that the supplements work well on other arthritic joints too.

Big money savings. These findings mean significant savings in money and health for arthritis sufferers, especially for people who take prescription NSAIDs. Using the vitamin supplements instead of NSAIDs, you'll save from $200 to

$800 per year, depending on what type of NSAID your doctor prescribes. (Prices may vary from region to region.) Unlike NSAIDs, the vitamin supplements did not cause any side effects. People who have taken NSAIDs for any period of time probably already know about the nightmares of NSAIDs, including ulcers, colitis, kidney and liver failure and even death.

You'll need a prescription. We don't recommend that you try vitamin supplementation on your own. You will need to get your doctor to write a prescription for the supplements and have him supervise your treatment, at least initially. "If you don't get a prescription, you'll have to take a lot of pills," says Dr. Flynn. Most pharmacies and herb shops don't carry folate and cobalamin supplement combinations. While cobalamin is fairly easy to purchase in the recommended doses, folic acid presents a problem.

The largest dose of folic acid that you can buy over the counter is 800 mcg. In a drugstore, you might pay $4.00 for 100 folic acid tablets.

This makes it easy to get the RDA of 400 mcg a day.

Remember that the Institute of Medicine recommends you don't get more than 1,000 mcg of folate in a day.

Watch out for side effects. Another reason you'll want to have a doctor's supervision is that some people experience side effects to large amounts of vitamins. Although none of the people in this study had any side effects, some people may have reactions to large amounts of folic acid.

Taking folic acid supplements can mask pernicious anemia. This disorder, which interferes with your body's ability to absorb vitamin B12, can lead to permanent nerve damage if it is not treated promptly.

Pernicious anemia is a rare condition, but if you or your doctor feel you may be at risk, you should have a test to measure the B12 levels in your body before you begin vitamin supplements.

Folic acid may hinder the effectiveness of medicines used to treat seizures. If you take these medicines, you should be closely supervised by your doctor if you decide to try B vitamin supplements.

There also has been some concern that folic acid may interfere with the uptake of zinc. Although the supplemental doses of folic acid are high, researchers don't think they are large enough to interfere with your body's absorption of zinc. Overall, the benefits of folic acid far outweigh possible side effects. In fact, most of the people who participated in Dr. Flynn's breakthrough study were so impressed with the results that they decided to continue using the vitamin supplements to treat their osteoarthritis.

So go ahead. Give B vitamins a try. You've got nothing to lose and everything to gain.

American Journal of Clinical Nutrition (50,2:353)
Food, Nutrition and Health (18,5:3)
Journal of the American College of Nutrition (13,4:351)

Ease arthritis with arnica

Want to test your knowledge of herbs with a short quiz? Then see if you know which herb relieves pain from bruises, sprains and aches; eases hemorrhoid pain; helps heal scrapes and cuts; stops the itching from insect bites; and soothes the discomfort of arthritis. Know the answer?

Go to the head of the class if you said arnica, one of the best medicinal herbs for treatment of external pain. A hardy perennial, its beautiful, large orange and yellow flowers bloom throughout the summer months. Widely found in Europe and in the northwestern and eastern areas of the United States, arnica has been used for centuries as an effective, safe external treatment.

Arnica

Use on the outside only! Remember, the emphasis is on external. If swallowed, arnica is poisonous, causing elevated blood pressure and cardiac arrest. But used externally in the form of moist compresses, it offers relief from a wide variety of ailments.

Get natural antibiotic action. Why is arnica so effective? Research has shown that it speeds the healing of cuts and bruises because of its antibiotic effect. It also increases capillary (the smallest blood vessel) circulation.

This is the reason moist arnica compresses are recommended for the pain and inflammation associated with hemorrhoids. And according to researchers, using arnica compresses on joints affected by chronic arthritis brings relief from soreness and stiffness because it acts like a painkiller.

Make an arnica compress. Arnica tincture is available at health-food stores or pharmacies that sell natural and homeopathic medicines.

To make your own solution for use in compresses, dilute a tablespoon of arnica tincture in two cups of water. Soak gauze pads or other clean, highly absorbent cloths and apply to the wound, bruise, rash or arthritic joint.

For treatment of hemorrhoids, apply the compress to the inflamed area and reapply after each bowel movement.

Arnica gel is also available and is best used as an ointment for relieving the pain of arthritis and bruises, as well as insect bites.

Try arnica compresses for relief from minor external aches and discomfort.

Watch out for a rash. But keep in mind that some people are sensitive to the compound helenalin, one of arnica's ingredients, and may get a mild rash.

If you develop a rash, discontinue use and see your doctor. And always consult your doctor for advice on treatment of chronic or prolonged painful conditions.

Herbal Medicine, Beaconsfield Publishers, Beaconsfield, England
King's American Dispensatory, Eclectic Medical Publications, Sandy, Ore.
The Honest Herbal, The Haworth Press, Binghamton, N.Y.

Combat gout with a low-purine diet

Some people may not be aware that gout is a type of arthritis. Gout mostly strikes men over the age of 40. It occurs when too much uric acid builds up in the blood and then lodges in a joint, usually the big toe.

Its symptoms are usually a very sore, swollen big toe. The symptoms can come on very suddenly, virtually overnight. The attack can last for just a few days and go away, but it may come back and be worse the next time.

Why the big toe? You may be wondering why gout prefers the big toe. It's because the toes are just a little cooler than the rest of the body. The uric acid forms crystals more easily in a cooler environment. The wear and tear on your feet from walking every day may also contribute to it. Gout can attack other areas, including the shoulders, elbows, wrists, fingers, spine, pelvis and some organs of the body.

Pass by the purines. Unlike osteoarthritis and rheumatoid arthritis, things that cause gout are a little easier to pinpoint. Being overweight and drinking too much alcohol on a regular basis are known to contribute to uric acid buildup.

Also, eating too many foods high in "purines" could cause gout or worsen its symptoms. The body converts purines into uric acid. Foods high in purines include:

➤ liver	➤ kidneys
➤ brains	➤ anchovies
➤ sardines	➤ scallops
➤ peas	➤ dried beans
➤ asparagus	➤ cauliflower
➤ mushrooms	➤ spinach

Drink six to eight glasses of water a day. Water dilutes uric acid and aids its removal by the kidneys.

Blood pressure drugs can cause gout. In some cases, gout may be caused by thiazide diuretics — drugs used to treat high blood pressure. This form of gout usually attacks older women who may have poor kidney function. The joints of the hands and knees are usually involved. If you are taking a thiazide diuretic and you get severe pain in your hands or knees, you should be checked for gout.

Bowes and Church's Food Values of Portions Commonly Used, 15th ed., HarperCollins Publishers, New York
FDA Consumer (29,2:19)
Western Journal of Medicine (150,4:419)

Special diet for arthritis

The role of diet in arthritis is a controversial subject. Some doctors do not believe diet is an important factor. The American College of Rheumatology's position is that nutritional therapy is "experimental." But even this organization agrees that it's worth looking into.

Go vegetarian. A number of studies seem to indicate that rheumatoid arthritis symptoms improve when people change to a vegetarian diet. In one study, participants fasted for a week and then ate a carefully controlled diet for about five months.

The diet in this first phase included foods such as herbal tea, vegetable broth, garlic, and extracts from carrots, beets and celery. Later they were allowed to add foods back into their diets one at a time. But they continued to avoid meat, fish, eggs, dairy products, citrus fruits, refined sugar, alcoholic beverages, coffee, tea, and foods containing gluten such as wheat, oats, barley and rye.

The results of this study were surprising. Pain and swelling decreased, and grip strength increased. There were also improvements in the participants' blood tests. The diet seemed very successful because after a year their symptoms were still improved.

Feel better when you fast? You may have food allergies. This study seems to suggest that food allergies may be a cause of rheumatoid arthritis. About half of the study participants believed they had certain food allergies. Most of them actually felt better while they were fasting, and they got worse when they started eating again.

If you have arthritis, you may want to consider whether food allergies are aggravating your symptoms. Pay particular attention to foods you don't digest well or that cause any unusual symptoms. But don't fast or drastically change your diet without consulting your doctor. If you have a known food allergy, ask your doctor how it might affect your arthritis symptoms.

Fatty diets at fault again. A study done on mice suggests a link between osteoarthritis and diet. A group of mice was fed a diet high in saturated fat. Another group was fed a diet high in unsaturated fat. The group that ate saturated fat developed more severe cases of osteoarthritis.

British Journal of Rheumatology (32,6:507)
The Lancet (338,8772:899)

Arthritis impostors exposed

Sometimes joint pain that seems like arthritis is actually caused by something else entirely. That is why it's called "false" arthritis. A doctor can do specific tests to determine whether you have real arthritis or a mimic.

It could be a curable illness. Among the imposters is the tiny human parvovirus. It causes a curable illness that seems like arthritis. The illness is called "chronic arthropathy" to distinguish it from arthritis.

Symptoms include a flu-like sickness and stiff joints. Those most vulnerable to getting human parvovirus are unborn babies and people with AIDS, chronic anemia or sickle cell anemia.

It could be food poisoning. The food poisoning sickness called "salmonella," which is caused by bacteria, can also cause joint inflammation. But the arthritis-like symptoms may not appear until after the salmonella illness is over. Doctors can diagnose it because of the presence of "antibodies," which are produced by the body in response to an attack by a foreign organism.

It could be a drug reaction. Strangely, some prescription drugs can cause joint pain that seems like arthritis. These drugs are listed on pages 20 and 21.

If you are taking any prescription drug and begin to get symptoms of arthritis, see your doctor. It may be true arthritis, or it may be a drug reaction.

Research Resources Reporter (15,8:1)
The Lancet (339,8801:1096)

A Natural Alternative

More herbal healing for arthritis

The most controversial self-help treatments for arthritis are herbal remedies. Why all the controversy?

Perhaps because herbs are so simple and natural, they seem threatening to the traditional medical community. Or maybe promoters of herbal treatments tend to exploit the fact that traditional medicine hasn't found a cure for arthritis. Either way, there are some treatments that work, despite all the controversy.

You may want to include herbal remedies in your plan for dealing with arthritis. Just use caution and discuss any treatments you are considering with your doctor. You should always discuss any treatments you take on your own with your doctor, even for simple things like colds and flu.

Tripterygium. A traditional remedy from China called tripterygium ("Thunder God Vine") has been studied by American researchers as a treatment for joint pain. An extract of the plant that is taken in pill form seems to decrease inflammation in rheumatoid arthritis, lupus and psoriasis.

Chinese studies have shown dramatic decreases in pain and other symptoms in people treated for 12 weeks. Mild side effects, such as a rash and diarrhea, were not serious enough to stop treatment. This plant grows wild in China, but it may be hard to find in an American herb shop.

Gammalinoleic acid. Another plant extract that may be useful in treating rheumatoid arthritis is gammalinoleic acid. It is found in borage seed oil and evening primrose oil.

In a 24-week study, this substance reduced joint inflammation. Although it is available in health-food stores, the Food and Drug Administration hasn't approved its use as a medicine.

Colchicine. Colchicine is a powerful old-time remedy for gout that has been used for centuries. It comes from the autumn crocus plant, which is native to Great Britain and Europe.

The Food and Drug Administration has approved its use in the United States as a generic prescription drug to treat and other inflammatory diseases. However, it should be used with extreme caution because it can be very toxic, causing nausea and diarrhea.

Capsaicin. Capsaicin is another very useful and popular herbal remedy. It comes from red peppers, but you can't get relief by eating them. You rub a cream containing capsaicin on aching joints and muscles. It deadens local nerves and, when used regularly, may reduce the amount of drugs you take for pain. You can buy capsaicin cream over the counter at your local pharmacy.

Other arthritis remedies your local herb shop may carry are black cherry juice concentrate, yucca and alfalfa.

Arthritis and Rheumatism (34,10:1274)
Geriatrics (44,7:14)
Annals of Internal Medicine (119,9:867)
Journal Watch (12,11:84)
FDA Consumer (29,2:22)
The Lawrence Review of Natural Products, Facts and Comparisons, St. Louis, Mo.

Generic drug name	Common brand name	What drug is for
acyclovir	Zovirax	kills viruses
amiloride	Midamor	reduces fluid retention
azathioprine	Imuran	suppresses immune system
carbamazepine	Tegretol	treats seizures
didanosine	Videx	kills viruses
doxycycline	Doryx, Vibramycin	kills bacteria
ethambutol	Myambutol	treats tuberculosis
famotidine	Pepcid	treats ulcers
hydralazine	Apresazide	treats high blood pressure
hydrochlorothiazide	Esidrix, Oretic	reduces fluid retention
hydroflumethiazide	Diucardin	treats high blood pressure
isotretinoin	Accutane	treats acne
lovastatin	Mevacor	treats high cholesterol
methylphenidate	Ritalin	treats attention deficit disorder and excessive sleepiness
metolazone	Zaroxolyn	reduces fluid retention
metronidazole	Flagyl	kills bacteria and parasites
mexiletine	Mexitil	treats irregular heartbeat
minocycline	Minocin	kills bacteria
neostigmine	Prostigmin	stimulates muscles
nicardipine	Cardene	treats high blood pressure
nicotine	Habitrol, Nicoderm	treats cigarette addiction
nifedipine	Adalat, Procardia	treats high blood pressure

Generic drug name	Common brand name	What drug is for
ofloxacin	Floxin	kills bacteria
olsalazine	Dipentum	treats colitis
paroxetine	Paxil	treats depression
penicillamine	Cuprimine	treats rheumatoid arthritis
pergolide	Permax	treats Parkinson's disease
phenytoin	Dilantin	treats seizures
pindolol	Visken	treats high blood pressure
piroxicam	Feldene	treats inflammation
pravastatin	Pravachol	treats high cholesterol
prazepam	Centrax	treats anxiety
sulfamethoxazole	Gantanol	kills bacteria
sulfamethoxazole with trimethoprim	Bactrim, Septra	kills bacteria
sulfisoxazole	Gantrisin	kills bacteria
timolol	Blocadren	treats high blood pressure

Exercise relieves arthritis pain

Years ago, doctors didn't advise people with arthritis to exercise. They thought that too much activity would cause the arthritis to get worse. But studies have shown that moderate, carefully planned exercise programs really help most people with arthritis.

Exercise can reduce the amount of medication needed to control pain and increase strength and flexibility. It may even delay or prevent arthritis from developing in other joints.

The most important principle to remember when exercising is to *respect your pain.* Even while you are trying to work around your pain and distract it, you have to stay aware of it. Pain should stop when you stop exercising. If it doesn't, especially if you still hurt the next day, you need to cut back on your exercise intensity.

The Arthritis Foundation recognizes a variety of different exercises that are helpful to people with arthritis. These exercises fall into three main groups:

range-of-motion, strengthening and endurance. We will examine each kind and see how they work together to make a well-rounded exercise program.

Keep your joints flexible. Range-of-motion exercises are important because they increase flexibility. These stretches encourage your joints to move from one end of their range to the other.

An example is bending your arm in at the elbow until your hand can touch your shoulder and then extending your arm out until it is straight. People with arthritis should do range-of-motion exercises for their affected joints each day.

You can begin each day by doing a set of stretching exercises while you are still in bed. Just after waking, do a mental assessment of your joints. Take a few minutes to stretch your legs, arms and back, including bending your knees,

Hot and cold therapy to the rescue

Hot or cold therapy, especially before and after exercise, can reduce pain, stop muscle spasms and reduce stiffness. You may need to experiment to see which works best for you. Heat should be applied for about 20 minutes. Cold can be applied for 10 to 15 minutes. Keep a timer nearby so that you don't overdo it.

Heat therapy. One form of heat therapy is dry heat, usually applied with an electric heating pad. Heat increases circulation in the joint. The joint should be protected from burning by placing an extra layer of cloth between the skin and the pad. After a heat treatment, your skin should be pink but not blotched or red. Moist heat, such as a hot bath, shower or whirlpool, can also be used to relieve aching joints.

Cold therapy. Cold therapy with an ice pack is good for reducing swelling. You should protect the skin from freezing with an extra layer of cloth, just like with heat therapy. And just like heat, cold therapy should make the skin pink.

Whether you are using heat or cold, follow these tips:

➤ Don't use heat or cold on skin that is blistered or has sores.
➤ Don't use any creams or gels before applying heat or cold.
➤ Always let your skin return to a normal temperature before reapplying either hot or cold therapy.
➤ Move the joint around gently afterward to restore mobility.

Arthritis Writings
Exercise and Your Arthritis, Arthritis Foundation, P.O. Box 19000, Atlanta, Ga. 30326

elbows, wrists and fingers.

Strengthen your muscles. Strengthening exercises help you build up your muscles and keep your joints stable. They are divided into two types: "isometric" exercises and "isotonic" exercises. Isometrics strengthen your muscles without moving your joints. Usually, you simply tighten a muscle while it is in a natural position. Pressing your palms together is an example.

Isotonics involve moving the joints and are much like range-of-motion exercises. The main difference is you do them faster and you can add weights for more resistance. Leg lifts are isotonic. Daily activities require both kinds of muscle movement — picking up a suitcase is isotonic and carrying it is isometric.

Strengthening exercises can also be done in a swimming pool because water provides resistance.

Build your stamina. Endurance exercises are the most challenging. This type of exercise strengthens your lungs and heart, giving you greater stamina. Examples include fitness walking, water aerobics, swimming and bicycling on a stationary bike.

You should be careful not to get too enthusiastic with this form of exercise right at first. Work at a moderate pace so you don't become breathless. If you haven't been exercising at all, the Arthritis Foundation recommends that you start out doing only range-of-motion and strengthening exercises. They will help you establish a foundation so you can gradually work your way up to endurance exercise. Eventually, you should include all three forms of exercise in your workout. Strive toward a goal of 20 to 30 minutes of endurance exercise per workout, three days a week.

———

Canadian Medical Association Journal (152,1:75)
Exercise and Your Arthritis, Arthritis Foundation, P.O. Box 19000, Atlanta, Ga. 30326
Medical Abstracts Newsletter (12,3:6)
The Physician and Sportsmedicine (21,4:104)
The Johns Hopkins Medical Letter: Health After 50 (4,4:6)

10 steps to a comfortable day

A significant part of your plan for living with arthritis should be finding new ways to cope. Your repetitive daily activities, such as bathing, brushing your teeth, cooking, cleaning, working, shopping and relaxing, should all be examined. You will probably find many ways to get organized and avoid unnecessary movements.

Organize your daily tasks. By organizing yourself and your day, you can accomplish goals more easily. Try these ways to get organized:

➤ Each morning, take a few minutes to plan out your day. List all the things you need to do in order of importance. Get the most important things done earlier in the day in case you get tired early.

➤ Organize your work space, such as your kitchen or living room, so all of your "tools" are nearby. Keep the television remote control in the same place so you can always find it. Store sewing supplies or cooking utensils in waist-level cabinets or shelves. Keep a notepad and pen on a table beside the telephone.

➤ Arrange chairs so that you can sit instead of stand while cooking, talking on the phone, ironing, cleaning, etc. That will take pressure off your joints. A high stool is useful in the kitchen for cooking or washing dishes.

➤ Avoid overly soft, deep-cushioned chairs. They can be hard to get out of, putting unnecessary strain on your arms and shoulders. Even in someone else's home, look for a chair that will allow you to sit down and get up easily.

➤ Try to do all the activities in one area of your home or work space before moving on to another area.

Think before you move. Each time you are about to do something, think about how you might do it more easily, without any extra stress on your joints:

➤ Avoid tight grasping movements that may strain your hands. Learn how to install larger handles on household objects. One simple way is to use soft foam rubber and wide tape. By building up handles with foam padding, you don't have to grip so tightly.

➤ Use your strongest joint and muscles to do a task. You could carry a small backpack or fanny pack instead of a purse with a handle. Start pushing open doors with your arm or shoulder rather than your hand.

➤ Always use good posture to avoid unnecessary strain. Make sure worktables are at the correct height. You should be able to work on a table with your arms comfortably at your sides, with your forearms at 90 degree angles from your upper arms. When lifting an object off the floor, bend your knees, rather than your back, and keep your back straight as you go down and back up.

➤ Don't sit in the same position for a long time. Get up and move every once in a while so you don't become stiff. Do a few range-of-motion movements to loosen up again.

➤ Find a balance between activity and rest. Alternate periods of work with periods of light activity or rest. Rest is just as important as keeping active; both should be done in moderation.

Arthritis, Farmers, and Ranchers, Arthritis Foundation, P.O. Box 19000, Atlanta, Ga. 30326
Using Your Joints Wisely, Arthritis Foundation, P.O. Box 19000, Atlanta, Ga. 30326

Unproven remedies and future possibilities

Sometimes new treatments for arthritis sound strange at first. But what may sound bizarre today may be tomorrow's miracle breakthrough. Arthritis remedies from ancient traditions and old wives' tales do occasionally have some truth to them when they are studied in laboratories. But some can be dangerous.

Unproven remedies may be harmful. The Arthritis Foundation divides unproven arthritis remedies into three groups: harmless, harmful and unknown. Harmless treatments include wearing a copper bracelet, sitting in mineral waters, and eating vinegar and honey. Treatments that may be harmful include snake venom, megadoses of vitamins, and DMSO, a drug used in the treatment of scleroderma that can cause skin irritation and diarrhea. It isn't known whether biofeedback or vaccines are of any benefit.

Some other treatments in the unknown category, such as fish oil and bee venom, are being studied scientifically. All researchers know right now about bee venom, for instance, is that beekeepers, who get stung an average of 2,000 times a year, suffer much less from arthritis than other people.

Regardless of the category, every remedy has its supporters.

The future looks promising. On the other hand, there are new treatments being thought up by researchers every day. Some scientists predict that within five years, doctors will be transplanting new cartilage into joints damaged by osteoarthritis. Research on animals has shown that collagen is a promising new treatment for rheumatoid arthritis. Collagen treatments in humans may begin soon.

Studies of the immune system are also bringing to light new information about how inflammation starts in rheumatoid arthritis. If researchers could figure out how it starts, they may be able to develop ways to stop it. And that would be the first step toward a cure.

So keep an eye toward new treatments and keep a positive attitude. But don't let your enthusiasm get you too carried away by experimental drugs and rediscoveries of bizarre ancient secrets. Read, study and think for yourself and then talk to your doctor.

Mayo Clinic Health Letter (13,1:5)
Medical Tribune (36,7:18)
Science News (138,19:294)
The Lancet (344,8930:1125)
Unproven Remedies, Arthritis Foundation, P.O. Box 19000, Atlanta, Ga. 30326

Asthma

Asthma attacks: How to fight back

Everyone with asthma knows the tight-chested, breath-stealing, panicky feeling of an asthma attack. Asthma sufferers may have a wheezing cough that lasts for days, but usually life is normal until an asthma "trigger" sets off a suffocating attack. Suddenly, your airways narrow as lung muscles contract, the airway walls swell, and thick mucus is produced.

Pollen, dust, exercise, stress, certain foods and medicines all serve as asthma triggers. The good news is, these triggers are all, to some extent, under your control. In other words, you can make a difference!

Keep your house clean and mold-free. Allergic reactions trigger most asthma attacks. Allergy triggers, or allergens, include pollen, dust, mold, animal hair and feathers. Clean your house regularly to keep dust and mold to a minimum.

➤ Vacuum at least once a week.

➤ Wash your linens, pillows and sheets once a week.

➤ Keep the damp places of your house, especially your basement and bathroom, clean.

➤ Keep the humidity in your house low. Humidifiers and vaporizers will make your house more humid and encourage mold to grow. Using an air conditioner is the best way to reduce humidity. Other ways to keep humidity low are using the exhaust fans in your bathroom and kitchen and limiting the number of houseplants you have. Use a dehumidifier for damp basements.

➤ Try to keep your pets outside as much as possible.

See the *Hay Fever* chapter for more housecleaning and allergen-avoiding tips.

But watch out for cleaning-product fumes! While cleaning your house is a must for eliminating allergens, be aware of the fact that certain housecleaning products contain chemical fumes that may bring on an asthma attack. Be especially careful when you buy and use new chemical cleaners.

Use caution in the great outdoors. Asthma triggers not only exist inside the house, they are outside as well. Air pollution and smog are terrible for asthma sufferers. Always carry your medication with you when you plan a long day outdoors. Stay indoors as much as possible when pollen and pollution are at their peak.

Avoid cigarette smoke like the plague. If your friends smoke, ask them politely to take their habit elsewhere. If you smoke, the best and only advice is to quit immediately. One cigarette can hinder your breathing and cause mucus to build up in your lungs. Always ask for nonsmoking sections in restaurants and on airplanes.

Figure out your food triggers and avoid them. Studies show that certain foods can bring on asthma attacks. In particular, seafood and some dairy products like milk and eggs have been linked to asthma flare-ups.

Eating foods with sulfites (food preservatives) and artificial coloring products can also trigger asthma. Manufacturers add sulfites to foods such as dried fruits and dehydrated potatoes to prevent discoloration. The Food and Drug Administration requires labels on foods containing large amounts of sulfites. Some foods that tend to have high sulfite levels are dried apricots, dried peaches, instant mashed potatoes, imported peppers, shrimp and hominy.

Cut back on salt. Although further studies need to be done, a high-salt diet may make asthma worse. Several studies show that this is especially true for men! In one 10-week study, men with asthma had to use a bronchodilator more often, exhaled less air, and wheezed more when researchers gave them a high-sodium tablet instead of a placebo.

Say no to alcohol. Substances in alcoholic drinks trigger asthma attacks in some people. People sensitive to sulfites can become short of breath after just one glass of wine.

Load up on cereals, dairy products, nuts and green vegetables. These foods contain magnesium — a mineral that can do wonders for your lungs. Eating magnesium-rich foods can prevent wheezing and reduce your chances of suffering an asthma attack. In one study, scientists exposed 2,600 people to a chemical known to irritate the lungs. The people with higher magnesium intakes were far less sensitive to that substance than those who consumed little magnesium.

How does magnesium help keep lungs and airways healthy? Researchers think the answer lies in the mineral's ability to relax smooth muscles in the lungs. In fact, one form of the mineral — magnesium sulfate — has been used by doctors to help open up the airways of asthma sufferers. Avoid eating too many processed foods. They tend to be very low in magnesium. The recommended daily allowance for magnesium is 350 mg for men and 300 mg for women.

Enjoy your morning cup of coffee. Caffeine has been found to reduce asthma attacks by widening the blood vessels in the lungs. During an asthma attack, caffeine can be particularly helpful as an emergency backup if you've forgotten your inhaler. Don't overdose on caffeine, but a can or two of cola or two cups of coffee can help. Now your morning coffee can serve the dual purpose of fighting asthma and giving you a jump-start on the day.

Chase away headaches with acetaminophen, not aspirin. Many people with asthma are sensitive to aspirin. Because aspirin is one of the most widely used drugs in the world, it is imperative that everyone with asthma be tested for aspirin-sensitivity. Doctors strongly recommend using acetaminophen in place of aspirin. Always ask your pharmacist about the possible aspirin content of any prescription or nonprescription medicine you take.

Take a cold-water bath. Cold-water baths, though they may not be the most comfortable, seem to ease asthma symptoms. Studies show remarkable improvements in wheezing and breathing after bathing in cold water for one minute or taking a 30-second cold shower every day. So if you can stand the chill, a cold shower a day can help keep the asthma attacks away!

Be careful with winter fires. Burning wood gives off tiny particles that can get into your lungs and cause shortness of breath. Some precautions: Don't let children with asthma sit close to the fireplace. Don't use chemicals, such as kerosene, to light the fire. Keep the chimney clean to prevent fumes. Air the room out after the fire, and dust and vacuum as soon as possible.

Protect your body from toxins. Cigarette smoke and other pollutants can be deadly for people with asthma. Vitamin C, the most important free-radical fighter in the lungs, helps protect your body from environmental pollutants. Make sure your diet is high in vitamin C. The recommended daily allowance is 60 mg, but most multivitamins contain much more than that.

Monitor your breathing with a peak flow meter. Most people with asthma have a mild case that they can control, but for some, asthma can be lethal. Some people with asthma can't tell when they're not getting enough oxygen until it's too late. If you have asthma, especially if you have trouble knowing when you are breathless, you need to use a peak flow meter every day. Peak flow meters measure how fast you blow air out of your lungs. They are portable and can alert you to the early signals of an asthma attack.

Although these changes may require some extra work on your part, the time and effort are definitely worth it. Asthma does not have to control your life. Instead of living with the chest pains, wheezing and coughing, you can fight asthma and win!

American Family Physician (48,5:865)
Asthma Facts, Whitehall Laboratories, No. 5 Giralda Farms, Madison, N.J., 07940
Asthma: What Every Parent Should Know, American Lung Association and Fisons Corp., P.O. Box 1766, Rochester, N.Y., 14603
British Medical Journal (306,6881:854 and 307,6913:1159)
Drug Therapy (24,6:20)
Food Safety Notebook (4,2:18)
Lungline (8,2:3)
Medical Tribune for the Internist and Cardiologist (35,7:12 and 35,16:19)
More Than Snuffles: Childhood Asthma, FDA Consumer Reprint, Publication No. (FDA) 91-3181, Dept. of Health and Human Services, Food and Drug Administration, Rockville, Md., 20857
One Minute Asthma, Pedipress Inc., Amherst, Mass.
The American Journal of Clinical Nutrition (61,3(S):625S)
The Lancet (344,8919:357)
The Physician and Sportsmedicine (22,9:15)

10 steps to easier exercising with asthma

Asthma may make exercise extra challenging, but definitely not impossible. Many people with asthma avoid exercise because they fear an exercise-induced asthma attack. But you don't have to miss out on good health and good times. In the 1984 and 1988 Olympics, 120 of the U.S. athletes had asthma. And those athletes won 57 Olympic medals.

Exercise-induced asthma is extremely common, but, fortunately, it can be prevented and controlled. Follow these suggestions, and you'll be able to enjoy a fun, daily exercise program.

Choose an asthma-friendly exercise. Some activities are going to be easier on your lungs than others. Most experts believe exercise-induced asthma occurs when your lungs lose heat and water. There are three reasons for this: long periods of hard breathing, breathing in allergens and breathing in cold air.

Therefore, sports such as running and bicycling, especially during the winter, will increase your chances of an exercise-induced attack. Long-lasting endurance sports, such as baseball and downhill skiing, are less likely to trigger asthma than a high-intensity sport like basketball or soccer.

Water sports cause the least problems because the moist, warm air prevents the airways from cooling. Plus, walking and weight training rarely trigger asthma.

The key to maintaining an exercise program is to choose an activity you enjoy. Experiment with different sports until you find your niche.

Choose the proper environment. Try to exercise in warm, humid, unpolluted environments.

On cold days, wear a face mask or scarf over your nose and mouth. This will make the air you breathe warmer and more humid. Foam nylon masks will help warm the air before it enters your lungs.

Use an inhaler five minutes to an hour before vigorous exercise. Always carry your inhaler in case you need it during exercise as well.

Always warm up thoroughly before starting vigorous exercise. Follow up with a long cool down after exercise. This is an excellent way to gradually increase your physical strength and lung capacity without triggering an asthma attack.

Follow a pre-exercise routine. Some athletes with asthma follow this routine: They use their inhaler, do five to 10 minutes of vigorous exercise, then completely cool down. Then they start playing their sport. This routine gives them a two-hour period during which they can exercise without suffering asthma symptoms.

Avoid eating certain foods up to two hours before exercise. Shrimp, celery, peanuts, egg whites, almonds and bananas are some of the foods that can trigger exercise-induced attacks. Eating these foods before exercise can actually cause breathlessness, a drop in blood pressure and extreme weakness.

Breathe through your nose. This will warm and moisten the air in your nasal passages. *Asthma and Exercise* by Nancy Hogstead and Gerald Couzens and *The Breath Approach to Whole Life Fitness* by Ian Jackson outline useful breathing techniques that will reduce your chances of asthma during exercise.

Keep a positive attitude and believe in yourself. Don't give up exercise altogether if you have a bad experience. One negative experience does not even compare to all of the positive benefits of exercise.

Finally, don't overdo it! Too much exercise isn't healthy for anyone. Fatigue, anemia, and the rapid deterioration of muscles are just a few of the adverse effects of too much exercise.

Asthma does not have to slow you down. A consistent exercise program will actually improve your asthma. You can still play your favorite sports, have fun, and compete with the best of them!

Emergency Medicine (26,2:40)
FDA Consumer (28,1:30)
Postgraduate Medicine (95,8:185)
The Physician and Sportsmedicine (21,10:27)
What Everyone Needs To Know About Exercise-Induced Asthma, UCLA School of Medicine, Los Angeles, Calif.

How to use your inhaler

The medicine in your inhaler can immediately relax your lung muscles and expand your airways — if you use it correctly. But over half the people who use an inhaler don't know exactly how to use it.

That means most of the medicine ends up in your mouth instead of your lungs. And one recent study revealed that only 4 percent of women with asthma used their inhalers correctly. Women may have more trouble because inhalers are often too large for them.

Here's the correct way to use an inhaler:
1) Holding the inhaler upright, shake thoroughly.
2) Tilt your head back and exhale.
3) Put the mouthpiece in a position that is comfortable for you. Doctors usually suggest one of three positions:
    ➤ Place the inhaler one to two inches away from your mouth.
    ➤ Place the mouthpiece inside your mouth with your lips firmly around it.
    ➤ Use a spacer. Spacers are tubes that connect the inhaler to your mouth. They will hold the medication until you inhale.

Don't forget to remove your inhaler cap!

Watch out asthma sufferers, you could be getting more than your breath back from your inhaler!

It's the middle of the night, and you are wheezing. Half asleep, you reach for your inhaler and take a deep breath. ... But wait, you forgot to take the cap off!

Sound hard to believe?

It was true for one 25-year-old asthma sufferer who woke during the night with shortness of breath. In his groggy state he forgot to remove the cap from his inhaler and then swallowed it.

Although this man was able to remove the cap, he caused considerable damage to his vocal cords.

Most breathing problems for asthma sufferers seem to occur at night.

Therefore, doctors advise you to take extra care when using your inhaler at night or when you are sleepy.

_____

The New England Journal of Medicine (325,6:431)

4) Start to breathe in slowly just as you press down on the inhaler to release the medicine. This simultaneous action seems to cause the most problems for people using inhalers. Concentrate on the activity and you will soon realize that it's not difficult at all. Remember to breathe in slowly, taking three to five seconds for each breath. You shouldn't see medicine in the air or feel it land on your tongue.

5) In order for the medicine to spread throughout the lungs, hold your breath for 10 seconds.

6) Repeat puffs as directed. You may want to wait one minute between puffs to get the full effect.

7) If you are buying inhaler refills earlier than the date suggested on the label, you may be overusing your inhaler. Consult your doctor because you may need another medication.

8) Finally, don't forget to clean your mouthpiece regularly to avoid buildup. Clean with warm water and soap, and air-dry. Keep the cap on your inhaler when you're not using it so dust and lint will stay out.

Once you start using the inhaler correctly, you will soon realize the medication really does work. It's simple, easy and provides immediate relief.

_____

Medical Tribune (35,24:7)
The Asthma and Allergy Advance
The New England Journal of Medicine (325,6:431)

Athlete's Foot

Relieving the itch of athlete's foot

Joining a gym was a great idea, you tell yourself. You can stop by on the way home from work and squeeze in a workout before dinner.

But one morning, you wake up and there's this red rash between your toes that itches like crazy.

That's athlete's foot. The most common fungal infection in people, about 10 percent of the population is scratching away at it at any one time.

The ailment got its name because "a lot of people, when they go into the gym or work out, they don't dry their feet off completely," says Dr. Chet Evans, dean of the School of Podiatric Medicine at Barry University in Miami, Fla., one of the nation's seven colleges of podiatric medicine. "They slip their socks on when their feet are still wet."

While the gym floor environment makes weekend warriors especially at risk for athlete's foot, the fungus can grow in any warm, dark, moist place, like your bathroom, says Dr. Bryant Stamford, director of the Health Promotion and Wellness Center and professor of allied health, School of Medicine, University of Louisville, Louisville, Ky.

You also increase your chances of athlete's foot by simply wearing shoes, especially without socks, wearing the same pair of shoes all the time, or forgetting to wash your socks often enough.

If you'd leave it alone, the fungus itself would be irritating, but not dangerous.

The fungus stays on the top layer of your skin, a layer that acts as your body's natural Band-Aid to keep the nasties out. Once you scratch off that Band-Aid, though, you risk a more serious infection.

"That's the potential," Evans says, "especially if you're a diabetic, have impaired circulation, if you have an immune system depression, such as AIDS, or you're on medication for cancer therapy."

Try Epsom salt soaks. When you have athlete's foot, try soaking your feet in Epsom salt, 10 to 15 minutes, three times a day for three to five days. You can also soak your feet in a gallon of warm water with two capfuls of bleach. After soaking, make sure you dry your feet completely.

After your bath, take a cotton ball and dry your feet with rubbing alcohol. "It burns like a son of a gun, but it's a good antiseptic and dries out the area," Evans says.

Sprinkle with cornstarch. You can sprinkle some cornstarch on your feet to help keep them dry when you have athlete's foot, but Evans warns against using baking soda or talcum powder if the infection is weeping. That can create a crust and allow the fungus and other bacteria to spread underneath.

Keep it clean and dry. The easiest way to prevent athlete's foot is to keep your feet clean and dry, wash your feet with soap and water, and change your socks.

You can use a foot powder, but make sure it's medicated, Evans says. Talcum powder smells nice, but that's about it. It won't kill the organisms on your feet.

Soak your feet in warm tea. If your feet sweat profusely, try putting a couple of tea bags in hot water just long enough to turn the water brown. Let it cool until it's warm and soak your feet for five to 10 minutes.

Tea contains tannins, natural chemicals that help pull excess moisture from your feet. A solution of one part vinegar to 10 parts water also works well. Dry your feet thoroughly after soaking. You also can spray your feet with an antiperspirant deodorant spray.

If your case of athlete's foot lasts for more than five to seven days, or seems to be affecting a toenail, go see your doctor.

Dr. Chet Evans, dean of School of Podiatric Medicine, Barry University, Miami, Fla.
Bryant Stamford, Ph.D., director of the Health Promotion and Wellness Center and professor of allied health, School of Medicine, University of Louisville, Louisville, Ky.
The Physician and Sportsmedicine (22,7:79)

Back Pain

Beat back pain without surgery

Your back pain started a few weeks ago. You try to rest and take it easy, but the pain just won't go away. Finally, you make a trip to the doctor and a magnetic resonance imaging (MRI) scan shows that you have a ruptured disk. Your doctor says you may need surgery.

Wait! Before you panic and undergo risky back surgery, you need to know the facts. Not all ruptured disks cause pain and problems. A recent study of 98 people with no back pain revealed that over half of them had one or more ruptured disks. Since a damaged disk does not necessarily hurt, it might be a coincidence that you have a sore back and a ruptured disk.

Disks are the soft, rounded cartilage between the bones of the spine. A ruptured disk occurs if the jellylike interior of the disk is pushed out of its usual place and extends beyond the bones of the spine. Ruptured disks also are called herniated, protruding or slipped disks. Often, ruptured disks shrink over time, returning to fit their normal spaces again.

Try rest and exercise before surgery. Most people with back pain improve without surgery. In fact, the long-term results of people who have surgery are identical to those who don't. Consider the results of another study of 126 people with ruptured disks. Half the group underwent surgery. The other half were treated without surgery. Four years later, the two groups showed very little — if any — difference.

Usually doctors don't know why your back hurts. Doctors aren't able to identify a definite cause of pain in 85 percent of the people who come to them with back complaints. In addition, the number of surgeries on the lumbar spine, or lower back, increases with the growth of new imaging techniques, such as MRI. When an MRI reveals a ruptured disk, doctors are likely to point to that as the cause of your back pain. The cure they will probably suggest — surgery.

But interpretations of an MRI scan can vary from doctor to doctor. So if your doctor suggests back surgery based on the results of imaging testing, get a second opinion. Keep in mind that 96 percent of all back injuries will heal with rest and rehabilitative exercises.

Get rid of bad habits to improve bad backs. Most back pain is self-inflicted, meaning years of poor posture, little exercise and bad lifting habits have finally caught up with you. However, you can help prevent future back attacks with a few simple lifestyle changes. Don't try to change all your habits at once. Include one or two changes at a time until you've mastered them all.

Exercise regularly. Get at least 30 minutes of aerobic exercise three or four times a week. Walking is an excellent alternative to running. It gives you the same benefits without the high-impact movements that compress disks or twist ligaments. Stretch before and after you exercise to prevent injury and strengthen your back.

Stand up straight. You've heard this since you were a child, but it really works. Try this exercise to check your posture. Imagine a string that extends from your ear down to your ankle bone. The string should go straight up the leg just behind the kneecap, over the hip and beside the shoulder to form a straight line. Remember to sit up straight too. Don't slump or sit with your back twisted.

Don't bend and twist your back when you rake, vacuum or mop. Keep your back straight, and move your arms and legs smoothly. Your job may take longer, but your back will appreciate it. Buy lightweight gardening tools and cleaning equipment with long handles.

When unloading your dishwasher, pivot on your feet so that you keep your hips and shoulders in a line and bend at the knees and hips.

To reach a high shelf, put your feet in a staggered stance (one foot in front of the other), then push off your back foot onto your forward foot as you reach up, keeping your hips and shoulders in line. Don't lift heavy objects above your shoulders. Stand on a stool or sturdy chair instead.

Try not to sleep on your stomach. If you absolutely must, put a small pillow under your stomach to keep your back straight. Put a pillow under your knees if you sleep on your back. The best way to sleep is on your side with your legs drawn up slightly toward your chest. You can use a pillow under your head and between your knees. Of course, make sure your mattress is firm and in good condition.

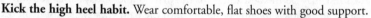

Let the knees have it. When lifting things from the ground, squat with a straight back while bending your knees. Let your legs do the lifting instead of your back.

Kick the high heel habit. Wear comfortable, flat shoes with good support.

Stretch your back every day. Stretching will control muscle spasms and relieve muscle tightness. Here are two easy stretches you can do at home or work:

➤ Push back into your chair's back support to stretch. Straighten your legs and flex your ankles and feet.

➤ Stretch like a cat. Stand up and place your hands about shoulder width apart on a table. Arch your back like a cat, looking at the floor, then push your back downward, looking at the ceiling.

Lose weight. Extra pounds around your stomach are a constant strain on your back. Excess weight is easier to lose if you regularly exercise than if you simply cut calories.

Give up cigarettes. If you are a smoker, you may be worsening your back pain. Some researchers think smoking decreases blood flow to the backbone. Less blood flow means more risk of injury. Others think that "smoker's c~ strains the muscles in your back.

As difficult as it may be to accept, many of the ~ ·

trouble you are a direct reflection of the way you treat your body. By slowly taking steps that show greater respect and care for your body, you should feel the improvements over time. A little prevention can save you a lot of pain.

American Family Physician (49,1:171)
Back Works, BookPartners, Seattle
No More Aching Back, Villard Books, New York
Surgical Neurology (1993,39:5)
The New England Journal of Medicine (331,2:69)

How to end a back attack

It's moving day, and your helpers haven't shown up yet. You really want to get started, so you carry the recliner to the truck by yourself. As you place the chair in the truck, you feel a sharp pain in your back. It hurts to stand up straight. It hurts to sit. It hurts. Period. Now what?

When you feel pain in your back, all hope is not lost. There are some things you can do at home to help ease your discomfort and avoid high medical bills. Of course, if your pain lasts for more than two or three days, if you drag your foot when you walk or lose bladder or bowel control, you should see your doctor. Your condition could require medical attention.

Take a painkiller and take it easy. Aspirin or ibuprofen, gentle massage and bed rest may be the best thing for the first couple of days after you hurt your back. No aerobics, jogging or tennis until the pain goes away. Just lie in bed on your back with a pillow under your knees or on your side with a pillow between your knees.

But don't get too comfortable. Too much bed rest may make your road to recovery longer than necessary. Try to get out of bed as soon as you can — even if it's just for short periods of time.

Stretch your back gently. Gentle stretching is the best way to get your muscles back in shape. Do the following stretches as soon as possible:

➤ Sit on the floor and draw your knees to your chest. Hold this position for 10 seconds, then relax. Repeat the exercise two or three times to stretch out your muscles.

➤ Relaxing your entire body is a great way to ease back muscle pain. Close your eyes and try to feel yourself contracting and relaxing each muscle in your body. Begin with your face muscles and work your way down to your toes.

➤ Lie on your back on a firm surface. Place your hands beneath the small of your back. Let your back rest on your hands while you tilt your pelvis upward. Hold for several seconds and relax. Repeat four or five times.

➤ Sit up straight in a chair. Raise both feet about one inch off the floor at the same time. Hold for several seconds. Repeat. This exercise can be done anywhere.

➤ Lie on your back with your rear end close to the wall. Lift your legs and place your heels against the wall. Do not bend your legs at the knee. If your legs bend, move back from the wall a little more. Hold this position for about 15 minutes and repeat every day. As your hamstrings loosen, you will be able to move closer to the wall.

Simple stretches and exercises can have you feeling like yourself again. Be sure to start slowly and work your way up to several repetitions. You don't want your recovery to put you on your back again!

Even after your back is pain-free, try to resist exercise that requires bouncing or jerking movements. Walking, bike riding and swimming are excellent exercises for a healthy back. These activities reduce the amount of stress on your muscles. If you have a history of back pain, check with your doctor before beginning any exercise routine.

Managing Back Pain, We Care for You, Baylor College of Medicine, Houston, Texas
Medical Tribune (34,10:10)
The Physician and Sportsmedicine (21,3:183)

Straight talk about posture

"Stand up straight!" "You're slumping again!"

We all heard it when we were younger, and we didn't give Mom's nagging much thought. But now that we're older and wiser, and our backs are tired and achy, we may be ready to listen to that good advice. Standing and sitting properly help more than just your looks. Good posture strengthens your bones, muscles and ligaments and helps you stay healthy all your life.

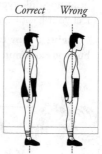

Correct   Wrong

Everyone knows that slouching on the couch in front of the television isn't the right way to sit. But standing as stiff as a United States Marine isn't proper either. A slouching position puts too much strain on your lower back muscles while a military posture puts too much arch in your back.

Practice good standing posture. To learn what good standing posture feels like, get to work on the following exercises:

➤ Stand with your back against a wall, heels 3 inches from the wall, feet about 6 inches apart.

➤ Let your arms hang at your sides, your palms facing forward.

➤ Keep your ankles straight and knees facing the front.

➤ Keep your lower back close to the wall.

➤ Straighten your upper back, lifting your chest and placing your shoulders against the wall.

➤ Place your head against the wall, tucking your chin.
➤ Pull up and in with your lower abdominal muscles, trying to flatten your stomach.
➤ Hold this for about 10 seconds, breathing normally.
➤ Relax and repeat three or four times.
➤ Repeat the entire exercise three times a day.

Sit like a beauty queen. To work on your sitting posture, try the following:

➤ Sit in a straight-back, armless chair, both feet flat on the floor, your back resting against the chair.
➤ Let your arms hang by your sides, your palms facing forward.
➤ Straighten your upper back by lifting your chest.
➤ Place your shoulders against the chair.
➤ Hold your head straight.
➤ Try to flatten your stomach by pulling your abdominal muscles up and in.
➤ Hold for about 10 seconds, breathing normally.
➤ Relax and repeat the exercise three or four times.
➤ Repeat the entire exercise three times each day.

It's easy for us to slump in our chairs at work or while watching television at home. Pay attention to your posture at all times. At work or school, keep your head up while typing or writing, and keep your chair close to the desk. If you feel your back begin to arch forward, put your feet on a stool.

Tighten your tummy. A poor posture weakens the lower stomach muscles, but you can improve your posture with the following tummy tightener:

A Natural Alternative
Icy massage soothes back pain best

The solution to your nagging back pain may be as close as the ice bin in your freezer. Believe it or not, rubbing the aches with a cup of ice can get you out of bed and back into the swing of things. One great way to make ice for this purpose is to freeze water in a paper cup. Once the ice is solid, peel away the paper from one end of the cup. Ask your wife, husband or friend to massage the painful area with the cup of ice for seven to 10 minutes. At first you will feel extreme cold, then a burning sensation. Hang in there because once your back gets numb, the pain goes away for a while. This is a safe way to relieve your back pain, and you can repeat the procedure about once an hour.

Geriatrics (49,2:22)

➤ Stand comfortably.

➤ Clasp your hands and cup them around your lower abdomen.

➤ Pull up and in with your lower stomach muscles, drawing in your abdomen.

➤ Hold this position for 10 seconds.

➤ Relax and repeat four or five times.

➤ Complete the entire exercise at least three times a day.

Working on your posture now can prevent a lot of pain later, so "Stand up straight!"

The Secret of Good Posture, American Physical Therapy Association, 1111 North Fairfax Street, Alexandria, Va., 22314

The shooting pain of sciatica

Many people think back pain is only caused by lifting heavy objects or somehow injuring your back. Not so. You can develop sciatica — pain in the lower back, buttocks and legs — during pregnancy or just from sitting at your desk all day.

The sciatic nerve runs from the lower back through the buttocks and down the back of your leg. Pressure on this nerve can shoot pain from the lower back to the feet. You may feel some numbness or tingling along the nerve too.

A back injury, poor posture or lack of exercise can cause a slipped disk to press on the sciatic nerve. Or a pregnant woman might suffer from lower back pain when the baby's head presses the sciatic nerve against the pelvic wall.

For most sciatica sufferers, treatment is not far away. Everyday pain relievers, such as aspirin and ibuprofen, can ease your discomfort, and bed rest will get you in the groove again quickly.

Sudden attacks of pain can be soothed by lying flat on your back for a while. Gentle stretches can also take the pain away. You should see your doctor if your pain doesn't go away after a couple of days.

Medical Update (16,9:4)

Bad Breath

Banish bad breath

Everyone has bad breath from time to time, especially after sleeping. Doctors call it halitosis, and although it sounds serious, it's not.

Most cases of bad breath are caused by bacteria in your mouth, or by the leftover effects of sulfur that is present in certain foods such as broccoli or garlic.

Most of the time, the odor-causing bacteria inside your mouth are kept in check, to some extent, by your own saliva. That's because your saliva is slightly acidic. But when you sleep, the normal flow of saliva slows down, and the environment inside your mouth becomes less acidic. This environment is a wonderful place for odor-causing bacteria to multiply and grow. The result: bad breath.

Most people can cure morning breath with a good toothbrushing. However, if you find that your morning breath tends to linger even after brushing, try these tips.

Don't regularly use deodorizing sprays or antiseptic mouthwashes like Listerine or Scope unless your dentist recommends it to help control gum disease. Using a mouthwash every day can actually make your bad breath worse by upsetting your mouth's delicate balances and drying out your mouth. Mouthwashes and deodorants will only temporarily cover up bad breath.

Drink plenty of water. Water will help keep your mouth clean and odor-free. If you can't brush your teeth after a meal, swish water around in your mouth to wash away food particles.

Other beverages, especially coffee and alcohol, tend to linger unpleasantly on your breath. After your body absorbs beer, whiskey or wine, your lungs spend hours trying to get rid of it.

Brush your tongue. Your tongue can contribute to bad breath by gathering food particles and bacteria. If your tongue becomes coated or furry, gently brush it when you brush your teeth. But don't get carried away — some people have brushed off taste buds and injured their tongues by brushing them too hard and too often.

Breathe through your nose at night. Mouth-breathing usually makes morning breath worse because it dries out your mouth even more than usual.

At night, your mouth moves very little and doesn't make much saliva, so food particles and bacteria tend to stay put. These particles break down while you sleep and cause morning breath. This is why it's so important to brush your teeth thoroughly at bedtime.

Eat something sweet. When you need to quickly cover up bad breath, something sweet will do the trick. The bacteria that cause cavities also fight bad breath. Sugars and other complex carbohydrates help keep bad breath at bay.

Drink buttermilk or eat yogurt with active cultures. The lactobacilli in these products make it hard for odor-causing bacteria to grow.

Is it serious?

Bad breath that never goes away may be more than embarrassing. It could be a sign of a serious health problem that needs a doctor's care.

Something as simple as sinusitis can cause bad breath, and treatment with antibiotics may be all you need. Or, bad breath could indicate something as serious as diabetes, kidney or liver failure, a lung infection or Sjögren's syndrome (a chronic inflammatory disease in which collagen — the connective tissue in skin, ligaments, cartilage and the mouth and gums — breaks down). A mouth ulcer or infection, gum disease or a dry socket left after you've had a tooth pulled can also be culprits behind bad breath.

Some prescription drugs, such as antidepressants or medication for angina, can cause your breath to smell bad. Many of these drugs cause dry mouth which can lead to bad breath. You can defeat the effects of these drugs by drinking more water.

If your breath constantly smells sweet and fruity or like ammonia or urine, see your doctor — this could signal serious medical problems.

Check your tongue too. Another clue to your health that's in your mouth is the color of your tongue. A normal, healthy tongue should be a deep pink color. A pale tongue may mean you're anemic and need iron. A bright red tongue may indicate a rare disease caused by a deficiency of the B vitamin niacin.

A brownish, hairy tongue could indicate tobacco stains or bacterial growth. "Black tongue" is also a harmless side effect of many prescription drugs. White patches on your tongue could signal a fungal infection or could simply be a result of breathing with your mouth open.

So there really is a reason your doctor says, "Say Aah"!

Bladder Infections

Healing powers of cranberry confirmed

Some old wives' tales are harmful, some contain a kernel of truth, and some hit the nail right on the head. One old home remedy has been proven absolutely correct in recent scientific studies: Drinking cranberry juice can prevent bladder infections, also known as urinary tract infections (UTIs).

A six-month study of 153 women age 65 or older found that those who drank 10 ounces of cranberry juice every day were much less likely to have a bladder infection than those who drank a similar beverage that did not contain cranberry juice.

Only 15 percent of the women drinking cranberry juice developed infections compared to 28 percent of those not drinking cranberry juice. Among those who did get infections, the women drinking cranberry juice recovered more quickly than the others.

Most bladder infections require antibiotics prescribed by your doctor. However, promptly applied home remedies can sometimes prevent a bladder infection while it's still in its early stages.

Give bacteria the slip. For decades people have believed that cranberry juice can ward off or treat a bladder infection because of its acid content. While it's true that bacteria cannot grow very well in an acidic environment, that's not how cranberry juice works.

Cranberry juice actually prevents bacteria from clinging to the walls of the urinary tract. It makes your urinary walls too slippery for bacteria. Since the bacteria cannot hold on inside the body, they are less likely to cause an infection or make an existing infection worse.

Drink at least two 8-ounce glasses of cranberry juice at the first sign of a bladder infection to give bacteria the slip.

Drink plenty of water. By drinking water, you may be able to flush the infection from your system before it gets a good grip.

Add a teaspoon of baking soda to a full glass of water to help relieve the painful burning sensation. Don't use baking soda for a long period of time or if you're sensitive to salt.

Don't use baking soda in your water and drink cranberry juice too. The two remedies cancel each other out.

Go to the bathroom every time you feel like it. Many people resist the urge to go to the bathroom when they have a bladder infection because of the painful burning they experience.

The tell-tale signs of a bladder infection

You're probably developing a bladder infection if you experience any of the following symptoms:

> ➤ a burning sensation when you urinate
> ➤ a frequent urge to urinate even though you only eliminate small amounts of urine
> ➤ a sense that your bladder is not completely empty even after you have gone to the bathroom
> ➤ cloudy urine

If your symptoms don't improve within 24 hours or if you have bloody urine, pain in your lower back, fever, nausea or vomiting, see your doctor immediately. Bladder infections that are not treated properly can cause permanent kidney damage.

_____

The American Medical Association Encyclopedia of Medicine, Random House, New York

But the more you go to the bathroom, the quicker you'll be rid of those bothersome bacteria.

Head off future infections. If you've had one bladder infection, you know you never want another one.

Here's what you can do to keep your urinary system running smoothly in the future.

➤ Drink at least eight glasses of water a day.
➤ Go to the bathroom every two to three hours and after sexual intercourse.
➤ Wipe from front to back. Wiping from back to front pulls bacteria from the rectum up towards the urethral opening and increases the risk of infection.
➤ Wash yourself and your undergarments with a mild soap.

_____

Before You Call the Doctor, Random-Ballantine, New York
The American Medical Association Encyclopedia of Medicine, Random House, New York
The Journal of the American Medical Association (271,10:751)

Blisters and Calluses

When you've pushed too hard, check out these blister busters

Most car owners know that warning lights on the dashboard are there for a good reason. When a light comes on, you either stop or risk damage to your car. Our bodies are the same way, with some wonderful built-in warning lights. One of the most common biological warning signals is the blister — your body's way of telling you that you've pushed too hard or gotten too hot. Just about everyone has gotten blisters at one time or another. In fact, they're so common that most people — especially athletes — assume they're unavoidable.

Fortunately, blisters can often be prevented, and when they do occur, there's plenty you can do to treat them. Friction blisters can occur anywhere on the body, although the feet and hands are the areas most prone to problems. They're caused by rubbing between a foot and a sock, a hand and a hammer, or even a bottom and a bicycle seat.

The rubbing causes stress on the surface of the skin because the tissue underneath pretty much stays in one place. The rubbing separates the skin and tissue into two layers, and the space in between fills with fluid.

(You rarely get friction blisters on your inner thighs because the tissue under the skin is elastic, and gives way. In those kinds of areas, you're more likely to get a scrape like rug burn than a blister.)

Should you pop it? The age-old question of whether to drain a blister or leave it alone depends on its size and location.

If the blister is smaller than the eraser on the end of a pencil (less than one-fourth of an inch), it's probably better to leave it alone. Anytime you open the skin, you run the risk of infection. Tape a doughnut-shaped pad over the blister. Besides protecting the blister, it will ease any discomfort. The blister should begin to dry up and grow new skin in about a day.

If the blister is bigger than a pencil eraser or it's in a place where it could get torn open, you probably should drain it. Sterilize a needle or razor blade with alcohol or a flame and cut a hole just big enough to allow the fluid to drain out.

Then treat the blister with a triple antibiotic, like Neosporin, and put on an adhesive bandage or a gauze pad to keep the blister from refilling with fluid.

Should you remove the blistered skin? The only time doctors recommend cutting the top off a blister is if it's already torn, if there's an infection, or if it's on the ball of your foot. In such situations, remove the blister tissue up to the edge of the normal tissue, using sterilized scissors. Trim the edges until they are smooth and wash the area with surgical soap to prevent further infection. Then, for 10 to 14 days or until new skin forms, you'll need to bandage the area.

Dr. Bryan P. Bergeron of Cambridge, Mass., recommends applying an over-the-counter product called Second Skin. Second Skin is a spongy material that absorbs pressure and reduces friction against blisters. You can tape the material in place with waterproof tape. If the bandage gets wet, change it.

Prevent blisters with a layer of "goo." Keep the skin lubricated and protected, and you'll cut down on the number of blisters. Apply petroleum jelly, A&D Ointment or adhesive tape to your feet to give shoes and socks something to rub against besides your skin. One wear tester for an athletic shoe company says smoothing a lubricant on his feet keeps his blisters at bay. But he suggests using nonpetroleum lubricants instead of the petroleum-based varieties. He says the petroleum-based products can break down the rubber in your running shoes.

Use antiperspirant to keep feet dry. Moist skin (as opposed to very wet or very dry skin) puts you at risk for blisters. Try spraying antiperspirant or sprinkling baby powder on your feet.

Wear fitted acrylic socks. Acrylic socks are better than cotton because they are made in layers designed to absorb friction. Recent research has shown that cotton socks produce twice as many blisters in runners as acrylic socks, and the blisters made by cotton socks are usually three times as big. Stay away from tube socks made of any material. They don't fit right and cause more friction.

Finally, break in that new pair of shoes by wearing them around the house a little while each day before you take them on a long workout.

The Physician and Sportsmedicine (22,7:23 and 23,2:37)

Shoestring techniques prevent foot pain

Step into any shoe store and you will find a wide variety of athletic shoe styles — and prices. You can find shoes for walking, running, hiking, aerobics, basketball, tennis, and many other specific activities. But if you're a woman, what you won't find is an athletic shoe designed just for you. According to one researcher at the University of California at Los Angeles, nearly all shoes are proportioned to fit men's feet. Even if the box says "women's" and the colors are feminine, it's probably just a man's shoe made in a smaller size.

So what's the problem? Feet are feet, right? Not exactly. Men's and women's feet tend to be shaped differently. Men's feet are rectangular, while women's feet are wider at the ball and skinnier at the heel. So women, forced to wear shoes designed for men, often suffer the agony of the feet. A pair of shoes that fits at the ball may slide on the heel, and a pair that holds the heel in place is probably too tight in front. Poorly fitting shoes can cause calluses, bunions and blisters.

If you have these problems, you're not alone. One study showed that 73 percent of women have some type of foot pain. Nearly seven in 10 have a deformity caused by poorly fitting shoes. More than 85 percent of the women in the study were wearing athletic shoes that were one width size too small so that their heels wouldn't slide.

So what's a woman to do? You could always write your shoe company to complain about the injustice in shoe design. Or you could pay a cobbler to custom fit a pair of shoes for you. But if you're on a shoestring budget, the best solution is right at your feet. The pattern you use when lacing your shoes can really take a load off your aching feet. These tips work best in shoes with double rows of eyelets (the holes you run your laces through).

For narrow feet: Thread the laces through the outside set of eyelets for a snugger fit.

For wider feet: Thread the laces only through the inner set of eyelets.

For narrow heels: Use two sets of laces, one for each set of eyelets. Start one set at the bottom and one at the top. Tie the top laces tight to fit the heel and the bottom laces loose to fit the ball of your foot.

For high arches or a sore spot on top of the foot: Skip the set of eyelets closest to the highest part of your foot. You can also feed the laces straight across rather than in a crisscross pattern.

For toe problems: Start the lace in the upper right eyelet. Run the lace down through the bottom left eyelet. Run the lace straight across through the bottom right eyelet. Continue threading the lace diagonally up the shoe until you reach the top. This should help relieve the pressure that causes hammertoes or corns.

For heel problems: Thread the laces in the normal crisscross pattern, starting at the bottom. At the eyelet that's next to the top feed the lace through, then feed the lace through the top eyelet on the same side. Then run the lace diagonally down to the eyelet that's next to the top on the opposite side.

Follow this pattern on both sides of the shoe. The laces should feed through each other at the top. This lets you tie the shoe snugly without putting too much pressure on the heel.

The Associated Press

Blood Clots

You can beat a blood clot

An 86-year-old man sails through gallbladder surgery like a champ, only to die a week later of a blood clot in his lung.

On New Year's Day, a 40-year-old bartender watches three consecutive bowl games on television while lying on the sofa and then goes right to bed, spending over 40 hours in a horizontal or near-horizontal position. Next day he is hospitalized with a blood clot in his lung. Even a former vice president is not immune. Dan Quayle's doctors attribute the blood clots in his lungs to long hours sitting in cramped quarters on an airplane. The bartender and Dan Quayle survived. They were correctly diagnosed and treated. They were the lucky ones.

Each year there are about 630,000 cases of pulmonary embolism (the medical term for a blood clot that plugs the arteries supplying blood to the lungs) in the United States. About 70,000 people die within an hour of their first symptoms.

Surprisingly, blood clots in the lungs are usually first formed somewhere else in the body. This fact puzzled doctors for centuries. The mystery was solved in 1845 when a German doctor, Rudolf Virchow, described how the clot formed in a leg vein, then worked its way up to the right side of the heart where it was pumped to the lungs. Further research proved him correct. About 95 percent of the time, clots that end up in the lungs develop in the large vein deep inside the muscles of the leg and pelvis.

Keeping deep vein clots from forming is the best way to prevent a blood clot in your lungs, since most deaths due to the disease occur before treatment can begin.

Keep your blood circulating vigorously. Normally, your calf muscles help your blood circulate by squeezing the deep veins in your legs. That helps push the blood back up to your heart. When you are inactive, blood can stagnate in your veins. It thickens and slows down, and then clots are able to form.

About half the people with deep vein blood clots have no symptoms. When symptoms do occur where the clot has formed, they may include slight swelling of the leg or calf, tenderness, cramp-like pain, chills, fever, a bluish skin color and protruding leg veins.

When you've been in the hospital, try to get on your feet as soon as possible — ordinarily the day after surgery or childbirth. If you aren't allowed out of bed for a few days, move your feet and legs in bed as much as you safely can.

Try these hospital-bed exercises. Bending the knees and straightening your legs, squeezing the muscles in your calves, and repeatedly pressing the balls of your feet against the footboard of the bed are some easy exercises that lower the risk of clot formation.

Prop your legs up after surgery. Most people in the hospital lie flat with their heads propped up. To reduce the risk of blood clots, lie flat with your legs tilted up about six inches. This position will get your blood flowing better. This position is recommended after you come home from the hospital too.

Take care when traveling. Healthy, active people don't usually have to worry about blood clots in the lungs. Traveling, however, especially when you sit for a long time, has its dangers.

Two doctors reported that over a three-year period at Heathrow Airport, about 18 percent of 61 sudden deaths in passengers traveling long distances were due to blood clots in the lungs.

Don't smoke when you are traveling by air. Smoking thickens the blood and makes it more likely to clot.

Drink plenty of nonalcoholic liquids. Liquids will counteract the dehydrating effects of low humidity in the cabins.

Stretch your legs and wiggle your toes. Frequent walks around the plane will keep blood from pooling in leg veins and feet from swelling. Other exercises that can be done in place are moving the feet up and down, toe-wiggling, and extending the lower legs. Squeezing the muscles in the stomach and buttocks encourages blood flow in the pelvic veins, while deep breathing increases the flow of blood to the upper part of the body.

Though the risk of blood pooling is slight in the upper body, people whose hands swell should do reaching exercises or open and close the fingers occasionally.

Who gets deep vein clots?

Any of these conditions put you at risk for deep vein clots.

- ➤ overweight
- ➤ inactive
- ➤ pregnant
- ➤ congestive heart failure
- ➤ cancer

By the way, deep vein clots are not the same as blood clots that form from fat buildup in arteries and block the flow of blood to the brain, causing a stroke, or to the heart, causing a heart attack.

FDA Consumer (23,9:22)

Prevent blood clots with these easy-to-do exercises

Extend your lower legs

Close and open your hands

Breathe deeply

Contract the muscles in your stomach & buttocks

Stretch your arms

The same goes for long trips in other vehicles. Walking up and down the train, or stopping the car occasionally to stretch the legs, helps the circulation.

Wear comfortable clothes when traveling. Leave tight girdles and pantyhose behind because they can interfere with blood flow. If your doctor has advised you to wear elastic stockings, you should wear those while you travel.

Don't nap during commercial breaks. If you like to watch TV or read for long stretches of time, remember to get up and move around every hour or so. If you have a desk job, try to get up and move around at least a few times during the day. Take a five-minute brisk walk during your lunch hour.

The body requires activity to keep itself in good condition, and that's not really asking much. When it comes to blood clots, a little prevention goes a long way.

FDA Consumer (23,9:22)
The Lancet (337,8756 and 345,8947:419)

Blood Pressure

Lower your blood pressure naturally

In the 1970s, Nathan Pritikin and his Pritikin program made the news with a plan to stop high blood pressure and high cholesterol in their tracks. The successful plan included a low-fat, low-calorie, low-salt diet and moderate daily exercise.

When a team of researchers from Loma Linda University studied the first 893 people to participate in the 26-day Pritikin Longevity Center program, they were amazed at the results:

✔ After the program, 83 percent of the people who were taking high blood pressure drugs were able to stop taking these drugs with their doctors' permission because their blood pressures had dropped to acceptable levels.

✔ Overweight participants lost an average of 13 pounds.

✔ Cholesterol levels dropped 25 percent. Many people who had been taking drugs to control their blood cholesterol were able to stop taking medicine.

✔ The level of other blood fats also dropped nearly 25 percent.

✔ Fifty percent of the diabetics were able, under medical supervision, to stop taking insulin.

✔ The study participants became more mentally alert and performed better on tests of mental ability.

✔ Many people lost their tiredness and required much less sleep.

The Pritikin diet plan. The diet worked to help reduce high blood pressure in three ways. It was low in:

➤ Calories so people could lose weight.

➤ Sodium to help sodium-sensitive people.

➤ Fat and cholesterol to limit damage to the heart and arteries.

Since the '70s, tens of thousands of people have gotten good results with the Pritikin Program. It just goes to show that simple changes in your diet and exercise habits can turn your health around.

Drugs aren't always necessary. The Pritikin findings have been confirmed by many studies over the past 20 years. In the late 1980s, Dr. Dean Ornish developed a program that helped people actually reverse heart disease and improve the blockages in their arteries. (You'll find the details of Ornish's plan in the *Heart Disease* chapter.)

A Natural Alternative

Magnesium and your blood pressure

If you are one of the unlucky thousands whose blood pressure soars way past the normal range, you may be able to lower it easily by losing a few pounds, saying no to salty food and alcohol, and exercising. But if that doesn't work, you could be faced with taking powerful drugs, which are often loaded with unpleasant side effects. Before turning to a prescription solution, however, talk to your doctor about the possibility of a natural alternative — magnesium. Evidence is mounting that the mineral can lower blood pressure safely.

Studies have shown that people who don't get enough magnesium from their diets tend to have higher blood pressure than folks who eat magnesium-rich foods. So researchers looked to see if taking magnesium supplements would lower blood pressure in a group of women with hypertension who were not taking any medication for their condition.

Half the women received a dose of magnesium equal to about twice what most of us get in our meals; the other half received an inactive pill known as a placebo. The blood pressure of the women taking the magnesium supplements dropped by about three points.

Just how does magnesium work its blood-pressure-reducing magic? Researchers aren't sure but suspect part of the reason is that magnesium helps neutralize stress-induced hormones that are known to hike blood pressure.

Circulation (90,1:225)
Medical Tribune for the Internist and Cardiologist (35,14:4)
The American Journal of Clinical Nutrition (60,1:129)

In a smaller study at the University of Minnesota, the researchers found that even people with mild high blood pressure who had been taking prescription blood pressure lowering drugs could keep their blood pressures down without drugs.

How? Simply by losing weight and reducing salt and alcohol.

The people who were able to quit taking drugs lost an average of five to 10 pounds and kept the weight off during the four-year study. They reduced their salt intake by 36 percent, and they reduced the amount of alcohol they consumed.

They also had improved levels of cholesterol, potassium and uric acid in the blood, an unexpected but pleasant side effect, the doctors noted.

All these studies prove that you can lower your high blood pressure naturally, even if you are already taking blood pressure medications.

A healthy lifestyle will lead to lower blood pressure and, therefore, lower your risk of heart, blood vessel and kidney diseases.

The New Pritikin Program, Pocket Books, New York
The Journal of the American Medical Association (262,13:1801)

Get it checked

If you have normal blood pressure (less than 130/85), you should have your blood pressure measured once every two years, although once every year is better.

If your blood pressure is in the high-normal range (130/85 to 139/89), you should have it checked at least once every year.

If you have one or more risk factors for high blood pressure, many doctors recommend that you have your blood pressure checked every six months, even if your blood pressure is currently normal. Those risk factors include:

➤ A family history of high blood pressure.

➤ Obesity.

➤ High cholesterol.

➤ High triglycerides.

➤ Sedentary lifestyle

➤ African-American race.

➤ Male sex.

➤ High-salt diet.

➤ High-fat diet.

➤ Use of birth control pills and other medications that can raise blood pressure.

Any one of these risk factors should prompt you to write a reminder on the calendar to have your blood pressure checked at least every six months.

People who have high blood pressure need to follow a more rigorous schedule of follow-up blood pressure checks. The following chart represents the most current follow-up recommendations.

Note: If a doctor is already treating your high blood pressure, disregard the chart's recommendations and follow your doctor's advice about follow-up visits.

Archives of Internal Medicine (153,2:154)
The Fifth Report of the Joint National Committee on Detection, Evaluation and Treatment of High Blood Pressure

The shakedown on salt

Salt itself isn't bad for your health. Roman soldiers were sometimes said to be "worth their salt" because they were often paid in salt rather than actual money.

Initial blood pressure		Category	Follow-up recommendations
Systolic (Top number)	Diastolic (Bottom number)		
Less than 120	Less than 80	Normal	Recheck in one year.
120-139	80-89	Prehypertension	Begin some simple lifestyle modifications to avoid high blood pressure.
140-159	90-99	Stage 1	If you are over 50, and your systolic pressure (the top number) is more than 140, your doctor should begin treating you for high blood pressure — regardless of your diastolic pressure (the bottom number).
160 and higher	100 and higher	Stage 2	

What you can do about high blood pressure
- Lose weight if you're overweight.
- Eat a healthy diet low in saturated fat, cholesterol, and salt.
- Limit your alcohol. For women, that means no more than one drink per day and two drinks a day for men.
- Become more physically active.
- Follow your doctor's orders on medication.

Without salt, we would die. Salt maintains fluid levels between the cells and the blood system and is necessary for healthy bones, teeth and muscles.

Why, then, all the fuss about removing salt from your diet? What has happened is that we have simply overdosed on a good thing to the point that it has become a bad thing. Our bodies are equipped to handle only so much salt.

Normally, the kidneys handle any extra salt by allowing the salt to be flushed out in the urine. Diets containing large amounts of salt over long periods of time tend to overwhelm the kidneys' ability to regulate salt. Over time, this can lead to high blood pressure.

Train your taste buds. A low-sodium diet is one of the basic, natural ways to lower high blood pressure, but many people are hesitant because they think that a salt-free diet is bland. However, researchers at the University of Minnesota discovered that your desire for salt decreases when you stick to a low-salt diet.

Many participants in earlier studies said that after they were on a low-salt diet, many foods they once enjoyed were now too salty.

Participants on a low-salt diet compared salted crackers at regular intervals. After a short time, the crackers with the most sodium were considered too salty. By the sixth week, the participants experienced a change in taste, preferring less salt.

As you reduce the amount of salt in your diet, you will experience new flavor sensations that were masked by the large amounts of salt you ate. The true flavor of vegetables can be hidden by cooking with too much salt. In this sense, excessive salt can be a taste destroyer rather than a flavor enhancer.

Measure your "salt sensitivity." According to many scientists, some people are "salt-sensitive." These people react more quickly to smaller amounts of salt in their diets and develop high blood pressure much sooner than people who are not salt-sensitive.

If you are wondering if you are one of those salt-sensitive people, try this three-step test:

1) Record blood pressure and salt intake under normal circumstances.
2) Restrict salt to one teaspoon a day and record blood pressure.
3) If your blood pressure went down when you restricted your salt, increase salt by one gram per day to determine when salt begins affecting your blood pressure.

According to Dr. Hugo Espinel of the Blood Pressure Center in Metropolitan

A Natural Alternative

Calcium and high blood pressure

Think calcium only works on your bones? Think again.

Calcium may also fight high blood pressure. Calcium may even be better for you than some medicine that fights hypertension because it has no side effects.

People who have high blood pressure caused by eating too much salt seem to get the most benefits from calcium. So if you have high blood pressure and you eat a lot of salt, make sure you eat a calcium-rich diet.

In addition, sodium seems to compete with calcium for absorption by your bones. Getting more sodium than calcium in your diet can speed bone loss and deterioration. Eating a high-calcium diet while you're expecting a child may help cut down on pregnancy-related high blood pressure too. Of course, you can overdo anything. Taking very large calcium or vitamin D supplements can cause hypercalcemia, and that can cause high blood pressure.

Archives of Internal Medicine (155,5:450)
Hypertension (24,1:83)
The Journal of Optimal Nutrition (3,1:34)
The Real Vitamin and Mineral Book: Going Beyond the RDA for Optimum Health, Avery Publishing, Garden City Park, N.Y.

Washington, this test can help you find the level of salt intake that is safe for your blood pressure.

Cut back to 500 mg a day. Getting salt down into the range of 500 milligrams (mg) per day (1/4 teaspoon of salt = 500 mg) seems to be the most effective. Since most Americans consume between 6,000 and 12,000 mg of salt each day, it shouldn't be too difficult to cut back some.

Recent studies indicate that some people need as little as 200 mg a day. A healthy amount for most people is from 500 mg up to no more than 1,000 mg of salt per day. However, there are exceptions. Hard labor, profuse sweating, pregnancy and breast-feeding might increase the need for salt up to 2,000 mg per day.

You may find it hard to believe that you eat a lot of salt every day, but the processed foods that we eat are usually filled with salt. This can account for up to 75 percent of salt intake. Any food that comes in a can, a frozen package or a box is likely to have salt added as a preservative or flavor enhancer.

Check the labels on the foods you buy. The higher salt appears on the ingredients list, the higher the content. A slice of bread may contain over 200 mg of salt, a bowl of cornflakes over 300 mg, a bowl of canned soup over 1,000 mg, a chicken dinner from a fast food restaurant over 2,000 mg and a large dill pickle over 1,000 mg.

Eat less salt without sacrificing flavor. If you are concerned about giving up flavor in your cooking, a little creativity can help add spice to your food while lowering the salt content. You do not have to sacrifice flavor if you follow these suggestions:

➤ Try using half the amount of salt a recipe recommends.
➤ Don't add salt to pasta or other starchy foods that will be topped with a sauce, vegetables, cheese, etc. The toppings usually add enough flavor so that you don't even notice the missing salt.
➤ Remove the salt shaker from your table.
➤ Use lemon juice on food instead of salt.
➤ Don't use onion salt or garlic salt as spices because they are just flavored salt. Use real onion or garlic for more flavor without the salt.
➤ Avoid store-bought mixes for biscuits, cakes, pancakes, muffins, cornbread, etc. If you prepare your own, you can control the ingredients.
➤ Learn about the many natural herbs, spices and fruit peels that are available. You may decide to grow your own or experiment with store-bought products.
➤ Don't use a potassium chloride salt substitute. They can increase potassium levels in your body and perhaps even cause heart rhythm abnormalities.
➤ Enjoy Mexican, Cajun and Tex-Mex foods. The strong spices give flavor without adding salt. Beware of Oriental food. It can be high in MSG (monosodium glutamate), which is high in sodium.
➤ To spice up chicken dishes, add fruits such as mandarin oranges or pineapples.

➤ Marinate chicken, fish, beef or poultry in orange juice or lemon juice. Add a honey glaze.

➤ Marinate meat in wine or add wine to sauces or soups. If you thoroughly cook the dish, the alcohol will evaporate, but the flavor will be enhanced.

➤ Use fresh or frozen vegetables instead of canned.

➤ Sprinkle on some green pepper, parsley, paprika or red pepper. Just a little can add a lot of flavor to a meal.

➤ Be sure to keep the meals attractive and include a variety of colors and textures. Most people are more tempted to add salt when the meal appears bland.

➤ Drink water with your meals and avoid soft drinks. Soft drinks are high in sugar, which dulls your taste buds and makes it more difficult to give up salt. Also, many carbonated drinks are high in sodium. Even some sugar-free soft drinks contain sodium as sodium saccharin, an artificial sweetener.

The Food Guide Pyramid, United States Department of Agriculture

Could a low-salt diet send your blood pressure soaring?

A few very rare people are salt-resistant.

Dr. Brent M. Egan, a blood pressure specialist, told the audience at a recent annual American Heart Association meeting that a low-salt diet may actually be harmful for some people. He and his colleagues studied 27 men who were put on a very low-salt diet for one week. They then ate their regular diet for two weeks and then repeated the low-salt diet once more.

Some of the men with normal blood pressure were "salt-resistant," says Dr. Egan, meaning that their blood pressure did not automatically fall when their salt intake was reduced. In fact, blood pressure actually increased by as much as five points in some men who reduced salt intake, he reports.

Studies have shown that insulin, a hormone produced by the pancreas, in some cases contributes to hardening of the arteries by helping the body produce excessive cholesterol. Insulin also encourages the body to retain salt in the kidneys, the report says.

Many men in the study had higher levels of insulin, and Dr. Egan suggests that the body may "adapt" to a low-salt diet by producing more insulin.

If your blood pressure doesn't fall after two months on a low-salt diet, talk with your doctor. Dr. Egan says, the diet "apparently is not helping."

American Heart Association

The protective role of potassium

Eat your bananas and you'll lower your blood pressure. Bananas are rich in potassium, and many scientific studies suggest that a diet high in potassium can help protect against high blood pressure.

Potassium appears to work by stimulating the body to get rid of excess sodium, which directly lowers blood pressure. Unfortunately, societies which have high levels of salt consumption also have low levels of potassium consumption and vice versa.

Potassium also may affect the release of certain hormones and chemicals into the blood that can influence blood pressure.

Don't buy potassium supplements. In spite of all the good news about potassium, don't run out and buy potassium supplements. Too much potassium in the blood (called hyperkalemia) is much more serious and life-threatening than low potassium (called hypokalemia).

Several medications can cause a buildup of excess potassium in the blood, including potassium-sparing diuretics, ACE inhibitors, beta-blockers, heparin and nonsteroidal anti-inflammatory agents (NSAIDs), such as aspirin and ibuprofen.

People using these medications or people with diabetes or kidney disease should use extreme caution in eating large amounts of potassium-rich foods or taking potassium supplements.

Get extra potassium naturally. The recommended dietary allowance for potassium is from 1,600 to 2,000 mg. But you might need to raise your potassium intake to about 3,500 mg a day for it to help lower high blood pressure.

A diet that includes more fresh fruits and vegetables, rather than canned or processed ones, will automatically raise your potassium intake and lower your sodium intake.

Multivitamins should also contain potassium.

Annals of Internal Medicine (115,10:753)
Hypertension (19,6:749)
Recommended Dietary Allowances, 10th ed., National Academy Press, Washington, D.C.

Foods high in potassium

Vegetables	asparagus, artichoke, broccoli, carrots, cauliflower, eggplant, romaine lettuce, mushrooms, peppers, baked potato, spinach, turnips
Fruits	apples, apricots, bananas, cherries, grapefruit, grapes, oranges, peaches, pears, plums
Peas and beans	broad beans, chickpeas, kidney beans, lentils, peas, pinto beans, string beans

The strengthening power of vitamin C

Vitamin C should get at least a B for its role in regulating blood pressure. Two studies have shown that people with high levels of vitamin C in their blood tend to have low blood pressure.

Researchers at the Medical College of Georgia found that 67 men and women with high levels of vitamin C in their blood averaged a blood pressure reading of 104/65. Others with one-fifth those blood levels of vitamin C, but still within acceptable, healthy levels, averaged blood pressure readings of 111/73.

Researchers at Tufts University checked 241 elderly Chinese-Americans and found the same result: The lower the blood levels of vitamin C, the higher the blood pressure. In two very small studies, people who took 1,000 mg of vitamin C a day reduced their systolic blood pressure by four to eight points over four weeks. In another study, people took 400 mg a day for four weeks, but they weren't able to reduce their blood pressure.

Foods high in vitamin C

Foods	Vitamin C (mg)
Kiwi fruit (2)	145
Orange juice (1 cup)	105
Papaya (1 cup)	87
Strawberries (1 cup)	83
Orange (1)	82
Broccoli, raw (1 cup)	79
Grapefruit juice (1 cup)	76
Green or red pepper (1/2)	76
Cantaloupe (1/4)	57
Brussels sprouts, cooked (1/2 cup)	53
Grapefruit (1/2)	53
Tangerines (2)	52
Snow peas (1/2 cup)	51
Cauliflower, cooked (2/3 cup)	47
Cabbage, shredded (1 cup)	40
Raspberries (1 cup)	35
Honeydew (1/10)	33
Sweet potato, baked (1)	32
Watermelon (2 cups)	27
Spinach, raw (1 1/2 cups)	24
Pineapple (1 cup)	22
Lettuce, romaine (1 1/2 cups)	20
Potato, baked, with skin (1)	19

Vitamin C builds strong blood vessels. The jury is definitely not in on vitamin C, but chances are good that it may help lower blood pressure slightly.

Scientists think that vitamin C might protect against high blood pressure because it helps maintain healthy connective tissue, known as collagen, within the blood vessel walls. Vitamin C helps keep the collagen healthy, which strengthens and supports the blood vessel walls and makes them more resistant to high blood pressure.

The current recommended daily allowance for vitamin C is 60 mg per day, although some scientists think that number should be higher. Some natural sources of vitamin C are citrus fruits and dark-green vegetables like broccoli. Check the chart on the previous page for foods high in vitamin C.

Nutrition Action Healthletter (21,9:10)
Recommended Dietary Allowances, 10th ed., National Academy Press, Washington, D.C.

Don't mix coffee and exercise

A hot cup of coffee can cheer the soul, especially on a cold winter morning, but if you have high blood pressure, you may be better off not drinking it — at least before you exercise.

Researchers studied the effects of caffeine on 28 men between the ages of 30 and 45. Seventeen of the men had hypertension (their blood pressure ranged from 140/90 to 160/105) and 11 had normal blood pressure (130/80 or less).

The heart rates of the men with high blood pressure rose higher during exercise after they drank coffee than when they didn't drink it. However, caffeine didn't affect the heart rates of the men with normal blood pressure during exercise.

As for blood pressure, the systolic pressure of both groups rose higher during exercise after coffee was consumed, and the diastolic pressure of the men with hypertension was also higher. (Systolic is the pressure in the arteries *during* a heartbeat, diastolic the pressure *between* beats.)

The point is that during exercise, caffeine may place additional stress on the cardiovascular systems of men with hypertension. The effects may start within 30 minutes and last three hours.

American Family Physician (47,1:210)

When lowering high blood pressure can be dangerous

Just how much should high blood pressure be lowered? That's the question being asked by doctors at Albert Einstein College of Medicine in New York City after a study there indicated some dangers associated with both very big and very small drops in blood pressure. The moderate declines seemed to be safest, says the report.

Has your doctor told you ...

Allergic reactions to medications can occur even after years of use

Taking medication for high blood pressure is a necessary way of life for many people, but it isn't totally risk-free. Doctors are warning consumers about the possibilities of potentially fatal reactions associated with ACE inhibitors occurring several years after the beginning of treatment.

Allergic reactions are most common in the first few months of treatment. But don't be lulled into thinking your tolerance of the drug is "guaranteed" just because you've taken it for a number of months or even years.

You can develop a sensitivity to a drug after years of use and suddenly experience an allergic reaction. Allergic reactions can take the form of severe tongue swelling, airway blockage and inability to swallow.

Check with your doctor or pharmacist to learn what allergic reaction symptoms are most common for the medications you use.

If you are taking ACE inhibitors for regulation of your blood pressure, make sure you report any strange reactions — even a mild reaction, such as tongue swelling that goes away on its own — to your doctor immediately.

Emergency Medicine (22,21:11)

Researchers say many more people eventually had severe or fatal heart attacks following blood pressure treatment that resulted in drops of less than six points or more than 18 points. People whose diastolic blood pressure dropped from seven to 17 points had the least amount of heart attacks.

People with very large and very small drops in blood pressure face three to four times the risk of heart attack compared with people with moderate declines, the study says.

Big blood pressure drops are hard on heart. Seen another way, the risks of fatal heart attack were about the same for those whose high blood pressure remained virtually unchanged as for those with a large fall in blood pressure. Why those with big drops in blood pressure should face the same risks as those whose blood pressure remained high is unknown.

The research indicates that an "ideal" blood pressure figure may be an unrealistic goal and may even be dangerous for many people.

One speculation was that a big blood pressure drop may result in poor blood flow through heart arteries, starving the heart muscle and leading to a heart attack. They downplayed other possible factors like reaction to the medicines, other diseases and behavior like smoking and drinking.

That's because those same factors were present in the ones who had moderate drops in pressure and fewer heart attacks. The doctors tracked 1,765 patients, three-quarters of them male and with an average age of 52 years.

Blood pressure drugs can cause dangerous drop. All patients had blood pressure higher than 160 systolic or 95 diastolic when they entered the study, the report says. Most of them took standard drug treatments, like diuretics, calcium channel blockers or beta-blockers, to lower their blood pressures.

The researchers say there was no direct time relationship between the big drop in blood pressures and subsequent heart attacks. Some attacks took place within a few weeks of the treatment; some occurred many months later.

The doctors make two suggestions:

➤ Your doctor should seek a very specific treatment tailored to each patient that will protect the heart while trying to lower blood pressure, and

➤ "Until this goal is attainable, the cautious physician should seek modest (in the range of seven to 17 mm Hg of diastolic blood pressure) ... reduction for those with mild to moderate hypertension."

The Journal of the American Medical Association (262,7:920)

Body Odor

Banish body odor

Long, long ago, humans could sweat, go through hormone changes and not bathe for weeks, and nobody minded the smell. In fact, our pungent scent was one of the ways we attracted the opposite sex.

Today, research shows that the way you smell matters more to the people around you than any other physical aspect, including the way you look. But that doesn't mean your wife will think your sweaty odor after you mow the lawn on a hot summer day is sexy.

With the arrival of running water, deodorant soaps and chemical antiperspirants, our tastes have changed. Most people can take care of body odor with a good daily bath, antiperspirants, deodorants and clean clothes. If you practice good hygiene and you're still not happy with the way you smell, you may be ready for stronger measures.

First, get feedback from a friend. Do you really smell bad, or do you just think you do? Some people's noses "hallucinate." It doesn't mean you're crazy; it just means you think you're smelling something that's not actually there.

Next, ask your doctor about your odor. Body odor can be a side effect of a drug you're taking or a sign of a serious disease. If bacteria or fungus is causing your body odor, your doctor may be able to prescribe antibiotics to help you.

Take a look at your diet. Garlic and onions are, of course, the biggest food offenders. The smell can drift from your skin hours after you've eaten them.

Some people get a fishy odor when they eat eggs, fish, liver and beans. These foods are high in choline, which produces a substance called trimethylamine. Some people can't metabolize this substance properly, so they give off a funny smell when they eat certain foods.

Try some natural astringents. The author of the book *30-Day Body Purification* suggests bathing or rubbing with certain herbs which work to close the pores of the skin. These natural astringents are witch hazel, arnica lotion, calendula and coriander extract. These herbs may also help fight odor-producing bacteria.

Find odor-fighters in your kitchen. Dabbing lemon juice under your armpits or powdering with cornstarch or baking soda should absorb some odors.

Powder away foot odor. Having problems with foot odor? Dust your feet with cornstarch each morning before putting on your socks. Change socks and repowder your feet midway through the day.

Mind your minerals. Some people have improved the way they smell with mineral supplements. Make sure your daily multivitamin contains calcium, magnesium and zinc.

The Journal of the American Medical Association (273,15:1172)
30-Day Body Purification: How to Cleanse Your Inner Body & Experience the Joys of Toxin-free Health, Parker Publishing, West Nyack, N.Y.

Breast Cancer

Lower your risk of breast cancer naturally

It's time women got a clear picture of what they can do to help lower their risk of breast cancer. Listed below is information that might help you sort through the maze of research.

What about family history? First of all, if your mother, and even your grandmother, had breast cancer, you are not doomed. Researchers used to think that women with a strong family history of breast cancer had five times the risk of getting the disease. But new research shows that those women are only 2.5 times more likely to develop breast cancer by age 70.

Smoking and alcohol increase risk. Smoking will single-handedly shoot your risk of breast cancer through the ceiling. Scientific studies also show that drinking alcohol, about 1 1/2 to two drinks a day, could increase your risk of getting breast cancer by 50 percent. Alcohol seems to boost your estrogen levels, which increases your breast cancer risk.

Eat less fat, more vegetables. Dietary habits can affect your risk. Certain types of cooking — namely, frying or grilling foods — can release cancer-causing substances from foods more easily than stewing or roasting those same foods.

Eating more carrots, cabbage, brussels sprouts, broccoli and cauliflower and other foods rich in calcium, vitamin A and vitamin D appears to lower the risk of breast cancer. Vitamin A-rich foods are especially important — yellow squash, sweet potatoes, spinach and carrots. Eating one serving of these vegetables a day may lower your risk of breast cancer by 20 percent. A low-fat diet seems to offer protection against breast cancer. The National Cancer Institute suggests that all Americans get 30 percent or fewer of their daily calories from fatty foods.

Exercise early and often. If you are willing to start exercising as a teen-ager and keep it up until at least age 40, you can cut your risk of breast cancer by more than half. A convincing study of over 1,000 women has shown that women who exercise four hours a week from the time they start their periods until age 40 reduce their risk of breast cancer by 60 percent.

The theory is that teen-age girls who exercise regularly and vigorously don't ovulate even though they are having periods. No ovulation means reduced amounts of female hormones that have been linked to breast tumors. Plus, older women who exercise ovulate later in their monthly cycle. Later ovulation means that smaller amounts of these hormones are present in the body.

The study didn't address whether exercise after age 40 reduces breast cancer risk.

Food, Nutrition and Health (18,7:6)
Journal of the National Cancer Institute (85,9:722)
Journal Watch (12,4:25)
Medical Tribune (34,10:13; 34,15:3; 34,19:6; and 34,23:6)
Medical World News (34,6:41)
Pharmacy Times (60,1:78)

Slash your risk of breast cancer with regular self-examinations

Early detection of breast cancer still remains the best way to beat the ravaging disease that affects one out of every eight women in the United States. And when it comes to early detection, you hold the most important key.

"Me?" you ask. "What about mammograms and all those other medical tests?"

Mammograms and yearly breast exams at the doctor's office are great ways to detect early cases of breast cancer. However, your monthly breast self-examination could be even more important. Chances are, you can detect changes in your breasts long before a doctor ever could, just because you are familiar with what is "normal" for you. The bottom line is this: Monthly breast self-examinations are a must for all women, regardless of age. Listed below and on the following page are answers to some common questions about breast self-examination.

What am I looking for in these exams? Quite simply, you are looking for any changes from what is "normal" for you. This could include lumps or knots in the breast tissue, any discharge from the nipple or any change in the skin, such as dimpling or puckering. Call your doctor right away if you notice any of these (or other) changes.

When is the best time to do these monthly exams? If you are still having monthly menstrual cycles, the best time is one or two days after your period starts. That's when your breasts will be the least lumpy or tender from monthly changes. If you are past the age of menopause, just pick a day (the first, 15th or 30th) each month that you can remember and stick with it. If you are taking hormones, talk with your doctor about when to do breast self-examinations.

If you have naturally lumpy breasts, should you perform monthly breast exams anyway? The answer is a hearty "yes." Even though lumpy breasts are a little harder to examine, and it's a little harder to notice new lumps or changes, you will be better at it than anyone else, just because you know your own lumps. Just take a little extra time each month to get to know your "normal" lumps so you'll know when an "abnormal" lump appears.

If I am over age 50 and get yearly mammograms, can I stop performing monthly breast self-examinations? Absolutely not! Mammograms are not foolproof. Nothing can replace your careful, monthly self-examinations. You might find something six months before your next mammogram — that's too long to wait for a mammogram to pick it up. No matter how old you are or how often you get mammograms, you need to perform monthly breast self-examinations.

American Family Physician (49,2:53)

How to do a breast self-exam

1) Stand in front of a mirror that is large enough for you to see your breasts clearly. Check each breast for anything unusual. Check the skin for puckering, dimpling or scaliness. Look for a discharge from the nipples.

Do steps 2 and 3 to check for any change in the shape or contour of your breasts. As you do these steps, you should feel your chest muscles tighten.

2) Watching closely in the mirror, clasp your hands behind your head and press your hands forward.

3) Next, press your hands firmly on your hips and bend slightly toward the mirror as you pull your shoulders and elbows forward.

4) Gently squeeze each nipple and look for a discharge.

5) Raise one arm. Use the pads of the fingers of your other hand to check the breast and the surrounding area firmly, carefully and thoroughly. Some women like to use lotion or powder to help their fingers glide easily over the skin. Feel for any unusual lump or mass under the skin. Feel the tissue by pressing your fingers in small, overlapping areas about the size of a dime. To be sure you cover your whole breast, take your time and follow a definite pattern: lines, circles or wedges.

Some research suggests that many women do breast self-examination more thoroughly when they use a pattern of up-and-down lines or strips. Other women feel more comfortable with another pattern.

The important thing is to cover the whole breast and to pay special attention to the area between the breast and the underarm, including the underarm itself. Check the area above the breast, up to the collarbone and all the way over to your shoulder.

Lines: Start in the underarm area and move your fingers downward little by little until they are below the breast. Then move your fingers slightly toward the middle and slowly move back up. Go up and down until you cover the whole area.

Circles: Beginning at the outer edge of your breast, move your fingers slowly around the whole breast in a circle. Move around the breast in smaller and smaller circles, gradually working toward the nipple. Don't forget to check the underarm and upper chest areas too.

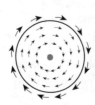

Wedges: Starting at the outer edge of the breast, move your fingers toward the nipple and back to the edge. Check your whole breast, covering one small wedge-shaped section at a time. Be sure to check the underarm area and the upper chest.

6) It's important to repeat step 5 while you are lying down. Lie flat on your back, with one arm over your head and a pillow or folded towel under the opposite shoulder. This position flattens the breast and makes it easier to examine. Check each breast and the area around it very carefully using one of the patterns described above.

7) Some women repeat step 5 in the shower. Your fingers will glide easily over soapy skin so you can concentrate on feeling for changes underneath.

If you notice a lump, a discharge or any other change during the month — whether or not it is during breast self-examination — contact your doctor.

What You Need to Know About Breast Cancer, National Cancer Institute, Building 31, Room 10A24, Bethesda, Md. 20892

Say nuts to cancer

Nuts have fallen out of favor recently because they contain so much fat. But at least one kind of nut is such an effective cancer preventive that you may want to add it to your diet. Brazil nuts are high in selenium, a well-documented anti-cancer mineral. In several studies, scientists exposed rats to chemicals known to cause cancer and gave some of the rats high doses of selenium. The rats fed selenium developed cancer at a much lower rate than the other rats.

It's impossible to conduct those kinds of studies on people, but researchers have found that people who live in areas where the soil contains a lot of selenium have a much lower risk of cancer than people who live in low-selenium areas. Other studies have shown that people who have cancer generally have low levels of selenium in their blood.

Selenium is especially good at preventing cancer of the breast, colon and lungs. It is also a strong preventive of cancer of the ovaries, cervix, rectum, bladder, esophagus, pancreas, skin, liver and prostate. It may help prevent leukemia.

Selenium is an antioxidant, which means it protects the body against damage from "free radicals." Free radicals are elements produced in the cells as byproducts of your body's normal activities. They have been linked to the aging process and may lead to the development of cancer.

While many foods contain some selenium, Brazil nuts seem to be the best source. Foods grown in selenium-rich soil also have high levels of the mineral, but there's no practical way to know if the dirt in your garden contains high levels of selenium.

How many Brazil nuts does it take to prevent cancer? Three to six nuts a day are enough to increase your body's selenium content to cancer-fighting levels. But before you go nuts over Brazil nuts, consider a couple of warnings.

First, nuts' high-fat reputation is well-deserved. Either make sure you cut down on other sources of fat in your diet, or consider taking selenium as a dietary supplement. Check your local pharmacy or health food store. Many multivitamins contain selenium.

Second, don't take too much of a good thing. You probably won't overdose on selenium with three to six Brazil nuts a day, but you should watch for fatigue, nausea, vomiting, sour-milk breath or loss of nails. If you have these symptoms, stop eating Brazil nuts.

Nutrition and Cancer (21,3:203)
The Real Vitamin & Mineral Book: Going Beyond the RDA for Optimum Health, Avery Publishing, Garden City Park, N.Y.
Complete Guide to Vitamins, Minerals and Supplements, Fisher Books, Tucson, Ariz.

Season with soy to reduce cancer risk

In addition to dumping extra vegetables into your Chinese stir-fry dinners, research suggests that you may want to throw in a little tofu and sprinkle on the soy sauce.

Tofu, tempeh, soy sauce, soy milk, miso and textured vegetable protein — all products made from the lowly soybean — may contain compounds that help prevent cancer, especially breast cancer.

In a recent study at the University of Wisconsin, scientists found that soy sauce acted as an antioxidant, preventing the growth of cancer. Several components of soy sauce reduced the number of stomach tumors in rats by 66 percent.

In a recent Japanese study, scientists showed that miso, a type of fermented soy paste used as a seasoning or pickling ingredient in Asian cuisine, is an antioxidant. It absorbs the free radicals associated with tumor growth.

Large population studies have shown that eating miso soup is associated with a lower death rate from stomach cancer. Miso is also associated with preventing breast tumors in lab rats. Miso contains vitamin E and other types of antioxidants called isoflavones and saponins.

Unfortunately, the soy picture is not all rosy. Many experts are concerned about the connection between soy and forgetfulness discovered several years ago. The research suggests soy makes your brain age faster — the more soy you eat, the greater your memory and learning difficulties and the greater your risk of developing senility. While you don't have to avoid soy altogether, talk to your doctor about keeping to moderate amounts.

Soy causes longer menstrual cycles? A large population study also indicates that eating lots of soy products may account for the decreased risk of breast cancer among women in China and Singapore. That view was supported by a recently published British study that links eating soy protein with a lower risk of breast cancer.

In that study, women who ate textured vegetable protein containing isoflavones began to have longer menstrual cycles, meaning they may have less exposure to the female hormone estrogen. High estrogen levels are linked with higher risk for breast cancer.

Tofu is perhaps the most popular soy product consumed in the United States. It comes in cake-like form and is available in the produce departments of most grocery stores, and in health food stores. It has a chewy texture and takes on the flavor of foods and sauces that are cooked with it. You can stir-fry it, or use it in lasagna and chili. Soft tofu can go in salad dressings, dips and even milkshakes.

Soy flour is also a good source of anti-cancer agents. In most recipes, you can substitute soy flour for one-third of every cup of wheat flour with no change in taste. Try mixing soy milk with your regular milk for your cereals, puddings, cream soups and sauces.

Consumer Reports on Health (5,4:37)
Food Safety Notebook (4,2:23)
Medical Tribune for the Family Physician (35,15:8)
Nutrition Research Newsletter (12,3:28)
The American Journal of Clinical Nutrition (60,3:333)

Timing your breast cancer surgery to the menstrual cycle may improve results

Your natural body rhythms may play a vital role in combatting deadly cancer cells that spread after breast cancer surgery.

Respected researchers believe that having breast cancer surgery in the last half of your menstrual cycle may keep cancer from spreading after the surgery. The "last half" means the time after you ovulate and before you start your period. In a recent study, over 75 percent of the women who had surgery during the last half of their menstrual cycles were cancer-free five years later. Only 63 percent of the women who had surgery during the first half of their menstrual cycles were cancer-free in five years.

Why does your menstrual cycle affect survival after surgery? Researchers give two main reasons why your chances of beating breast cancer may be better if you have surgery after you ovulate and before you start your period:

➤ You have a high level of estrogen and very little progesterone in your body in the first half of your cycle — from the time you start bleeding to the time you ovulate. Estrogen seems to encourage the growth of cancer cells that may escape during surgery, while progesterone discourages the cancer from growing.

The extra progesterone you have in the last half of your cycle helps protect you against spreading cancer cells.

➤ A woman's immune system may be at a low point in the first half of her cycle, making it harder to battle cancer cells that escape during surgery. Your immune system may be low at this time so it won't accidently attack a newly fertilized egg when you ovulate.

After you ovulate, your immune system gets stronger. You have a larger number of natural killer cells that can hunt down and get rid of any escaping cancer cells.

Talk to your doctor about the findings. Some studies have reported conflicting results, and not all doctors are ready to accept the notion that your chances of cancer-free survival are better when you time your breast cancer surgery to your menstrual cycle.

However, many studies are revealing that your body's natural rhythms affect your odds of beating cancer. One of the most recent studies looked at over 1,000 women and was reported in the highly respected medical journal *The Lancet*. If breast cancer surgery is in your future, you'd be wise to talk to your doctor about these findings. Scheduling your surgery in the last half of your cycle — after you ovulate and before you start your period — may help you beat breast cancer for life.

Annals of Internal Medicine (116,3:268)
Archives of Surgery (128,3:309)
British Journal of Surgery (80,1:43 and 80,5:670)
Journal of the National Cancer Institute (85,8:605)
The Lancet (343,8912:1545)

Is your bra giving you breast cancer?

Think you've heard it all about what may cause cancer? Get ready for a shock — an anthropologist has published a new book blaming breast cancer on the bras you wear.

Wearing a bra that's too tight for too long can greatly increase your risk of cancer, says astonishing new research by Sydney Ross Singer and his wife Soma Grismaijer. Women who wear bras more than 12 hours a day are 21 times more likely to develop breast cancer, says the pair. And women who wear a bra to bed are 125 times more likely to get breast cancer than women who don't wear a bra at all.

Singer believes that tight bras smash the lymph vessels that lie close to the breast's surface. Lymph fluid normally flows through these vessels and cleans toxins from the body. Bras prevent that cleansing action.

Bras also squeeze the large clusters of lymph nodes in your armpits, which produce the killer immune cells you need to fight toxins in your body.

Singer developed his theory after questioning women about their bra-wearing habits. He surveyed over 2,000 women without breast cancer and over 2,000 breast cancer survivors.

The link between bras and breast cancer needs to be examined by medical experts before we can be sure it really exists.

Be a bra burner. But, according to Singer, here's what women who wear bras can do to cut their risk of breast cancer:

➤ Wear a bra as little as possible.

➤ Never wear a bra to bed.

➤ Don't wear underwire, push-up or strapless bras (except perhaps on special occasions).

➤ Buy loose bras. Bras should never leave a red mark on your skin.

➤ If your breast size changes during your menstrual cycle, buy different-sized bras so you'll always be comfortable.

➤ When you take your bra off, massage your breasts to get your lymph fluid flowing.

Dressed to Kill: The Link Between Breast Cancer and Bras, Avery Publishing, Garden City Park, N.Y.

Bunions

Barefoot and bunion-free

If you're a woman and you can remember back to when you were a young girl, you probably remember teetering around in your mother's high heels and then wobbling in your own. You also remember sitting down and rubbing your feet after a few hours, reciting the famous line, "Beauty knows no pain."

It's somewhat ironic that something done in the name of beauty can result in something as ugly as bunions. Once thought to be the result of genetics, doctors are now pointing the finger at our shoes.

In a report presented in 1993, Dr. Michael Coughlin studied his own orthopedic practice and barefoot populations. Women who go barefoot, it seems, don't get very many bunions. He concluded that bunions come from wearing shoes that don't fit right. Annual medical cost of treating conditions related to shoe wear? Two billion dollars.

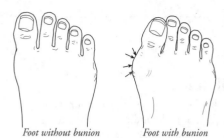

Foot without bunion   *Foot with bunion*

Hang up your high heels. "I have a lot of my female patients trace their foot on a sheet of paper and then trace their shoe," said Dr. Bret Ribotsky, a podiatrist at Cleveland Clinic Florida. "Nine times out of 10, it doesn't fit. ... The ratio (of bunion patients) is eight to one women over men, and 80 to 85 percent of them have been wearing heels for years."

Pointed-toe high heels throw a woman's center of gravity to the front of her foot, Ribotsky said, and are a leading cause of bunions, an inflammation and thickening of the joint where your big toe attaches to your foot.

The joint becomes enlarged and forces the big toe inward. That cramps the remaining toes on the foot, and a big red bump comes up on the side of the foot at the base of the big toe. It hurts like the dickens and can interfere with your ability to walk. Real pretty.

Okay. Enough bashing. You get the message. What's there to do about the problem?

Feel free in flats. If you want to avoid bunions, the answer is to switch from heels to flats or lace-up shoes. Older women may be horrified by the popular "grunge" look that pairs dresses with clunky Army boots, but at least feet in Army boots aren't in pain. If you wear running shoes, wear those sold for men. They have more room in the toes than the shoes made for women.

You may also want to try orthotics, individually fitted inserts that conform to the bottom of your foot and keep your toes in place.

Going barefoot beats bunion surgery. Surgery for bunions is recommended only when you have substantial pain and problems with walking, and even then, there's a controversy about what kind of doctor — a podiatrist or an orthopedist — is best qualified to do the job. Recovery time can be lengthy; the results are decidedly mixed; and the doctors still recommend swearing off high heels.

Your best bet is to go barefoot at home and wear flat, comfortable shoes whenever possible. That way, you may not have to foot the bill for painful bunion surgery.

Bunion Fact Sheet, National Institute of Arthritis and Musculoskeletal and Skin Diseases, Office of Scientific and Health Communications, Box AMS, 9000 Rockville Pike, Bethesda, Md. 20892
Dr. Bret Ribotsky, podiatrist, Cleveland Clinic Florida
The Physician and Sportsmedicine (22,2:32)
Washington Post

Bursitis

How to heal those painful joints

You worked in your yard for one hour too long, or you let your tennis partner talk you into one too many games last week, and now you're paying for it. Your shoulder is so sore that you have to hold your arm close to your body, with your forearm resting motionless across your chest.

Chances are good that you have bursitis. It is an inflammation of the bursa, the fluid-filled sacs between a joint and the supporting ligaments around the joint. These little sacs (160 of them in all!) cushion the muscles and bones so they can move easily.

A sharp blow or too much exercise can cause the bursa to swell and hurt. While the pain may feel like arthritis, bursitis is different. Arthritis involves swelling of the joints themselves, but bursitis involves the fluid-filled sacs that cushion the joints. Arthritis can last a long time, but bursitis generally goes away with treatment.

The shoulder and the hip are the most common sites of bursitis, but the knee, elbow, groin and foot joints (bunions are a form of bursitis) are also vulnerable. You'll feel severe pain and tenderness, and you'll have trouble moving the joint. Overuse or straining is usually at the root of bursitis, but it can be caused by an infection or connective-tissue disease. If it is not allowed to heal, bursitis can lead to calcium deposits in the fluid-filled sacs, making your joint painful and stiff.

With proper treatment, the pain usually subsides in a few days, and all symptoms usually disappear within two weeks. The problem can return, however, and may take longer to respond to treatment the second time. To avoid this, you should stop the activity that caused the bursitis for several weeks to a month and continue to do the recommended gentle exercises.

Rest is essential. To avoid further damage to the bursa, stop the activity that caused the problem until the pain is gone and the inflammation is allowed to heal. Try to find alternative ways to perform activities that irritate the inflamed area.

Ice it. For the first 48 hours of treatment, use ice or cold packs to stop the swelling. After that, you can use a heating pad to stimulate blood flow and ease the pain.

Give it support. You may want to use a splint or sling to keep your shoulder or elbow still, or add padding to protect from bumps. An elastic bandage may help decrease swelling and provide support to the area. You may also want to try using an elbow, wrist, ankle or knee brace for support.

Aspirin can help. Any anti-inflammatory, such as aspirin or ibuprofen, can help ease the pain and speed healing.

Gentle exercises promote healing. As the pain subsides, you can begin gentle range-of-motion exercises. Do the exercises slowly, and stop if you feel pain.

➤ *For shoulder pain*, lie on your back, and raise one arm over your head, keeping your elbow straight. Keep your arm close to your ear. Return your arm slowly to your side. Repeat as needed. You can also do this from a standing position.

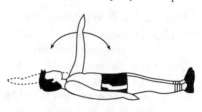

➤ *For hip pain*, lie on your back with your legs straight and about six inches apart. Point your toes up. Slide one leg out to the side and return. Try to keep your toes pointing up. Slide your leg only. Do not lift it. Repeat as needed. This also can be done from a standing position. (This exercise isn't recommended if you have low back problems, osteoporosis or a total hip replacement.)

➤ *For the hip and the knee*, lie on your back with one knee bent and the other as straight as possible. Bend the knee of the straight leg. Use your hands to pull your knee to your chest. Push the leg into the air and then lower it to the floor. Repeat as needed. If you feel pain in your knee, do not kick it into the air. Just lower it to the floor.

➤ *For your shoulder and elbow*, try the back pat. Reach one palm over the shoulder to pat your back and place the back of the other hand on the lower back. Slide your hands toward each other, trying to touch your fingertips together. Don't worry if you can't quite reach. Many people are not able to actually touch the fingertips together.

Exercise and Your Arthritis, Arthritis Foundation, P.O. Box 19000, Atlanta, Ga. 30326
The Johns Hopkins Medical Letter: Health After 50 (4,11:6)
U.S. Pharmacist (20,1:33)

Caffeine Dependence

How to be a wise caffeine consumer

Caffeine is just as addictive as cocaine, scientists are saying these days.

"Uh-oh," you're probably muttering. "Now the health police are after my last indulgence, my morning coffee!" You needn't worry — much. If you're healthy, you don't have to give up caffeine.

Caffeine, unlike cocaine, is fairly harmless. However, too much caffeine can make you jittery, anxious and headachy, give you a stomachache, or interfere with your sleep. Withdrawing from a caffeine addiction can be extremely painful, so it's smart to know how much caffeine you're getting every day.

How much is too much? Almost every person in America takes in caffeine in one form or another every day. Most coffee lovers drink about three and a half cups a day. A five-ounce cup of automatic drip coffee contains about 103 milligrams (mg) of caffeine. (That's *cup*, not mug. Mugs hold 10 ounces, or up to a whopping 206 mg of caffeine.) Most experts recommend you get no more than 250 to 450 mg of caffeine per day, depending on your weight, age and general health.

Overdoing it. Too much caffeine can cause abnormal heart rhythms or raise blood pressure, especially in people who aren't used to the jolt. It can affect cholesterol levels slightly, but recent research has suggested that any rise in LDL ("bad") cholesterol that it causes is offset by an equal rise in HDL ("good") cholesterol.

Drinking more than two cups of coffee a day can cause calcium loss, increasing the chance of osteoporosis and hip fracture. Coffee lovers, especially women, should drink a glass of milk a day to offset coffee's effect on bones.

Caffeine can also hinder the absorption of certain kinds of iron, including iron from supplements. If you're anemic, don't take your iron with your morning coffee! And if you are pregnant or soon plan to be, it's best to avoid caffeine. Heavy use can increase the risk of miscarriage or low birth weight. It may also make you less fertile.

Caffeine and other drugs. Caffeine can intensify the effects of some stimulants, common cold remedies and hormones. It can cause extremely high blood pressure when combined with certain antidepressants. Make sure your doctor or pharmacist knows how much caffeine you drink.

Cold turkey ... er, coffee. Someone who consumes a lot of caffeine can find quitting, or even cutting back, rough going. Flulike symptoms, insomnia, jangling nerves and a nasty headache are frequent consequences. Withdrawal symptoms usually start within 18 to 24 hours, but can begin earlier. In fact, the

Has your doctor told you ...

Drugs and caffeine can clash

Many common medications interact with the caffeine you consume and cause harmful side effects. Some drugs slow the body's disposal of caffeine. These can result in insomnia, irritability, nervousness or heart palpitations when combined with caffeine.

> ➤ Birth-control pills
> ➤ Ciprofloxacin (Cipro) — prescribed for bacterial infections
> ➤ Cimetidine (Tagamet) — prescribed for ulcers

Drugs that stimulate the nervous system can also cause insomnia, anxiety or palpitations when combined with caffeine.

> ➤ Appetite suppressants (Acutrim, Dexatrim)
> ➤ Theophylline (Slo-Phyllin, Theo-Dur) — prescribed for asthma
> ➤ Oral decongestants (Contac, Propagest)

Caffeine can interfere with the sedative effects of the benzodiazepine tranquilizers (Halcion, Valium, Xanax). Perhaps most dangerous of all, when combined with the antidepressant monoamine oxidase (MAO) inhibitors (Nardil, Parnate), caffeine can lead to extremely high blood pressure or abnormal heart rhythms.

Nursing95 Drug Handbook, Springhouse Corp., Springhouse, Pa.
Physicians' Desk Reference, Medical Economics Data Production, Montvale, N.J.

"lift" your morning cup of coffee gives you may be simple relief from early withdrawal symptoms. If you need to cut down, do it gradually.

Now for the good news. Caffeine's stimulating effect can be useful. It can improve mental and physical performance, make a dull task go faster and help with fatigue on long drives. In military combat, it can keep soldiers alert and save lives. It helps some pain relievers work more efficiently, and research has shown it to "rev" the metabolism slightly. Dieters always appreciate even a slight metabolism boost.

The trick to healthy coffee consumption is balance and constancy. Since it is possible to develop a tolerance for caffeine, it's best not to get too much. Be aware that caffeine "hides" in unexpected places, and you may be consuming much more than you know. Read labels, and check the caffeine chart on page 77.

Let's say you want to limit yourself to no more than 350 mg of caffeine per 12-hour day. Suppose you like to have a mug of coffee in the morning and a cup after lunch. You're already near 309 mg — almost your limit. You could have a chocolate cupcake and a cup of hot tea, at 35 mg, for your total of 344, but no more coffee.

Or ... you *could* make that lunch cup decaf and "bank" about 103 mg — enough for a double cappuccino later. However, if you took Excedrin for a headache that day, you're a little over your limit, so better make that after-dinner coffee decaf. (But you could still have the chocolate cupcake.)

Moderation, as in most things, is the key. In an age of "don'ts," isn't it nice to know that you can have your coffee — and eat your cake, too?

American Family Physician (47,5:1262)
Food Safety Notebook (4,9:88)
Medical Tribune (33,5:19)
The Journal of the American Medical Association (266,8:1070 and 267,6:811)
U.S. Pharmacist (17,12:34)

Coffee in the 21st century

Coffee houses, coffee bars and cafes are springing up all over America. What's the appeal? Conversation, for one thing. Alcohol-free socializing. A comfortable place to play games, read or just think. And, in supermarkets and specialty stores, you can now buy coffee by country of origin, type of roasting process, even type of bean.

Are you watching your caffeine intake?

Surprise! Gourmet coffees, espresso, cappuccino and all the rest have less, not more, caffeine than plain, all-American joe.

One reason is the beans. Arabica bean, the usual base for such coffees, have about one-third less caffeine than robusta beans, the mainstream bean. Another is the roast. The darker roasts burn off more caffeine, so although the coffee tastes stronger, it isn't.

And espresso, which looks and tastes strongest of all, is made by forcing water so quickly through the grounds that it doesn't absorb much caffeine. Because it's usually sipped slowly from 1 1/2 oz. demitasse cups, an after-dinner espresso is a much better choice than a cup of regular drip coffee. Cappuccino, café au lait and the like are made with espresso, so you can safely consume one — even two — as part of a healthy, managed caffeine intake.

Hippocrates (3,6:18)

The caffeine calculator

Beverages	Milligrams caffeine
Coffee, automatic drip (5 oz. cup)	80 - 150
Coffee, perked (5 oz. cup)	64 - 124
Coffee, instant (5 oz. cup)	40 - 108
Coffee, decaf (5 oz. cup)	2 - 5
Cocoa, hot (5 oz. cup)	4 - 6
Tea, brewed, 3 min. (5 oz. cup)	36 - 40
Tea, brewed, iced (12 oz. glass)	36 - 40
Cola drinks (12 oz. can)	36 - 46
"Specialty" Coffees	
Espresso, 1.5 oz. (demitasse cup)	15 - 30
Cappuccino (3 oz. espresso, 3 oz. milk)	30 - 60
Foods	
Chocolate bar, average size	15 - 30
Baking chocolate, unsweetened, 1 oz.	25
Chocolate cake, slice	20 - 30
Drugs (adult dose)	
No-Doz	200
Aqua-Ban	200
Excedrin	130
Fiorinal	80
Anacin, Empirin, Midol	64
Darvon Compound	60
Norgesic	60

Bowes and Church's Food Values of Portions Commonly Used, 15th ed., HarperCollins, New York
Physicians' Desk Reference for Nonprescription Drugs, Medical Economics Data Production, Montvale, N.J.

Expectant mothers take a break from coffee

While "the best part of waking up" might be some coffee in your cup, it might not be the best thing for your baby if you're pregnant. Researchers have discovered that your daily "fix" of caffeine might increase your risk of miscarriage if you are pregnant or are planning a pregnancy.

Caffeine doubles chance of miscarriage. Researchers at McGill University in Quebec found that even a moderate amount of caffeine — the equivalent of as little as one and a half cups of coffee a day — doubled the chance of miscarriage in the first three months of pregnancy. They also discovered that the risk of having a miscarriage was doubled by drinking as little as three cups of coffee a day during the month before conception. While caffeine is relatively harmless under most circumstances, even small amounts during pregnancy might cause a decrease in the normal blood flow from the mother to the fetus.

Caffeine is toxic to growing baby. The caffeine crosses through the placenta from the mother to the fetus rather easily, but the growing fetus can't detoxify the caffeine since its still-developing liver isn't able to produce the required enzymes. Once the caffeine reaches the fetus, it interferes with the normal development of the cells, and it might intensify the dangerous side effects of other chemicals or substances that may be present.

How much caffeine is too much? Doctors advise women to play it safe and cut way back, since the study indicates that even moderate amounts of caffeine consumed on a regular basis can increase your risk of having a miscarriage.

If you are considering pregnancy, if you are already pregnant, or even if you are breast-feeding, you should keep your intake of caffeine to a minimum.

Science News (145,4:61)
The Journal of the American Medical Association (270,24:2940)

Cancer of the Esophagus

Ancient Chinese custom combats cancer

Good news is brewing for tea lovers. Researchers say as little as one cup of green tea a week can slash your risk of developing cancer of the esophagus (the tube that carries food from your throat to your stomach) in half.

Not as common as colon cancer, esophageal cancer is, nevertheless, gaining ground. Deaths from this digestive tract cancer have almost doubled over the last 30 years. An estimated 11,000 people will develop esophageal cancer this year. Of these, over 10,000 will die.

Earlier animal studies had linked consumption of green tea to a reduced risk of esophageal cancer. A recent study reports that the tea has the same protective benefits for people.

Researchers studied a group of people's tea-drinking habits and noted that among those who regularly drank green tea, but also drank alcohol and smoked, the risk for developing esophageal cancer was reduced 20 percent for men and 50 percent for women.

In the nonsmokers and nondrinkers, risks were reduced 57 percent for men and 60 percent for women. The more tea the study participants drank, the lower their risk.

Scientists prove a 4,000-year-old remedy. While these findings may be a cause of celebration among tea lovers everywhere, scientists weren't too surprised. Rumors of tea's natural healing properties have been passed down about 4,000 years.

Chinese emperor Shen Nung, often called "The Divine Healer," discovered this delightful drink in 2737 B.C. when tea leaves accidently fell into some water he was boiling.

Since then, healers worldwide have used tea to treat digestive disorders, relieve headaches, fight infections and prevent cavities, just to name a few.

Why is tea protective? It may be the polyphenols, substances which possess antioxidant properties and can also stop or slow down cancer-causing reactions at the cellular level in your body.

Although black tea, the tea most Americans use to make hot and iced tea, also bestows health benefits, some researchers believe that green tea packs a slightly greater protective punch than black tea because of the way it is processed.

Control your risk of esophageal cancer. In addition to having a cup of tea or so a week, here are some additional ways you can reduce your risk of esophageal cancer:

➤ Avoid alcohol or limit your intake to one or two drinks a week at most.
➤ Stop smoking.
➤ Limit your consumption of salt-cured and smoked foods, such as hot dogs, ham, sausage and bacon.
➤ Don't eat or drink foods that are burning hot. Such foods appear to damage your esophagus and can increase your risk of esophageal cancer five times.

Cancer Facts and Figures, American Cancer Society, 1599 Clifton Road N.E., Atlanta, Ga. 30329-4251
Journal of the National Cancer Institute (86,11:855)
Medical Tribune for the Family Physician (35,12:6)
Two Leaves and a Bud, Tea Council of the U.S.A., 230 Park Ave., New York, N.Y. 10017

Take time out for tea

Whether you like your brew hot or iced, the Tea Council of the U.S.A. has some suggestions for making tip-top tea every time.

Hot tea:

You don't have to cook up a tempest in a teapot to brew an excellent cup of tea. Follow these four golden rules, and you'll always find yourself sipping an exquisite blend.

➤ Prerinse the teapot or teacup you'll be using for your tea with hot water. This will ensure that your tea stays warm while brewing.

➤ Fill your teakettle with fresh cold water. Reheated water gives tea a flat taste. Bring water to a rolling boil. Only boiling water will draw out the full flavor of the tea leaves.

➤ Use one tea bag or one teaspoonful of tea for every 5 1/2 ounces (about one cup) of water. Pour boiling water over the tea.

➤ Watch the clock. Tea should be brewed for three to five minutes. The color of tea is not a good indicator of its strength. If you find that the tea is too strong for you after it's finished brewing, add a little warm water.

Iced tea:

When making iced tea, you need to use 50 percent more tea than you would in making hot tea. For example, if you wanted to make eight glasses of iced tea, you would need to use 12 tea bags or 12 teaspoonfuls of loose tea instead of the eight you would use to make hot tea.

The extra tea will allow for melting ice and help maintain the full flavor of the tea. If you don't have an automatic tea maker, use the easy saucepan method below to make a two-quart pitcherful of tea.

➤ Bring one quart of fresh cold water to a rolling boil.

➤ Remove water from heat and add one-third cup of loose tea or 15 tea bags.

➤ Stir, cover and let stand five minutes.

➤ Fill your pitcher with one quart of cold water. Stir tea again and then strain into pitcher.

➤ Keep tea at room temperature until ready to serve. (Refrigerated tea often turns cloudy.) Pour over ice. If your tea should cloud up, add a little boiling water to restore its clear amber color.

Enjoy!

Two Leaves and a Bud, Tea Council of the U.S.A., 230 Park Ave., New York, N.Y. 10017

Canker Sores and Fever Blisters

Natural therapy for unsightly sores

They're painful and unsightly. They pop up unexpectedly and last for two or three weeks before healing. Eight out of 10 people have had a bout with them. And there's no known medical cure. What are they?

Fever blisters and canker sores — two very similar ailments with some important differences. Fever blisters (also called cold sores) can appear both inside and outside the mouth, usually on your lips or at the corners of your mouth. Canker sores are found only inside the mouth, most often inside your cheeks or on your tongue. The biggest difference is what causes the sores. Fever blisters are caused by the herpes simplex virus. The blisters can be spread easily, especially by kissing.

Even after your first fever blister heals, the virus can lie hidden in a nerve in your face. It may stay there or it may travel down the nerve and cause a new outbreak every once in a while. Unlike fever blisters, you can't catch a canker sore. Some evidence suggests they are caused by bacteria that live in your mouth. One study found that about 20 percent of canker sores are caused by deficiencies of folic acid, vitamin B12 and iron.

Other studies point to a problem in your immune system that causes it to attack normal cells in your mouth. Or, your canker sores may be caused by allergies to acidic foods (such as tomatoes and citrus fruits). Since there are no cures, the best you can do is treat the symptoms and be patient.

Try menthol, phenol and benzocaine. You can buy these balms and salves without a prescription, and they will provide temporary relief of the pain and itching. Don't use them for more than a week without consulting your doctor. Fever blisters often respond to an ointment containing 5 percent acyclovir, a virus-fighting drug. Corticosteroid creams may be helpful in the treatment of canker sores.

Avoid products that contain silver nitrate. Silver nitrate actually slows or prevents the healing process.

Don't stress out. Stress seems to trigger outbreaks of both canker sores and fever blisters.

Avoid salty, spicy and acidic foods. Salty potato chips, spicy tomato sauce and acidic orange juice can quickly aggravate the sores. Other problem foods may include chocolate, seeds, nuts and gelatin.

Stay out of the sun. Research shows that fever blisters may also be activated by an increase in body temperature. This often occurs during sunbathing and outdoor activities. Sunlight itself may be a cause, so wear a hat and use sunblock with a sun protection factor (SPF) of 15 or more when you are outdoors.

Brush gently. Try not to irritate your sores when you brush your teeth.

Heal with foods high in lysine and lactobacillus. Nutritional/herbal therapies may hold the most promise for controlling outbreaks of fever blisters and canker sores. If you have recurring fever blisters, you may be able to speed the healing process with lysine (found in dairy products, potatoes and brewer's yeast), as well as with foods that contain lactobacillus such as yogurt.

Try some melissa-leaf tea. Melissa is a fragrant flowering herb that has been shown to shorten healing time in fever blisters and to cut down on the number of new outbreaks. This herb has been used for more than 2,000 years for its antibacterial qualities. To prepare the tea, add two or three teaspoons (two or three grams) of finely cut melissa leaves to one-half cup of boiling water. Let the solution cool, and use cotton balls to apply to blisters several times a day.

Discover any vitamin deficiencies. If you constantly suffer from canker sores, you may want to get blood and allergy tests to try to find the cause. You may be deficient in folic acid, vitamin B12 or iron. Vitamin supplements could do wonders for you.

Make a goldenseal mouthwash. Goldenseal is widely known for its ability to kill certain bacteria. Mix two teaspoons (six grams) of goldenseal in one cup of boiling water. Let cool. Rinse your mouth with this mixture several times a day to relieve pain of canker sores and help them heal faster.

Mend a sore with myrrh. Myrrh is an antibacterial that is almost always contained in an alcohol solution. You can apply it directly to sores or use it as a mouthwash. To make a mouthwash, mix five to 10 drops of the solution in a glass of water and rinse.

Soothe with sage. Sage's antiseptic and anti-inflammatory properties can bring relief as a gargle or mouthwash. Make a mouthwash by mixing two teaspoonfuls of finely cut sage in a cup of boiling water. Let cool, then gargle.

Wait them out. You'll be glad to hear one good thing about fever blisters: New outbreaks tend to decrease after the age of 35. Getting older does have many advantages!

Dermatologic Clinics (7,1:71)
Fever Blisters and Canker Sores, American Academy of Otolaryngology — Head and Neck Surgery, Inc., One Prince St., Alexandria, Va. 22314
Fever Blisters and Canker Sores, National Institute of Dental Research, Bethesda, Md. 20892
General Dentistry (42,1:40)
Herbs of Choice: The Therapeutic Use of Phytomedicinals, The Haworth Press, Binghamton, N.Y.
Herbs, The Reader's Digest Association, Pleasantville, N.Y.
Journal of Oral Medicine (27,4:113)
The Medical Letter (14,16:59)
U.S. Pharmacist, (18,5:37 and 19,1:Patient Teaching Aid)

Carpal Tunnel Syndrome and Wrist Pain

Help for hard-working hands

You wake up in the middle of the night and your hands are numb and tingling. If you try to write a check, swing a tennis racket or a hammer, you're in pain in a matter of minutes. Twist the lid off a jar? Forget it.

These kinds of symptoms describe carpal tunnel syndrome, a repetitive motion injury that affects thousands of people every year. In its minor form, it's an irritation. At its most serious, it can be disabling.

Don't take it lightly. The carpal tunnel is a ligament that circles the median nerve and tendons running down your arm and into your fingers. Sometimes, when you use your wrist the same way again and again, the tunnel swells and clamps down on the nerve. Long known as an occupational hazard for meat cutters (the industry in which the highest incidences have been reported), carpal tunnel syndrome has become a serious workplace health issue.

With half of the nation's jobs in information-based categories, it's easy to see why more and more people are showing up at the company doctor complaining about pain in their wrists and hands. The U.S. Bureau of Labor Statistics reported that there were nearly 90,000 cases of repetitive motion injuries, including CTS, in 1992.

Blame it on your job, your sport or your hormones. Some people at high risk are keyboard operators (including writers), carpenters, gardeners, cooks, musicians, assembly workers, electricians, butchers, beauticians and homemakers.

Pregnant and menopausal women, whose hormones are changing, may also get CTS because fluid retention puts pressure on the nerve.

Athletes who play racquetball and other racket sports, go bicycling, canoeing or kayaking, bowl, play baseball, or perform gymnastics also run the risk of developing CTS.

"Hey, doc. It hurts when I do this." Sometimes, treatment is as simple as the old joke about the person who goes to the doctor and says, "It hurts when I do this," and the doctor says, "So, don't do that." When the activity that causes you pain is a basic part of doing your job, though, a different approach is needed. The main goal of treatment is to relieve pressure from the nerve so the pain will stop and you can regain full use of your fingers, hands and wrists.

Many times, CTS can be relieved just by changing the height of your desk chair, adding a wrist pad to the front of your keyboard, doing some simple exercises, taking an anti-inflammatory like aspirin or ibuprofen, or a combination of all of the above. For more advanced cases, a doctor could prescribe wearing a wrist splint at night or during the day, steroid injections, or, in the most severe cases, surgery to cut the tunnel and release the pressure on the nerve.

Read this before you choose surgery. A recent report says surgery to correct carpal tunnel syndrome is inadequate. The surgery does nothing to correct muscle problems in the neck, shoulders and back. The researchers argue that imbalances in these muscles and abnormal postures are what cause carpal tunnel syndrome. Change the way you sleep, improve your body positions at work, and strengthen your muscles. You'll get better results than you'll get from surgery, the researchers say.

Try these pain-relief tactics. Here are some techniques you can try yourself that can make a big difference:

➤ Keep your wrists straight when you're performing repetitive tasks like typing, sewing or swinging a tennis racket. (Hmm. Isn't that what the pros say to do anyway?) When typing, don't let your wrists go slack or rest them on your desk.

➤ Take frequent breaks when you use your hands a lot for work or sports. Rest your hands by doing other tasks, like filing or making phone calls.

➤ If you work at a computer, add a wrist rest to the front of your keyboard, and adjust your chair so that your wrists and forearms are parallel to the floor.

➤ Sit up straight at your computer. If you slouch or lean into your keyboard, you strain the nerves and muscles in your wrists and hands. Roll your shoulders back occasionally to relax.

➤ Eat a low-salt diet to reduce swelling and pressure on the nerve.

➤ Squeeze a tennis ball several times a day to help strengthen your hands.

➤ Massage the palm and back of your hands often during the day. Shake your hands periodically if they feel stiff.

Easy exercises will keep your muscles toned and flexible. You should do these exercises several times throughout the day.

1) Make a fist and hold it for 10 seconds. Unclench your hand for a few seconds, then make a fist again. Do this five times with each hand.

2) Make a fist, and bend your wrist up and down slowly as far as you can comfortably. Repeat five times with each wrist.

3) With your hands in a fist, rotate your hands inward in a circle 15 times. Then rotate outward 15 times. Repeat the rotations with your fingers extended. Then, with your fingers relaxed, gently shake your wrists to the sides.

4) Hold your hand up like you're taking an oath, with the fingers facing away from you. With the other hand, pull the fingers back toward you and hold for 10 seconds. Release the hold for a few seconds. Do this five times with each hand.

Diet away wrist pain

Painful wrists are yet another reason to shed those extra pounds. Wrist pain is a common problem for tennis players or golfers because of the constant gripping motion. But sports enthusiasts aren't the only people suffering from wrist pain. In fact, you may be more at risk of developing wrist pain if you are inactive. It may sound strange, but a new study suggests a simple reason for the increased risk: being overweight.

More weight equals more risk. The heavier you are, the greater your risk of developing osteoarthritis. Those who aren't overweight tend to develop fewer wrist and hand problems. The study also suggests that those extra pounds may increase your body's hormone levels, especially estrogen. Excessive amounts of estrogen may lead to stiffer, more mineralized bones, causing osteoarthritis in the joints. That's why women are more likely to have problems than men.

Most of the stresses that occur across a joint are related to muscle contractions and not how much weight they must support. Even though your wrists are not weight-bearing joints, the amount of stress they experience is directly related to your body size. The heavier you are, the more likely you are to produce extra stress on your wrists.

If you're overweight, consider shedding a few pounds. And see your doctor if you are experiencing pain or swelling in your wrists or hands.

American Journal of Epidemiology (139,2:119)

5) Hold your hand up the same way as in Exercise No. 4, and pull your thumb toward your body using the other hand. Hold for 10 seconds, then rest. Do five times with each thumb.

6) Stretching your arms is important too. Lace your fingers and stretch your arms in front of you (palms should face forward). Hold for 10 seconds. Then stretch your arms above your head with your fingers laced.

Next, relieve your shoulders by lacing your fingers behind your head and pushing your elbows back, pressing your shoulder blades together. Relax your elbows by placing your hands on your shoulders with your elbows facing forward. Make about 10 slow circles in front of you.

American Family Physician (49,6:1371)
HealthSmart, Prudential Health Care System
Journal of the American Osteopathic Association (94,8:647)
Medical Tribune (35,8:8)
Medical Tribune for the Family Physician (36,6:20)
"Self care for hard-working hands," *Taking Care* (12,6) Center for Corporate Health
The Physician and Sportsmedicine (23,1:27)

Vitamin B6 eases carpal tunnel pain

For more than 20 years, doctors who prefer a conservative approach to treating carpal tunnel syndrome have prescribed vitamin B6. In fact, the vitamin has been used to treat everything from premenstrual syndrome to sickle cell anemia.

In a recent small study, 16 adults with mild to moderate cases of carpal tunnel syndrome were given a daily dose of 200 mg of vitamin B6 for three months. The study, done by researchers at the Kaiser Permanente Medical Center in Hayward, California, found that everyone felt better when they were taking B6.

B6 raises pain threshold. The vitamin didn't make their carpal tunnel syndrome any less severe, but it had a significant effect on the people's pain thresholds. As a result, the condition caused them less discomfort, so they were able to resume their activities.

"Pain scores improved dramatically during this study," the researchers reported in the *Journal of the American College of Nutrition*.

What they didn't find was a link to a B6 deficiency, long thought by some doctors to be at the root of carpal tunnel. In animals, vitamin B6 deficiencies have been associated with abnormal electroencephalograms (EEGs).

All the participants underwent EEGs before and after the study. They showed no abnormalities before treatment and no changes after treatment.

High doses can be toxic. Since past studies had shown that high doses of vitamin B6 could be toxic, everyone was carefully monitored for nerve damage. Nobody experienced any negative side effects during the study, even though 200 mg is more than 100 times greater than the U.S. recommended daily allowance of 1.5 to 1.7 mg.

Some doctors prescribe taking 150 mg a day for six months, then backing off to 25 mg a day. Since high doses of vitamin B6 can be toxic, treatment should only be done under a doctor's supervision.

The researchers concluded that carpal tunnel sufferers could safely and effectively be treated with vitamin B6 for relief of hand and wrist pain.

Journal of the American College of Nutrition (12,1:73)

Get a grip on wrist pain

If you experience pain in your wrists from overuse, pay attention to your body's warning signs. Catching an injury early and dealing with it quickly can prevent more serious problems later.

If you've simply overdone it, try these tips, and you'll be back in the swing of things in a matter of days.

➤ Stop doing what hurts, and try to find what's causing your pain.

➤ Check out your sports equipment and your form to help identify the cause of your problem. Your racket or clubs may be worn out, or you may need more instruction on the proper grip. The right equipment and the proper form will improve performance and enhance your enjoyment of the activity.

➤ Treat the pain with nonprescription painkillers like ibuprofen or aspirin.

➤ Apply ice to the painful area to help relieve pain (See "Hot and cold therapy to the rescue" in the *Arthritis* chapter for guidelines on applying ice.)

➤ Try this exercise. Keeping your hand and palm face down, place your wrist over the edge of a table. Holding a 1 to 2 lb. weight, bend your wrist as far down as possible. Slowly lift the weight. Continue moving your wrist up and down without stopping. See if you can do three sets of 10 once or twice a day. Try it with your palm up too.

In most cases, controlling the pain and getting your wrist back up to par should only take several days. But if your wrist, hand or forearm is swollen or if it feels warm, tender or numb, see your doctor.

The Physician and Sportsmedicine (22,2:41)

Cataracts

Conquer cataracts with vitamins

The multipurpose multivitamin adds another advantage to its list of life-enhancing benefits: A daily dose can reduce your risk of developing cataracts.

Cataracts cloud the lens, the part of the eye that focuses light to produce a clear, crisp image. Half of all people over 65 develop cataracts, the leading cause of blindness in the world. Vision impaired by cataracts may be improved with prescription eyeglasses, a special type of contact lens, or surgery.

Doctors perform one million surgeries each year. Cataract surgery is the most common procedure performed among older people. In fact, doctors routinely perform more than 1 million cataract surgeries in the United States each year.

However, the Agency for Health Care Policy and Research (AHCPR) believes cataract surgery may be overprescribed.

Just because you're diagnosed with a cataract doesn't mean you need surgery. Most experts recommend that you put off surgery until the cataract begins to interfere with your daily activities, such as reading or driving.

A clear look at cataract facts and myths

➤ As you grow older, chemical changes often take place in the lens of your eye. These changes make your lens cloudy and discolored. That's called a cataract.

➤ Cataracts are not a film or coating on the eye.

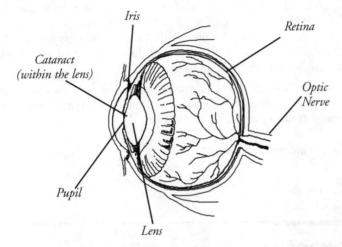

Iris

Retina

Cataract (within the lens)

Optic Nerve

Pupil

Lens

➤ Cataracts are associated with the natural aging process, certain diseases, poor nutrition, exposure to sunlight, inherited tendencies and certain drugs.

➤ Cataracts are not caused from overusing your eyes.

➤ Normally, light passes through your lens and produces a sharp image on your retina, the tissue that lines the inside of the back of your eye. When your lens becomes cloudy, light can't pass through it as well, and you get blurred vision.

➤ As far as is known, you can't reverse cataracts once they begin to develop.

➤ Cataracts usually develop in both eyes around age 50. But they may not damage your vision until 15 or 25 years later.

Cataracts, National Eye Institute, National Institutes of Health, Building 31, Room 6A32, Bethesda, Md. 20892

Microsurgery and laser surgery make implantation of a plastic replacement lens faster and easier than ever. Still, complications from cataract surgery can be very serious, ranging from a drooping eyelid to blindness.

The eye may become infected, causing the retina to detach. While 95 percent of laser surgeries are considered successful, this figure includes people who still have to wear prescription eyeglasses afterward.

Protect your eyes with daily multivitamin. But if you take a daily multivitamin, you may never have to worry about cataract surgery.

A recent Harvard study found that taking a daily multivitamin can cut your risk of cataracts by 27 percent. Smokers and diabetics, two high-risk groups, gain the greatest rewards from long-term use of multivitamin supplements.

Earlier studies linked vitamins C and E to a decreased risk of cataract surgery. In addition, the AHCPR reviewed 8,000 studies and found that people with cataracts are often deficient in those vitamins.

But the Harvard researchers found that taking vitamins C and E alone or in combination with a multivitamin didn't seem to have as good an effect as taking only a multivitamin.

The researchers suggest that something in the multivitamins besides vitamins C and E may offer protection against cataracts.

American Journal of Public Health (84,5:788)
The American Medical Association Encyclopedia of Medicine, Rartdom House, New York
The Atlanta Journal/Constitution

Keep clear vision for life

You can better your 50-50 chance of contracting cataracts in your later years with a few simple precautions.

> ➤ Protect your eyes from the sun and limit exposure to X-rays and microwaves.
> ➤ Limit your alcohol intake. One study suggests that drinkers are four times more likely to develop cataracts than people who do not consume alcohol.
> ➤ Stop smoking.
> ➤ Avoid corticosteroid drugs, diuretics and tranquilizers whenever possible. You may want to talk with your doctor about alternatives to these drugs, but never stop taking a prescribed medicine without consulting your doctor.

The American Medical Association Encyclopedia of Medicine, Random House, New York
The Atlanta Journal/Constitution

Chapped Lips

Kiss chapped lips goodbye

Couples do it. Parents and kids do it. Some animals even seem to do it. Everybody loves kissing. But nobody likes kissing dry, chapped lips. How can you keep your lips healthy? It's easy when you know a few facts.

Beware the three enemies of healthy lips. Enemy number one is the sun. Unlike the rest of your exposed skin, your lips don't have any melanin. This means they cannot tan to protect themselves from harmful ultraviolet sunlight. But they can burn very easily. Enemy number two is dry air. Lips don't have any sweat or sebaceous glands to help keep them moist and lubricated in dry or windy weather.

Enemy number three might be you. Your lips are crammed full of nerve endings. Whether you realize it or not, you probably lick, bite or wipe your lips more frequently when they're irritated. This leads to further irritation.

Lick your lip enemies with balms and sunscreens. How can you stop the assault on your lips? A little prevention goes a long way. Make it a habit to apply a lip balm with sunscreen several times a day. Look for a lip balm with a sun protection factor (SPF) of 15 or higher. Lip protectants relieve and prevent dryness and chapping. Petrolatum, allantoin and cocoa butter are common ingredients found in lip balms. Lip ointments also may contain local anesthetics, camphor, phenol or menthol, which will provide soothing relief from irritation. Apply the lip balm with sunscreen about an hour before going outside. Reapply every hour and after swimming or eating.

Don't forget your lip sunscreen in the winter months. Even if it doesn't feel warm and sunny, the sun's rays can still burn your lips. And snow reflects up to 90 percent of the sun's rays. So wear your sunscreen in the winter too. Some people have allergic reactions to certain sunscreens. If your lips become red or swollen while using one, discontinue use. If the condition persists, see your doctor.

Drink at least eight glasses of water a day. Extra water helps keep your lips and skin moist and supple.

Protecting your lips every day is the best way to keep them kissably soft.

U.S. Pharmacist (19,3:36)

Cholesterol

19 ways to lower high cholesterol naturally

If you're thinking you don't have to worry about cholesterol because you don't have heart trouble, you may want to think again. About 25 percent of American adults over age 20 have blood cholesterol levels that are considered high. More than half of all Americans have levels that are borderline-high.

Eating the typical American diet of fatty meats; processed cold cuts; dairy products; fried foods; eggs; and commercially baked breads, cakes and cookies can lead just about anyone down the high-cholesterol path. Only a fraction of the population can eat high-fat diets and have low cholesterol.

You don't have to eat any cholesterol, a waxy substance that is vital for hormones and cell membranes. Your body makes all it needs. Any extra you get is either eliminated from your body or deposited in your arteries. That's when problems begin.

Of course, even if your cholesterol is a little high, it doesn't mean you'll have a heart attack, but elevated cholesterol is one of the main risk factors. And if your cholesterol isn't high, you may want to take steps to keep it that way.

Fortunately, that's fairly easy to do. Most people can lower or maintain their cholesterol just by making a few additions and subtractions to their diets. Here are several ideas, along with a primer on cholesterol terms and numbers.

Don't chew the fat. Strangely enough, eating cholesterol doesn't raise blood cholesterol nearly as much as eating a type of fat called saturated fat. Like cholesterol, saturated fat is found mainly in animal products, like cheese, butter, cream, whole milk, ice cream, lard and marbled meats.

Some vegetable oils — palm oil, palm kernel oil, coconut oil and cocoa butter — are also high in saturated fat. These oils are often used in commercially baked goods, coffee creamers and nondairy whipped toppings, so read the labels.

Unsaturated fats, both polyunsaturated and monounsaturated, have been shown to reduce blood cholesterol levels. They are found in many vegetable oils, including corn oil, olive oil and canola oil.

Buy the leanest cuts of meat, and regularly substitute poultry (without skin) and fish, which are lower in saturated fat, for red meat. Switch to low-fat cottage cheese and yogurt, reduced-fat hard cheeses and skim or 1-percent milk.

Simply switching from whole milk to skim milk can lower your total cholesterol 6.9 percent and your LDL "bad" cholesterol 10.8 percent.

Stick to four egg yolks a week. Most people don't have to worry about eating cholesterol. Our bodies adjust to higher dietary intakes of cholesterol by cutting back on internal cholesterol production.

However, one-third of Americans are "cholesterol responders." Their blood cholesterol does go up when they eat cholesterol, although saturated fat is still the biggest villain for them too.

Since you probably don't know if you're a cholesterol responder, the American Heart Association says play it safe — don't eat more than four egg yolks a week. (An average egg yolk contains 213 mg of cholesterol.)

Forgo frying. Buying low-fat foods is only the first step. You need to use low-fat cooking methods to keep fat from creeping back in. Trim all fat off meat before cooking. Remove fatty skin from chicken and turkey.

Don't fry foods. Roast, bake, broil or poach them instead. Use fat-free basting or marinating liquids, such as wine, tomato juice or lemon juice.

If you use oil for sautéing or baking, use olive or canola, both very low in saturated fat. Use diet, tub or squeeze margarines instead of regular. Watch out for the term "hydrogenated," which means some of the fat has been made saturated. (For more information on oils, see the "Some oils are better than others" story.)

Eat your vegetables and complex carbohydrates. The lowest-fat foods of all are vegetables, fruits, grains (rice, barley and pasta), beans and legumes. Substitute these for meat and high-fat dairy products.

Don't douse your pasta in butter or your baked potato in sour cream. Use tomato-based sauces instead of cream-based. Use lemon juice, low-sodium soy sauce or herbs to season vegetables. Make chili with extra beans and seasonings, and leave out the meat.

Lose weight. People who are overweight usually have high cholesterol levels. Most can lower their LDL "bad" cholesterol and raise their HDL "good" cholesterol by dropping a few pounds. Eat fewer fatty foods and more fruits, vegetables, grains and beans, and you will slowly but surely lose weight.

Include the family. Children older than age 2 can join in the low-fat lifestyle. Eating habits carry into adulthood, so get your kids started on a healthy eating pattern early. Don't, however, start before age 2. Babies need extra fat calories to develop properly.

Snack to your heart's content. Don't be afraid to snack several times a day on low-fat foods, such as yogurt, fruit, vegetables, bagels and whole-grain breads and cereals. As a matter of fact, evidence points to lower cholesterol levels in people who eat small meals several times a day. Eating often keeps hormones like insulin from rising and signaling your body to make cholesterol. Just make sure your total intake of calories doesn't go up when you eat more often.

Go a little nutty. If you like nuts, especially walnuts or almonds, sprinkle a few on your cereal, bake them into muffins or pancakes, or add them to casseroles or stir-fries. In one study, eating about three ounces of walnuts a day was shown to decrease blood cholesterol levels by 10 percent more than an already low-fat, low-cholesterol diet.

While walnuts are high in fat, it is mostly polyunsaturated fat, the kind that lowers cholesterol. Another study showed that about three ounces of almonds, which are rich in monounsaturated fat, lowered LDL cholesterol by nine percent.

Be sure to decrease other sources of fat to allow for the extra calories from the nuts.

Even some chocolate is OK. Studies indicate that the primary type of saturated fat in chocolate, stearic acid, has no effect on cholesterol levels. When a chocolate bar was substituted for a high-carbohydrate snack on a low-fat, low-cholesterol diet, the chocolate did not increase LDL cholesterol (the bad type), and even seemed to raise HDL cholesterol (the good type), according to one study. But chocolate is high in fat and calories, so take it easy.

Quench your thirst with fruit juice. A low rate of heart disease in France — despite a high-fat diet — led researchers to investigate the French habit of drinking red wine with meals. It seems that some of the nonalcoholic ingredients in red wine raise your HDL cholesterol levels and keep your body from producing LDL cholesterol.

Purple grape juice works like red wine to lower the level of fat in your blood. The cholesterol-lowering effect of red wine and grape juice comes from a naturally occurring compound that helps grapes resist mold. The darker the grape juice, the better.

Grapefruit juice can also lower the level of cholesterol in your blood. It even improves the ratio of "good" cholesterol to "bad" cholesterol in your body.

Grapefruit juice may also help your body get rid of a fatty substance called plaque that can build up in your arteries and cause a heart attack.

Eat the "stinking rose." The cholesterol-lowering effects of garlic have been repeatedly demonstrated in people with normal and high cholesterol, so don't hold back. Garlic seems to raise your "good" HDL levels too. If the odor bothers you, try it in tablets. These have been shown to be almost as effective as the cooked or raw cloves.

Niacin works, but be careful. Niacin, one of the B vitamins, is proven to lower total cholesterol and raise HDL. It is one of the cheapest and most effective cholesterol-lowering drugs around.

But without a doctor's supervision, it may not be safe. Doses high enough to lower cholesterol have been shown to cause very high blood sugar or liver damage. In one study, liver problems developed at 1500 mg a day. If you have very high cholesterol, check with your doctor about this treatment.

Give flaxseed a whirl. The seeds from the flax plant amazingly lower your cholesterol levels and your blood pressure at the same time. Loaded with soluble fiber that lowers cholesterol, flaxseed is also the best plant source of omega-3 fatty acids. These fats, found mainly in fish, keep your blood from sticking, regulate your heartbeat, and lower your blood pressure. They've also been shown to lower cholesterol.

Whether because of the soluble fiber, omega-3 fatty acids, or some other ingredient, flaxseed works. Studies have shown flaxseed can lower cholesterol by as much as 14.7 percent. Just remember, to get the benefits, you must grind up the seeds first.

It's easy to sneak flaxseed into your diet. Here's an instant way to keep your arteries free of clogging plaque. Just whip flaxseed up in your smoothies. You can also mix ground flaxseed into oatmeal, rice pilaf, applesauce, or yogurt. Or add it to salads, soups, cereals, and baked goods.

For example, bake some flaxseed bread. This amazing bread works exactly like cholesterol-lowering drugs, but without the side effects. One study found that people who ate six slices of flaxseed bread a day significantly lowered their cholesterol.

Calcium can help. In one study, when 56 people took a calcium carbonate supplement, their total cholesterol went down 4 percent and their HDL (good) cholesterol went up 4 percent. They took 400 mg of calcium three times a day. No side effects were reported.

Might as well take a multivitamin. While you are boosting your calcium and vitamin E intake, don't forget good old vitamin C. Vitamin C, the No. 1 immune system booster, also drives up your good cholesterol. In a recent study, the people who took in more than 60 mg of vitamin C a day (60 mg is the recommended dietary allowance) had the highest HDL levels.

Fill up on fiber. Oat bran caught the national fancy a few years ago when some studies showed that it drastically lowered cholesterol levels. Later studies showed inconsistent results, but scientists generally believe that soluble fiber, the kind found in oat bran, helps lower LDL cholesterol and raise HDL cholesterol.

As little as three grams per day of fiber from oat bran or oatmeal can be effective. There are 7.2 grams of soluble fiber per 100 grams of dry oat bran, and five grams of soluble fiber per 100 grams of dry oatmeal. (Read labels to check the number of grams in a serving.)

Other sources of soluble fiber are barley, beans, peas and many other vegetables. Corn fiber is a good cholesterol reducer. It lowered cholesterol 5 percent in a recent study. The researchers used 20 grams of corn fiber a day. You'd be hard pressed to eat that much in a day (one serving of corn has three grams of corn fiber), but every little bit helps.

Pectin (a soluble fiber found in fruits such as apples and prunes) and psyllium (the fiber you'll find in many breakfast cereals and bulk laxatives) seem to lower cholesterol even better than oat bran. To get the best cholesterol-lowering results from bulk laxatives containing psyllium, mix it with your food instead of taking it between meals. (See the ***Constipation*** chapter for a list of high-fiber breakfast cereals.)

Keep moving. Evidence shows that exercise can lower LDL cholesterol and boost HDL cholesterol. But exercise alone can't perform this magic. People who exercise and still eat high-fat diets or who are overweight may not reap the cholesterol-lowering benefits.

Both aerobic exercise — walking, jogging, swimming, bicycling and cross-country skiing — and strength training — lifting weights or using weight machines — improve cholesterol levels. An analysis of 11 studies on weight training showed that this exercise lowered LDL cholesterol by 13 percent and raised HDL cholesterol by 5 percent. If you lift weights, use light to moderate weights and do many repetitions.

Serve a savory dish of soy. You will probably lower your cholesterol if you can learn to cook with soy products. People in a recent study lowered their cholesterol 12 percent by eating 50 grams of soy protein a day, baked into muffins, breads, cookies, cakes and fruit bars.

You have to substitute the soy protein for the animal proteins you normally eat. Soy proteins are high in fat just like animal proteins, but they are full of good quality nutrients.

Tofu is the most common kind of soy protein you'll find in the grocery stores. It comes in cake-like form, has a chewy texture, and takes on the flavor of foods and sauces that are cooked with it. You can stir-fry it, or use it in lasagna and chili. Soft tofu can go in salad dressings, dips and even milkshakes.

Take time for tea. Green tea, and possibly black tea, may lower your cholesterol and improve your HDL to LDL ratio.

———

ACP Journal (119,3:68)
American Heart Association news release
Archives of Family Medicine (2,2:130)
Archives of Internal Medicine (153,17:2050)
Arteriosclerosis, Thrombosis, and Vascular Biology (15,3:325)
British Medical Journal (303,6805:785)
Cholesterol and Your Heart, American Heart Association, 7272 Greenville Ave., Dallas, Texas 75231-4596
Cholesterol in Children: Healthy Eating Is a Family Affair, National Institutes of Health, 9000 Rockville Pike, Bethesda, Md. 20892
Food, Nutrition and Health (18,2:1 and 18,4:3)
Harvard Health Letter (18,3:3)
HerbalGram (30:11)
Journal of the American Dietetic Association (94,4:425 and 94,1:65)
Medical Abstracts Newsletter (13,11:3)
Medical Tribune (35,2:12 and 36,8:21)
Nutrition Forum (10,3:22)
Nutrition Research Newsletter (12,11/12:122)
Nutrition Today (28,3:30)
So You Have High Blood Cholesterol, Eating to Lower Your High Blood Cholesterol and *National Cholesterol Education Program's Report of the Expert Panel on Blood Cholesterol Levels in Children and Adolescents,* National Institutes of Health, National Heart, Lung and

Blood Institute, National Cholesterol Education Program, NHLBI Information Center, P.O. Box 30105, Bethesda, Md. 20824-0105
Stay Healthy (6,12:47)
The American Journal of Clinical Nutrition (57,6:868; 58,4:501; 59,1:66; 59,5:1055; and 60,1:100)
The Atlanta Journal/Constitution
The Journal of Nutrition (124,1:78)
The Lancet (341,8843:454 and 341,8836:27)
The New England Journal of Medicine (328,9:603)
The Physician and Sportsmedicine (21,10:103 and 22,7:15)
The Wall Street Journal
U.S. Pharmacist (18,9:100)
University of California at Berkeley Wellness Letter (11,1:2)

The cholesterol test: What your numbers mean

Cholesterol tests can be tricky. Simple screening tests, done without fasting, measure only your total cholesterol and your HDL cholesterol, the "good" kind. They can be inaccurate, but they give you at least a ballpark figure.

Even the complete cholesterol test, called the lipid profile, can vary each time you take one. These measure total cholesterol, HDL cholesterol, LDL cholesterol (the "bad" cholesterol) and triglycerides. For accurate numbers, you should not eat or drink anything except water for 12 hours before the test, and you shouldn't exercise vigorously for 24 hours. Also, if you're taking any medication, such as blood-pressure pills or birth-control pills, make sure the person testing you knows. These will affect the results.

Relax and sit still. Relax when blood is being drawn and sit still. Say something if the tourniquet stays on your arm more than a minute. This can also

Cholesterol safe after 70

Getting older definitely has its perks: time to travel, time for grandkids, time for hobbies, and time to stop worrying about cholesterol. Wait. Hold on. Did we just say time to stop worrying about cholesterol?

Yup, that's just what the most recent medical research has revealed. During a four-year study of nearly 1,000 adults with an average age of 79, scientists discovered that age may lessen the impact of high cholesterol. For years, medical researchers have been sounding the cholesterol alarm: If you have high blood cholesterol, you must lower it. High levels of "bad" LDL cholesterol can lead to heart disease, stroke and death.

As a result of these warnings, millions of patients with high cholesterol have been put on restricted diets and medication. And these treatments have been routinely prescribed for everyone with high cholesterol — regardless of age or sex.

Save worry and money. Today, however, that approach to cholesterol management may be changing. Researchers at Yale University have uncovered some startling new facts about the effects of age on cholesterol. And the new findings could save many seniors both money and worry. The men and women in the study had high cholesterol, but were otherwise healthy. And the study results showed they had no increased risk for heart attack or stroke simply because they had high cholesterol.

In fact, the older women in the group demonstrated few links between high cholesterol and heart disease.

Ask your doctor to re-evaluate treatment. No one is disputing the fact that high cholesterol levels can be debilitating — or deadly — for the young or middle-aged. But this new study suggests that the same high levels of cholesterol that threatened you at 40 may not be a problem as you reach your 70s or 80s.

Today, millions of otherwise healthy seniors are being treated for high cholesterol with drugs and diet control. And if you're one of them, you might want to check with your doctor about re-evaluating or discontinuing your cholesterol control program. However, don't stop taking your cholesterol medicine without first talking to your doctor.

Enjoy benefits of getting off cholesterol drugs. If you've never had heart disease, stroke or other circulatory problems, you could benefit in several ways by reducing routine cholesterol screenings and getting off drug and diet treatments. You could:

➤ Enjoy eating again. Strict diet controls to limit fat intake make it hard for many seniors to find appealing foods or eat sufficient amounts and varieties of foods. Malnutrition can be a problem.

➤ Save money. Cholesterol-lowering drugs can cost hundreds to thousands of dollars each year.

➤ Reduce your risk of cancer. Some cholesterol drugs may be associated with increased cancer risk.

➤ Decrease your chances of drug interactions. The more drugs you take, the greater the possibility you'll suffer unpredictable reactions or side effects.

Many people following prescribed treatments for high cholesterol will have to fight the problem for years. The risks are too high if they stop. But if you're in good health and a senior over 70, you could be a candidate for reduced cholesterol therapy. Ask your doctor.

Geriatrics (49,12:14)
Nutrition Research Newsletter (13,11/12:129)
The Journal of the American Medical Association (272,17:1335,1372)

affect the results. Finally, get tested more than once, especially if readings are not normal. Studies show that cholesterol levels may vary by season, so try again in a month or so.

Now that you know your numbers are accurate, you just need to know what they mean. First, let's get some terms straight. Dietary cholesterol means the cholesterol you eat. The American Heart Association (AHA) recommends no more than 300 mg per day if you do not already suffer from heart disease. If you have heart disease, make sure you get less than 200 mg a day of cholesterol from food. Most nutrition labels on food list cholesterol.

Serum cholesterol, blood cholesterol, and total cholesterol all mean the same thing — the cholesterol in your body. This is what is measured when you have a cholesterol test, in milligrams per deciliter of blood (mg/dL).

When your doctor discusses your cholesterol, she probably refers to it in four different ways — total cholesterol, high-density lipoprotein (HDL) cholesterol, low-density lipoprotein (LDL) cholesterol, and triglycerides.

Here's how the AHA categorizes total cholesterol:

➤ less than 200 mg/dL — desirable. Your heart attack risk is relatively low unless you have other risk factors. Still, watch your saturated fat and dietary cholesterol and exercise regularly.

➤ 200 - 239 mg/dL — borderline high. Talk to your doctor about these numbers. Depending on other factors, you may or may not be at higher risk for a heart attack. Try to get your cholesterol level below 200 through diet and exercise. Get your LDL cholesterol checked.

➤ 240 mg/dL and above — high. Your risk of heart attack and stroke is high — generally twice that of people with cholesterol below 200. Have your doctor check your other risk factors and discuss a strategy to bring this number down.

HDL cholesterol is often referred to as "good" cholesterol because it carries cholesterol away from your arteries to your liver, where it is eliminated. Your HDL numbers are always lower because there is less HDL in your blood. Average, healthy HDL levels range from 40 to 60 mg/dL. Less than 40 is considered low and puts you at high risk for heart disease. Over 60 is considered high and reduces your risk for heart disease. If you have low HDL cholesterol, raise it by losing weight, exercising regularly, and not smoking.

Your LDL (bad) cholesterol greatly affects your risk of heart attack and stroke since it carries cholesterol primarily from your liver to various places within your body. Too much LDL means an excess of cholesterol in your arteries. Over time, it builds up on your artery walls (a condition called atherosclerosis), causing blockages and leading to heart attack or stroke. Here are LDL cholesterol levels according to the AHA:

➤ less than 100 mg/dL — ideal

➤ 100 to 129 mg/dL — near/above ideal

➤ 130 to 159 mg/dL — borderline high

➤ 160 to 189 mg/dL — high

➤ 190 mg/dL and above — very high

Triglycerides are fats that provide most of the fuel for your body. You get some from the fat in your diet, and your liver makes the rest from the carbohydrates you eat. Like all fats, they are necessary, within limits, for good health. But studies have found a link between elevated triglyceride levels and heart disease. And high triglycerides plus high LDL cholesterol deals a double whammy to your heart's health. On the other hand, the combination of low triglycerides and high HDL cholesterol is a plus. It puts you at less risk for heart disease even if your LDL cholesterol is high.

See where you fall within the AHA categories for triglyceride levels.

➤ less than 150 mg/dL — normal

➤ 150 - 199 mg/dL — borderline high

➤ 200 - 499 mg/dL — high

➤ 500 mg/dL and above — very high

Consumer Reports on Health (6,3:24)
Food, Nutrition and Health (16,12:1)
Geriatrics (48,6:18)
Medical Tribune (34,7:21 and 34,13:1)
Medical Tribune for the Internist and Cardiologist (35,22:7)
So You Have High Blood Cholesterol, National Institutes of Health, National Heart, Lung and Blood Institute, National Cholesterol Education Program, NHLBI Information Center, P.O. Box 30105, Bethesda, Md. 20824-0105
The Lancet (342,8885:1455)

Some oils are better than others

In all the contradictory nutrition advice that's out there these days, one thing has remained constant — cooking with oils low in saturated fat is definitely a plus.

Canola, sunflower, corn and olive oils are all fairly low in saturated fat. Sesame oil and peanut oil are a little higher, but butter and coconut oil are the worst possible choices for people trying to lower their cholesterol levels.

Unsaturated fats can be called either polyunsaturated fats or monounsaturated fats. Studies show that foods high in polyunsaturated fats (such as sunflower, corn and soybean oils, bagels, fish, walnuts, air-popped popcorn, squash and sweet potatoes) can reduce total cholesterol levels but may also reduce your levels of HDL cholesterol (the "good" kind).

Foods high in monounsaturated fats (such as canola, olive and peanut oils, oatmeal) also reduce cholesterol levels. Plus, they don't lower your HDL levels, according to some experts. New research is coming out every day regarding ways to lower your cholesterol levels.

The American Journal of Clinical Nutrition (59,3:667)
The Atlanta Journal/Constitution
The Complete and Up-to-Date Fat Book, Avery Publishing Group, Garden City Park, N.Y.

Cooking oils comparison chart

Although all of the oils listed in this chart (except butter) contain no measurable amounts of dietary cholesterol, to lower your cholesterol level, you must use oils low in saturated fat. Canola oil (7 percent saturated fat) is one of the best available cooking oils. Olive oil (14 percent saturated fat) is also good to use.

This chart is deceptive in one respect. Any fat that is hard at room temperature, such as stick margarine, is not good for your cholesterol. Margarine has been hydrogenated, or hardened, and that process adds trans fatty acids.

Trans fatty acids may be almost as bad for you as saturated fat, so stick margarine is about the same as butter as far as your cholesterol is concerned. Diet margarines and soft margarines are better choices. Also, look for brands of margarine or shortening that top the ingredients list with oils rich in monounsaturated fat, like canola.

Science News (147,8:127)
Composition of Foods: Fats and Oils — Raw, Processed, Prepared, Agriculture Handbook 8-4,
United States Department of Agriculture, Science and Education Administration

Product	Saturated Fat	Cholesterol	Polyun- saturated Fat	Monoun- saturated Fat
Canola Oil	7%	0 mg	35%	58%
Safflower Oil	9%	0 mg	78%	12%
Sunflower Oil	11%	0 mg	42%	47%
Corn Oil	13%	0 mg	62%	25%
Olive Oil	14%	0 mg	12%	74%
Hydrogenated Sunflower Oil	14%	0 mg	40%	48%
Sesame Oil	15%	0 mg	44%	42%
Soybean Oil	15%	0 mg	60%	24%
Margarine, bottled	17%	0 mg	47%	36%
Margarine, tub	17%	0 mg	37%	46%
Peanut Oil	18%	0 mg	33%	49%
Margarine, stick	19%	0 mg	33%	47%
Cocoa Butter	62%	0 mg	3%	35%
Butter	66%	31 mg	4%	30%
Palm Kernel Oil	87%	0 mg	2%	11%
Coconut Oil	92%	0 mg	2%	6%

Chronic Pain

Conquer pain without painkillers

Pop a pill at the first sign of pain?

If that's your approach to pain control, you could be heading for some serious health problems. Those reassuring over-the-counter painkillers with the familiar brand names may dissolve the ache, but if not handled carefully, they can be dangerous, even life threatening.

The two main nonprescription pain relievers Americans rely on are acetaminophen (as in Tylenol and Excedrin) and nonsteroidal anti-inflammatory drugs (NSAIDs), including those containing ibuprofen (such as Advil and Motrin) and those which contain salicylates (aspirin). All are safe if taken according to the label's directions, but you should be alert to certain side effects, some of them serious.

More is not better. Researchers at the University of Pittsburgh Medical Center discovered that under certain conditions taking just two more acetaminophen pills per day than the label recommends can seriously damage your liver.

The maximum number of acetaminophen pills an adult should take in one day is eight extra-strength tablets. If you take 10 of those tablets one day and diet or drink alcohol that same day, you're posing a serious risk to your liver.

Another study, conducted at Johns Hopkins University in Maryland, indicated that people who take more than one acetaminophen tablet a day for one year double their risk of kidney failure.

As for the NSAIDs containing ibuprofen, such as Advil, research shows that people who have taken as many as 5,000 pills in their lifetime (about one pill every three days for 44 years) have an 8.8 times higher risk of kidney failure than those who have taken fewer than 1,000 pills (about one pill every two weeks for 44 years).

No relationship has been found between aspirin and either liver or kidney damage, but aspirin can irritate the stomach lining and cause internal bleeding, nausea and ulcers. And some people are allergic to aspirin.

It's important to remember that both types of painkillers can be beneficial and are safe if taken correctly. But even if you're careful not to exceed the recommended dose, you should not take the pills for more than a couple of days.

If you take painkillers regularly, you may begin to experience the "rebound effect." When this happens, you may find that after your pain medicine wears off your pain returns worse than ever.

See your doctor for long-term pain. You should see your doctor for any pain that lasts longer than a few days. You need to rule out any serious underlying problems that could be causing your pain. It may be that all your body needs is time to heal. In some cases, you may have to learn to live with a little pain. However, there are natural ways you can ease pain. Take a look at the six different strategies outlined below:

Keep it moving. If you favor the hurting area by holding it immobile, you may lose strength and muscle tone and experience more pain when you do have to move it. If you know you aren't in danger of reinjuring the area, exercise it daily. Daily exercise can prevent the pain from getting worse and keep you prepared for recovery.

Get a mental grip on your pain. Shut your eyes and get comfortable and deeply relaxed. Focus lightly on your pain. How big is it? Is it round, oval, square? What color is it? Can you shrink it? Picture yourself lifting it out and dropping it into a pond. Now return to the area. How big is the pain now? What color? You can also picture the pain becoming warm and friendly.

Appreciate the art of acupuncture. This ancient Chinese therapy involves the usually painless insertion of small needles at key points in the body. The practice is said to stimulate the release of the body's natural painkillers, known as endorphins, and to block pain messages to the brain.

Master massage therapy. This is especially good for chronic pain of unknown origin. Massage can relax muscles that have been hard or tense for years. It can also clear out scar tissue and cellular debris. Acupressure may be part of a massage, stimulating pressure points with fingertips and knuckles rather than needles.

Beat pain with biofeedback. This technique uses electronic devices to enable you to monitor, and therefore learn to control, such functions as brain waves, blood pressure and, possibly, pain.

Your local libraries and bookstores will have additional information on natural pain control. Check your Yellow Pages for more information on specific treatments mentioned here. And for further help, write: National Pain Outreach Association, 7979 Old Georgetown Road, Suite 100, Bethesda, MD 20814-4948.

Alternative Medicine: The Definitive Guide, Future Medicine Publishing, Puyallup, Wash.
American Family Physician (51,1:203)
Powers of Mind, Random House, New York
The Alternative Health Guide, Alfred A. Knopf, New York
The Journal of the American Medical Association (272,23:1845,1866)
The New England Journal of Medicine (331,25:1675,1711)

Nature's powerful painkillers

More and more scientific research supports what home healers have known for a long time. The same foods that please your palate can sometimes put a stop to your pain. Take a look at five of Mother Nature's most powerful painkillers.

Hot peppers — Researchers have found that the active ingredient in red peppers, capsaicin, effectively relieves discomfort caused by arthritis, diabetes and shingles. Made from dried cayenne peppers, capsaicin (distributed under the name Zostrix) is available as a nonprescription cream. It is absorbed through your skin and works by deadening local nerves.

Some herbalists say you can get similar relief from hot pepper capsules, available in herb shops. If you want to try this remedy, take two capsules with milk or apple juice three or four times a day. Take capsules on a regular basis. At first you may notice an increase in pain, but this side effect will lessen with time.

Ginger — This savory spice is one of the most effective food remedies for relieving arthritis and headaches. To relieve arthritis, take about 1/3 teaspoon of ginger three times a day. Dissolve the ginger in liquid or mix with food. Straight ginger can burn your mouth. At the first sign of headache, mix 1/3 teaspoon of powdered ginger into a glass of water and drink. If you have headaches frequently, especially migraines, you may benefit from including ginger in your diet regularly. You can also relieve headaches by combining powdered ginger and cold water together to make a paste. Apply to your forehead

Pain-causing foods

In your quest for pain relief, you may find that knowing what *not* to eat can be just as helpful as knowing which foods act as natural painkillers. Listed below are some of the most common foods that can provoke headaches and arthritis symptoms.

Headache triggers: caffeine, chocolate, cheese, yogurt, nuts, cured meats (hot dogs, bologna, etc.), alcohol, monosodium glutamate (MSG), citrus fruits (oranges, lemons, etc.), sauerkraut, yeast-containing baked goods, and the artificial sweetener aspartame.

Top arthritis triggers, listed in order of most common trigger to least: corn, wheat, pork, oranges, milk, oats, rye, eggs, beef, coffee, malt, cheese, grapefruit, tomato, peanuts, sugar, butter, lamb, lemon and soybeans.

To test a food you suspect may be causing you problems, eliminate that food from your diet for one week. If your symptoms subside, you may have identified one of your food triggers. You can double-check by reintroducing the suspect food into your diet to see if your symptoms return.

Headache Q&A, The National Headache Foundation, 5252 N. Western Ave., Chicago, Ill., 60625
Rheumatic Disease Clinics of North America (17,2:273)

and temples with the back of a large teaspoon. Lie down for a while.

Peppermint tea — Peppermint tea works wonders for relieving headaches, especially migraines. To make peppermint tea, boil one pint of water. Remove from heat and add two tablespoons of fresh or dried peppermint leaves. Cover mixture and let steep for 50 minutes; strain. Drink one to two cups of tea. You can also obtain relief by rubbing a little peppermint oil on your forehead, temples and back of your neck.

Fish — This is a long-term cure, which means that a bite of fish when you have a headache won't relieve the pain right away. However, regularly including fish, such as mackerel, sardines, salmon and tuna, in your diet can help lessen the frequency of migraine headaches. Eating fish can also prevent or relieve rheumatoid arthritis and osteoarthritis symptoms.

Turmeric — To relieve arthritis, add one teaspoon of turmeric to some juice. Drink this mixture in the morning and evening. You can also mix two tablespoons of turmeric with one tablespoon of lime juice and enough boiling water to make a warm paste. Apply mixture to sore area. Cover with plastic wrap to retain heat.

Food — Your Miracle Medicine: How Food Can Prevent and Cure Over 100 Symptoms and Problems, HarperCollins, New York
Heinerman's Encyclopedia of Fruits, Herbs and Vegetables, Parker Publishing, West Nyack, N.Y.

Colds

15 ways to comfort a common cold

Doctors can transplant organs, put in artificial joints and use drugs to control anything from an earache to high blood pressure. Simple childhood vaccinations prevent smallpox and polio.

But for all its miracles, modern medicine still can't do much for the illness that affects more people more often than any other: the common cold.

Nearly everyone falls victim to the cold. Sneezes, coughs and handshakes send cold germs jumping from person to person in homes, schools and offices. The average child catches a cold six to eight times a year. And while a cold may not be life-threatening, it is one of the leading reasons people call in sick for work.

Unlike bacterial infections that go away when you take antibiotics, colds are caused by viruses. There are no drugs to cure colds, though they usually go away on their own in about a week or 10 days. While you wait for scientists to discover a cure, there are a few things you can do to help prevent colds or to help your body recover faster if you catch a cold.

Take your vitamin C. Studies show that vitamin C can help prevent colds. Citrus juices like orange and grapefruit are excellent sources of vitamin C. You could also take vitamin supplements. Even if vitamin C doesn't keep the cold away, researchers say it can make the cold less severe and go away faster.

Keep your cool. A group of researchers found that people under stress are more likely to catch a cold. The hustle and bustle of the holiday season is very stressful for many people. Try to relax as you do your shopping, and take slow, deep breaths when your mother-in-law calls to say she's spending the holidays at your house.

Keep it clean. Scrub all the surfaces in your house, especially doorknobs, staircase railings and counters. Use soap and hot water to get rid of germs. You might even consider using a solution of water with a little bleach on your counters.

Ventilate your house. Cold germs prefer stagnant, cool air. Keep the furnace going to warm the house and move the air around. Also consider using a humidifier, since germs don't like moist air. Open pans of water placed near your furnace vents or radiator will also help keep your house moist.

Wash your utensils. Use very warm, soapy water to kill all the germs. Let them air dry, because cold germs often live in drying cloths.

Keep your children's toys clean. A water and bleach solution will kill germs. You should consider washing the toys as they are put away.

Wash your hands. Your mother was right when she told you hand washing was important. You touch hundreds of surfaces each day, and each one harbors germs. We don't notice it, but most of us also touch our mouth or nose many times each day, creating an interstate highway for cold germs right into our bodies. Washing your hands puts a road block in the way of those germs.

Antibacterial or liquid soap is the best for ridding your hands of germs. Cold germs can actually live on the surface of regular soap. If your hands become irritated and dry, wash them without soap. The rinsing action can wash away many germs even without soap.

Don't smoke. Smoking can lower your body's resistance to infection. It also irritates your airways and makes your cold more likely to turn into something serious, like bronchitis.

Have a hot toddy. Alcohol (in small amounts) can increase your body's resistance to colds. Be careful not to overdo it for the sake of preventing a cold, because the cure may be worse than the disease. You may be the cleanest and most cautious person in the world, but you will probably still catch a cold or two each year. Once the sniffles start, there are a few things you can do to make yourself more comfortable.

Breathe hot, moist air. A vaporizer or similar device for inhaling hot, moist air may help you breathe easier if your chest is tight. Hot showers can also help your airways open. Unfortunately, two recent studies show that breathing hot, moist air won't help the cold go away faster.

Or try a T! Breathing the moist air steaming from a pot of hot water will help unstuff your nose, but you don't always have time for this luxury. Instead, find an old T-shirt for a ready-made remedy.

Cut a strip from the old T-shirt and soak it in hot water. Tie the wet strip around your head, covering up your nose, then breathe deeply. The T-shirt will hold water but still allow you to breathe. You'll get the same effect as sitting with your head over a steaming pot, but you'll be able to read, cook or work at the

Is it a cold or the flu?

Symptom	Cold	Flu
Fever	Rare	Common — begins suddenly, can rise to 102 degrees F to104 degrees F, lasts three to four days
Headache	Rare	Usual
General aches and pains	Slight	Usual — can be quite severe
Fatigue and weakness	Mild	Extreme — can last two to three weeks
Runny, stuffy nose	Common	Sometimes
Sneezing	Usual	Sometimes
Sore throat	Common	Sometimes
Chest discomfort, cough	Mild to moderate — hacking cough	Common — can be severe
Complications	Sinus congestion or earache	Bronchitis, pneumonia, can be life-threatening

U.S. Pharmacist (14,12:33)

same time.

Drink lots of fluids. Most people don't drink enough fluids when they are healthy, but your body is strong enough to manage. When you are sick, however, it's very important to drink so that your body has the strength to fight the illness. Eight to 10 glassfuls of liquid each day is a good guideline. Hot drinks are better than cold. Use the color of your urine as an indicator. If your urine is dark yellow, you need to drink more. If your urine is clear, you are drinking enough.

Get plenty of rest. If you feel tired, your body is trying to tell you something. Take a nap, or take a day off work. Your body will appreciate it, and your co-workers will thank you for not spreading your cold throughout the office.

Use disposable tissues instead of handkerchiefs. Cold germs can live for hours in your handkerchief.

Gargle with warm, salty water. Your sore throat will thank you for this time-tested remedy.

Wash out your nostrils. This will help prevent stuffy sinuses from becoming infected. Take a syringe and fill it with warm water, then gently inject the water into one nostril. The water (and mucus) will drain out through your mouth into the sink. Repeat a few times on each nostril until the drainage is clean. It sounds kind of unpleasant, but it really will help clear your sinuses. If the plain water irritates your skin, try mixing two cups of warm water with a spoonful of salt and a pinch of baking soda.

Take advantage of medicine. You won't find a cure at your local pharmacy, but you will find a variety of medicines that can help ease the symptoms of a cold. Cough suppressants (to keep your cough down), decongestants (to help reduce congestion and swelling of nasal linings), expectorants (to help clear your chest), throat lozenges and pain/fever relievers are available in many forms. Ask your pharmacist if you aren't sure which one is best for your symptoms.

Many of these over-the-counter drugs have side effects, such as drowsiness. Be sure to read the label before taking any medicine.

Be careful with children's medicine. Don't give aspirin or any drug containing aspirin to children or teen-agers. If your child's fever goes above 101 degrees Fahrenheit, call your doctor. Don't downsize the dose of adult medicine for children unless the label says it's OK, and keep all medicine out of the reach of children.

Medical World News (34,3:31)
Nutrition Research Newsletter (12,3:29 and 12,11/12,121)
Parent's Guide to Cold-proofing Your Home, Dixie Child Care Challenge, James River Corporation
Postgraduate Medicine (91,5:281 and 91,6:55)
The Journal of the American Medical Association (271,14:1109)
The Lancet (338,8765:522)
U.S. Pharmacist (18,101:35)

Herbal remedies for the common cold

Researchers have struggled in laboratories for years to find a cure, or even an effective treatment, for the common cold. They may have been better off growing an herb garden. Three herbs have been proven to relieve some cold symptoms. And with these safe, natural remedies, you won't have to worry as much about drug side effects.

Hyssop

Hyssop, a common perennial garden plant, grows along the sides of roads in the United States as a shrub. Its leaves and flowers contain a minty oil that gives off a camphor-like odor. The taste is bitter, so many people add honey to tea made from hyssop leaves. Drink hyssop tea for relief of coughs, hoarseness, fever and sore throats. It is especially effective as an expectorant, helping you get rid of fluid in your chest.

Hyssop

To grow it yourself, pick a site with lots of sunlight. Hyssop prefers light, well-drained, alkaline soil. Sow seeds in spring. You can divide the roots in spring and take stem cuttings from spring to autumn. Trim the bush down to 8 inches after flowering. To harvest, pick the flowering tops just as they begin to blossom. You can gather leaves anytime. Use dried flowers and leaves to make hyssop tea.

Horehound

Horehound

Horehound is a perennial herb native to the Mediterranean region, but it grows well in the United States. Its minty leaves and flowering tops are often used as a folk medicine. In fact, horehound is such an effective remedy that German health officials approved it as a drug to fight colds.

You've probably heard of horehound lozenges to relieve sore throats and coughs. Lozenges containing horehound may be available at your pharmacy, natural health food store, or herbal remedy store. If you can't find the lozenges, you can grow it yourself. Find a site in full sunlight that is protected from cold winds. Horehound prefers dry, alkaline soil. Divide the plant in midspring and sow in late spring.

You can take stem cuttings at the end of summer. Pruning should be done in spring. Pick the leaves as you need them and let them dry. To use as a medicine, finely chop nine leaves. Mix the leaves with one tablespoon of honey and eat slowly. Repeat as you feel necessary.

Echinacea

Echinacea works by stimulating your body's defenses against germs. It doesn't relieve symptoms of a cold, but it may keep the cold from becoming severe or lasting a long time, especially if you take the herb in the early stages of your cold.

Also known as the cone flower, echinacea is a perennial member of the daisy family. It has narrow leaves and a strong stem that grows up to 3-feet high.

Echinacea

Has your doctor told you ...

Cold medicine for children may not help

The next time your child catches a cold, you might think twice about spending money on over-the-counter drugs. Recent studies conclude that cold medicine may not do much for children.

More than 800 cold medicines are available in the United States. Parents spend millions of dollars on these remedies hoping they will make their children more comfortable. If you're like most parents, you probably have between four and eight different cold remedies in your medicine cabinet right now. But one recent report says the usefulness of these drugs has not been proven in children. In fact, no good evidence was found to show that the drugs work at all in preschool children. There were signs, however, that the drugs did help children over the age of 6. Teen-agers and adults seem to feel the full effect of cold remedies. So if you catch a cold from your child, at least the drugs will help you.

Another study looked only at cough suppressants. The children in the study were between 18 months and 12 years old. Children who took cough suppressants didn't feel any better or get well any sooner than children who didn't take the drugs. Another reason to think twice: The drugs in this study, dextromethorphan and codeine, can have serious side effects including drowsiness, diarrhea and hyperactive behavior.

So the next time your child has a cold, don't waste your money or your time on a trip to the pharmacy. Your child won't suffer more because he's not medicated, and you won't have to struggle with your child to get the medicine down.

Journal Watch (12,1:5)
Journal of Pediatrics (122,5:799)
American Family Physician (48,7:1302)
The Journal of the American Medical Association (269,17:2258)

A single, large purple flower grows at the top of the stem. It grows wild in the central United States. It's not practical to grow echinacea yourself, because you need to take a concentrated extract of fluid from the herb to feel any results. You can find echinacea in a liquid or tablet form in stores that sell herbal remedies. If you choose the liquid, take 10 to 25 drops per day. If you choose tablets, take one or two a day.

Chamomile

Cold sufferers will feel better under the influence of the healing and soothing powers of chamomile. Chamomile clears clogged sinuses and stuffy noses. Place a handful of chamomile flower heads into a bowl and pour boiling water over them.

Place a towel over your head, lean over the bowl, and inhale the steam. Chamomile also soothes minor irritations of the mouth, gums and throat. To relieve discomfort, gargle with a cup of hot chamomile tea every hour.

To prepare chamomile tea, pour boiling water over one heaping tablespoon of chamomile flower heads. Cover and let steep for 10 to 15 minutes. Strain. You may find the tea more enjoyable if you add a spoonful of honey or sugar.

To grow your own chamomile, select a sunny area with well-drained soil. Sow the herb in spring. Plant German chamomile 9 inches apart; plant Roman chamomile 6 inches apart. Divide in either spring or fall. Pick flowers that are fully open. The yellow center of the flower contains the active ingredients.

Horseradish

For quick and natural sinus relief, grate some fresh horseradish. A few whiffs and your sinuses will open right up. You can also grate horseradish into a mixture of honey and water and gargle with it to relieve hoarseness.

Herbal Medicine, Beaconsfield Publishers, Beaconsfield, England
HerbalGram (30:45)
Herbs of Choice: The Therapeutic Use of Phytomedicinals, The Haworth Press, Binghamton, N.Y.
Herbs, Reader's Digest, Pleasantville, N.Y.
The Honest Herbal, The Haworth Press, Binghamton, N.Y.
The Lawrence Review of Natural Products, Facts and Comparisons, St. Louis, Mo.

Colon Cancer

Filling foods help prevent colon cancer

Add several helpings of filling, low-fat, high-fiber foods to your diet every day, and you'll reduce your risk of colon cancer. Getting plenty of fiber in your diet can help keep you regular and lower your cholesterol too.

You may be tired of the news about the benefits of a high-fiber diet, but most of America hasn't gotten the message. Less than half of all Americans eat enough grains, and just over a quarter eat enough fruits and vegetables, says the latest U.S. Department of Agriculture survey.

Find fiber in beans, peas, other vegetables, grains and fruits. You can't digest the fiber, or "roughage," in these foods, and that's what makes it good for you. An analysis of 13 studies concluded that your risk of cancer would be reduced by about 31 percent if you increased your fiber intake to 39 grams a day. (See the *Constipation* chapter to find out how many grams of fiber different foods contain.)

Scientists separate fiber into two categories — water-soluble fiber and water-insoluble fiber.

Some foods have both kinds of fiber, but most foods are higher in one than the other. It's important to eat both kinds. Soluble fiber, the kind that dissolves in water, works best to lower your cholesterol.

> **Try these good food sources of calcium.**
>
> 1 cup plain, low-fat yogurt, 415 mg.
> 3 ounces canned sardines, with bones, 371 mg.
> 1/2 cup part-skim ricotta cheese, 334 mg.
> 1 cup skim milk, 302-316 mg.
> 1 cup 2 percent low-fat milk, 297-313 mg.
> 1 ounce Swiss cheese, 272 mg.
> 1 cup soft-serve ice cream, 236 mg.
> 1 ounce cheddar, Muenster or mozzarella cheese, part skim, 203-207 mg.
> 1/2 cup slivered almonds, 179 mg.
> 1/2 cup cooked and chopped collard greens, 178 mg.
> 3 ounces canned salmon with bones, 167 mg.
> 3/4 cup cooked broccoli, 132 mg.
> 3 1/2 ounces tofu, 108 mg.

Insoluble fiber, however, is the clear winner when it comes to reducing your risk of colorectal cancer. Insoluble fiber doesn't dissolve in water. It passes through your digestive system pretty much unchanged from the way it went into your mouth.

Speed harmful wastes through your bowels. When the insoluble fiber gets into the intestines, it dramatically reduces the amount of time food spends in the digestive tract. This reduces the possible harmful effects of wastes staying in the intestines longer than necessary.

That's one reason researchers believe insoluble fiber helps prevent colon cancer. The insoluble fiber should come from fruits, grains, beans, peas and other vegetables. A balanced diet of these foods provides about a 3-to-1 ratio of insoluble to soluble fiber. It's a good idea to get insoluble fiber from a variety of these healthy foods.

The scientific world is still trying to decide exactly what helps prevent cancer:

1) the fiber, or
2) the other good things in these foods, or
3) a combination of both.

Journal of the American Dietetic Association (93,12:1446)
Journal of the National Cancer Institute (87,7:477)
Nutrition and Cancer (19,2:213 and 19,1:11)
The Lancet (344,8914:39)
The Physician and Sportsmedicine (22,7:15)

Fight colon cancer with calcium and vitamin D

Here's a new twist on mother's advice to "drink your milk so you'll build strong bones and teeth."

Research has shown for years now that the calcium and vitamin D in milk products may also help prevent colon cancer, particularly among older women.

Colon cancer is the second most common cause of cancer deaths in the United States, and it appears to be strongly affected by your diet. Calcium — and, to a lesser extent, vitamin D — has reduced the growth of cancer-causers in laboratory rats and in humans.

Two different recent studies found that eating and drinking dairy products, or taking a supplement with calcium and vitamin D, could play a part in reducing the risk of colon cancer. In one study, people took a supplement of 1,200 mg of calcium carbonate a day (about the same as three Rolaids tablets) and suffered no negative side effects.

At least one small study has indicated that extra calcium doesn't help prevent colon cancer, but the researchers admitted that all 30 people in the study got plenty of calcium in their diets anyway. You may especially need vitamin D if

A Natural Alternative

Pooh Bear had the right idea

Licking the last drop out of the honey jar may have kept Pooh Bear healthy all those years. Honey has many healing properties — it seems to fight fungi, bacteria and inflammation.

Now, researchers at the American Health Foundation in Valhalla, N.Y., report that an ingredient of honey works against precancerous changes in the colons of rats.

The honey ingredient is called "caffeic esters." These esters come from the thick, brown material that honeybees get from trees to cement together their hives.

The researchers plan on studying the effects of the honey ingredients on colon cancer more closely. For now, it's safe to assume that natural sweeteners like honey are the healthiest too.

Science News (144,13:207)

you live in an area with high air pollution or in a northern climate without much sunlight. Less sunshine means lower levels of vitamin D in the blood-stream.

American Journal of Epidemiology (137,12:1302)
Journal of the National Cancer Institute (84,17:1355; 85,2:132; and 87,8:598)
Nutritive Value of Foods, HG-72, U.S. Department of Agriculture, HNIS, Room 325A, 6505 Belcrest Road, Hyattsville, Md. 20782

Folic acid turns off colon cancer

Folic acid is so important to the health of unborn babies that the Food and Drug Administration has proposed that all bread and grain products be forti-fied with it.

It only makes sense that something so essential for pregnant women is impor-tant to your good health too. Large amounts of folic acid, a B vitamin found in many green, leafy vegetables, can reduce your chances of getting colon cancer.

Folic acid seems to help "turn cancer genes off," according to researchers at Harvard. On the other hand, as few as two alcoholic beverages a day can increase the chances of colon cancer in men and women. The alcohol gets in the way of folic acid's good effects.

Other vitamins also seem to fight cancer, including vitamins C and E and an amino acid called methionine (found in fish and chicken).

Eat food high in folic acid. Many of the foods you already enjoy contain folic acid, including broccoli, spinach, collards, oranges, lemons, grapefruit, beans and whole-grain breads and cereals.

Other foods may soon be fortified with folic acid to make sure everyone gets an ample supply of the vitamin. (Check labels on food you buy to see if this important vitamin is found inside!)

If you absolutely hate eating fruits and vegetables, vitamin supplements can give you folic acid. Vitamin supplements should never take the place of foods naturally rich in vitamins, but, unfortunately, many people don't eat a well-balanced diet every day.

Folic acid needs to be replenished every day in order to help fight cancer and other illnesses.

Of course, extra vitamin B in your diet is no guarantee against cancer, but if it lowers your chances, why not give it a try?

The bottom line on lowering your chances of colon cancer is to maintain good health by eating nutritious foods, including foods rich in folic acid.

FDA Consumer (28,4:11)
Journal of the National Cancer Institute (85,11:875)
Stay Healthy
The Wall Street Journal

Constipation

Seven daily habits to prevent constipation

Do you want to stay regular, save money on laxatives and avoid hemorrhoids? Try this menu plan: Eat a bowl of wheat bran cereal in the morning; make your lunch sandwich out of whole-grain wheat bread; and eat several vegetables at lunch, at dinner, or as snacks throughout the day.

Get your fill of fiber. That way, you'll get your fill of "insoluble fiber" — the kind of fiber that works best to prevent constipation. Fiber is the indigestible parts of plants. The insoluble type of fiber doesn't dissolve in water. When you eat it, it enters your intestines and holds water there. The water makes the stool soft, bulky and easy to eliminate. And, since you don't digest fiber, the food goes through your system much more quickly.

You'll find the most insoluble fiber in wheat bran, vegetables, and whole-grain wheat breads and cereals. The cheapest and probably best source of insoluble fiber is raw, unprocessed wheat bran, which is one of the few high-fiber foods that really does call to mind those ugly images of rough, gritty, tasteless foods.

But you can easily cover it up by mixing it with your cereal, hot or cold, or baking it into low-fat muffins or breads. It also adds an interesting texture to thick soups and stews.

Psyllium is the type of fiber you find in many bulk laxatives and bran supplements. It's a soluble fiber, which means it dissolves in water and lowers cholesterol, but it's an oddity. The bacteria in your stomach don't break it down as quickly as other soluble fibers, so it also works like an insoluble fiber to increase stool bulk and prevent constipation. A good food source of psyllium is Kellogg's Bran Buds.

Add about 10 grams of fiber to your diet a day until you regularly eat 20 to 35 grams of fiber a day. Take care to introduce extra fiber into your diet gradually. Adding too much fiber too quickly could cause more constipation, gas and bloating. Make sure you drink plenty of water as you increase the amount of fiber. If you don't, the fiber may just make the problem worse. Check the accompanying chart for high-fiber foods you should eat every day.

Drink six to eight glasses of liquids a day. Caffeine and alcohol don't count because they cause you to lose water. You need enough water in your body to help keep your stools soft, so you can pass them easily.

Exercise regularly. Spend at least 20 to 30 minutes three times a week walking or engaging in some other aerobic exercise that you enjoy. Regular exercise helps move food through your intestines faster.

Go when you gotta go. Try to go to the bathroom as soon as you feel the urge to have a bowel movement. Constantly ignoring the urge leads to hardened stools and constipation.

Get on a schedule. Pick a convenient time about 10 to 60 minutes after one of your regular meals to spend about 10 minutes in the bathroom. Go to the bathroom every day after the same meal. Many people find that after breakfast works well. If nothing happens right away, don't worry and don't strain. After a while, your bowels will catch on.

Keep a step stool in the bathroom. Some people find that propping their feet on a footrest during bathroom visits makes bowel movements easier.

Ask your doctor if any of the medicines you're taking could cause constipation. Some common culprits include antidepressants, antihistamines, antiparkinson-ism drugs, diuretics, and antacids that contain calcium or aluminum. Your doctor may be able to recommend an alternative that's easier on your intestines.

High-Fiber Foods	Fiber (grams)
Selected High-Fiber Cereals	
General Mills Fiber One (1 oz. or 1/2 cup)	12
Kellogg's All-Bran (1 oz. or 1/3 cup)	8.5
Loma Linda 100% Bran (1 oz. or 1/3 cup)	8.4
Kellogg's Bran Buds (1 oz. or 1/3 cup)	7.9
Ralston Purina Bran Chex (1 oz. or 2/3 cup)	6.1
Post Bran Flakes (1 oz. or 2/3 cup)	5.6
Quaker Corn Bran (1 oz. or 2/3 cup)	5.4
Ralston Purina Raisin Bran (1.3 oz. or 3/4 cup)	4.8
Kellogg's Cracklin Bran (1 oz. or 1/3 cup)	4.3
Post Fruit and Fiber (1 oz. or 1/2 cup)	4.2
Kellogg's Bran Flakes (1 oz. or 3/4 cup)	4
General Mills Bran Muffin Crisp (1.2 oz. or 2/3 cup)	4
Kellogg's Raisin Bran (1.3 oz. or 3/4 cup)	4
Beans and Peas (1 cup)	
Broad beans	8.7
Lentils	7.9
Black beans	7.2
Lima beans	7
Pinto beans	6.8
Baked beans	6.6
Kidney beans	6.4
Green peas	6
Chickpeas	5.7
Black-eyed peas	4.4
High-Fiber Fruits	
Blackberries (1 cup)	6.6
Raspberries (1 cup)	5.8
Blueberries (1 cup)	4.4
Dates (10)	4.2
Pear	4.1
Apple	3

Bowes and Church's Food Values of Portions Commonly Used, 15th ed., HarperCollins, New York

Pass the cheese, please. Cheese and constipation may not go hand in hand after all. In a recent study of 21 people aged 68 to 87, researchers found that not one of the study participants complained of constipation or excessive gas even after eating 10 times as much cheese as they normally did. So feel free to enjoy your cheese.

Inside Tract: Maintaining Your Digestive Health, Glaxo Institute for Digestive Health, P.O. Box 899, West Caldwell, N.J. 07007-0899
Journal of the American Dietetic Association (93,12:1446)
The Atlanta Journal/Constitution
The Physician and Sportsmedicine (22,7:15)

Laxatives linked to cancer

Think you can't live without your laxative? Well, think again.

Recent research indicates you'll probably live a lot longer if you lay off the laxatives.

Laxatives can cause disease. Researchers speculate that laxatives interfere with your body's ability to absorb proteins from your regular diet. Your liver needs these proteins to make albumin, a simple protein that appears to offer protection against cancer.

Regular use of laxatives can cause other problems as well, including nutritional deficiencies and chronic diarrhea. Laxatives can also severely damage your intestines and make your constipation much worse. People who depend on laxatives often develop "lazy colon," meaning they simply *can't* have a bowel movement without taking a laxative. As people get older they frequently turn to laxatives because they're concerned that they don't have the same number of bowel movements they did when they were younger.

Be careful about diagnosing yourself with constipation too quickly. A decreasing number of bowel movements is normal as colon and rectal muscles weaken with age. While most young people often have at least one bowel movement a day, it's not uncommon for older people to have only three bowel movements a week.

Are you addicted? "Well, I'm OK," you may be saying to yourself. "I only use laxatives once a week or so." The truth is, if you're using laxatives once a week, you're not OK. Doctors define laxative abusers as people who use laxatives as least once a week for several months.

If you want long-lasting, natural relief that won't harm your health, throw out your laxatives and try the natural remedies we recommend.

Archives of Family Medicine (2,8:853)
Journal of the American Geriatrics Society (42,1:50)
Medical World News (31,1:19)

Coughing

How to halt your hacking

From a dry tickle at the back of your throat to a never-ending hacking to a gut-wrenching, sputum-producing heave — coughing is one miserable symptom that seems to accompany a variety of health problems. Colds, flu, heartburn and even some drugs such as ACE inhibitors cause coughing.

Coughing can lead to serious health problems like urinary incontinence and rectal and vaginal muscle strain. But even without additional problems, coughing is irritating enough in itself to warrant some cures.

Here are some ways to relieve your discomfort when coughing strikes.

Get that chicken soup comfort. If you are coughing up phlegm, you need to let nature take its course and even help it along. Warm soup will help speed the process of coughing up the phlegm and mucus caught in your lungs. When your body coughs productively, it can clean out unwanted substances in your lungs.

Drink warm liquids and plain water. Warm liquids and water are the best ways to loosen mucus in your lungs so that it's easier to cough up. If your cough accompanies other cold and flu symptoms, try to drink at least eight to 10 glasses of liquids a day. Liquids will help keep a fever down, soothe a sore throat, and help your body flush out germs.

Take the right kind of cough medicine. If you are coughing up phlegm, you need to take an expectorant that will help you cough. If you have a dry cough that doesn't bring up any mucus, you can use a cough suppressant. Suppressants are also called antitussives, and they come in both liquid form and lozenge form.

Sip some herbal teas. Hyssop and chamomile teas will soothe your throat and relieve a cough. Horehound works well too. You can usually find horehound lozenges at health-food stores.

Take a hot shower or a steamy bath. Use a humidifier or sit in a steamy room to help loosen the mucus in your lungs.

Eat a banana. Heartburn is the culprit for about one in every 10 chronic coughers, and researchers have found that bananas are a great natural solution for heartburn. Banana powder, a dried, ground-up form of the fruit, also works well. Other heartburn remedies include raising the head of your bed, avoiding food and drink before bedtime, losing weight and eating more slowly.

Put down that cigarette. Have you ever met a smoker who doesn't have a chronic cough? Even if you don't smoke, if you work or live with people who do, passive smoke could be the culprit for your cough. Put your foot down about your smoky environment, or you could be coughing and wheezing forever.

If your cough goes on and on and gets worse instead of better, make sure you see a doctor. Coughing up blood, shortness of breath when you cough or sharp pains in your chest when you cough are all sure signs that a doctor's visit is in order.

British Medical Journal (298,6683:1280)
Health Letter (6,2:1)
The Lancet (336,8710:282)

Cuts, Burns and Scrapes

The miracle herb

Aloe Plant

Ever wonder why Cleopatra was so beautiful? According to legend, one of her beauty secrets was aloe vera. Today, centuries later, many people choose lotions containing aloe vera to ease sunburns or moisturize dry skin. But aloe vera isn't just a cosmetic — the plant itself is a natural remedy for many minor ailments.

So what's the "magical" ingredient in aloe? It's called aloe vera gel, and it's the clear, jellylike sap inside aloe leaves. The outside of the leaves produces a bitter yellow substance called aloe latex or juice.

People often confuse aloe gel and aloe juice because of their similar names. But aloe juice has an entirely different makeup than aloe gel and acts differently, producing a "not-so-magical" laxative effect when swallowed.

If you have a minor cut, burn or other skin irritation, you may want to try aloe gel. Studies suggest that aloe gel can ease pain, reduce swelling, prevent blistering and combat bacteria and fungi. Because aloe gel seems to regenerate damaged skin tissues, it prevents scarring in many cases.

Use aloe to stop bleeding. Aloe can also stop minor cuts from bleeding. If you apply it directly to your cut, the aloe will dry immediately and slow the escape of blood. You can even use aloe gel as an insect repellant.

Stick with fresh aloe. Researchers debate whether or not commercially prepared aloe products lose their healing effects over time. While most studies suggest that these solutions have some positive effects, one study found that they actually disrupt the healing of human cells.

For best results, stick with fresh aloe. The aloe plant is inexpensive, easy to maintain and looks great in a kitchen window.

It's handy too. When you need it, just break off a leaf segment and squeeze the sap onto your injury. Of course, you should consult your doctor if your wound is serious. But maybe you can't find an aloe plant, or perhaps you just have a brown thumb. Then you might want to pick up an aloe-based cream at a natural-foods store. Just read the labels carefully.

Steer clear of aloe vera extract. Aloe vera extract may be highly diluted. Likewise, avoid reconstituted aloe, which is made either from powdered or liquid concentrate. Ideally you want to buy a product with an aloe concentration of at least 70 percent; otherwise, it won't do much good.

If you want to try cosmetics with aloe, look for concentrations of at least 40 percent. If the product you're interested in doesn't print percentages on the label, read the list of ingredients. If aloe vera doesn't appear near the top of the list, there probably isn't much aloe in the product.

Whether your goal is timeless beauty or timely first aid, remember aloe vera: a fresh and natural alternative.

Herbs, The Reader's Digest Association, Pleasantville, N.Y.
Miracle Medicine Herbs, Parker Publishing, West Nyack, N.Y.
The Honest Herbal, Pharmaceutical Products Press, Binghamton, N.Y.

At-home first aid for minor wounds

Most cuts and scrapes get well without much attention. But some wounds need more than a Band-Aid, but don't need a doctor's attention. Here are a few tips:

Clean the wound. It's important to clean the wound to remove any dirt or other foreign materials that might cause infection. Mild soap and water are best. If the pressure of running water isn't enough to remove all the dirt and debris, use a sterile pad to gently brush the dirt out.

For easy cleaning of dirty wounds, keep a can of aerosolized saline solution in your first-aid kit. You'll find it in the eye care section of the pharmacy. The preservative-free saline for sensitive eyes is safest.

Stop the bleeding. Many minor wounds stop bleeding on their own. If it is still bleeding after you clean it, apply pressure directly to the wound for a couple of minutes. If you can't easily stop the bleeding, you should see a doctor.

Kill the germs. You can help prevent infection in wounds by applying antiseptic to kill the germs as soon as possible after the wound occurs. You probably have a bottle of isopropyl alcohol or hydrogen peroxide in the medicine

A Natural Alternative

A scar-free diet

The American Academy of Cosmetic Surgery warns health-conscious Americans to make sure their diets contain wound-healing nutrients. Your body requires certain nutrients in order to heal quickly without ugly scars.

The Academy recently reported on two vegetarians who scarred after receiving chemical peels, a procedure where a plastic surgeon uses chemicals to peel off the top layer of skin to expose the tighter, smoother skin underneath. People normally heal quickly and don't scar at all after a chemical peel.

If you're a vegetarian or a chronic dieter, make sure your diet isn't hindering your body's ability to heal. It takes less than one week on a poor diet to lower the production of an essential wound healer in your body. Your diet must include albumin (contained in proteins); glucose (in carbohydrates); essential fatty acids; vitamins A, B complex, C and K; and the minerals zinc, copper, iron and manganese.

All these nutrients are essential to help you avoid scars that last a lifetime.

The Journal of the American Medical Association (273,12:910)

cabinet. Both are excellent antiseptics, but they may sting.

Iodine is also used as an antiseptic, but it burns and discolors the surrounding skin. Iodine and hydrogen peroxide can be dangerous if used on large areas. Decolorized iodine does not kill germs. If you or your children can't stand the sting, you can find nonstinging antiseptic ointments, creams and sprays at your pharmacy.

If you are really worried about infection, several antibiotic creams are available without a prescription. Apply a small amount (enough to cover your fingertip) one to three times a day. If your wound is too large to be covered by a fingertip's worth of antibiotic cream, you probably should see a doctor.

Cover the wound. Dressings are important for several reasons. They can be used to apply pressure to a wound to stop bleeding. Once the bleeding is stopped, they can absorb any fluid that oozes from the wound. They also help protect the wound from further damage and keep it clean.

Most minor wounds should be covered with a dressing that won't stick. First-aid kits usually contain this kind of dressing, and it is readily available at any pharmacy. This dressing is especially useful on hairy areas and on wounds that might tear easily. Most nonstick dressings don't absorb oozing fluids from the wound. Fluid can pass through the dressing. Wounds that drain may require additional absorbent dressing on top of the nonstick dressing. Don't put gauze directly on a wound because it might stick. Change the dressing daily, or more often if the wound is draining.

Secure the dressing. Use tape to firmly secure all four sides of the dressing. You can choose from several kinds of first-aid tapes. Cloth tapes won't cause allergic reactions, and they are very strong. Use cloth tape if the dressing is bulky.

Plastic tapes stretch with the skin, and the clear plastic lets you examine the wound without removing the tape. Paper tape isn't as sticky, so it doesn't irritate the skin as much as the other kinds. But it may come loose in areas where the skin moves. Don't use household tapes, like Scotch tape or masking tape, to secure dressings.

Emergency Medicine (25,7:45)
U.S. Pharmacist (19,10:1 Supplement)

How to care for burns at home

When you stumble into a hot iron or spill boiling water on yourself, your first instinct should be to head for cool water. That's smart — the sooner you get the temperature of your skin back to normal, the less damage you'll have.

Get cold water on the burned area as quickly as possible. You can soak the area in cold water or use wet towels that have been soaked in cold water. You should keep the burned area in cold water until the pain stops.

For first-degree burns, just dry the burn off and for the next day or two, keep it covered loosely with some gauze. After the first day, you can use something like aloe vera cream to relieve the stinging.

For second-degree burns, smooth on a layer of antibiotic cream, preferably

First-degree burns involve only the top layers of skin and usually leave no scars. The skin is red and turns white when touched.

Second-degree burns look white or white with some redness, and they feel wet or waxy dry. Flames, oil or grease are often the cause of second-degree burns, and they usually do scar. You might not be able to tell the difference between a deep second-degree burn and a third-degree burn. If you're not sure, go ahead and see your doctor. He'll treat the burn in the office and show you how to care for it at home.

Third-degree burns usually look white or charred. You will only be able to feel deep pressure in a third-degree burn. The nerves are destroyed so you can't feel pain. You must see your doctor for these burns.

silver sulfadiazine ointment. Use something sterile instead of your bare hands to apply the cream (such as a tongue depressor from the doctor's office).

Then cover the burn with a dressing like a Telfa pad and wrap the burned area loosely with gauze. Completely wash off and reapply the antibiotic cream every day. Repeat this process until your wound begins to heal.

More hot tips for burns:

➤ Gently cleanse broken skin. Mild soap and water works well.

➤ Try not to scratch. If the burn itches as it starts to heal, you may want to take an antihistamine.

➤ Never pop a blister. If a blister does pop, clean it gently with soap and water, then put antibiotic cream on it.

➤ Don't put butter, shortening or yogurt on a burn. Anything that's not sterile could cause an infection.

➤ Watch for signs of infection like fever, chills, vomiting and swollen glands.

➤ Have a tetanus shot if your immunization is not current.

➤ Remember that burned skin is sensitive to sun for a full year.

American Family Physician (45,3:1321)
U.S. Pharmacist (17,4:28)

When to blaze a trail to the doctor's office

Most burns are merely a painful nuisance that you know will heal in time. But sometimes it's hard to know if a burn is superficial or deeper and more damaging than it appears. You can treat first-degree burns and most second-degree burns at home. For third-degree burns, you must see your doctor.

You also need to see a doctor for a burn if:

➤ The burn is from electricity or from a chemical. Burns from electricity can cause heart problems and damage that you may not see to tissues deep in the body. Chemicals such as hydrofluoric acid, commonly used in the semiconductor industry, cause burns that are initially painless, but can severely injure deep tissues.

➤ The burn goes all the way around your neck, trunk, leg or arm, or covers a large area.

➤ You are burned on the eyes, ears or genital area.

➤ You have diabetes, heart disease or an immune system disorder.

➤ The burn is on a baby under 2 years old or on a person over 60.

➤ You have inhaled enough smoke to damage your lungs.

American Family Physician (45,3:1321)

Dandruff

Rescue from dandruff disasters

You've got a big date tonight. You want to wear that new black outfit. You try it on and brush your hair into place, and then you see it: You have dandruff! It's 6 p.m. and you have to be ready by 9. What can you do?

If you've never seen flakes in your hair before, then you may only have a temporary condition. Consider trying one of these herbal home remedies for dandruff before buying a more potent dandruff shampoo.

Make an herbal treatment with burdock root oil. Mix together two tablespoons of plain vegetable oil with six drops of burdock root oil. Warm the mixture and then gently massage it into your scalp and hair. Put a shower cap over your head. Soak a towel in hot water and wring it out. Then wrap your head with it. If the towel cools off, get it wet again in hot water, wring it out, and wrap your head again. Keep the towel and shower cap in place for 20 minutes.

Then wash your hair with a *mild* shampoo. Rinse thoroughly, two to three times. Style as usual. Other herbal oils that may be mixed with vegetable oil to treat dandruff include rosemary, parsley, chamomile and licorice.

Rinse with bay laurel tea. You've probably cooked with sweet bay or bay laurel. For dandruff shampoo, the thick, aromatic leaves should be dried and crushed. Mix three teaspoons of the crushed leaves into a quart of boiling water. Cover the pot and let the leaves soak for about half an hour. Strain the leaves and pour the "tea" into a plastic container.

After shampooing, rinse your hair well and then slowly pour about a cup of the mixture over your head. Distribute it well, all through the hair and over the entire scalp. Rinse out after one hour. If used regularly, the bay mixture should control common dandruff. Keep the "tea" in your refrigerator, and mark the container.

Try a medicated shampoo. If dandruff is a frequent uninvited guest, you may have eczema or psoriasis. You should probably try one of the "medicated" dandruff shampoos. They contain ingredients like salicylic acid or coal tar. A dandruff shampoo will loosen those dry flakes and cleanse your scalp and hair. Always rinse thoroughly, two to three times, and follow up with a hair conditioner.

But use these stronger shampoos with caution: Shampoos containing coal tar can discolor lighter hair. They shouldn't be left on your skin for long periods, and they can make your skin and hair sensitive to sunlight.

If regular use of a dandruff shampoo doesn't control your flaky scalp, make an appointment with a dermatologist.

Alternate your dandruff shampoo with a regular shampoo. Keep both in the shower. Leave the cap flipped up or turn the bottle upside-down to show which one you used last, in case you forget.

Experiment to see which product works best for you. There are several different products available to control dandruff, including shampoos, rinses and leave-in treatments. Always carefully read and follow the instructions on the dandruff shampoo bottle. Don't let the lather get in your eyes.

Wash your hair frequently. Fighting dandruff can be an ongoing battle. Part of your battle plan should be washing your hair every day. Dandruff occurs more often in people with oily hair, not dry hair. Too much oil may promote dandruff. Frequent washings will help remove the oil.

Resist the urge to scratch. If itching develops, you may need a prescription drug to control your dandruff. Keep fingernails trimmed to avoid breaking the skin of the scalp.

FDA Consumer (28,8:25)
Heinerman's Encyclopedia of Fruits, Vegetables and Herbs, Parker Publishing Company, West Nyack, N.Y.
Herbal Medicine, Beaconsfield Publishers, Beaconsfield, England
Herbs, The Reader's Digest Association Inc., Pleasantville, N.Y.
Mayo Clinic Health Letter (11,9:4)
The American Medical Association Family Medical Guide, Random House, New York
The Lawrence Review of Natural Products, Facts and Comparisons, St. Louis, Mo.

Depression

When it's more than the blues

If you are human, you feel sad sometimes — when a loved one dies, a marriage ends, a job promotion doesn't come through, or a tear-jerker movie wrenches at your heartstrings.

There are, fortunately, a host of natural ways to help remedy a down mood. But when you just can't shake feelings of hopelessness, helplessness and fatigue for weeks and months, it may be more than a simple case of the blues. You could be suffering from clinical depression — a medical disorder (just like heart disease, diabetes or high blood pressure) that can affect both your behavior and physical health.

One in 20 people in the United States suffers an episode of clinical depression each year, and about 15 percent of Americans will suffer from a major depressive disorder sometime during their lives. Unfortunately, fewer than a third of depressed people will ever be properly diagnosed and receive the help they need.

Left untreated, depression can wreak havoc on your life. In fact, only heart disease results in more days spent confined to bed, and only arthritis is blamed for more chronic pain. And clinical depression can be a killer: Researchers say more than 18,000 people who take their lives each year in the United States suffer from severe depression.

But there's good news. Researchers at the National Institute of Mental Health have concluded that treatment of depression is almost always successful.

Recognize depression's warning signs. The first step toward conquering clinical depression is to recognize its signs. If you are suffering from a major depressive disorder, you will have at least one of these symptoms nearly every day, all day, for a minimum of two weeks — a loss of interest in things you used to enjoy (like a hobby or a sport) and blues that you simply can't shake. Feelings of hopelessness and excess worry are also common.

You'll also probably have at least three of the following symptoms:

➤ Feeling either slowed down or restless and unable to sit still.
➤ Feelings of guilt and worthlessness.
➤ An increase or decrease in your appetite or weight.
➤ Thoughts of death and suicide.
➤ Difficulty in going to sleep or staying asleep, or sleeping too much.
➤ Feeling fatigued all the time.

In addition, several physical symptoms are frequently associated with depression: headaches, other all-over aches and pains, digestive problems, and a lack of interest in sex.

Remember, clinical depression is not a sign of weakness. Depression affects people of all income levels, races and religions. You can't make it go away by just "cheering up" or "toughing it out" because clinical depression is an illness.

Researchers speculate it results from complex interactions involving brain chemicals and hormones that are set in motion by traumatic events or prolonged stress (although in some cases, no trigger can be identified). They also believe the risk for the disorder can be inherited.

Do the signs of clinical depression sound far too familiar? Then don't hesitate to seek help and discuss your symptoms with your doctor. Successful treatment of depression can include the use of antidepressant drugs, light therapy, dietary changes and psychotherapy.

It can take time and patience for symptoms to disappear. But the odds are overwhelmingly on your side that depression's fog of hopelessness and fatigue will finally lift, and you'll soon be on the road to recovery and wellness.

Answers to Your Questions About Clinical Depression, National Mental Health Association, 1021 Prince Street, Alexandria, Va. 22314-2971
Depression is a Treatable Illness: A Patient's Guide, U.S. Department of Health and Human Services, 2101 East Jefferson Street, Suite 501, Rockville, Md. 20852
Depression in Primary Care: Detection, Diagnosis, and Treatment, U.S. Department of Health and Human Services, 2101 East Jefferson Street, Suite 501, Rockville, Md. 2085
The Lancet (341,8852:1087)

Natural ways to beat depression

Does it ever seem like the whole world is on Prozac? While severe depression may require treatment with antidepressant drugs, there are a host of natural ways to boost your spirits if you have a case of the blues.

When you feel down, your natural instinct may be to retreat and be alone — but that's a strategy researchers say rarely helps. Instead of becoming a TV-watching, snack-munching couch potato, get moving. A recent study of over 400 people concluded that the top way to change a bleak mood to a bright one was exercise.

Move your body to heal your mind. In fact, according to the Canadian Fitness and Lifestyle Research Institute, evidence is mounting that exercise can actually prevent depression, as well as help people already experiencing mild to moderate symptoms of depression.

Exercise even helps those with severe emotional illness, when used in combination with other treatments. The Canadian researchers noted that depressed people often show marked improvement after two to six months of regular exercise.

How can moving your body heal your mind? No one knows for sure, but scientists suspect the brain counters the stimulus of exercising your muscles by exerting an opposite stimulus — possibly by releasing chemical messengers known as endorphins that cause pleasurable sensations and elevate mood.

Men and women talk a different language when battling blues. Researchers studying how people battle the blues list tackling chores, pursuing hobbies and getting out around other people as ways that often work to fight depression. But, they note, strategies for combatting a bad mood frequently differ along gender lines.

For example, women, who suffer from depression twice as often as men, are most likely to try snacking, shopping, and having a heart-to-heart talk with a friend. Men, on the other hand, more frequently seek distracting, pleasurable activities — like sex — to zap depression. And males are far more likely than women to turn to potentially dangerous behaviors to alter their moods, including abusing drugs and alcohol.

The problem is, recreational drugs and alcohol not only don't work, but researchers have concluded they can actually cause — as well as worsen — depression.

Soothe your soul with music. "Music alone with sudden charms can bind the wand'ring sense, and calme the troubled mind," wrote 17th century dramatist William Congreve.

Twentieth century scientists say that's more than a poetic idea. In fact, when researchers asked over 500 adults what worked best to overcome a bad mood, listening to music was high on the list, topped only by exercise.

A recent study of 30 depressed elderly adults, between the ages of 61 and 86, concluded that music can lift depression. Research subjects were divided into two groups. One received no treatment while the other relaxed by listening to music. The untreated group didn't get better, but those who used music as part of their therapy soon had improved moods and higher self-esteem.

Let in the light. Another way to help rid yourself of depression is to check into the possibility of light therapy. If your blues seem linked to the dark, bleak days of autumn and winter, you may have a form of depression known as SAD (Seasonal Affective Disorder).

According to the U.S. Department of Health and Human Services, mild or moderate seasonal depression due to a lack of natural light can be successfully treated using a special bright light bulb.

It "tricks" the body into thinking you've experienced a few extra hours of daylight each day. To find out if you are a candidate for light therapy, talk to your doctor.

Is your medication dragging you down? Another subject to take up with your doctor if you are feeling down in the dumps is the possibility that any prescription drugs you're taking could be causing or contributing to your bad mood. Depression has been linked to beta blockers, drugs widely prescribed for high blood pressure. Researchers now say beta blockers may only cause depression in a few people, but many other prescription drugs list depression as a side effect.

So if you suspect a drug is behind your blues, discuss alternatives with your doctor — like discontinuing the drug, changing your dosage, or switching to a drug less likely to cause depression.

Be good to yourself. Perhaps the best way to help yourself feel better when you are down is simply to be good to yourself. And don't hesitate to seek professional counseling if you need help. Ask your doctor or local mental health center for a referral. You may also want to ask them to put you in touch with a local support group so you can learn how other people are handling their depression.

Most of all, remember that your depression didn't develop overnight, and it won't be gone magically in a split second either. But with the right help —

including doing everything you can to help yourself feel better, naturally — you will win the battle of the blues.

_____

Depression is a Treatable Illness: A Patient's Guide, U.S. Department of Health and Human Services, 2101 East Jefferson Street, Suite 501, Rockville, Md. 20852
Medical Abstracts (15,1:8)
Medical Tribune (306,6878:655)
Physician Assistant (17,1:62)
Science News (141,13:213)
The Atlanta Journal/Constitution
The Canadian Medical Association Journal (151,8:1163)

Eat right to fight depression

Most people, unless they've been living in a cave somewhere for the past couple of decades, have heard the news that what you eat can have a profound effect on your health. A lack of calcium may result in bone-crumbling osteoporosis, for example, and a high-fat diet seems to increase your risk of heart disease.

But it's not so well-known that what you eat can also affect your mood. Consuming the wrong foods can contribute to depression while making some specific diet changes may boost your mood back to the sunny side.

Crush those comfort-food cravings! It's perfectly normal to turn to food for comfort occasionally, and munching on a chocolate chip cookie every now and then when you are blue is relatively harmless.

But for people who have a serious problem with depression, using sweets as a kind of "self-medication" can start a dangerous cycle of not only overeating — but also eating foods that actually make depression worse.

Why do many people get the munchies for candy bars when they are depressed? And why do women suffering from premenstrual syndrome, who often feel depressed and anxious, crave sweets? Scientists believe that carbohydrate-rich foods, including sweets, boost levels of serotonin — a hormone-like brain chemical that helps calm irritable feelings and gives you a "feel-good" lift.

Don't crash down from a sugar "high." But this doesn't mean sugar is a healthy prescription for depression. Sure, eating sugar makes you feel better for a while. But then you may feel worse — until you eat more sugar.

Researchers suspect that sugar causes your body to release endorphins — those same chemicals that produce a "runner's high." A sugar-triggered endorphin rush, however, unlike one produced by exercise, soon disappears. And endorphin levels drop even lower than before you had that candy bar or cola.

(Also, caffeine can make a normal drop in blood sugar seem worse — so eliminating or reducing consumption of coffee and caffeine-containing colas may help improve mood swings, as well.)

In one study, even people who were not depressed felt better when they stopped eating sugar. (If you decide to eliminate sugar from your diet to help your mood, remember to check labels. It's a "hidden" ingredient in many products — including flavored yogurt, catsup, cereals, fruit drinks and granola bars.)

Lift your mood with complex carbos. So how can you get the mood-lifting benefits of increased serotonin that come with eating carbohydrate-rich foods without eating sugar? Easy. Eat complex carbohydrates like whole-grain breads and cereals.

Researchers at the University of South Alabama found that although simple carbohydrates, like sugar, and complex carbohydrates both stimulate serotonin production, it's the complex carbos that have a long-lasting mood-lifting effect.

Another reason to fill up on complex carbohydrates is that you'll be increasing your body's supply of tryptophan, an amino acid that can help banish depression. In fact, in a Scandinavian research trial, the amino acid worked just as well in treating depression as the prescription drug imipramine.

A few years ago, the U.S. Food and Drug Administration (FDA) pulled supplements containing tryptophan off U.S. store shelves when contaminated batches of the pills were found to be the cause of a painful muscular disorder.

But you can increase your body's supply of the amino acid naturally by eating more complex carbohydrates like oatmeal, brown rice and whole-wheat muffins.

Protein may perk you up. Not everyone responds with a sunnier disposition after trying a diet that relies heavily on complex carbohydrates, however.

Some people feel better when they eat more protein. So if high-carbo eating doesn't improve your mood, try a lean turkey sandwich and some low-fat milk.

The reason? Researchers theorize that the amino acid tyrosine, found in abundance in milk and poultry, increases the body's ability to use more of the mood-raising brain chemical norepinephrine.

For some people, that change in diet is just what their particular body chemistry needs to banish fatigue and depression.

B vitamins beat the blues. Another reason to forget about sweets are all those empty calories. You may end up lacking important nutrients, including calcium, magnesium and selenium, and that can contribute to lethargy and depression.

The group of vitamins best known for beating the blues is the B's. Researchers have found that people who take in the least vitamin B12 are the most likely to suffer from depression and other mental problems, including memory loss. And a deficiency of folic acid, a member of the B complex family, has been linked to mood swings and depression.

In fact, British scientists studying a group of people suffering from depression-related psychological problems found that over 30 percent of the research subjects had low levels of folic acid. When these people were given folic acid supplements, they improved dramatically.

Some foods rich in folic acid are broccoli, spinach, collards, oranges, lemons, grapefruit, beans and whole-grain breads and cereals. Other foods may soon be fortified with folic acid to make sure everyone gets an ample supply of the vitamin. (Check the labels on the food you buy to see if this important vitamin is found inside.)

B vitamins build brain power. We don't know for sure how B vitamins improve mental health, but University of Arizona psychiatrist Iris Bell has come up with some tantalizing clues. She discovered that 27 older people suffering from depression all had high blood levels of an amino acid called homocysteine.

The depressed people with the most homocysteine scored the lowest on mental tests and showed symptoms of declining brain power — including memory loss and the inability to learn. So homocysteine may damage blood vessels in the brain, or it might even convert into another substance that destroys brain cells.

What brings down high levels of homocysteine? Correcting any lack of the depression-busting B vitamins — including B6, B12 and folic acid. You can get B6 and B12 in chicken, fish, pork, eggs, whole-wheat breads and cereals, dairy products, peanuts and walnuts.

Don't wait too long to eat. Skipping meals not only robs you of needed vitamins and minerals but it can make a bad mood worse by causing blood sugar levels to drop. If you wait too long to eat, researchers have found, blood-sugar levels may fail to rise back to normal. And that can increase fatigue and depression.

Dieting can be a downer. One more way food can lead to the blues is that great American pastime — dieting or trying to lose weight. Not eating what you want or feeling guilty about eating fattening foods is no fun.

Seriously overweight people have a higher than average risk of depression due to the stress of repeatedly going on diets.

Using common sense can go a long way toward solving food-related blues. Don't follow fad diets. You can learn to eat nutritious, low-fat meals to keep your weight down. Fill up on complex carbohydrates, lean meats and poultry, and snack on fruit, veggies and low-fat dairy products.

Learn to control your sweet tooth, especially if you are sensitive to the "crash" after a sugar high. And remember, scientists are learning more and more that we really are what we eat — physically and mentally.

Annals of Internal Medicine (117,10:820)
British Medical Journal (308,6940:1328)
Food and Mood: The Complete Guide to Eating Well and Feeling Your Best, Henry Holt and Co., New York
The Atlanta Journal/Constitution

Depression and your heart

For centuries, the heart was thought to be the seat of your emotions. While we now understand that the heart's mission is to pump blood through our bodies, scientists have discovered that emotions and your heart are profoundly linked.

In fact, feelings of despair and hopelessness not only boost your risk of developing heart disease but increase the odds that you'll die if you do have a heart attack.

Researchers from the Centers for Disease Control studied nearly 3,000 adults, ranging in age from 45 to 77, and found that about one-fourth of them reported symptoms of depression.

Although none of the volunteers had heart disease when the study began, over the next 12 years the participants who suffered from depression — whether it was mild or severe — were four times more likely to die from heart disease.

Work hard at happiness after heart attack! Having a heart attack and feeling depressed afterwards can be a lethal combination.

Montreal Heart Institute and McGill University investigators studied 222 patients about a week after they suffered heart attacks and discovered that 16 percent were clinically depressed. Just six months later, these depressed people were almost five times more likely to die than the nondepressed people.

Did the depressed people have more severe heart disease? Or were there more smokers in the depressed group? The answer to both questions is no.

The only important difference the researchers could find between the two groups was depression.

Get back to work. Researchers at the University of Arkansas have come up with one way heart attack survivors can fight depression — as soon as your doctor says it's OK, go back to work.

In the Arkansas study, over 60 percent of the people went back to work within four months of their attack. No matter how depressed these people were at first, going back to work made them much happier and more content.

The people who gave up their jobs didn't fare so well, mentally or physically. In fact, at their one year checkup, they had more health complications.

No one knows exactly why depression, left unchecked, can spell danger for the heart.

If you are depressed, you may be less likely to follow your doctor's orders or to change risky behaviors — like giving up smoking or a fat-filled diet.

Depression may bring on abnormal heart rhythms. Or it could increase the risk of blood clots.

Don't ignore signs of depression. While scientists unravel the exact connection between depression and heart disease, one fact is clear: Since depression can increase your risk of developing heart trouble and lessen the odds you'll survive if you do have a heart attack, never ignore it.

Especially following a heart attack, any symptoms of depression should be reported immediately to your doctor so that you can be properly diagnosed and treated. Your life could depend on it.

Low blood pressure puts you at risk for the blues? Another possible link between your heart and depression has recently been reported — and the findings have scientists scratching their heads. While it's well-documented that having low blood pressure is good for your heart, some research suggests it may increase your risk for depression.

When University of California scientists studied nearly 600 men between the ages of 69 and 89, they found that those with the lowest diastolic blood pressure (the second number in a blood pressure reading) had the most symptoms of depression — including sadness, fatigue, and a preoccupation with their health.

In fact, those with low diastolic pressures were four times more likely to be depressed than those with higher diastolic pressures.

But there are still many questions researchers need to answer before depression can be blamed on low blood pressure. For example, no one knows yet if low blood pressure can cause symptoms of depression, or if depression may actually cause low blood pressure.

It is also possible that people with low blood pressure are simply more sensitive to bodily sensations than folks with higher blood pressure and more likely to report any symptoms they experience.

There is no doubt among health professionals that having low blood pressure lowers your risk of heart disease.

So if your diastolic number runs on the low side, don't worry about it. However, you may want to look out for any symptoms of depression and discuss them with your doctor.

Archives of Internal Medicine (152,2:381)
British Medical Journal (306,6878:655 and 308,6926:446)
Journal Watch (12,10:74)
Medical Tribune (34,14:16 and 35,6:18)
Medical World News (34,11:13)
Science News (144,5:79 and 144,17:263)

Diabetes

Describing diabetes — the sugar disease

What you don't know *can* hurt you when it comes to diabetes. You have no idea anything is wrong with you, then one day, your life is in danger because your blood sugar is out of control.

Nearly one out of five adults over 65 is diabetic, but more than half of them don't even know it.

Normally, your pancreas produces insulin, a hormone that helps your cells take in sugar. That gives your cells the energy they need.

But when you have diabetes, your pancreas may not produce any insulin at all. That's called type 1 diabetes. When your pancreas doesn't produce enough insulin or your cells don't respond properly to it, it's called type 2 diabetes.

For both types the result is the same: Too much sugar circulates in your bloodstream.

Type 1 diabetes usually strikes before age 20. Nine out of every 10 people with diabetes have type 2. It usually surfaces after you're 40.

Most type 1 diabetics and about one-third of all type 2 diabetics require insulin injections, usually once or twice a day.

Your risk of developing diabetes is greater if you:

➤ Are over 30 years old.
➤ Weigh more than 20 percent over your ideal weight.
➤ Have given birth to more than one baby weighing over 9 pounds.
➤ Are of Native-American, Latin-American or African-American descent.
➤ Have a parent, brother or sister with diabetes.

Look for these diabetes warning signs:

➤ Frequent urination, especially at night.
➤ Fatigue, or the sense that something is wrong.
➤ Unexplained weight loss.
➤ Blurry vision.
➤ Slow healing of cuts and bruises.
➤ Frequent bladder, gum and yeast infections.
➤ Unusual hunger or thirst.
➤ Tingling or numbness in the hands and feet.
➤ Unexplained itchiness.

If you notice any of these symptoms, don't wait for your yearly checkup — see your doctor at once! Unfortunately, diabetics have to worry about high blood pressure too. Together, diabetes and high blood pressure can cause serious health problems.

Heart disease. Your risk of heart disease doubles if you're diabetic. To fight back, quit smoking, lower your cholesterol levels, control your blood pressure, and monitor your fat intake.

Kidney disease. Reduce your chances of kidney damage and dialysis treatments by controlling your blood pressure and treating urinary tract infections early.

Eye disease. Head off glaucoma, cataracts, blurry vision and even blindness by visiting your eye doctor regularly.

Nerve damage. Since diabetes can damage the blood vessels and nerves in the feet, your sensitivity to pain isn't what it should be. Take extra-special care of your feet, and treat minor cuts and blisters promptly.

Tooth and gum problems. Your teeth and gums are more prone to infection if you have diabetes. See your dentist regularly, brush and floss often, and massage your gums with a triangular rubber gum stimulator (found on the end of some toothbrushes). Put the rubber tip between two teeth, point it away from your gums, and massage gently.

Your main goal as a diabetic is to control your blood sugar level. You may need a carefully planned diet, regular blood sugar testing, weight control, exercise and insulin injections. The hardest part of treatment, doctors say, is sticking to it. But even minor changes can make a major difference in your health.

Cardiac Alert (16,10:3)
Consumer Reports on Health (6,4:44)
Diabetes. Take the test. Know the score., American Diabetes Association, 1660 Duke Street, Alexandria, Va. 22314
Journal of the American Dietetic Association (94,5:504)
The New England Journal of Medicine (329,14:977)

New diet is sweet news for diabetics

Deciding what to eat can be a problem for everyone, and it's worse for those of us with diabetes.

But the latest word offers new hope for those with the diabetic-diet blues.

Doctors used to recommend a standard, very strict diabetic diet to everyone who had diabetes. Now, researchers have learned so much about the effects of carbohydrates, proteins and fats that the American Diabetes Association (the ADA) revised its guidelines.

The new guidelines let you create an individual diet, using advice from a registered dietician. Your ideal diet will depend on what type of diabetes you have, your lifestyle and your health profile.

Satisfy your sweet tooth sometimes. The ADA is relaxing its restrictions on sugar, the simple carbohydrate once considered to be a diabetic's biggest no-no. Experts used to believe that simple carbohydrates like sugar entered the blood more quickly than the complex carbohydrates you find in breads and vegetables.

They thought that, because diabetics can't process sugar efficiently, eating too many simple carbohydrates caused a sugar surge. But the truth is that all sugars enter your blood at nearly the same rate. Moderate amounts of sugar are no more damaging for diabetics than other carbohydrates.

But the total amount of carbohydrates you consume is important, say the experts. So while you used to keep track of how much complex and simple carbohydrates you were eating, now you just have to remember that carbohydrates can make up 55 to 60 percent of your total calorie intake.

So satisfy your sweet tooth every now and then, but be sure to adjust your diet accordingly. Cut back on calories from starches by a corresponding amount and watch your fat intake, since many sweets contain large amounts of fat.

Unlike Jack Sprat, you can eat some fat. But you must keep track of the kind of fat you're eating, similar to the old way of monitoring your carbohydrates. Stay away from saturated fats, which are found in animal products and in coconut, palm and palm-kernel oils.

They're more likely to increase the amount of cholesterol and triglycerides in your blood.

Instead, choose one of the two types of unsaturated fat. The first type, polyunsaturated fat, is found in corn, safflower, sunflower and soybean oils. Monounsaturated fat, now thought to be the healthier of the two, is found in olive and canola oils and in some deep water fish.

 A Natural Alternative

Hot pepper cream brings
cool relief for people with diabetes

If you're one of those people who puts red chili peppers on everything, listen up! Doctors have come up with a remarkable new way to use them: on your burning ankles and feet.

Don't worry — they're not suggesting that you actually rub yourself with peppers! Instead, they're recommending a cream derived from red chilies — one that effectively reduces the pain of diabetic neuropathy.

Diabetic neuropathy is one of the most uncomfortable complications of diabetes. Nearly 8 percent of all diabetics already have the condition by the time their diabetes is diagnosed, and after 25 years, one-half of all people with diabetes experience it.

Diabetic neuropathy is a severe burning in your ankles and feet. It's usually worse at night. The pain can keep people from sleeping and working, and it can lead to infections and amputations. Unfortunately, doctors still don't know what actually causes it. Some people improve on their own in six to 10 months, while others battle pain for years.

Deaden painful nerves with capsaicin cream. Ask your doctor about using capsaicin, a substance that comes from red chili peppers. (It's the ingredient that makes peppers hot.) In one study, 71 percent of the people who used capsaicin felt relief after eight weeks.

When you apply capsaicin to your skin, it deadens the nerves beneath it and keeps pain impulses from traveling to your central nervous system. Capsaicin reduces your pain, but it doesn't affect your nervous system's other processes.

Look for *capsaicin* only in list of ingredients. One popular brand name for capsaicin cream is Zostrix. Make sure the product you buy lists capsaicin as an ingredient. Some similar-sounding ingredients, such as capsicum, capsaicin oleoresin or capsaicin nonivamide, don't work as well.

Don't give up too early. The cream may cause some burning or stinging when you first apply it, but these symptoms are normal. They'll subside if you keep using it. You may not notice relief from pain for two weeks or more.

Capsaicin can't make your diabetic neuropathy go away, but it can free you from its day-to-day discomfort. If you carefully follow the directions in your capsaicin package, it's certainly a safe home remedy:

➤ Capsaicin shouldn't interact with other medications you may be taking.

➤ You won't "overmedicate" yourself with capsaicin. It comes in low concentrations. The concentrations lower than .01 percent are the most effective. Actually, a highly concentrated capsaicin solution is out of the question — it would burn like fire!

➤ Capsaicin isn't a numbing agent. It reduces pain, but not overall sensation.

Annals of Internal Medicine (116, Supplement 2:50)
Health Gazette (16,3:3)
Postgraduate Medicine (93,1:89)
The Physician and Sportsmedicine (21,4:13)
U. S. Pharmacist (18,8:20)

Whether you're diabetic or not you should get no more than 30 percent of your daily calories from fat. No more than 10 percent of these should come from saturated fat, no more than 10 percent from polyunsaturated fat, and no more than 10 percent from monounsaturated fat.

Some researchers believe that fat isn't so bad for you after all. One study found that a high-fat diet low in saturated fats can lower LDL (bad) cholesterol levels just as much as a high-carbohydrate diet.

Load up on fiber. Researchers say fiber helps you regulate your blood sugar, and possibly decreases your need for insulin. Apples, berries, figs, oranges, pears, prunes, broccoli, brussels sprouts, carrots, cauliflower, lettuce and potatoes are a few of the many natural sources of fiber.

A high-fiber diet will require motivation on your part, however. To get results, you'll have to eat between five and seven times your normal amount of fiber.

When you increase the fiber in your diet, drink lots of water, at least six glasses a day, to avoid constipation. It's also a good idea to increase your fiber intake gradually, to avoid cramping or bloating.

Work the following suggestions into your diet plan one at a time.

➤ Eat at least five servings of fruits and vegetables every day.

➤ Switch to whole-grain breads and cereals, and eat brown rice.

➤ Rediscover oatmeal, bran muffins and popcorn.

➤ Eat a very high-fiber bran cereal for breakfast.

➤ Add 1/4 cup wheat bran to foods like applesauce or meatloaf.

➤ Give beans such as lentils, black beans, lima beans, pinto beans and baked beans a permanent spot on your weekly menu.

Eat four to six small meals instead of three square meals. Participants in a recent study lowered their blood sugar levels and insulin requirements by grazing instead of eating three square meals a day. This doesn't mean you get to eat more. Just eat smaller quantities more frequently.

If you're taking insulin, remember that you must eat at regular times, according to the time and amount of your injection.

Alcohol and smoking are still taboo for diabetics. Alcohol can cause hypoglycemia, interact with medication, and lead to liver damage. Smoking cigarettes doubles the risk of diabetes. Smoking damages the pancreas, where your insulin is produced. Kicking the smoking habit certainly helps, but don't count on quitting someday to bring your diabetes risk back to normal. The damage you've done to your pancreas apparently remains even after you've quit.

While many of the nutrition rules have changed, the game remains the same: Your diet is important. Counting calories and hezalthy eating can prevent complications and, for type 2 diabetics, reduce your need for insulin.

American Family Physician (51,2:419)
Journal of the American Dietetic Association (94,5:504)
Medical Tribune for the Internist and Cardiologist (36,7:18)
Nutrition Today (29,1:6)
The American Journal of Clinical Nutrition (55,2:461)
The Journal of the American Medical Association (271,18:1421)

Coffee, tea ... not for baby!

Do you need your morning coffee or tea to keep up with those energetic kids? Don't share that cup with your children!

Children who drink one or more cups of coffee or tea each day greatly increased their risk of developing type 1 diabetes. So keep that coffee break for the adults; children have enough energy on their own.

Journal of the American Dietetic Association (94,11:1331)
Nutrition Research Newsletter (13,6:78)

Omega-3 fatty acids fine-tune insulin

Fatty, cold-water fish — like salmon, trout, tuna, halibut, herring, sardines, and mackerel — is a top source of omega-3 fatty acids. Researchers have shown that you need this type of polyunsaturated fat to process insulin. Without it, you run the risk of not using your insulin properly. And insulin resistance is often the first stop on the road to diabetes.

In addition, omega-3 fatty acids help lower triglycerides — a major factor in heart disease. Remember, triglycerides are a kind of fat in your blood stream, which comes from the fats in food you eat, and from excess carbohydrates. A high triglyceride level is a pretty powerful indicator of heart disease risk. Many think fish oil may work by interfering with your liver's ability to change the carbohydrates into triglycerides. That's another reason fish is an important food for diabetics.

Supplementing with fish oil is one way to get those important omega-3 fatty acids. However, researchers are still working to shed some light on just how much fish oil is most beneficial. In earlier studies, the tested amounts ranged from 3 to 18 grams a day.

Replace some of the red meat in your diet with fish to reduce triglyceride-raising saturated fats. And avoid processed foods, margarine, and baked goods — all loaded with trans fatty acids, another factor in type 2 diabetes. Try eating fatty fish three times a week, and use canola oil for cooking. That's a smart, healthy way to cut your risk of both diabetes and heart disease.

Has your doctor told you ...

Cow's milk for babies can cause diabetes

Could switching your baby too early to cow's milk ... or to solid food ... trigger diabetes years later? Recent studies from around the world suggest such a risk. Scientists in Sweden and Finland found that babies who were breast-fed for less than three months had a higher rate of type 1 (insulin-dependent) diabetes than those who were given only mother's milk for at least three months.

Researchers in the United States and Canada reported similar results for babies who were given cow's milk or solid foods before four months. Early introduction of solid foods increased the risk of diabetes even more than cow's milk. This risk is greatest when diabetes runs in the family.

These doctors recommend that babies who are genetically at risk of developing diabetes should be exclusively breast-fed for at least three months. The University of Colorado School of Medicine estimates that if all parents waited until after the age of four months to begin introducing cow's milk or solid foods into their baby's diet, between 10 percent to 25 percent of the cases of insulin dependent diabetes could be prevented.

But how could wholesome cow's milk be harmful to your baby? Researchers believe that the problem is caused by an allergic reaction to milk proteins. Babies have immature digestive systems and immune systems. In the early months of your baby's life, the immune system is learning how to distinguish foreign substances from the body's own cells.

In babies who are genetically predisposed to developing diabetes, the infection-fighting system seems to confuse the milk proteins with its own insulin-producing cells of the pancreas.

The system backfires when the baby's immune system attacks both the foreign protein and the pancreas cells, destroying both. Without these cells, your child's body cannot produce insulin and will develop diabetes.

If type 1 diabetes runs in your family and you cannot breast-feed your baby, be sure to talk to your doctor about what kind of formula to use.

Researchers recommend that you delay feeding your baby formulas based on cow's milk.

Diabetes (42:288)
Diabetic Medicine (9,9:815)

Nuts help fight diabetes

Researchers with the Nurses' Health Study recently looked at the relationship between nuts and diabetes risk, and they liked what they saw. Women in the study who ate an ounce of nuts — about a handful — at least five times a week had a 27 percent less chance of developing type 2 diabetes, compared with women who almost never ate them.

"We were not really surprised by our findings," announces Rui Jiang, one of the study's authors. "Nuts contain lots of fat, but most fats in nuts are mono- and polyunsaturated fats, which are good for insulin sensitivity and serum cholesterol. Nuts are also rich in antioxidant vitamins, minerals, plant protein, and dietary fiber."

Jiang suggests adding these nutrient powerhouses to your diet. "To avoid increase in caloric intake," she advises, "people should not simply add nuts on the top of the diet. Instead, people should substitute nuts for less-healthy foods such as refined carbohydrates, like white bread, and red meats."

Say goodbye to low blood sugar

More than just a thickener for gravy, cornstarch may help control blood-sugar levels and keep you from having an attack of hypoglycemia. This starch is digested and absorbed slowly so it's especially effective for type-1 diabetics prone to low blood-glucose levels overnight.

Researchers found that diabetics who drank a mixture of uncooked cornstarch dissolved in a non-sugary drink, such as milk or sugar-free soda, had fewer problems with low blood sugar when they woke up in the morning. If you have this problem, talk to your doctor about trying this natural solution.

You can also look for snack bars that contain sucrose, protein, and cornstarch. These ingredients release glucose at different speeds, giving you both immediate and long-term help for low blood sugar.

Hope for aspirin cure

It may be the latest medical miracle. Researchers at Harvard Medical School and the University of California San Diego reversed insulin resistance in overweight mice by using extremely high doses of aspirin. Trials of aspirin therapy are now underway on diabetics and obese people who are insulin resistant.

When your body resists insulin, a hormone that turns blood sugar into energy, sugar builds up in your blood. Even though weight loss and exercise can often reverse the problem, many people can't seem to trim down and shape up. Doctors say that puts them at risk for type 2 diabetes, a disease that is growing at an alarming rate.

High doses of aspirin blocked a particular enzyme in the mice, making them responsive to insulin again and causing their blood sugar levels to drop. Since aspirin is known to fight inflammation, the mice study suggests inflammation could be a source of type 2 diabetes and obesity.

If aspirin therapy does prove successful in people, you must only receive it under a doctor's care. The necessary doses are high enough to cause intestinal bleeding, and liver and kidney damage. Researchers hope to develop a drug similar to aspirin, but without these dangerous side effects.

Lip-smacking spice adds healthy kick

Fenugreek, a bitter-tasting legume, has been used for thousands of years in Asia, Africa, and parts of Europe to treat a variety of ailments — to settle a gassy stomach, improve appetite, increase a mother's milk production, and soothe inflamed skin. Now Western medicine learns fenugreek may help diabetics in two important ways.

When people with mild, type 2 diabetes took fenugreek, their blood sugar levels fell significantly. It's important to note that healthy people saw no change, and people with severe diabetes experienced only a slight decrease.

As a diabetic, you're at risk of heart disease and must be especially careful of your cholesterol levels. Research shows taking fenugreek every day can lower total and LDL (bad) cholesterol.

Experts aren't sure exactly how fenugreek brings about these benefits, but think its soluble fiber and plant steroids, called saponins, could be the answer.

You can buy fenugreek at many natural foods stores, and at markets that specialize in foods from India. Diabetics in this study took about one-half teaspoon (2.5 grams) of fenugreek twice a day for three months to get these health-saving results.

Be sure to talk to your doctor before taking fenugreek if you are on any medication for diabetes. In addition, if you are pregnant, avoid this folk remedy completely. Some cultures use fenugreek to bring on labor.

Arteriosclerosis and Thrombosis (14,9:1425)
Journal of the American College of Nutrition (13,4:344)
Journal of the American Dietetic Association (94,11:1259)
Nutrition Research Newsletter (11,10:113)
The American Journal of Clinical Nutrition (55,6:1161 and 57,5:650)
The Diabetes Educator (18,5:420)
The Journal of Nutrition (123,4:626)

Smart workouts for diabetics

Need another reason to exercise? How's this for motivation: Aerobic exercise just once a week will greatly reduce your chances of developing type 2 diabetes in middle age. And even better — the more you exercise, the more control you have over your blood sugar. Even people with type 1 diabetes may need less insulin if they exercise regularly. Exercise also lowers your risk of complications like eye disease, heart and circulatory disease, and neuropathy.

As we grow older, our insulin becomes less effective in controlling our blood sugar levels. Aerobic exercise "works out" this problem by making insulin more efficient. In fact, a recent study found that people at risk for developing diabetes can clear up to 11 percent more sugar from their blood with the same amount of insulin after regular aerobic exercise.

Ideally, you should exercise between three and five times a week for 30 minutes at a time. Aim for a heart rate of around 100 to 160 beats per minute. Pushing yourself over this rate increases your risk of fatigue, injury and hypoglycemia. Here are some other guidelines for exercising safely:

Ease into it. Begin with light exercise for a few minutes each day. Slowly increase how hard and how long you work out.

Warm up and cool down. Before and after exercise, spend five to 10 minutes stretching and doing light exercises such as sit-ups and shoulder shrugs.

Don't dehydrate. Drink three or four cups of water before exercise, 1/2 cup every 15 minutes during exercise, and enough afterward to regain any pounds you sweat away.

Be light on your feet. Choose activities that are easy on your feet, like walking, swimming or cross-country skiing. Wear comfortable shoes and socks during exercise and inspect your feet afterwards.

Don't exercise on an empty stomach. Three hours before your workout, eat a high-carbohydrate, low-fiber, low-fat meal. Snack on fruit juice or low-fat crackers 30 minutes to an hour before you exercise. Always eat something two or three hours after you exercise.

Head off hypoglycemia. Avoid alcohol and beta blocker drugs around the time of exercise. Both promote hypoglycemia. Exercise with a buddy who knows the signs of hypoglycemia. To prevent nighttime hypoglycemia, exercise earlier in the day and reduce your evening insulin dose after you are through exercising. You may need extra carbohydrates before you go to sleep.

Know your numbers. Log your blood sugar level, insulin dosage (if you use it), diet and exercise for a few months. Learn how changes in your exercise (such as a hard workout) affect your blood sugar, and adjust your preworkout diet and insulin dosage accordingly.

Check your blood-sugar level before exercising. If it's less than 100 mg/dl, eat a slice of bread or piece of fruit and check it again. Don't exercise if your blood-sugar level is less than 60 mg/dl.

Create an exercise kit. Keep hard candy or fruit juice and diabetic identification with you while you exercise.

Follow two tips for insulin shots. Inject your insulin at least an hour before you start exercising, and try to keep the injection away from active muscle groups. If you're unable to exercise (or if you're just not enthusiastic about it), try to be as active as possible. Doctors have pinpointed a direct relationship between low levels of activity and type 2 diabetes.

But if you're willing and able to start an exercise program, make sure you stick with it. A few days without exercise can erase all of the benefits you've achieved.

American Family Physician (47,1:216)
Consumer Reports on Health (6,7:79)
Journal of Gerontology (48,3:M84)
Journal of the American Dietetic Association (94,7:752)
Journal of the American Geriatrics Society (42,12:1235)
Medical Abstracts Newsletter (13,8:6)
The Physician and Sportsmedicine (23,3:41)

Diabetics, don't forget your feet

Adults suffering from diabetes frequently develop ulcer-type sores on their feet. These foot ulcers are caused by poor circulation, hardening of the arteries, loss of nerve sensitivity, and a weakened immune system. If not cared for properly, foot ulcers can become quite serious. They can lead to gangrene (an infection in dead tissue), and, eventually, amputation.

No injury should be ignored. The only sure method for preventing foot problems is constant vigilance against injury to your feet, careful foot hygiene, and frequent foot checkups by your doctor or podiatrist. You must care for even the most minor injury to your feet to ensure rapid and complete healing.

Pass on that barefoot stroll. As a diabetic, you should never walk barefoot or in sandals. Shoes protect your feet from injury.

If the shoe fits ... Shoes must be fitted carefully by a professional familiar with your special needs as a diabetic. A good fit is extremely important since nerve damage can prevent you from feeling the comfortable snugness of a properly fitting shoe.

Shoes should be sturdy with ample toe room, good support, and should have soft leather uppers. Running or walking shoes are generally a good choice, but you may require specially designed orthopedic shoes. Break in new shoes gradually to prevent blisters. Wear them for short periods of time at first.

Treat your feet well. Keep your feet clean and dry at all times. Daily foot care should include careful inspection, washing in lukewarm water, and the use of moisturizing lotion. Your feet should never be exposed to extreme temperatures such as hot water soaks, heating pads, or very cold outdoor weather. Nails should be trimmed straight across, not rounded. Corns or calluses should only be removed by your doctor or podiatrist.

A diet fit for your feet. Diabetic foot problems can also be prevented by controlling the underlying causes. Tight control of your blood sugar levels can reduce damage to your nerves and circulatory system.

Geriatrics (50,2:48)
Postgraduate Medicine (96,5:177)

Diaper Rash

Dealing with diaper rash

Obviously, the villain that causes the distress of diaper rash is the diaper. But a diaperless infant is a disaster in the making. Fortunately, you can take some steps besides doing away with diapers that will lessen the likelihood of diaper rash for your baby.

Keep 'em dry with disposables. Whatever their environmental impact, disposable diapers do a better job of keeping moisture away from your baby's skin. Babies in reusable cloth diapers get diaper rash more often and more severely.

Change those dirty diapers. A dirty diaper that's left on your baby can cause diaper rash, so frequent changes are extremely important. The worst kind of dirty diaper is a mixture of urine and stool. The mixture can produce ammonia, which really makes diaper rash worse.

Give the rubber panties a rest. Avoid the use of plastic or rubber pants, since these trap moisture against the baby's skin. Not only does the moisture irritate the skin, it also lets irritants enter the skin more easily.

Ask your doctor about zinc. One study showed that infants who often get diaper rash have lower than normal levels of zinc in their bodies. In another study, babies given 10 mg of oral zinc gluconate crushed and mixed with milk had less diaper rash than babies who didn't get the zinc.

Try breast-feeding? For pregnant women debating breast-feeding vs. the bottle: You may want to know that breast-fed babies have fewer diaper rashes because their urine and stool are more acidic.

Blot or blow your baby dry. If your baby has already developed diaper rash, your major focus should still be keeping his skin dry. Don't wash the diaper area when your baby is only wet. Simply blot the urine dry. You can also use a blow dryer set on its coolest temperature. If you use a blow dryer, don't hold it too close to your baby's skin. You should just barely be able to feel the air against your baby's skin.

Wash with a mild soap. After a bowel movement, when washing is necessary, use a mild soap (such as Dove, Tone or Caress) instead of baby wipes, since the wipes may contain irritating chemicals.

Watch out for these harmful products. Cornstarch can help keep a baby dry, but don't use talcum powder. It's so light that it can be inhaled by your baby and cause chemical pneumonia, which can be fatal. When using any kind of powder, be sure to keep it away from your baby's face.

Other harmful products you should never use are boric acid, baking soda, egg whites (an old home remedy) and ointments such as Vaseline or A & D ointment. These ointments don't allow moisture to evaporate. Don't use antibiotic ointments, products containing hydrocortisone, or nonprescription antifungal products until you've checked with your doctor.

Lastly, take heart! Incidences of diaper rash become less and less common as your baby grows older and needs less frequent diaper changes.

U.S. Pharmacist (19,3:27)

Diarrhea

The pink cure for diarrhea

When you or your child has diarrhea, you could be in for a long, messy, crampy night. But a good remedy for diarrhea may be as close as your medicine cabinet. In a recent study, children admitted to a hospital with severe diarrhea improved faster and were released sooner when they were given bismuth subsalicylate, the ingredient in Pepto-Bismol. All the children, who ranged from 5-month-old to 5-year-olds, were given liquids for dehydration and easily digested, high-calorie foods.

Most children who received even low doses of bismuth subsalicylate improved by the third day. One-fourth of the children not given the pink stuff were still sick five days later. There are no negative side effects if you use the recommended dose. Higher doses do not provide faster or better results, so follow package directions. What else should you do if you or your child has diarrhea?

Stay away from medicine right at first. Diarrhea usually doesn't last very long, and you shouldn't try to stop it right away. You may be interfering with the body's effort to get rid of an infection. Diarrhea that drags on or is severe needs treatment.

Swallow plenty of clear liquids such as Gatorade or Pedialyte. Diarrhea places both adults and children at risk for dehydration. Symptoms of dehydration are dry skin that may feel leathery, dry lips or sticky mouth, dark circles under sunken eyes, weakness, irritability, lack of tears when crying, and less urine. Urine may have a strong smell or be darker than usual.

Children under 2 years old definitely need an oral rehydration solution such as Pedialyte. It contains the right mix of salt, sugar, potassium and other elements. Gatorade is usually OK for older children and adults. Don't drink anything with caffeine. Caffeine makes you lose even more salt and water.

Get back to regular foods quickly. After you get some liquids down, you need nutritious, high-calorie foods. Breast milk or regular-strength formula is good for babies. You may have heard that you should water down the baby's formula, but recent studies show that regular-strength formula is better for your child. Older children and adults should eat carbohydrate-rich foods such as rice, cereal, bananas, noodles, bread and potatoes. However, it isn't necessary to stick to the old BRAT diet (bananas, rice, applesauce and toast). You or your child should eat nutritious foods that appeal to you.

Avoid sugary foods and drinks — ice cream, juice, soda pop and candy could make diarrhea worse. In some cases, milk can aggravate diarrhea symptoms, so

Has your doctor told you ...

Children can drink too much juice

There's no doubt that fruit juice is healthy, and parents should encourage their children to drink juice to get the nutritional benefits. But researchers now say it may be possible for children to get too much of a good thing.

Too much fruit juice may cause bouts of diarrhea. Apple juice in particular contains diarrhea-causing compounds that children's bodies can't absorb in large quantities. Pear and prune juices can be hard to absorb too.

Also, large amounts of fruit juice can make children feel full, so they don't eat enough foods that contain more calories and nutrients. Without enough solid food, children may lose weight and fail to grow properly. But don't rush to take that cup of juice away from your child.

The study showed that it takes 12 or more ounces of fruit juice a day to cause problems, and not every child who drinks that much juice will have health problems. But if your child drinks more than 12 ounces of juice a day and is not interested in solid food, or has frequent diarrhea, you may want to limit juice intake.

A final warning: Children with diarrhea can quickly become dehydrated — a very dangerous condition. You must give them plenty to drink. At the drugstore, you can buy "rehydrating solutions" for children with diarrhea. Some popular brands are Pedialyte, ReSol and Lytren.

Nutrition Research Newsletter (12,2:21)
Pediatrics (93,3:438)

you may want to use lactose-free formula or milk. Some children will not want to drink or eat at all. Very young children may want to eat too much. Both undereating and overeating may aggravate diarrhea.

What if vomiting is a problem? Too much liquid can make vomiting worse. Small amounts of liquid every few minutes works the best. When your child is vomiting, try giving one teaspoon of oral rehydration solution every minute. Then when he's able to keep the drink down, slowly increase the amount.

If the diarrhea has not improved after two days, consult your doctor.

_____
American Family Physician (51,5:1115)
Athens Regional Medical Center Parent's Information Handbook and Pediatrics' Unit
Teaching Tool: Gastroenteritis, Athens, Ga.
Medical Abstracts Newsletter (13,8:4)
Pediatrics (92,2:241)
The New England Journal of Medicine (328,23:1653)

Diverticulosis

How to prevent 'left-sided' appendicitis

Imagine your doctor prescribing apples as crisp and tart as an autumn afternoon, peaches so juicy their nectar runs down your chin, oranges bright as a tropical island sunset and sweeter than heaven itself. Well, that's just what medical researchers recommend for preventing a disease that occurs in one-third of all people older than 45 — diverticulosis.

Diverticula are small sac-like growths that develop on the lower part of the colon. These small pouches can cause cramps, pain, tenderness in the left side of the abdomen and gas. A bowel movement or passing gas may bring temporary relief. Bowel movements may be small and hard, alternating with attacks of diarrhea. If a diverticulum bleeds, you may pass vivid red blood with your bowel movements. The most severe form of diverticulosis, called diverticulitis, is rare. Complications from diverticulitis can be fatal. Many people develop the small pouches called diverticula and never even know it.

To keep diverticula from becoming a problem, or to relieve the crampy, painful symptoms of diverticulosis, follow these two easy steps:

Eat more fiber. The most important prevention measure and treatment is a high-fiber diet. Dietary fiber is the part of plants that cannot be broken down by the digestive processes. Symptoms of diverticulosis usually disappear within a week or two after you start eating whole-grain breads, oatmeal and bran cereals, fibrous fresh fruits and vegetables.

It's especially important to eat fresh fruits because they stimulate the growth of "good" microbes in the intestines. These microbes increase bowel movements and keep food waste moving through your system, which helps avoid diverticula problems. High-fiber fruits, listed with fiber grams per serving, include:

> Blackberries, 6.6 grams of fiber per cup
> Raspberries, 5.8 grams per cup
> Blueberries, 4.4 grams per cup
> Dates, 4.2 grams per 10 dates
> Pear, 4.1 grams per medium fruit
> Apple, 3 grams per medium fruit
> Banana, 2 grams per medium fruit
> Orange, 2 grams per medium fruit

Beans and peas are good sources of vegetable fiber. For a complete list of high-fiber cereals and vegetables, see the **Constipation** chapter. Increase your fiber intake slowly, otherwise bloating and gas may occur. Drink lots of water because dietary fiber may cause constipation and aggravate digestive problems.

Eat less red meat and fat. A diet low in fat and red meat is the second way to prevent diverticulosis. According to a recent study of nearly 50,000 doctors ages 40 to 75, men who ate a lot of fatty, red meat and little fiber were most likely to experience crippling forms of diverticulosis.

Medical researchers believe that red meat causes intestinal bacteria to produce substances that weaken the colon so diverticula form more readily. Eating chicken and fish does not increase your risk of diverticulosis. Fats from meats are more likely to lead to diverticulosis than those from dairy products.

Diverticulosis is a disease you may never think about — until you lie doubled over on your sofa, crippled by stomach cramps. A high-fiber diet has so many other benefits, why not start changing the way you eat right now?

Dietary fiber prevents heart disease and cancer and is an effective treatment for all colon diseases, constipation, hemorrhoids, hiatal hernia, varicose veins and diabetes mellitus. It even helps you lose weight because fiber makes you feel full.

If saving yourself from diverticulosis and a host of other ailments is not reason enough for a high-fiber, low-fat diet, imagine how much fun you'll have enjoying meals made with garden-fresh vegetables and luscious fruits for dessert.

American Family Physician (51,2:419)
Cecil Textbook of Medicine, 19th ed., W.B. Saunders Co., Philadelphia
The American Journal of Clinical Nutrition (60,5:737)
The American Medical Association Family Medical Guide, Random House, New York

Dizziness

How to stop the merry-go-round

Most people can remember riding a merry-go-round as a child. Standing on the platform, you held on, leaned your head back and looked at the sky. Then, when you got off the ride, you staggered around for a few minutes while the playground spun around you.

Balance and orientation are controlled by the vestibular system, an intricate and magnificent relationship between our eyes and inner ears. When the system is disrupted, the result can be dizziness.

The causes behind dizziness fall into one of several categories, including: physiological vertigo, benign paroxysmal positional vertigo, acute labyrinthitis, post-traumatic vertigo, vascular insufficiency and Meniere's disease. See *What's causing your dizziness* for an explanation. No matter what the cause of your dizziness, try these few proven methods to stop your head from spinning.

Ask for the canalith redistribution procedure. Sufferers of BPPV (benign paroxysmal positional vertigo) should ask their doctor to try a painless five- to 10-minute procedure called either a liberatory maneuver or a canalith redistribution procedure.

The procedure involves lying on a table with your head hanging off the end, and having the doctor turn your head in a sequence of positions to try to move the "ear rocks" out of the semicircular canal. It's reported to be effective in about two-thirds of patients after just one or two treatments.

But, be prepared to sleep sitting up for a couple of days after the treatment and to spend the day keeping your head as vertical as possible. Then, for a week, avoid dizziness-provoking positions, such as lying flat on your back (including getting your hair shampooed at the beauty parlor or having dental work done), exercise like sit-ups or swimming, or praying with your head down.

If that doesn't work, try Brandt-Daroff exercises. These simple movements reportedly are successful 95 percent of the time. You have to do them for 30 minutes a day for up to two weeks.

Sit on a bed or couch in an upright position for 30 seconds. Keep your feet on the floor and lay to one side, with your chin pointed up toward your shoulder. Stay there for 30 seconds or longer, until dizziness subsides. Go back to the sitting position, stay there for 30 seconds, and then lay down on the opposite side, again with your chin pointed up toward your shoulder. Repeat the series four more times, for a total of 10 minutes. The suggested schedule is five repetitions morning, noon and evening.

What's causing your dizziness

➤ *Physiological vertigo* is when the information coming into the eyes and inner ears gets mismatched, like on the merry-go-round. Astronauts moving around in weightlessness have reported dizziness that dissolves by simply touching a wall or other surface, what's often referred to as "getting your bearings."

➤ *Benign paroxysmal (par-ox-IZ-mul) positional vertigo, or BPPV,* is one of the most common types, accounting for about 20 percent of dizziness cases. If people act a little goofy, sometimes we say they've got rocks in their head. As amazing as it sounds, we really do have "rocks" in our heads, and if they roll around, they can make people act and feel very goofy indeed.

BPPV is caused by debris called otoconia, more commonly known as ear rocks, which are the result of head injury, infection or other disorders of the inner ear, or just advancing age.

The ear rocks float along in fluid to a part of the inner ear called the semicircular canal, a vital part of our balance system. When you move your head in a certain way, the ear rocks roll and stimulate the nerve endings in the ear canal, producing the feeling of severe, sudden spinning.

➤ *Acute labyrinthitis* affects all age groups, is known to occur in epidemics, and is thought to be viral or bacterial. Most people recover within a few weeks.

➤ *Post-traumatic vertigo* is dizziness caused by a blow to the head. In the early 1960s, astronaut John Glenn accidentally fell and hit his head on the bathtub. It caused such disabling dizziness and nausea that he was confined to his bed for months and was forced to give up his bid for the Senate.

➤ *Vascular insufficiency* is a change in the blood vessels supplying blood to the inner ear and brain stem, normally as the result of advancing age.

➤ *Meniere's disease* is an abnormal increase in inner ear fluid, creating some of the most severe vertigo. It often lasts for hours, as opposed to BPPV attacks that are over in just about a minute.

Dizziness can also be the result of exposure to chemicals such as welder's fumes, carbon monoxide or solvents, or it can be caused by alcohol or certain medications, such as anticonvulsants or drugs used to treat heart disease.

If you don't bring on dizziness during a session, stop the exercises for the day. If you can't make yourself dizzy during the first session of the next day, stop them entirely.

Give your nervous system a workout. Besides doing specific exercises for your dizziness, you should do aerobic exercise, like walking, several times a week. Active exercise has been found to help the body's central nervous system recover from vertigo (the medical term for dizziness) more quickly.

Wear your bedroom slippers. Some people find that wearing thin-soled shoes helps them feel the ground better and retain their balance.

Cut down on caffeine and salt. These measures help people with dizziness caused by Meniere's disease.

Sleep on your good side. Use two or more pillows at night and avoid sleeping on the "bad" side. (Lying on one side usually makes you more dizzy than lying on the other.) Get out of bed slowly, and sit on the edge of the bed for a minute before standing up.

Keep a straight head on your shoulders. Try to squat instead of bending over to pick things up, and use a step stool to see into cupboards instead of tipping your head back to look for things.

Professional Nurse (8,8:506)
R-4: Canalith Redistribution for Treatment of BPPV, R-5: Benign Paroxysmal Positional Vertigo, Vestibular Disorders Association, P.O. Box 4467, Portland, Ore. 97208–4467
The Western Journal of Medicine (162,1:73)

Drowning

10 steps to water safety

If you don't have a lake or swimming pool in your backyard, you may think your child is safe from drowning. But there may be some hazards inside your home that need your attention.

Drowning is a leading cause of accidental death in children. That may not surprise you, but did you know that toddlers under 1 year of age most often drown in bathtubs and buckets?

A toddler left alone can't resist splashing and playing in a large bucket filled with water. But it's only too easy to fall headfirst into the bucket.

If the baby can't get himself out in time, he can die in just a few inches of water. Toilets and bathtubs can pose a similar threat to very small children.

The good news is you can prevent such tragedies. As soon as your baby starts to get around on his own, start thinking about water safety in your home. Use only small buckets (under five gallons) for household chores. When you're through with a container of water, empty it.

Never leave a child alone, even for a few minutes, in the bathtub. In fact, because of the potential danger from toilets, toddlers should never be alone in the bathroom at all. If the doorbell or phone rings, ignore it or take your baby with you to answer it.

The American Academy of Pediatrics has released some other recommendations for preventing childhood drowning:

4 years and under:
➤ Never leave children alone near any standing water, including spas, wading pools, irrigation ditches, post holes, etc.
➤ Fence all four sides of your pool so your children can't wander in from the house. This one strategy has been shown to reduce pool injuries by as much as 50 percent.
➤ Swimming lessons are not recommended for children this young. They may give a false sense of security to both you and your child.
➤ Learn cardiopulmonary resuscitation (CPR) and keep a telephone and Coast Guard-approved equipment — such as a life preserver and a shepherd's crook — by the pool.

5 to 12 years:
➤ Children at this age should learn to swim, but should never swim alone or without an adult.
➤ Teach your children about water safety in various environments. They may be fine in pool water, but they need to learn about tides at the beach and hazards hidden under dark lake waters.
➤ Make sure they wear approved personal flotation devices when riding in a boat and, preferably, when playing near water.
➤ Teach them to be careful when they jump or dive into water, and teach them the dangers of water covered by ice.

13 to 19 years:
➤ Reinforce all the safety rules outlined above, but, in addition, teach them that alcohol, drugs and water sports don't mix.
➤ Make sure they learn CPR.

Hidden Hazards, The Coalition for Consumer Health and Safety, 1424 16th Street, N.W., Suite 604, Washington, D.C. 20036
Pediatrics (92,2:292)
The Physician and Sportsmedicine (22,5:26)

Dry Eyes

Six simple ways to defeat dry eyes

Many things bring tears to our eyes — watching a sad movie, seeing our children graduate, or just chopping a pungent onion. But what if those tears don't come? What if your eyes don't even produce enough tears to keep your eyes moist from day to day?

If your eyes have been feeling dry, irritated, tired or itchy, you may be one of 10 million Americans who suffers from "dry eye" each year. Dry eye is not any specific disease, but a general term used to describe the symptoms that occur when your body doesn't produce enough tears to properly lubricate your eyes.

As we age, our eyes typically become somewhat drier. By the age of 45, people lose up to 50 percent of their normal tear-producing ability. Menopausal and postmenopausal women commonly experience dry eyes.

A large number of conditions may lead to dry eye, including cigarette smoke, smog, wind, allergies, airplane travel and air conditioning. Occasionally, dry eyes can be a sign of a serious health problem. You should check with your doctor just in case.

Check the medicine cabinet for culprits. Sometimes medicines are the sneaky culprit causing dry eyes. Look out for dry eyes as a potential side effect if you take diuretics, antihistamines, anticholinergics or antidepressants. If your eyes are really bothering you, talk with your doctor about changing your medication.

Don't develop a vitamin A deficiency. You also may develop dry eyes if you have a deficiency of vitamin A, which is essential for healthy eyes. Most people get enough vitamin A through diet or supplements.

However, some disorders may prevent you from absorbing all the vitamin A you need. People with chronic pancreatitis, liver disease, alcoholism and cystic fibrosis often have vitamin A deficiencies.

You'll get plenty of vitamin A by taking a daily multivitamin.

Perk up your peepers with a humidifier. Dry eyes react badly to dry air. Avoid dusty, smoky areas if you can. A humidifier will keep the air in your office and home moist. Airplane air can be extremely dry. Drink plenty of water and fruit juices when flying. Avoid alcohol as it tends to dry out your eyes.

Take blink breaks. Don't strain your eyes for hours at a computer screen or a book without a break.

Don't rub those itchy eyes. Dry eyes are easily infected, so you need to keep your hands away.

Try tear substitutes. Tear substitutes are a low-cost, safe and effective way to replenish eye moisture. These eye drops soothe and protect the eye the way natural tears do. Because they are gentle, they can be used by most people every day, as often as needed.

Don't purchase artificial tears that contain preservatives. These eye drops may cause allergic reactions. Be sure to keep unpreserved eye drops in the refrigerator. Always wash your hands before applying eye drops. Don't confuse tear substitutes with vasoconstrictors, the eye drops that are used to reduce redness. They limit the amount of oxygen to the eye and can actually worsen dry eye.

Check with the pharmacist on duty to make sure you are using the product that is right for you.

Before You Call the Doctor, Random-Ballantine, New York
Emergency Medicine (24,7:33)
U.S. Pharmacist (17,1:35 and 19,3:22)

Dry Mouth

7 ways to wet your whistle

Was it fear or shock or perhaps physical stress that caused it? Suddenly, you couldn't speak. The words literally stuck in your throat. Your tongue felt swollen. And you could barely swallow.

Most people, at one time or another, have experienced stress-related dry mouth. At worst, the temporary condition is frustrating, even embarrassing, but certainly not physically damaging.

Just imagine suffering these symptoms continuously. For millions of people — especially older adults — dry mouth syndrome is a permanent problem. And, if it's left untreated, it can have some serious consequences. Dry mouth just means that you don't have enough saliva in your mouth. The condition can lead to mouth pain and infections, tooth and gum decay, reduced appetite and loss of sleep.

Saliva is just one of those things you take for granted — until your mouth goes dry. Then you begin to realize that saliva is truly your body's miracle mouthwash. It helps you taste, digest and swallow food. It fights cavities. It keeps viruses and funguses from attacking the lining of your mouth and throat. You need it in order to speak. And if your throat is too dry to swallow, you may not be able to sleep at night.

Diabetes and radiation treatments for cancer can permanently destroy saliva glands and cause irreversible dry mouth. But no matter whether your condition is permanent or temporary, you're going to want as much relief as possible.

Fortunately, there are several easy, inexpensive ways you can ease the discomfort of dry mouth. You can buy nonprescription saliva substitutes or try some home remedies proven to bring mouthwatering relief.

Try these tips to get your juices flowing:

As usual, check your medicines. Medicines are a common dry-mouth culprit. If you're taking drugs for high blood pressure, weight loss or depression, you may have noticed that dry mouth is a problem. If it is, discuss it with your doctor. Changing dosages or substituting other medications, when possible, may be your answer. Remember, as long as your saliva glands are intact, dry mouth syndrome may be reversible.

For a long time, the theory was that the older you got, the more your mouth was likely to dry up. Recent studies show that if most older adults weren't taking drugs that cause dry mouth, they'd have no problem producing saliva.

Suck on hard fruit candies, lozenges or even fruit pits between meals. But make sure they're sugar-free. Remember, without the protective chemicals in natural saliva, you're going to be a sitting duck for more cavities and gum disease.

Eat yogurt, milk or cheddar cheese before and after meals. Studies show these foods increase saliva and fight cavities.

Put an ice cube wrapped in gauze inside your cheek. Or put margarine or oil in your mouth.

Drink extra liquids. Try sipping water with every bite of food at mealtime.

Avoid aggravating the condition. Say no to spicy, salty or dry foods, alcohol and tobacco products.

And finally, add a little extra moisture to your air. If your home is dry from air-conditioning or heating, use a vaporizer, especially at night when you sleep.

Dairy Council Digest (65,1:1)
Dysphagia (8,3:225)
U.S. Pharmacist (19,5:16)

Dry, Irritated Skin

Moisturizing basics to relieve dry skin

It cracks easily, flakes and itches. It's unsightly. And sometimes, it even bleeds. That's dry skin. It's a common problem. Unfortunately, it's also one of those minor irritations that can become a serious medical problem if neglected.

Dry skin might be nothing more than a tight, scratchy sensation on your hands and fingers after washing dishes or spending a long time in the bath. Or it can have more serious symptoms: Cracking, scaling, roughness and redness often appear on the face, hands, shins, back or sides of the body.

When the skin becomes severely dry, deep surface cracks develop that let bacteria in. And that can lead to skin infections. Infections also occur more frequently in dry skin because it loses its flexibility and is prone to injury.

Fortunately, for most people there are several easy, common-sense remedies available to relieve dry skin before it becomes serious. Successful treatment depends upon a three-pronged approach:

➤ Try to change the outer conditions that cause dry skin.
➤ Use lotions to replace your skin's oily evaporation barrier.
➤ Replenish — or rehydrate — the water inside the cells.

Don't get too much water! The most important factor underlying dry skin is water — too much and too little of it. An adequate amount of water inside each skin cell is absolutely critical to healthy skin. Water gives shape to the cells. It provides elasticity and nourishment.

The problem is, water passes easily into the cells, but it also moves quickly to the skin's surface and evaporates — if it isn't stopped. That's why you have oil glands in your skin. Natural lipids form a barrier on your skin that keeps the water in.

Unfortunately, each time you take a long, hot shower, soak in the tub or spend the day in the pool, you wash off those protective oils. And once those oils are gone, you start losing moisture to evaporation. To complicate matters, you start losing your ability to produce those skin oils as you get older.

Don't linger in the bath or shower — we recommend 15 minutes maximum. And keep water temperature warm or cool — not hot.

Be stingy with the soap. Apply soap sparingly and rinse it off well. If you're suffering from very dry skin, wash only your face, feet, hands, underarms and genital area with soap. Pay special attention to the soap you use. Stay away from deodorant soaps, antibacterial soaps and products with fragrance additives. Instead, try nonsoap cleansers or mild soaps containing moisturizers.

Beautify with bath oil. You can moisturize your skin by adding bath oil to your bath water. But don't add the oil right away. Wait 10 minutes to let your body pull in the water like a sponge, then add the oil to seal the moisture into your skin. If you add oil too early, the slick coating on your skin will seal the moisture out. Be careful, oil makes the surface of the tub slippery.

Try the "soak-grease" method. If you don't like bathing in bath oil, take a two-step approach. After soaking in water for at least 10 minutes, dry off, but don't rub your skin with towels, washcloths or rough-textured clothing. Don't air-dry either, but pat or blot with a soft towel until your skin is slightly damp.

Then apply a good moisturizer — a thin layer of lotion, oil or petroleum jelly. The "grease" will seal the moisture in to keep your skin fresh and young-looking.

Pull on gloves to tackle the dirty work. Limit your contact with dish detergents and household cleansers. Protect your hands with cotton-lined rubber gloves.

Eat a well-balanced diet. Good nutrition will strengthen your skin from within.

Enjoy the humidity. Ever noticed that people who live in the tropics have beautiful skin? Today many people suffer dry skin because of constant exposure to air-conditioned or heated homes, cars and offices. Heating lowers the amount of relative humidity in the air, and air-conditioning actually removes moisture.

Usually, you can't control the humidity levels in your workplace. But you can alter the air at home. Room humidifiers are efficient and cost relatively little. Also, ask your air-conditioning/heating contractor about adding a whole-house humidifier to your central heating and air.

Block out the elements. Use sunblock and moisturizers to protect your skin from drying if you spend time outdoors in cold, windy or sunny weather.

Reapply moisturizers frequently throughout the day. Select appropriate moisturizers and body oils that act as sealants, attract moisture and don't clog your pores. Effective alpha hydroxy acids, humectants and oils are available in many products. Even inexpensive white petroleum jelly works as a good moisture barrier.

Just make sure that the product has been tested to be noncomedogenic — it won't clog your pores. And if you're using alpha hydroxy acids, find the concentration that you can tolerate. Some people experience severe stinging reactions with higher doses of alpha hydroxy acid.

And finally, don't scratch. Dry skin often itches, but scratching only makes matters worse. Try bags of ice water applied to the skin to reduce itching. Or ask your pharmacist about over-the-counter products that contain antihistamines. Topical corticosteroid preparations are also available and may work well for you.

Consumer Reports on Health (7,1:5)
Cutis (54,4:229)
The Physician and Sportsmedicine (23,1:53)

Oatmeal is not just for eating

What's good for your insides also can benefit the wrapper — that is, your skin. Natural ingredients, untouched by processing or chemical additives, can create excellent beauty treatments as well as save you money.

For instance, the creamy oatmeal that gives your tummy a soothing start on the day can give your skin some much-needed tender loving care. Whether your skin is normal, oily or acne-prone, try an oatmeal-based facial mask customized for your skin type.

These masks help absorb excess oil and dirt from the skin's surface. As the mask tightens, circulation is stimulated. The result? A smooth, even surface that reflects light more fully for fresher-looking skin.

For the mask base, you'll need a special form of the grain called colloidal oatmeal. The finely-ground, powdery product is available in the bath section of major drugstores. Or, you can make your own by putting a cup or so of uncooked oats into your food processor or blender. Start with a base of one tablespoon of ground oatmeal. For normal skin, add two tablespoons of distilled water and one tablespoon of powdered milk.

For oily skin, mix in two tablespoons of skim milk. Acne-prone skin could benefit from adding one tablespoon of distilled water and a half tablespoon of calamine lotion. Mix all ingredients into a paste and spread gently on your cleansed face with fingers or a soft cosmetic brush. Take care to avoid stretching your skin. Leave the mask on your face for approximately 20 minutes.

Remove by splashing your face with room temperature water. Pat, do not rub, your face dry.

The Complete Book of Natural Cosmetics, Simon and Schuster, New York
The New Medically Based No-Nonsense Beauty Book, Henry Holt and Company Inc., New York

A rash from your loofah

Love the squeaky clean feeling that washing with a loofah gives you? Just the thoughts of scrubbing the day's troubles away with a well-soaped loofah make you want to jump in the shower?

Well, wait just a second. If you're not careful, you could end up with a blister-like rash all over your arms, legs and upper body. Loofah sponges that are not allowed to dry between uses can harbor the *Pseudomonas aeruginosa* bacteria, the same culprit responsible for rashes among hot tub and whirlpool users.

Loofah sponges are made from natural cellulose fibers derived from vegetable gourds. Many people use them as an exfoliant, which removes the outer layers of dead skin cells, giving the skin a healthier-looking, smoother appearance. Often the loofah sponge hangs somewhere inside the shower stall. This prevents it from drying out and encourages dangerous bacteria to multiply.

A Natural Alternative

Soothe irritated skin with aloe

Snap off a stem of your aloe plant or smooth on an aloe-based cream from your natural foods store to relieve the discomfort of any of these skin problems:

> - acne
> - bed sores
> - chapped skin
> - cuts and scrapes
> - dermatitis
> - eczema
> - poison oak and ivy
> - burns
> - ringworm
> - shingles
> - sunburn

Aloe plants are easy to grow, and they are the best possible source of the soothing aloe gel. Aloe products you can buy may lose their healing effects over time. But if you do buy an aloe product, choose one with an aloe concentration of at least 70 percent. And avoid aloe vera extracts and reconstituted aloe products.

Herbs, The Reader's Digest Association, Pleasantville, N.Y.
Miracle Medicine Herbs, Parker Publishing, West Nyack, N.Y.
The Honest Herbal, Pharmaceutical Products Press, Binghamton, N.Y.

To use your loofah safely, store it in a dry, well-ventilated place so that it may dry out between uses. You may occasionally want to disinfect your loofah with a mixture of one part chlorine bleach and 10 parts water. Be sure to rinse your loofah with water after cleaning it.

Sloughing off with a loofah sponge in the shower may be a chic and sensible way to nurture supple skin. But beware of the mishandled loofah that can be bacteria's best friend.

Cutis (54,1:12)
Journal of Clinical Microbiology (31,3:480)

The bug from the hot tub — how to avoid whirlpool folliculitis

Whirlpools, hot tubs and saunas have become more and more popular recently. Health clubs, tanning parlors and even private homeowners are installing more of them than ever before.

Unfortunately, the increase in the number of whirlpools has increased the number of people suffering from an infection known as whirlpool folliculitis.

Whirlpool folliculitis is a skin infection caused by the bacteria *Pseudomonas aeruginosa*. This bacteria is extremely hearty and can grow in a variety of settings, including the water in hot tubs and whirlpools.

Although the high water temperature in whirlpools and hot tubs kills many types of molds and bacteria, the *Pseudomonas aeruginosa* bacteria can survive the high temperature and the high chlorine content in the water.

The bacteria will cause a skin infection only if it enters the skin — through tiny breaks in the skin, open sores or even through the tiny pores in the skin around each hair follicle.

You'll notice a rash. If the bacteria enters the skin, you will usually notice a rash within one to four days.

The rash usually is hives-like in nature, and it involves all areas of the body that were exposed to the bacteria except the head and neck. The hive-like bumps sometimes look very much like insect bites.

Often people who are infected also suffer from a low-grade fever, headaches, general fatigue and achiness, breast tenderness (in men and women), and upper respiratory complaints (coughing, wheezing, etc.).

Don't bother with antibiotics. If you get the aggravating skin infection, don't bother with any antibiotic creams or pills — the bacteria is not affected by the antibiotics. Fortunately, the infection clears up on its own in about two to 10 days. It does not leave scars, and it rarely occurs in the same person twice.

So should you avoid whirlpools from now on to avoid getting this infection? No, not exactly. Just follow some simple tips:

Limit the amount of time you spend in the whirlpool. The more time you spend in the water, the more likely you are to get an infection.

Avoid a hot tub party. Hot tubs or whirlpools that have had a lot of people in them are likely to carry the infection. Don't use them late in the day after people have been in the water all day.

Look for cloudy water and a lack of chlorine. Stay out of any whirlpool or tub that has cloudy water. Sometimes the bacteria will grow in water that contains the proper amount of chlorine, but the recommended amount of chlorine

Skin care for runners
Applying petroleum jelly to your legs will help protect your skin when you run in shorts during cold weather.

certainly helps to discourage it. The Centers for Disease Control's Suggested Health and Safety Guidelines for Public Spas and Hot Tubs suggest a chlorine concentration of 1 to 3 milligrams per liter and a pH of 7.2 to 7.8.

Don't scrub in the shower afterward. If you have used a pool late in the day or a pool that did not have clear water, don't scrub yourself in the shower trying to get rid of the bacteria.

Vigorous scrubbing and bathing with antibacterial soap can actually break the skin and alter the normal protective skin barrier. Remember that the bacteria have to get into the skin to cause infection, so try to avoid breaking the skin while bathing.

Earaches and Earwax

Getting rid of earwax

A lot of people spend a lot of time trying to clean earwax out of their ears. The simplest solution for earwax is to leave it alone. Earwax helps protect your ears against infection by trapping dust, sand, insects and other particles before they can travel deeper into your ears and cause serious problems. Wax is naturally pushed out of the ears by everyday jaw movements like chewing and talking.

Most people only produce small amounts of wax. But some people produce so much that it blocks the ear canal, making the ears feel as though they were stuffed with cotton and causing hearing difficulties. People who have narrow or very hairy ear canals may experience more than their fair share of problems. Some people who don't chew their food properly can get a buildup of wax in their ears.

No digging allowed. When you do suffer from the symptoms of excessive earwax, the urge to remove the stuff may become almost unbearable. But don't try to dig the wax out with your finger, a hairpin, a pencil, tweezers, sharp objects or even cotton swabs. They can push the wax deeper into the ear and even damage the eardrum.

Oil your ears. To remove excess earwax, use an eyedropper to apply a few drops of olive oil or baby oil twice daily. Gently insert a cotton ball in the ear to hold in the oil. The wax should soften up in a couple of days.

Hose 'em out. If your ears don't seem to be expelling wax naturally, you may want to clean them with a bulb syringe, available at drug stores.

➤ Fill a three-ounce syringe with warm water.

➤ Lower your chin to your chest. Pull your earlobe up and back.

➤ Gently squeeze the bulb syringe, and squirt a steady stream of water into your ear canal. Do not squirt water so hard that it causes pain.

The wax should flow right out of your ears into the sink or shower.

Don't attempt to remove excess earwax or use any over-the-counter ear medication if you've ever had a broken eardrum.

American Family Physician (48,2:254)
Postgraduate Medicine (91,8:58)
U.S. Pharmacist (18,12:26)

Swimmer's ear is summer hazard

Water lovers beware! Exposing your ears to too much water can cause swimmer's ear. This disorder is common during the summer months and in humid climates. It can also occur with frequent showering.

Excessive moisture causes earwax to swell up and block the ear canal. When dirt or bacteria get caught in the earwax, an infection usually results. If your ear becomes itchy, red, swollen or begins to drain, you've probably developed an infection and need to see your doctor.

The best way to prevent swimmer's ear is to keep your ear canals dry. There are several over-the-counter eardrop formulas that absorb excess moisture from ears. If you don't have any problems with excessive earwax, a few drops of 70 percent alcohol also works well.

American Family Physician (48,2:254)
Postgraduate Medicine (91,8:58)
U.S. Pharmacist (18,12:26)

Head off air traveler's earache

Flying can cause terrible ear pain if you suffer from sinus troubles or have allergies or a cold. During a plane's takeoff or landing, you may experience popping noises in your ears.

Force a yawn or wiggle your jaw. You can relieve popping noises and other pain by yawning or by moving your jaw in a circular motion. When you find a position that relieves your discomfort, hold your jaw there for a few seconds.

Pinch your nose closed and swallow. If yawning doesn't work, you can try one of these two techniques: Close your mouth, pinch your nostrils and push your tongue against the roof of your mouth. Or you can try pinching your nostrils closed and swallowing. But don't try the outdated technique of closing your mouth, pinching your nostrils, and trying to blow air out your nose. This can injure your middle ear.

Take a decongestant. If you must fly when you are congested, take a decongestant the night before your flight. Taking a nasal spray decongestant 10 to 15 minutes before landing can also help.

Put warm compresses on painful ears. Sometimes pressure changes can slightly damage your ears, causing you to experience pain, hearing loss and ringing in your ears. These symptoms normally disappear after a few hours or days. In the meantime, you may want to take an over-the-counter pain reliever. Putting warm compresses over the affected ear and on the sides and back of the neck can also be helpful.

If you have a persistent earache, itching, drainage or hearing difficulties, see your doctor. Continuing to self-treat a problem that is not improving could permanently damage your ears and hearing.

American Family Physician (48,2:254)
Emergency Medicine (27,2:64)
Postgraduate Medicine (91,8:58)
U.S. Pharmacist (18,12:26)

Has your doctor told you ...

How to apply eardrops

➤ Wash your hands thoroughly.
➤ Hold the eardrop container in your fist for a few minutes to warm the solution. Never put eardrop medication in boiling water.
➤ Lean your head down toward your shoulder. Apply five to 10 drops (only two or three drops if you're using mineral or olive oil) to the affected ear. Keep your head in the same position for several minutes. If you use cotton, insert it gently and do not push it down into the ear canal.
➤ Don't let any eardrops get into your eyes.

American Family Physician (48,2:254)
Postgraduate Medicine (91,8:58)
U.S. Pharmacist (18,12:26)

Enlarged Prostate

Evaluating your options

Let's face it. Women's bodies tend to be more of a problem than men's. Women have to worry with monthly hormone cycles, childbirth, breast cancer and menopause. But men have the prostate gland — and that little gland does its best to even the score.

In their 20s, men deal with inflamed prostates and prostate infections. By their 50s and 60s, they must contend with enlarged prostates that make urinating difficult. Then prostate cancer looms as a threat. The prostate seems harmless enough — it's a small, doughnut-shaped gland that surrounds the urethra, the tube that carries urine to the penis. The prostate is responsible for producing most of the whitish-colored fluid that carries sperm.

The problem comes as you grow older and your prostate grows larger than normal. The prostate begins to squeeze the urinary tube, making it difficult to urinate and possibly causing a urinary infection or bleeding. Eventually, you may have trouble emptying your bladder completely, and that can cause bladder or kidney problems. Some men can't urinate at all. Take the following test to see if you have symptoms of an enlarged prostate:

➤ I feel that I have not completely emptied my bladder after I stop urinating.
➤ I urinate often.
➤ I stop and start when I urinate.
➤ I have a strong and sudden desire to urinate that is difficult to delay.
➤ My urine stream is weak.
➤ I need to push or strain to start the urine stream.
➤ I often wake up at night to urinate.

If you have any of these symptoms, you should see a doctor. But just having an enlarged prostate is no reason to get treatment. If you're not bothered by your symptoms, you and your doctor may decide on a program of watchful waiting.

That means you'll just get regular exams to make sure your prostate isn't getting worse or causing more problems. Here are some other ways to cope with an enlarged prostate:

Stay away from spicy foods, alcohol, coffee and other caffeinated drinks. These will irritate your prostate gland. Many pain relievers also contain caffeine, so only use caffeine-free cold, headache and hay fever medicine. If you can't resist caffeinated coffee, tea or cola, don't drink the beverages right after dinner.

Give yourself several uninterrupted minutes to urinate. This will help you empty your bladder completely.

Use caution with decongestants and diuretics. Don't take over-the-counter cold and sinus remedies that contain decongestants. And avoid diuretics if possible. If your doctor believes you need them, take your pill early in the day.

Consider your treatment options. You may get to a point where you can't urinate, you're getting infections often, or your bladder or kidneys are becoming damaged. Then you'll need treatment. You still have plenty of options. Major surgery isn't always necessary.

New treatments appear every year, like laser surgery. Using a laser to destroy the excess prostate tissue seems to lead to fewer complications than other types of surgery, but doctors are waiting for the results of long-term studies to know for sure. One procedure is so new that it's still experimental. It's called TUNA — transurethral needle ablation — and it takes about 30 minutes in an outpatient setting.

Low-level radio frequency energy goes through a catheter device directly into your prostate. It produces a high temperature that "melts" away your prostate's extra tissue. This procedure worked for four out of five men in a Belgian study.

The most common type of prostate surgery is TURP — transurethral resection of the prostate. The doctor removes part of the prostate with an instrument he inserts through the penis.

Protect your prostate. The smartest move you can make is to take good care of your prostate before it starts to give you trouble. That basically means eating low-fat, high-fiber foods and exercising. Carrying an extra 7 inches around your waist — about 35 extra pounds — gives you a 75-percent greater risk of an enlarged prostate after age 50. That's a high risk for extra baggage you don't need anyway.

Turn to the *Prostate Cancer* chapter for more ways to protect your troublesome prostate gland.

Treating Your Enlarged Prostate, AHCPR Publication No. 94-0584, U.S. Department of Health and Human Services, Agency for Health Care Policy and Research, 2101 East Jefferson Street, Rockville, Md. 20852
Urology (45,1:28)

Falling Accidents

Fall prevention after 50

A slip in the shower or fall down the front steps often leaves you breathless and shaken, especially as you grow older. If you're lucky, that's all it leaves you.

If you're injured in a fall, with severe muscle strain, fractured ribs or a broken hip, the fear of falling can practically paralyze you.

People who've suffered severe injuries in a fall tend to avoid situations where they might fall again. In some cases, that's wise. You may never want to try roller-blading again.

However, other people stay home, away from family and friends and fun activities, trapped as much by the memory of their fall as they are by soreness and stiffness. Don't be a prisoner to the fear of falling. The 10 common-sense tips listed below will help make sure you stay steady on your feet.

Don't drink a lot of liquids right before bedtime. You're more likely to have to go to the bathroom several times during the night. A study conducted by the Florida Geriatric Research Program concluded that nighttime trips to the bathroom are one of the leading causes of serious falls in older people. Plus, the more often you wake up to go to the bathroom during the night, the less sleep you get. Being tired and sleepy during the day also increases your risk of falling.

Install wall outlet night lights along the path from the bed to the bathroom. When you wake up at night, you're often groggy and disoriented. Having a lighted path to the bathroom decreases your chances of stumbling and falling.

Tape down rugs. Secure loose carpeting and tape down all loose throw rugs with double-sided tape.

Make sure no furniture, electrical cords or other odds and ends block walking paths. This becomes especially important during those late-night trips to the bathroom.

Add handrails and grab bars. Handrails along hallways and stairways and grab bars in bathtubs and showers will help you keep your balance.

Use only nonskid floor wax on your floors.

Wear your shoes. Studies show that it's easier to slip and fall when barefoot. Wearing sturdy, flat-heeled shoes with nonslip soles can help you keep your balance indoors and out. Thin-soled shoes seem to give a greater feeling of balance than shoes with cushioned soles, such as running shoes. Keep a pair of nonskid slippers beside your bed for nighttime bathroom trips.

Watch for falling blood pressure. After a meal, your blood pressure can drop extremely low. Low blood pressure makes you dizzy when you stand up. This drop in blood pressure after eating is more common the older you get and the more heart medicines you take. Make sure you rise slowly from the table, and be especially careful for a full hour after a big meal.

Talk to your doctor about any medicines you're taking. Some drugs cause dizziness or interfere with your vision. Your doctor may be able to prescribe a different medication, or you may simply have to take extra precautions.

Have your vision and hearing checked. Poor eyesight or an inner-ear condition can cause balance problems.

Exercise regularly. You can cut your risk of falling in half. Being in good shape not only helps you avoid falls, it also reduces your risk of injury if you do fall. Low-injury exercises include walking, swimming and bicycling.

Walking is an excellent choice because it strengthens your calf and ankle muscles, which are particularly important in maintaining balance and avoiding falls. Before beginning an exercise program, get a full checkup and physical exam from your doctor.

For more information on the causes and prevention of falls, send for a free copy of "Why Do We Fall?," a booklet available from the American Academy of Otolaryngology — Head and Neck Surgery, Inc., One Prince Street, Alexandria, VA 22314. Include a self-addressed stamped envelope with your request.

American Family Physician (50,5:1085)
Journal of the American Geriatrics Society (40,12:1217)
Journal Watch (14,8:59)
Medical Tribune for the Family Physician (35,20:20)
The American Journal of Medicine (94,6:646)
The Journal of the American Medical Association (271,2:128)
The New England Journal of Medicine (331,13:821)

Fatigue

Feel healthier and happier with vitamins

If you've been feeling a little under the weather lately, you could be suffering from a slight deficiency of several important vitamins, including vitamin C and the B vitamins. Studies show that people who are just barely deficient in these important nutrients tend to feel under the weather, irritable, fearful, and even more nervous and depressed.

A team of researchers from the Institute of Nutrition in Germany studied the effects of slight vitamin deficiencies on 1,082 otherwise healthy young men (ages 17 to 29 years), and they found some encouraging results.

The men were more depressed, nervous, irritable, fearful, forgetful and unable to concentrate. The good news, however, is that the men began to feel a greater sense of well-being after receiving vitamin supplements. Folic acid (vitamin B9) supplements helped the men be more self-confident, more active, better able to concentrate, and just be in a better mood overall.

Vitamin C supplements helped the men be less nervous, less depressed and more emotionally stable. And the men who received vitamin-B supplements reported feeling more sociable and more sensitive to others.

Older people may need extra vitamins. The researchers report that vitamin supplements did not really help the men who were not suffering from vitamin deficiencies. But levels of some vitamins, such as vitamin B12, decrease with age, leaving many older people vitamin deficient. A healthy diet should provide almost all of your nutritional needs.

Foods high in vitamin C	collard greens broccoli spinach strawberries	green and red peppers tomatoes potatoes oranges and other citrus fruits
Foods high in vitamin B	sweet corn egg yolks brewer's yeast brown rice liver fish	corn meal green vegetables unrefined cereal grains seeds and nuts lean cuts of pork poultry and dairy products

Some natural sources of the B and C vitamins are listed on the previous page. Good sources of folic acid, one of the most important B vitamins, are liver, yeast, leafy vegetables, legumes (peas and beans) and fruits.

Annals of the New York Academy of Sciences (669:352)
Nutrition Research Newsletter (13,11/12:122)

Tired and worn out? Here's how to regain your energy

Think of all the places you could go, the projects you could accomplish, and the friends you could make if you were never tired. What's the key to a high-energy life? Exercise! If you're a senior, you're no doubt aware of changes in yourself. You've slowed down, you have less energy, more aches and pains, more ailments to take to the doctor.

However, recent research shows that many complaints of old age are severely aggravated or even caused by physical inactivity, not by age itself. The old adage, "Use it or lose it," holds true. You can control the condition of your body, no matter how old you are.

Plan a three-part exercise program. There are three distinct types of exercise that you need: aerobic, resistance and flexibility. You know what the aerobic exercises are: walking, jogging, swimming, cycling, etc. They strengthen and condition your cardiovascular system and improve your body's ability to use oxygen, which gives you energy. Resistance or strength exercises consist of pushing or pulling against resistance, as in weight lifting. You need these to strengthen your muscles and increase (or avoid losing) muscle mass and to maintain bone density.

Flexibility exercises consist of stretching the muscles and joints to keep them pliable and able to move smoothly without pain or stiffness. If you aren't exercising at all, devising a three-part program may seem far too formidable. Be content to start out with an aerobic exercise you enjoy. Walking is an outstanding choice for most people.

Build up to at least 20 minutes of brisk exercise three times a week. Aim for six times because you'll miss sessions now and then. Then start thinking about resistance and flexibility exercises.

British Medical Journal (6950,309:331)
Geriatrics (47,8:33)
NCRR Reporter (18,4:9)
The American Journal of Clinical Nutrition (60,2:167)
The New England Journal of Medicine (330,25:1770)
The Physician and Sportsmedicine (22,10:111)

Easy anti-fatigue exercises

Exercise gives you the strength and energy to enjoy life. And the flexibility you develop from stretching exercises gives you extra grace and poise. Take a few minutes of your day to relax and soothe yourself with exercise you enjoy.

In addition to your aerobic activity, try the following exercises. The first three improve flexibility of key areas; the last two develop muscle strength. Start with five repetitions of each exercise and gradually work up to 25. Never strain to stretch or lift.

➤ For lower back, hip joints and hamstrings. Sit on the floor with your legs straight in front of you, toes up. Lean forward from the hips (not your waist) and place your hands on your legs, as far as they can reach without strain. Pull your body forward till you feel a pull in your hamstrings, lower back or hip joints. Hold for several seconds, then release gently.

➤ For the neck. Sit or stand. Lower your chin toward your chest, hold for a few seconds. Then roll your head up and to the right till your chin is over your right shoulder. Tilt your head over till it's above your left shoulder. Roll down to starting position and begin again.

➤ For the shoulders. Sitting or standing, raise your arms high above your head, clasp your hands together, and lock your elbows so that your arms are squeezing your head. From the shoulders, bend as far to the right as comfortable, then to the left.

➤ For the biceps and forearms. Stand erect, palms forward at your sides, holding in each hand a light dumbbell (or a can of soup or a brick). Curl your hand to your shoulders, then lower slowly to your sides.

➤ For the triceps and shoulders. Hold a dumbbell in each hand at your shoulders. Raise arms up to full length, then lower to shoulders.

Eventually, you'll want to include more stretching and strength-training activities in your routine, but these exercises form a great foundation for a long, healthy, energized life.

Exercises for Non-Athletes over Fifty-One, Schocken Books, New York
Exercises for the Elderly, Emerson Books, Verplanck, N.Y.
The Physician and Sportsmedicine (22,10:11)

Is your iron too low?
If you've been feeling tired and worn down lately, check the color of your tongue. A pale tongue may mean that you have anemia and need more iron.

How to fight chronic fatigue syndrome

We all feel tired and on the verge of getting sick at times, but some people live with this feeling year round. Chronic fatigue syndrome (CFS) is a devastating disease that affects between one and 10 of every 10,000 Americans.

Diagnosis is difficult and no cure or cause is known. The symptoms of CFS are:

> extreme fatigue
> headaches
> sore throat
> slight fever
> weakness
> muscle and joint pains
> lymph node pains
> stomach trouble
> memory loss
> difficulty in concentrating

Basically, your immune system isn't functioning quite right. All these symptoms must last for at least six months to be regarded as CFS — however, they often continue for years.

While there is no cure yet, if you suffer from chronic fatigue syndrome, you can take action now to boost your energy. Energy "sappers" include sleep problems, smoking, drinking, stress, negative emotions, medications and poor eating and exercise habits.

Make a good night's sleep a priority. Most chronic fatigue syndrome sufferers seem to have some type of sleep disorder. They either sleep too much or have difficulty getting to sleep or staying asleep at night. The abnormal sleep patterns may have a lot to do with causing their CFS. If you keep healthy people from getting enough sleep, they have many of the CFS symptoms.

To combat these fatiguing culprits, make your bedroom a cozy, comfortable haven for sleep and swear off caffeine, cigarettes, sleeping pills and alcohol. See the *Insomnia* chapter for more tips on getting a good night's rest.

To reduce stress, learn how to say "no" to activities you don't enjoy. Take a class or learn a new skill, meditate, pray, or talk to a friend or therapist. A sure way to reduce stress in your own life is to donate your time and energy to others. You may not have the energy for extra activities, though. At certain times of the day, you will feel more energetic than usual. Learn your energy pattern, and plan important activities for the times when you feel your best.

Fight off bad emotions and bring on endorphins. Endorphins are the energy-creating chemicals released when we feel love and joy. Think of something that gives you a lift, rediscover an old friend, forgive yourself for making mistakes, go to the zoo, or go for a walk out in the sunshine. You'll need emotional support. Ask family and friends to give you encouragement and support. Every once in a while, take advantage of a kind listener and grieve for the energy you've lost.

Ask your doctor about getting off medicine that can cause fatigue. Some common culprits are antidepressants, antihistamines and blood pressure drugs. Also, buy all your prescriptions from the same place, so your pharmacist can watch out for fatigue-causing interactions between drugs.

Take a pain reliever occasionally. An aspirin may help with the aches and pains that can make you feel tired.

Eat properly — lots of carbohydrates and very little fat — and get regular exercise. Foods high in carbohydrates, such as bread, cereal and pasta, will give you more energy. Many people with chronic fatigue report that exercise makes them feel worse in the short term. Once they stick with it for a while, though, they begin to feel better. You may be tempted to drop out of your exercise program too early, but hang in there.

Chronic Fatigue and Immune Dysfunction Syndrome Association of America
P.O. Box 220398
Charlotte, NC 28222
800-442-3437   <www.cfids.org>

National Chronic Fatigue Syndrome and Fibromyalgia Association
P.O. Box 18426
Kansas City, MO 64133
816-313-2000   <www.ncfsfa.org>

British Medical Journal (306,6886:1161)
Medical Update (16,9:2)
The American Journal of Medicine (96,6:544)
The Physician and Sportsmedicine (21,11:47)

Has your doctor told you ...

'Red wine fatigue' is common for allergy sufferers

Do you enjoy red wine with your meals? Your beverage may be the culprit behind that tired and worn-down feeling you haven't been able to explain, especially if you're troubled by allergies or constant sinus problems.

A full one-third of a group of 300 people complained of fatigue the day after they drank a moderate amount of red wine. They also felt pressure in their sinuses. Many people in the group had been suffering from daily fatigue that completely went away when they quit drinking red wine.

Red wine tends to make your blood vessels dilate, which could cause the sinus pressure. Achy sinuses can cause fatigue.

Archives of Internal Medicine (154,10:1163)

Fever

Is your baby too hot?

If you're wondering whether or not your baby is running a fever, keep a few things in mind when taking his temperature. A baby's normal body temperature may vary by a few degrees, depending upon his age and the season.

For example, three-month-old babies have a normal body temperature of half a degree more than one-month-old babies. In the hot summer months, baby's temperature might be a little higher, on average, than it is during the winter months.

Here are some quick guidelines: For babies less than one month old, fever is defined as a temperature of about 100.4 degrees Fahrenheit. For one-month-old babies, fever is a temperature greater than 100.6 degrees Fahrenheit. And for three-month-old babies, fever is defined as anything over 100.8 degrees Fahrenheit.

The Journal of the American Medical Association (270,22:2680)

Food Allergies

Food allergies: Rare but risky

Do you start itching when you eat peanuts? Does seafood cause your stomach to churn?

Symptoms like these cause millions of Americans to suspect they have a food allergy. However, true food allergies affect only about two out of every 100 adults and eight out of every 100 children.

Food allergies are often confused with food intolerances. True food allergies can be fatal. Food intolerances are not. Obviously, it pays to know the difference. The fact is, these terms actually describe very different conditions. And their misuse can cause a variety of problems — everything from a lifetime of unnecessary food avoidance to fatal reactions.

Misunderstandings about food allergies too often lead to overreaction. Some children don't develop properly because their mothers incorrectly diagnosed food allergies and strictly limited the children's diets. Often, the foods in question, such as milk, fruits and grains, were critical to healthy growth.

At the other extreme, some people don't know enough to take food allergies seriously. They disregard the warnings about food allergies, assuming that allergic simply means a slight sensitivity. In some instances, people have died from consuming as little as one-fifth to one-five-thousandth of a teaspoon of the offending food.

What is a true allergy? A true allergic reaction means your body activates your immune system to fight off a food it identifies as foreign and dangerous. Your immune system produces antibodies to halt the "invasion." The resulting chemical release can cause skin reactions, breathing problems and digestive difficulties.

Food intolerances are much more common than allergies although the symptoms of the two disorders are often very similar. If you have a food intolerance, your body doesn't have an immune response to the food; it simply cannot digest it. For example, people who have trouble digesting milk usually don't have the intestinal enzyme lactase, which is needed to digest milk sugar. Unlike allergies, food intolerances often grow worse with age.

While people with true food allergies must avoid the offending food altogether, people with food intolerances can often eat some of the problem food without suffering symptoms. The amount a person can eat is usually small and varies from individual to individual.

How does your body react? If you have a food allergy, you probably won't have a reaction to the food the first time you eat it. After the first exposure, your body classifies a particular food as foreign and will be prepared to attack quickly at the next encounter. The second time you eat the offending food your body may respond in a number of ways, including:

> ➤ swollen lips
> ➤ stomach cramps, vomiting or diarrhea
> ➤ skin reactions, including hives or rashes
> ➤ wheezing or breathing difficulties
> ➤ migraine headache
> ➤ fluid buildup behind the ear drum — this reaction is usually only seen in children

How do you stop an allergic emergency? In worst cases, an allergic reaction may trigger anaphylactic shock. Without immediate treatment, breathing becomes extremely difficult, blood pressure drops, the mouth and throat swell, the victim has a feeling of impending disaster and may lose consciousness. Anaphylaxis can be fatal.

This type of reaction often occurs within 15 minutes of eating the offending food. Symptoms can last for several hours. The quicker anaphylaxis is treated, the greater the chance of survival. Anyone with symptoms of anaphylaxis should go to a hospital emergency room, even if symptoms seem to subside on their own.

Treatment of anaphylaxis requires an injection of epinephrine, a synthetic version of the natural hormone adrenaline. If you have ever experienced a severe food allergy, you should carry an emergency dose of epinephrine with you at all times. Your doctor can write you a prescription for epinephrine if you need one.

Do you have a food allergy? If you suspect you have a food allergy, keep a food diary. Write down everything you eat or drink for a two-week period. Note any symptoms and how long it took for them to develop.

Even though you may identify a reaction you have to certain foods, you will not be able to correctly identify a food allergy without the assistance of a doctor who has specialized training in allergy and immunology.

Incorrectly labeling some reaction to food as a food allergy can lead to unnecessary avoidance of the food, which can cause nutritional deficiencies.

What precautions must you take? If you are diagnosed with a food allergy, you will need to completely avoid the offending food. It's critical that allergy sufferers, or their food preparers, take precautions:

➤ Read food labels carefully to detect possible sources of allergens.

➤ Consult restaurant staff concerning menu ingredients when you eat out.

➤ Warn school employees if your child is allergic.

➤ Instruct children, their friends and caregivers about the type and seriousness of the allergy.

➤ Keep epinephrine on hand and know how to administer it.

Children should be retested for their food responses, since they sometimes "outgrow" their allergies. In those instances, the allergy-causing foods may be reintroduced into the diet.

What are some common problem foods? The majority of allergies occur in response to just a few categories of food. Most allergies are triggered by eggs, peanuts, milk, fish, soy and wheat.

Recent studies show that some adults may also have cross-reactive allergies. For example, people who tested allergic to fruits such as avocados and bananas may also be allergic to latex used in clothing, in surgical gloves and in some medical equipment.

If you are allergic to these fruits and have surgery scheduled, let your doctor know that you may have an allergy to latex. Some people also don't respond well to various preservatives and additives used in food preparation.

The artificial sweetener aspartame, the flavor enhancer monosodium glutamate (MSG), the food dye FD&C Yellow No. 5 (listed as tartrazine on medicine labels), and the sulfur-based preservatives called sulfites cause adverse reactions in certain people. These reactions are not necessarily allergic; some people's bodies just don't like them.

Reactions to these foods and products vary from person to person. Learn to tune in to what your body is telling you. Knowing how to recognize a food allergy can mean the difference between life and death.

Food Allergies, FDA Consumer Reprint, Publication No. (FDA) 94-2279, Department of Health and Human Services, Food and Drug Administration, HFI-40, Rockville, Md. 20857
Journal Watch (14,12:93)
Science News (146,15:231)
The Journal of Allergy and Clinical Immunology (81,3:495)

Food Poisoning

Don't eat oysters raw from spring to fall — if at all!

You may remember the old adage: Eat oysters only in months with the letter "r." The Food and Drug Administration wants you to follow that advice, plus some. According to the old advice, you should avoid oysters from May through August. The FDA says don't eat them raw from April through October.

Raw oysters can cause food poisoning from bacteria called *Vibrio vulnificus*. This bacteria thrives in warm ocean water. Infected oysters can cause diarrhea, severe illness and even death. A current FDA proposal suggests that oysters harvested from the Gulf of Mexico between April and October should have warning labels.

Consumers would be warned that they should fully cook the oysters before eating them. Cooking the oysters kills the harmful bacteria, according to the FDA. People who have kidney disease, liver disease, diabetes or weakened immune systems have the highest risk of getting the infection. Some states already have laws about informing these high-risk people.

Spicy sauce makes oysters safer? Some Louisiana researchers think spicy cocktail sauces may kill some of the bacteria in raw oysters. They tossed spicy sauce into a test tube of bacteria and killed all the bacteria within one minute.

However, to throw cold water on the hot sauce idea — the researchers haven't tested their theory on people yet, so, in the real world, hot sauce may not make oysters safer at all.

FDA Consumer (28,9:4)
The Atlanta Journal/Constitution

Cook your eggs!

Try to avoid using recipes that call for raw or only slightly cooked eggs, which are the most common source of the salmonella infection. People likely to be severely affected by salmonella include pregnant women, infants, the elderly and the sick. These people should only eat well-cooked eggs.

Either modify a recipe so that cooked eggs may be substituted for raw or use pasteurized or dried eggs. Many grocery stores carry pasteurized egg substitutes, such as Egg Beaters. Specialty food stores often stock dried egg products.

British Medical Journal (308,6928:595)

Hold the honey for babies

You should never feed honey to babies, no matter how much they like the taste! Honey can cause a common form of food poisoning called botulism. In fact, botulism strikes infants more often than adults, and about one-third of the cases in babies are caused by honey.

Ten percent of honey contains the substance that can poison babies, causing symptoms ranging from sluggishness and slowed feeding to paralysis and death.

You may have heard of giving honey in water with a dash of salt for diarrhea. This is fine for older children and adults, but never for children under 12 months old.

The Merck Manual, 16th ed., Merck and Co., Rahway, N.J.

Forgetfulness and Poor Concentration

Thiamin beats the bad memory blues

If your memory won't mind you and your concentration has crumbled, take a look at what you've been eating lately. You may not be getting enough vitamin B1 in your diet.

Vitamin B1, also known as thiamin, is an important vitamin used by your body to help promote and maintain the normal functions and development of your muscles, heart and nervous system.

It plays a key role in the metabolism of carbohydrates, in the conversion of fatty acids into steroids, and it may also play a part in your body's natural resistance to disease.

Having trouble concentrating? If you're not getting enough thiamin in your diet, you may feel tired; nauseated; irritable; experience a loss of appetite; and have difficulty sleeping, remembering and concentrating. An advanced deficiency of thiamin may lead to more severe mental problems including depression and possibly even delirium, a state of mental confusion accompanied by frequent mood swings and anxiety.

In fact, a recent study of elderly people who were hospitalized found that those people with lower levels of vitamin B1 were more likely to suffer from delirium than people who had normal levels of the vitamin. Your nervous system, in particular, is very sensitive to your body's ability to break down carbohydrates. If you don't get enough thiamin to assist your body in breaking down carbohydrates, your brain and the rest of your nervous system may not work properly.

Doctors think that this could be the link between vitamin B1 intake and memory loss, the inability to concentrate, and other symptoms associated with a deficiency of the vitamin. Unlike some other vitamins, thiamin is not stored in the body in large amounts, so it's important to eat a thiamin-rich diet.

Where do you get thiamin? Natural sources of thiamin include liver, pork, salmon, poultry, fish, beans, peas, rice and whole-grain products. The chart in this chapter will help you figure out what you need to eat to get enough thiamin.

The U.S. Recommended Daily Allowance (RDA) is only 1.2 milligrams (mg) for men and 1.1 mg for women, and most people get more than enough thiamin from their diets. However, there are some people who may not be getting enough and may need to take a supplement in the form of a multivitamin.

You may need extra thiamin if you:

✔ Take antibiotics, birth-control pills or sulfa drugs.
✔ Eat a high-carbohydrate diet or a diet that's low in calories or nutrients.
✔ Need to eat large amounts of calories, such as endurance athletes or manual workers.
✔ Drink large amounts of coffee or tea.
✔ Are over 55.
✔ Use tobacco.
✔ Have recently had a fever.
✔ Are pregnant or breast-feeding.
✔ Are under unusual emotional or physical stress.
✔ Have recently had surgery.
✔ Have an overactive thyroid.
✔ Have kidney or liver disease.

If you're not getting enough thiamin in your regular diet, a supplement that supplies 50 mg a day or less should provide plenty.

Complete Guide to Vitamins, Minerals and Supplements, Fisher Books, Tucson, Ariz.
Gerontology (40,1:18)
The American Medical Association Encyclopedia of Medicine, Random House, New York
The Real Vitamin and Mineral Book: Going Beyond the RDA for Optimum Health, Avery Publishing Group, Garden City Park, N.Y.

False senility reversed

Are you over 55? Ever lose your eyeglasses? Forget your keys? Feel confused and disoriented about where you left your car? Get anxious about little things that never used to bother you? If you think these are normal signs of getting older, you may be able to turn back the clock. These and a host of other symptoms of "false senility" may actually be caused by thyroid problems that can be treated.

Doctors have long confused many of the signs of thyroid diseases with "normal aging." That's because thyroid problems are difficult to diagnose.

There are two types of thyroid disorders. Hyperthyroidism, when your thyroid gland pumps too much thyroid hormone into your system, may cause nervousness, anxiety, irritability, fidgeting, trembling, forgetfulness, heart disease or sluggish heart functions, diarrhea or constipation, loss of appetite, and depression.

Hypothyroidism, when production of the thyroid hormone slows down, may result in listlessness, dry skin, feeling cold when others around you are comfortable, tingling skin, carpal tunnel syndrome, deafness, puffy face, confusion, constipation and even anemia.

Nearly 9 percent of all adults over age 55 may have some form of thyroid disorder. Hypothyroidism occurs more often in older people than in younger people, and in more women than men. Your risk is higher if someone else in your family has a thyroid disease.

Ask for a blood test. Today, doctors don't have to rely on correctly identifying physical symptoms to diagnose thyroid disorders. Blood tests reveal whether too much or too little thyroid hormone is circulating through your body.

Treatments vary, depending on the disorder. Hypothyroidism is treated with replacement therapy for the thyroid hormone. Hyperthyroidism is frequently corrected with radioactive iodine therapy.

One study found low levels of vitamin A in young people with goiter, a symptom of hyperthyroidism, but not in older people. Eating foods high in vitamin A may help prevent goiter. Sweet potatoes, carrots, spinach and broccoli are good sources of vitamin A. It is not known whether eating foods high in vitamin A can prevent other symptoms of thyroid disorder.

Your best bet if you are over age 55 is to ask your doctor for a blood screening to test the level of your thyroid hormone.

Archives of Internal Medicine (13,10:1)
Geriatrics (45,8:86)
International Journal of Vitamin and Nutrition Research (58,2:155)
Journal of the American Geriatrics Society (41,12:1361)
Postgraduate Medicine (95,4:219)

Natural sources of thiamin

Food	Quantity	Mg of thiamin
Asparagus, boiled	1/2 cup	.15
Black-eyed peas, boiled	1 cup	.35
Bread, Italian	1 medium slice	.10
Bread, whole-wheat	1 medium slice	.10
Brewer's yeast	1 package	.17
Broccoli, boiled	1/2 cup	.05
Brown rice, cooked	1 cup	.19
Brussels sprouts, boiled	1/2 cup	.08
Cereal, Kellogg's All-Bran	1/2 cup	.36
Cereal, Kellogg's Product 19	1 cup	1.50
Chicken, white meat, roasted	1/2 breast	.06
Chickpeas, boiled	1 cup	.19
Eggs, poached	1 large	.04
Liver, beef, cooked	1 slice	.13
Navy beans, boiled	1 cup	.37
Noodles, cooked	1 cup	.30
Oatmeal, cooked	3/4 cup	.19
Peanuts, dry-roasted without salt	1 ounce	.12
Plums	1 medium	.02
Pork tenderloin, roasted	3 ounces	.80
Prunes	1 cup	.10
Raisins	1 cup	.15
Salmon, cooked	3 ounces	.29
Soybeans, stir-fried	3.5 ounces	.42
Sunflower seeds, dried	1 cup	1.05
Wheat germ, toasted	1 ounce	.47

How to supercharge your memory

Even in this fitness crazy age, people often neglect one of the most important organs — the brain. Just like the muscles in your body, your brain needs proper exercise and nutrition to stay in shape and function efficiently. Here are a few tips to make your memory work for you.

Stop pampering your mind by using lists. Memorize phone numbers, grocery lists and appointment dates. The more things you try to remember, the better your memory will be. Constantly seek new challenges for your brain. Read difficult books and play games. Do math problems in your head.

Eat well-balanced meals. Vitamin and mineral deficiencies can impair your mental abilities. Vitamin C and B vitamins are especially important to proper brain functioning. More than 100,000 chemical reactions occur in your brain each second. These reactions require huge amounts of energy.

Heavy thinking and intense concentration can use up as many calories as your muscles do during exercise. In fact, your brain uses one-fifth of the total calories you consume every day. And a hard day of mental work can leave you as exhausted as a strenuous physical workout.

However, some experts believe you can stop "brain drain" just by eating certain foods. Although some of the foods labeled as brain boosters may surprise you, give them a try.

Perk up with a cup of coffee. Studies conducted at Massachusetts Institute of Technology demonstrated that one cup of coffee improved mental functioning, reaction time, concentration and accuracy. Drink one cup of coffee in the morning for greatest mental alertness.

The effects from one cup of coffee will last for several hours, so you don't need to drink coffee continuously throughout the day. However, you may want to have another cup of coffee in the afternoon to combat that after-lunch slump.

Eat the best of the brain food: lean fish and shellfish. Since ancient times, fish has been praised as a brain food. Researchers have found that four ounces of broiled or grilled fish stimulate your brain chemicals and make you more alert. Fish fried in fat may lose some of its natural brain-boosting effects.

Lower your blood pressure to improve your memory?

If it seems like you just can't remember anything lately, have your blood pressure checked. Researchers have found that people who have diastolic (the lower number) pressures above 90 often have difficulty remembering and learning new tasks.

Stay sharp with sugar. Sugar makes many people sleepy. However, it has the opposite effect on certain people born with an unusual brain chemistry. Sugar actually makes these people more focused, concentrated and alert.

Two and a half tablespoons of sugar or two ounces of candy will normally do the trick. Eating more does not seem to be more effective. Even if sugar has this effect on you, don't rely on it as your primary mental booster. You'll gain weight, of course.

Milk it for all it's worth. Milk may not put you to sleep despite what you may have heard. Recent research reveals that it can actually perk up your brain chemicals. For maximum benefits, drink skim or low-fat milk. Because of its high fat content, whole milk may actually make you sleepy and sluggish.

As little as half a cup of skim or low-fat milk can rev your brain up into high gear. For best results, drink milk before eating an accompanying snack or meal. If you don't like milk or have trouble digesting it, low-fat yogurt has the same brain-boosting effects as low-fat or skim milk.

The Compass in Your Nose and Other Astonishing Facts about Humans, Jeremy P. Tarcher, Los Angeles
The Food Pharmacy, Bantam Books, New York

Breakfast boosts your brain power

How many times have you dashed out the door, rushed the kids to the bus stop, and zipped off to sit in traffic on the freeway without ever thinking about getting something to eat for yourself or your family?

If this sounds familiar, you may want to rethink your morning routine. Repeated scientific studies show that missing breakfast can be hazardous to your family's mental abilities.

Skipping breakfast is a common characteristic of the fast-paced American lifestyle of the 90s. One recent survey of 407 children in grades four through eight showed that nearly 60 percent said they skipped breakfast. More than a third of American adults may eat no breakfast or one of little nutritional value.

Both children and adults can suffer from skipping breakfast. Children who don't eat breakfast don't concentrate well, don't pay attention as long, and get lower scores on tests. Adults who don't eat breakfast show poorer performance at work too. Busy mornings don't have to mean going without breakfast. If you are going full-speed each morning, here are a few ideas for grabbing some nutrition along the way.

Save leftovers. Pizza, casseroles, pasta dishes, stews and soups are all easy-to-grab foods that can be popped in the microwave or toaster oven, or eaten cold. They can even be stored in single-serving containers and eaten on the road.

Crunch on carrots. Buy individual carrot sticks and set them out in the mornings with made-ahead yogurt or bean dip. Family members can snack while getting ready, or grab some to go.

Show children how to fix their own quick breakfast. Keep cereal, bowls, cups and utensils in a low cabinet, and put milk and juice in small pitchers on a low refrigerator shelf.

Make ahead a quick batch of low-fat muffins. Or pick muffins up in the "nutrition" or "natural foods" section of your grocery store. Keep them in the refrigerator or freezer already filled with fruit spread, peanut butter or low-fat cream cheese.

Make ahead sandwiches. Use bagels, whole-wheat bread, English muffins or tortillas, and freeze them already filled with peanut butter, low-fat cream cheese, other cheeses, fruit spreads, fruit slices or low-fat meats. Heat them in the microwave or toaster oven.

Dairy Council Digest (64,2:7)
Hamilton/Whitney's Nutrition: Concepts and Controversies, 6th ed., West Publishing, St. Paul, Minn.
Nutrition Research Newsletter (13,1:4)

Frostbite

Take the bite out of frostbite

When Christmas carolers sing "Jack Frost nipping at your nose," some cold-climate dwellers and winter-sports freaks get the shivers.

A nip or a bite from Jack Frost can mean serious injury to, or even loss of, the nose, toes, ears, fingers and cheeks of the hapless wanderer in a Winter Wonderland. Frostbite is your body's natural reaction to cold weather. Struggling to keep the center of your body warm, your blood vessels narrow and shut down circulation to your limbs and outer surfaces.

Without a proper blood supply, your tissues start to die. In extreme cold, even the water in your body starts to freeze. You can get frostbitten in less than a minute, especially if you're holding on to a metal tool or ski pole with a bare hand, but it's more likely that frostbite will develop over several hours or days.

Don't ignore the warning signs. With frostnip — the first stage of frostbite — your toes, fingertips or a patch of skin on your cheek will get cold, pale, firm and dry and will feel prickly or numb. Always ski, hike or work outside with a buddy, so he can look at your patchy-white face and tell you to warm up or go inside.

When Jack Frost is out with a vengeance, take these steps to reduce your risk of frostbite:

Get out of the wind. Besides cold temperatures, high wind and humidity are the two main weather risk factors for frostbite. Wind makes you lose heat five times faster than still weather, and rain or snow will chill your body 25 times faster than dry skies.

Drink plenty of water and other liquids. Dehydration is by far the No. 1 bodily cause of frostbite, say nurses in an Alaskan hospital's thermal unit.

Don't strain too hard and take regular breaks. Fatigue and sweating raise your risk of frostbite, whether you're working, playing or seeking shelter from the cold.

Avoid alcohol and cigarettes. Alcohol makes you think you're warm when you're not, so your body doesn't shiver. Shivering is a natural way to produce heat. Smoking makes frostbite more likely because it shrinks your outer blood vessels.

Be extra cautious in cold weather if you have any injury or illness or are simply out of shape. Even a common cold makes your body less able to generate and conserve heat. Medication you might be taking for an illness can make circulation worse too. Some conditions that particularly raise your risk of frostbite are:

➤ Raynaud's syndrome (An illness where the blood vessels in your hands and feet close up too much in response to cold weather or stress. Your fingers turn pale and feel tingly or numb.)
➤ Diabetes
➤ An old or new bone fracture
➤ Previous frostbite
➤ Head injury
➤ Heart disease
➤ Lung disease
➤ Kidney or liver disease

Make sure your clothes are well-insulated, dry and not too tight. You need to be able to move freely. Don't forget your hat and scarf — 80 percent of your body heat is lost from your head and neck.

Don't try to "be tough" and ignore the cold. You're more likely to get frostbitten when you're used to milder winters and your body isn't adjusted to freezing temperatures. You're also at high risk for frostbite if you're so used to the cold that you ignore it. Eskimos have an old tradition of exposing their ears on purpose so that they'll acquire frostnip.

Frostnip can actually make you more sensitive to the cold and better able to avoid frostbite. Be proud if you're sensitive to cold weather — you've got a built-in frostbite warning system.

First aid for frostbite

Your goal in treating frostbite is to thaw your frozen fingers, feet and ears as quickly as possible in warm water.

First, make sure refreezing isn't a risk. It's better to keep walking on a frozen foot than to stop and thaw it before you get to permanent shelter. Tissues that have frozen, thawed and refrozen probably won't recover.

Second, make sure the frostbitten person doesn't have hypothermia (extremely low body temperature — around 90 degrees Fahrenheit instead of the normal 98.6 degrees Fahrenheit). A person with hypothermia should never be soaked in warm water. If a person can talk clearly and answer questions logically, he probably doesn't have hypothermia.

On the other hand, a person whose body core is too cold will seem extremely lethargic — on the verge of unconsciousness. Wrap him in blankets and get him to a doctor as quickly as possible. Follow these steps to thaw frozen parts of your body:

➤ Soak in a tub of warm water — 100 degrees Fahrenheit to 106 degrees Fahrenheit. If possible, use a thermometer to check the temperature so you won't burn your numbed body. Since frostbitten skin is prone to infection, put a solution such as Hibiclens (an anti-infection solution) in the bath water.

➤ Thaw frostbitten ears with soft towels soaked in warm salt water.

➤ Don't try to thaw yourself with dry heat. Campfires, exhaust pipes and car heaters are likely to burn your tender, numb skin, especially since your frostbitten hand has no idea how hot that air is.

➤ You'll know you are thawed when your skin turns pink or red — the blood is flowing back into the frozen tissues. Gently rinse the frostbitten parts with clean water, then pat dry or allow to air-dry. Cover loosely.

➤ If you have blisters, don't burst them. Apply burn ointment such as Silvadene or Thermazene to open wounds and wrap loosely with sterile gauze and bandages.

➤ The more fluids you drink, the faster your body will heal. Avoid caffeine and smoking because they cause blood vessels to narrow — the last thing you want to happen.

➤ Make sure you eat meals high in protein, calories, vitamins and minerals.

➤ Take aspirin to ease pain.

➤ To help blood circulate in damaged feet and hands, exercise and stretch gently several times a day. Also, take warm 20-minute baths with an anti-infection solution, such as Hibiclens, twice a day to help blood flow to damaged tissues.

If you think you have frostbite, contact your doctor as soon as possible. You may need professional treatment.

Gas

Flavorful herbs get rid of gas

A high-fiber diet, gulping down your meals, no regular exercise, and hard-to-digest medications — any of these can give you painful intestinal gas buildup.

While most people suffer only occasional gas attacks, others suffer every day. Americans spend millions of dollars every year on over-the-counter treatments for gas attacks. But costly tablets and liquids don't have to be the only answer to gas problems. Instead of looking in your medicine cabinet, try some safe, inexpensive home remedies.

Increase fiber intake slowly. If you're increasing your intake of high-fiber foods, try slowly increasing the amount of fiber over a period of time. This makes it easier for your digestive system to adjust.

Don't eat so fast. Many people experience gas pains with bloating because they swallow too much air while eating. By simply slowing your eating, you can often relieve problems that develop from excess air in the stomach.

Watch out for the worst food offenders. Some foods are hard to break down and digest. Beans, broccoli, cabbage, bran and dried fruits are notorious for causing gas attacks in many people. These foods usually aren't completely digested and absorbed as they pass through the stomach and small intestine. When undigested sugars reach the colon, they are fermented by bacteria, resulting in gas.

When this occurs, the only way to get relief is by removing or absorbing the gas and quieting intestinal spasms. And that's where a special group of herbs can be very helpful.

Relieve gas with herbs. For centuries, scientists have known that some plants commonly used to flavor foods contain chemicals that aid in the absorption and removal of gas from the digestive system. Clove, allspice, black pepper, ginger root, cardamom, coriander, lemon balm, turmeric and angelica root are all considered mildly effective in aiding digestion and ridding the intestines of gas.

But the best herbal remedies for gas and digestion problems are made from the oils or seeds of anise, caraway, chamomile, fennel and peppermint. Researchers have found that teas and preparations made from these plants are often better at removing intestinal gas than over-the-counter charcoal and kaolin products.

Chemicals in these plants seem to improve the tone of the smooth muscle of the intestinal wall, which improves the absorption of gases and reduces spasms. Some chemicals actually help expel gas.

You may want to try one of these herbs if you have gas problems:

Anise. Anise is often used in blended teas with caraway and fennel to ease gas pain.

Caraway. Add caraway seeds to foods such as cabbage to add flavor and reduce gas buildup. Caraway may also be blended with fennel tea to improve its taste.

Chamomile. This plant is raised in the United States and Europe. It's often used in teas, inhalants and other preparations. The benefits may increase with long-term use. Use whole flower heads, not powder. To prepare chamomile tea, add one teaspoon of flower heads to boiling water and steep in a covered teapot for 10 to 15 minutes. Drink one cup at a time between meals. Be very careful with chamomile if you have pollen allergies because it can cause a reaction.

Fennel. You can mix anise and caraway with fennel seeds for a more pleasing flavor. To prepare fennel tea, pour boiling water over crushed seeds and steep. Drink 30 minutes before eating. Only use the seeds, since even small amounts of the oil can cause skin irritation, vomiting, seizures or respiratory problems.

Peppermint. Don't confuse this plant with spearmint (they look a lot alike). Besides relieving spasms, gas and indigestion, peppermint can also temporarily reduce hunger pangs, but they will return later, stronger than ever. To prepare peppermint tea, pour boiling water over two-thirds cup dried leaves and steep for five to 10 minutes. Peppermint teas should not be given to infants and small children because it can cause a choking sensation.

If you're going to treat yourself with these remedies, let your doctor know. Although they are considered safe, some herbs can interfere with the action of other medications.

Buy Beano to pass less gas. Now you may be able to enjoy that bowl of beans or plate of cabbage in comfort if the result of a new study on one anti-gas product proves correct. In a recent test, half the people were fed chili laced with a product called "Beano." After five hours, these subjects reported less gas passed than the people who ate chili without Beano. Beano seems to be an easy-to-use and low-cost way to relieve gas.

One word of caution: The enzyme in Beano releases higher levels of carbohydrates into your system when you eat high-fiber foods. This increase could be important if you are a diabetic. Also avoid Beano if you are allergic to mold, since some Beano ingredients are taken from mold cultures.

Herbal Medicine, Beaconsfield Publishers, Beaconsfield, England
Herbs, The Reader's Digest Association, Pleasantville, N.Y.
The Honest Herbal, The Haworth Press, Binghamton, N.Y.
The Journal of Family Practice (39,5:441)
Herbs of Choice: The Therapeutic Use of Phytomedicinals, The Haworth Press, Binghamton, N.Y.

Hair Loss

When you should be concerned about hair loss

"I've got so much to do I'm pulling my hair out!" How many times have busy women said something like this? Well, it's not too far from a true statement. Many times, working mothers and other women pile too much on their plates and can't seem to get anything done.

Get stress level under control. Too much stress is a very real cause of hair loss in women, according to recent research. Stressful situations also lead many people to neglect their diets, and rapid weight loss does not help keep the scalp and hair healthy. You may notice that you're losing extra hair about three months after a traumatic event, such as major surgery, severe illness or a high fever. This hair loss is not permanent, and your hair will grow back.

Check your medicines. Some medications can cause hair loss, so check with your doctor or pharmacist if you suspect a connection. Some medicines that may be the culprit include blood thinners, gout medicines, vitamin A (if you overdo it), birth-control pills and antidepressants.

Be prepared for after-pregnancy fallout. Women often notice healthier, thicker hair during pregnancy and are terribly disappointed when large amounts of hair begin to fall out after the baby is born. Those changing hormones during and after pregnancy can affect hair growth and loss. There is no need for alarm if you notice your hair falling out and you've just had a baby.

Menopause is another time in a woman's life when hair loss can begin.

Make sure thyroid and iron levels are normal. Anemia (iron deficiency), a low blood count or thyroid problems can cause hair loss. You may need a simple blood test to determine if you have normal hormone and nutrient levels.

Look for redness and rash. If you notice redness, scaling or a rash on your scalp, see your doctor. You may have a scalp infection. Many infections can be treated with anti-fungal medicines, and the hair will grow back.

Don't damage your hair follicles. To help keep your hair on your head and not in your brush, avoid hot curlers, curling irons, harsh chemicals and tight braids. They can all harm your scalp and hair. If you stop pulling your hair with braids or tight rollers before your scalp scars, your hair will grow back. Once your scalp has scarred, your hair loss may be permanent.

Hot oil treatments and permanents can cause hair loss. If you have a nervous habit of pulling or twisting your hair, stop it now!

Some people can't stop this habit on their own and need counseling or drug therapy.

Hair loss in women is a cause for concern, but not necessarily a cause for alarm. Think about what is taking place in your life now and what has happened in the last few months. You may just need to slow down, eat healthier foods, and take good care of your scalp and hair.

American Family Physician (51,6:1527)
Diseases of the Hair and Nails, Year Book Medical Publishers, Chicago
Hair Loss Journal (6,2:1)
Postgraduate Medicine (85,6:53)
The Journal of the American Medical Association (273,11:897)

Hangover

Hang the hangover

In the movies, hangover symptoms — headache, fatigue, nausea, vomiting, no appetite, raging thirst, sweating, poor vision, depression, giddiness — often seem amusing. But in real life, they are the unfunny and painful result of too much alcohol in the system, causing an unbalanced biochemistry in the body. The feeling of dehydration occurs because alcohol is a diuretic.

The first and best way to avoid a hangover is not to drink. The second best way is not to drink to excess. For many people, excess means when they "get a buzz."

Here are seven other ways to avoid a hangover:

✔ Set reasonable limits for yourself and learn to say no.
✔ Drink slowly.
✔ Dilute your drinks with water or other nonalcoholic beverages.
✔ Don't drink by yourself.
✔ Don't smoke. Smoking makes the hangover worse.
✔ Eat a full meal before drinking; fatty foods are good choices because the fat seems to coat the stomach and cut down absorption of alcohol.
✔ Drink plenty of nonalcoholic liquids.

Some drinks are worse than others. Most alcoholic drinks contain added coloring and flavoring substances. Different substances in different combinations combined with alcohol are an almost certain formula for a hangover, say medical experts. The alcoholic beverages with the highest amount of these headache-producing substances are brandy, bourbon and red wine.

Although there is little evidence that one alcoholic beverage causes less severe hangover symptoms than another, drinking several different kinds of alcoholic beverages at one sitting does seem to produce more severe hangovers.

How to deal with the morning after. Should you have a hangover, try:

➤ Two aspirin or buffered aspirin, or antacid for stomach upset.

➤ Lots of nonalcoholic beverages, particularly fruit juices loaded with vitamin C.

➤ Sweet, bland foods.

There is no evidence that a "hair from the dog that bit you" will do anything but make the situation worse. Obviously, if your hangover is caused by too much alcohol in the bloodstream, having more will not help.

The only "cure" for a hangover is aspirin, (nonalcoholic) liquids, sleep and time.

The American Medical Association Family Medical Guide, Random House, New York

Hay Fever

Home remedies for hay fever

There's nothing quite like the splendor of spring, when trees come alive again and flowers bloom — particularly if you are one of the millions who suffer from hay fever. Spending some time outside enjoying nature's rebirth could make you wish you could be reborn — without allergies this time, please!

Hay fever, or allergic rhinitis, is an allergic reaction (usually inherited) that causes the lining of your nose and sinuses to swell. Though pollen from blooming trees, shrubs, grasses and flowers makes spring the most likely time to have hay fever, other allergens like mold, dust mites and pet dander can cause hay fever at any time of the year.

The result is an itchy or runny nose, sneezing, dripping sinuses, sore throat, a stuffy head, and even a decreased attention span.

Many medications are available to treat hay fever, but side effects like drowsiness can make the cure worse than the disease. By evaluating your home and workplace, and adjusting your lifestyle a little, you can eliminate many of the things that cause your hay fever.

Wear a mask when you work in the yard, especially while cutting your grass. Blocking pollen and dust from your airways can provide significant relief, particularly during the growing season. Sunglasses can help protect your eyes from pollen too.

Not everyone is allergic to the same pollen, and different geographic areas have different "pollen seasons," so it's impossible to say when you should be wary of the outdoors. Note which time of year seems to produce the worst hay fever symptoms for you and be extra careful at that time.

Pollen is usually worst in the early evening, when it's settling back to the ground. The best time for allergy sufferers to go outside on hot, dry days is midmorning.

Wash your hair. Your hair, especially if it's long, acts as a pollen net. Washing it before you go to bed should help you rest easier.

Sunlight stops dust mites from bugging you. If dust mites are bugging you, sunlight may be the solution you've been searching for.

Dust mites are mighty irritating animals, especially to people with allergies or asthma. These tiny insects, which are related to spiders, live in bedding, carpets and mattresses. They eat small pieces of dead, sloughed-off human skin cells and produce waste material (feces), which is coated in enzymes made from the mite's intestines. This enzyme coating is mainly responsible for triggering allergic reactions.

When you change the sheets or vacuum, the mite feces blow around in the air for 30 minutes or so before settling down. If you *don't* inhale any of the mite stuff floating around, consider it a minor miracle. If you do, you're liable to start sniffling, sneezing or coughing or even have an asthma attack.

How can you get a handle on those nearly invisible bugs that love to cuddle up in your carpets and snuggle with you in bed?

The latest research from Australia suggests that sunlight may be the key. Researchers there found that leaving mite-infested rugs outdoors for four hours on a hot, sunny day killed 100 percent of the mites and their eggs. This approach would probably work well for bedding, curtains and pillows.

Try a tannic acid solution for rugs and carpets that you can't take outside. Researchers at the University of Virginia in Charlottesville found that the

Sneezeless plants

If you suffer from hay fever but can't bear to stay cooped up inside during peak pollen times, consider growing "sneezeless" plants. Some plants produce less pollen than others, or the pollen they do produce is less likely to cause hay fever. See the chart on the following page.

Plants	*Instead of these allergy producers*	*Consider these "sneezeless" plants*
Trees	Acacia	Catalpa
	Alder	Dogwood
	Almond	Fig
	Ash	Tulip Tree
	Birch	Redwood
	Cottonwood	Jacaranda
	Elm	Pine
	Fruitless Mulberry	Mulberry
	Oak	Fir
	Olive	Chinese Tallow
	Pecan	Palm
	Poplar	Plum
	Privet	Podocarpus
	Sweet Gum	Strawberry Tree
	Sycamore	Silk Tree
	Walnut	Pear
	Willow	Chorisia; Coral Tree; Crape Myrtle; Magnolia; Maidenhair; Mayten; Orchid Tree; Red Bud; Silk Oak
Shrubs	Elderberry	Oleander
	Juniper	Nandina
	Privet	Manzanita
	Rhamnus	Pyracantha
	Thuja	Yucca
	Ceanothus	Boxwood; Grevillea; Hibiscus; Pittosporum; Verbena; Viburnum
Ground Cover	Juniper	Cinquefoil, Sedum, Tradescantia
Grass	Bermuda	Bunch grasses — rye, fescue, blue, etc.; Dichondra; Hippocrepis comosa; Irish Moss; Mazus reptans
Ornamental	Amaranthus	Poppy
Flowers	Ceanothus	Azalea; Begonia; Bougainvillea; Bulbs — Tulip, Ranunculus, Iris, Daffodil, etc.; Camellia; Cymbidium; Pansy; Peony; Solanum

Sneezeless Landscaping, American Lung Association of California

Hay fever — how the sniffling got its start

Did you know that hay fever may not have even existed before the 19th century? Grass and pollen have been around forever, so you'd think hay fever would have been a common malady since the beginning of time. But it may have gotten its start with the Industrial Revolution.

Descriptions of hay fever in medical writing are extremely rare before 1800. Biblical, Greek and Roman writings don't mention it at all. Not until Dr. John Bostock, a London physician, published his own case history in 1819 was hay fever recognized.

Dr. Bostock wasn't sure what caused his symptoms. Dr. Charles Blackley, another English physician who suffered from hay fever, solved the riddle when he collected grass pollen in a bottle during the summer. In the middle of winter, he took the top off the bottle, breathed in the pollen and developed symptoms of hay fever.

Both of these men had spent time in the north of England, where the Industrial Revolution was born, leading to major chemical pollution for the first time in history.

Scientists now speculate that the damage to the nasal passages from industrial pollutants makes people more susceptible to hay fever.

_____

The Lancet (340,8833:1453)

product Allersearch ADS reduced dust mites in carpet by up to 92 percent. This product does not actually remove dust mites, it just makes the enzyme coating found on mite's feces inactive. This means dust mite droppings will no longer trigger an allergic or asthmatic reaction in people who are susceptible.

The product may not work as well if you keep a cat in the house. Cat dander, allergens that come from the cat's fur, skin and saliva, seems to interfere with the effectiveness of tannic acid. For more information on Allersearch ADS, call 1-800-422-DUST.

Here are some other tips to help you send your dust mites packing:

➤ Cover mattresses, box springs and pillows with airtight plastic casings.
➤ Wash your bed sheets, comforters and mattress pads and pillows in very hot water every week. You should also wash curtains when you do your spring cleaning.
➤ Sun or vacuum items that can't be washed, such as upholstered furniture. Be sure to throw away vacuum bags immediately after vacuuming.

Be healed with bee stings? You may find the latest natural treatment for allergies in your nearest beehive.

Researchers have discovered that beekeepers suffer much less from allergies and arthritis than other people. Beekeepers get stung an average of 2,000 times a year, so researchers are speculating that there may be mighty healing powers in everyday bee venom.

Stay tuned for more buzz about bee venom and allergies, and, in the meantime, if you're looking for a healthy hobby, consider keeping bees. (Keep in mind, however, that some people have life-threatening reactions to bee stings.)

Use air conditioning. If pollen causes your hay fever, opening your windows to let fresh air in is the worst thing you can do. Air conditioning can keep the pollen out while helping you keep your cool.

Use the air conditioner in your car as well. It may be fun to drive with the windows open or the top down, but that just blows pollen up your nose at the speed you are driving.

Air conditioning also keeps the humidity down in your house. By holding down the moisture, you prevent mold from growing.

Mold spores can cause severe hay fever in some people. Studies show that central air conditioning is better at preventing mold than window units, but a window unit is better than no air conditioning at all.

Vacuum your house once a week. Or even better, have someone who doesn't suffer from hay fever vacuum for you. Stirring up dust as the vacuum rolls along could make your hay fever worse. Vacuuming will help eliminate dust, dust mites and pet dander that might be causing your hay fever.

Some people swear by the special "anti-allergic" vacuum cleaners, but certain studies show that these vacuum cleaners don't work any better than regular vacuums. You should at least consider the small expense of a special bag for your vacuum. Some vacuum cleaner bags and filters do a better job of trapping microscopic particles.

Don't let furry or feathered pets inside. You may love Fluffy very much, but she could be the reason you always feel sick. Pet dander, or dead skin cells, ranks with dust mites as a primary cause of hay fever. Keeping Fluffy out of your bedroom is not a solution because the hair and dead skin cells can be blown through your house by heating or cooling systems.

Fleas carried by your pet can also cause hay fever. That's why you can be allergic to some pets but not others — it may be the fleas that make you sneeze, not the pet. For some people who are extremely sensitive to pet dander, even keeping the animal outside may not be enough to prevent hay fever.

If you insist on keeping a pet, consider those that don't cause allergies. Fish, turtles, frogs, snakes and sand crabs are ideal for hay fever sufferers. And if you absolutely can't part with Fluffy, be sure to bathe her often. You should also place filters over forced-air heating and cooling vents to keep the dander down.

Check your house for mold. The air conditioner will help keep mold down, but you should also check spots in and around your house where mold is likely to grow. Dark, damp areas such as basements are prime spots for mold growth. Also check sinks, shower and toilet areas, refrigerators and washing machines. Even the air conditioner, which can be so helpful, can be an area of concern if it does not drain properly. Wipe moldy surfaces with a solution of bleach and water.

Houseplants can also harbor mold, especially those in wicker baskets. You can purchase mold retardants from your local nursery for use in the home.

Don't forget to check your yard for mold as well. Compost piles, poorly landscaped or heavily shaded areas, along with areas that don't drain well, are susceptible to mold. Again, check with your local nursery for mold retardants.

Steer clear of smoke. People with allergies should not smoke and should ask smokers not to smoke around them. Avoiding smoke not only helps your allergies, it also helps prevent other respiratory problems like lung cancer and emphysema.

Use pump or roll-on products instead of aerosols. Breathing in the spray of aerosols irritates upper and lower airways.

Stay away from strong odors. Perfumes, scented soaps and tissues, paints, and insecticides all contain chemicals which can trigger allergic reactions.

Take a beach vacation. One of the best vacation spots for allergy sufferers is the seashore. Sea breezes keep pollen inland and away from the beach.

If your hay fever symptoms persist after you have done all you can to remove pollen, mold, pet dander and dust mites, you might resort to medicine.

A variety of drugs are available without a prescription. These antihistamines and decongestants can relieve your symptoms, but you may have to endure side effects such as drowsiness, nervousness or insomnia. If you have high blood pressure or urinary problems, you should talk with your doctor before taking these drugs. Nose drops or sprays can help you breathe easier, but they can be addicting and eventually make symptoms worse.

As a last resort, you might consider allergy shots. A doctor conducts tests to determine exactly what causes your hay fever, then injects you with extracts of those substances. The goal is to build up resistance to the substance. Relief usually begins four to six months after you start the allergy shots. You will probably need to have the shots regularly for several years to be cured. The shots don't work for everyone, but they can be a lifesaver for some people with severe hay fever.

Medical Tribune (33,6:112 and 36,7:18)
Medical Tribune for the Family Physician (35,7:24 and 35,18:22)
Physician Assistant (117,5:52)
Science News (1145,2:28)
The Allergy Book, Atlanta Allergy Clinic, P.A., Suite 200, 1965 N. Park Place, N.W., Atlanta, Ga. 30339

Headaches

Put the squeeze on a tension headache

Proposal due tomorrow. Briefcase. Laptop computer. Pencil. Paper clip. ... Am I forgetting anything? Oh yes, the headache.

Of all the items people bring home from the office at the end of the day, by far the most common is a headache.

Some people suffer from the crippling, one-sided migraine accompanied by nausea (see the *Migraines* chapter), the sinus headache which can be treated with nasal decongestants and antibiotics, or the intensely painful "cluster headache" which develops around the eyes and often hits in the middle of the night.

However, nine out of every 10 headaches are the "tension-type," says The National Headache Foundation. You're likely to get a tension headache during a stressful or tiring day at the office, after a confrontation that left you biting back words on the tip of your tongue, or after serving a Thanksgiving feast to 20 of your loudest relatives.

Everyone knows the signs of a tension headache — a dull, constant ache slowly grows on both sides of your head. You may feel as though a headband is squeezing tighter and tighter around your temples and the back of your skull.

Your shoulders, neck and head muscles often feel tight and tense. Extreme tiredness and sensitivity to light and sound may accompany your headache. There's no doubt about it — a tension headache can hurt worse than a migraine.

Stop the pain while you still can. The most important step in fighting a tension headache is to stop the pain before it gets out of control. As soon as you notice a headache coming on, immediately take aspirin, acetaminophen or ibuprofen.

Put your head on ice (or be a little hot-headed). Keep an ice pack or a hot pack at the office so you can place it on your head or neck at the first sign of pain. A long, hot shower will help ease tension and an aching head.

Get plenty of sleep. Stick to a regular sleeping schedule too.

Exercise! Strive for at least three times a week.

Take breaks during stressful situations. Stretch, go for a short walk, or just "take" five to relax.

Don't pass up a vacation or a day off work. When headaches become a daily trial, you need to give yourself some time off.

Reduce stress. Try deep breathing, gentle music or other relaxation techniques.

Keep tabs on your caffeine intake. A caffeine-withdrawal headache feels just like a tension headache. If you normally drink several cups of coffee, tea and soda a day, your head will probably ache dully when you miss your regular dose of caffeine. Too much caffeine can give you a headache too, so try to wean yourself off slowly.

Headaches and depression go hand in hand. Depression may be the cause of a daily tension headache that hits the moment you wake up or early in the morning. If your headache falls into this pattern, you may have a chemical imbalance that may be improved with medication or you may need to work with friends, family members, a local support group or a counselor to pull yourself out of the dumps.

Don't pop a pain reliever every day. For chronic headaches that occur more than 15 times a month, don't keep taking over-the-counter pain relievers without visiting your doctor. Pain relievers that you can buy without a prescription are generally less harmful than prescription medications, but they do have their side effects (see the ***Chronic Pain*** chapter).

Aspirin, ibuprofen and acetaminophen, especially those products that contain caffeine, can lead to a "rebound effect." Your body adapts to the pain reliever being in your system, and you become extra sensitive to pain when the medicine starts to wear off.

You need to see your doctor if you're taking a large number of pain relievers, if frequent headaches are interfering with your daily life, or if a severe or constant headache is accompanied by weakness, dizziness, numbness or other strange physical sensations.

American Family Physician (47,4:799)
The National Headache Foundation, 5252 N. Western Avenue, Chicago, Ill. 60625

Hearing Loss

Hearing loss protection: How to keep your ears listening for life

Did you grow up working on a farm, perhaps baling hay or filling grain sacks for hours near a noisy tractor? Or maybe you had a part-time job in a restaurant or factory, working near a roaring exhaust fan?

Your ears have had a hard life. Even when you were relaxing at a loud concert with friends, your ears weren't having fun. Many times during your life, noise has destroyed some of the sensory hair cells in your inner ear.

When loud noises have made your ears ring or feel stuffed with cotton, you've lost some of your hearing ability. You've always had enough healthy cells left for your hearing to return to normal, but now you may be on the road to lasting hearing loss, along with the one-third of all Americans who have hearing problems by age 65. It's time to begin pampering your ears.

Choose quiet leisure activities. Avoid noisy activities such as hunting or woodworking with power tools, especially if you work in a noisy place or drive to work in loud city traffic. How do you know a noise is too loud?

Here are two clues:

➤ You have to shout to be heard above the noise.

➤ You can't understand a person speaking to you who's less than two feet away.

Activity	Sound pressure level (in decibels)
Automobile interior	60-92
Firearm	130 or higher
Lawn mower	80-95
Manufacturing plant	85-105
Motorcycle/snowmobile	80-110
Music	
Rock concert	90-115
Stereo headset	60-115
Symphonic concert	80-110
Busy office	70-85
Power saw	95-110
Vacuum cleaner	70-85

A Natural Alternative

Help prevent hearing loss with vitamin A

If you want to make sure you don't lose your keen sense of hearing, make sure you get enough vitamin A in your diet.

Some cases of hearing loss may be linked to a vitamin-A deficiency. Studies show that a lack of vitamin A in the diet first increases the ear's sensitivity to sound. In other words, your hearing is actually more sensitive during the first stages of deficiency.

However, an increased sensitivity to noise increases the chances of noise-induced hearing loss. The very sensitive ear can be damaged more easily and quickly than a normal ear. So the vitamin-A deficiency does not actually cause hearing loss. It simply makes the ear more sensitive to sound — which increases the chances of hearing loss due to noise damage.

If you suspect you may have a problem with your hearing, even if your ears seem supersensitive, talk to your doctor immediately. He can help you determine whether you need more vitamin A in your diet.

Go fishing for vitamin A. Vitamin A is found in many sources. Cod liver oil is loaded with vitamin A, so much, in fact, that it can be toxic if you take too much. After cod liver oil, salmon, mackerel, tuna and other fish also contain vitamin A. Fish also contains vitamin D. Vitamin D helps prevent bone loss and may help strengthen the bones in the ear's hearing mechanism, which can help keep your hearing sharp as you age.

Other good sources of vitamin A are butter; egg yolks; cod liver oil; liver; yellow vegetables; and green, leafy vegetables. Some fruits are also good sources of vitamin A including prunes, pineapples, oranges, limes and cantaloupes.

The Journal of Nutrition (120,7:726)

Compare the common noises listed on the previous page (a noise that an average young adult can barely hear is zero decibels; the pain threshold is about 140 decibels).

Any noise over 85 to 90 decibels is hazardous when you're exposed to it for several hours a day. Very loud noises, such as firearms and fireworks, can cause "acoustic trauma," which means your ears are damaged immediately.

Never start a loud activity immediately after a noisy workday. Your ears need time to rest and begin to recover their hearing ability. They don't need total silence, but they do need a low-noise environment.

Wear earplugs when you know you'll be around loud noises. Disposable foam earplugs, around $2 a pair, can shut out 25 decibels of sound. That can make the difference between a safe noise and one that causes hearing loss. Always use earplugs when riding snowmobiles, motorcycles or other loud vehicles and when using power tools, lawn mowers or leaf blowers. Hunting without protecting your ears can be extremely harmful. If you aren't willing to wear earplugs while in the woods, purchase a headset or earmuffs you can quickly pull on and off.

Reduce noise at home and work with sound-absorbing materials. Put rubber mats under loud dishwashers, computer printers and typewriters. Hang heavy curtains at the windows and quilts, decorative rugs or blankets on the walls. Thick, plush carpets over dense padding absorbs indoor noise well. Storm windows or double-pane windows reduce outdoor noises.

Break the habit of loudness. Get used to a lower volume when using the television set, stereo or headset. Don't use several noisy machines at once. You know your stereo headset is too loud when a person standing near you can hear sounds from it when it's on your head.

Don't use loud noises to drown out other, unwelcome noises. Don't crank up the volume on the car radio to drown out traffic noises, or turn the TV volume up so that you can hear it over the vacuum cleaner.

Exercise! Regular exercise will protect and even improve your hearing. Exercise improves your blood circulation, which helps keep the sound-detecting hair cells in your inner ear healthy.

Don't strain too hard. Strenuous activities, such as lifting heavy boxes, can raise the pressure in your ears too high. That can cause hearing loss.

Get a free hearing test over the phone. Here's an easy way to test your hearing without making an expensive trip to the doctor. Call Dial a Hearing Test at 1-800-222-EARS (3277). An operator there will give you a number in your area to call to take a free, two-minute hearing test over the phone.

You should have your hearing tested every year if you're regularly exposed to loud noises. Children should have their ears checked before they start kindergarten, especially if they have chronic ear infections or a family history of hearing problems. You'll first know that you've started a decline toward deafness when you can't understand high-pitched noises — singing birds, the voices of women and young children. Eventually, men's voices and other lower-pitched noises will become hard to understand. It's particularly difficult to hear what others are saying to you when you're surrounded by loud background noise.

Check your medicines. Some drugs can damage your ears. If you regularly take salicylates (such as aspirin), furosemide, neomycin or gentamicin, you should get your hearing tested often.

Clean out that earwax. Some people have had their hearing completely restored when they had their ears cleaned! Earwax can completely block your ears. See the ***Earaches and Earwax*** chapter for tips on getting rid of earwax.

Be aware of these warning signs of hearing loss. How can you know when you're hurting your ears? Hearing loss isn't often painful, so people tend not to notice the damage. Plus, a noise that causes severe hearing loss in one person may not cause any damage at all to another person. These sensations are warning signs of hearing loss. They may last a few minutes or a few days after exposure to loud noises.

➤ Ears feel full or under pressure.
➤ Voices sound muffled and far away.
➤ You hear a ringing sound in your ears when all is quiet.

Converse in corners. When conversing, position yourself in a corner or some place where you have two walls behind you that can reflect sound. Cupping your hand around your ear and turning your ear in the direction of

Help for the hard of hearing

When you start to lose your hearing, it's easy to feel cut off from the outside world. Some of these mechanical devices can help you get back in touch:

➤ Amplifiers for telephones, televisions, VCRs, dictating machines and microphones.
➤ Loud bells, buzzers and ringers for telephones, doorbells, security alarms and smoke alarms.
➤ Flashing lights, vibrating devices, fans and bed shakers for alarm clocks, doorbells and smoke alarms.
➤ Closed-caption television receivers, relay services, message centers and other devices to keep you informed.

You can learn more about these hearing helpers from many national organizations:

➤ **National Association of the Deaf**, 814 Thayer Avenue, Silver Spring, MD 20910 (telephone: 301-587-1788; telecommunication device for the deaf [TTY]: 301-587-1789).
➤ **Alexander Graham Bell Association for the Deaf**, 3417 Volta Place N.W., Washington, D.C. 20007 (telephone: 202-337-5220; TTY: 202-337-5221).
➤ **National Information Center on Deafness**, Gallaudet University, 800 Florida Avenue N.E., Washington, D.C. 20002-3625 (telephone: 800-241-1044; TTY: 800-241-1055).

American Family Physician (46,3:851)

the speaker can also help. Ask people talking to you to lower the pitch of their voices instead of talking louder.

Hear what you're missing with hearing aids. A hearing aid can dramatically improve your quality of life. You need to buy your first hearing aid from a physician (an otolaryngologist) or an audiologist, even though it may cost you more than going to a hearing-aid dealer. At least visit an audiologist or doctor first.

Dealers, even though they have a lot of practical experience in fitting hearing aids, can't tell you if you have a serious health problem that's causing your hearing loss or if you have a type of hearing loss that hearing aids won't help.

If you've totally lost the ability to hear certain frequencies, a hearing aid will not help you understand speech clearly again. It will only make the sounds you can hear louder. Hearing aids do help when you've only partially lost the ability to hear certain frequencies. If you have trouble distinguishing between D's and B's and between L's and R's, you probably have a problem with low frequencies and would not benefit from a hearing aid. If your hearing aid quits working, check the batteries first. Another common problem is a buildup of earwax in the ear or on the hearing aid.

No surgery or medical device can restore hearing loss due to loud noises, but if you think you're losing your hearing, you can take extra precautions to save the hearing you have left.

American Family Physician (46,3:851 and 47,5:1219)
Emergency Medicine (24,15:165)
Journal of Gerontological Nursing (19,4:23)
Medical Tribune for the Family Physician (34,22:2)
The American Medical Association Encyclopedia of Medicine, Random House, New York
U.S. Pharmacist (18,4:101)

Heart Disease

Reverse heart disease without drugs or surgery

Want to lose weight without dieting, lower your risk of heart disease to nearly nothing and feel better than you ever have in your life?

Then Dr. Dean Ornish has the miracle you're looking for. Author of *Dean Ornish's Program for Reversing Heart Disease*, he is director of the Preventive Medicine Research Institute in Sausalito, California, and assistant professor of medicine at the University of California's School of Medicine.

Stress management, diet and exercise. Ornish has developed a program that focuses on stress management, diet and exercise as the keys to preventing and reversing heart disease. His healthy-heart diet also works wonders for people who want to lose weight.

In addition, this program can improve your sex life, help you sleep better, give you more energy, make you more productive and boost your brain power.

How soon will you feel better if you follow Ornish's program? About seven days, he estimates.

Are you isolated or connected? Dr. Ornish says the real key to the many health problems Americans are experiencing these days is isolation. Feelings of isolation lead people to engage in health-destroying behaviors, such as smoking, drinking alcohol, overeating and putting themselves under constant stress.

Ornish recommends stress management techniques as a way to increase your awareness of what's happening inside your body. This way, you notice and deal with potential problems, such as stress, before they lead to serious health complications. These techniques also teach you to relax, which can help you perform at the peak of your ability.

Learn to communicate. How you approach people every day plays a big part in whether you feel isolated or connected. He offers some tips to help you feel closer to other people:

➤ Learn to communicate your feelings and wants clearly. Many times the way we express ourselves makes other people defensive and very unlikely to understand our real concerns and worries.

➤ Don't expect other people or yourself to be perfect. Be forgiving.

➤ Be kind and giving to others. Find enjoyable ways to help people. Studies have shown that helpful people live 2 1/2 times longer than ungiving people. However, you should resist helping people when you feel forced into it.

➤ Don't expect a big thank you for everything you do.

➤ Find or create a support group that communicates openly.

Diet and exercise also play important roles in making you feel good and helping you stay healthy. The low-fat, high-carbohydrate diets Ornish recommends can make you more energetic and improve your mental and physical powers. They can also reduce your risk of cancer, diabetes, high blood pressure and stroke.

A heart-healthy diet. For people who have been diagnosed with heart disease, Ornish recommends a vegetarian diet that is less than 10 percent fat. This food plan, which Ornish calls The Reversal Diet, is a dieter's dream come true. You can eat whenever you feel hungry and still lose weight.

The diet includes fruits, vegetables, grains, legumes and soybean products. There are a few high-fat vegetarian choices you should not eat such as avocados, olives, coconut, nuts, seeds and cocoa products.

You should also avoid all animal products with the exception of egg whites and one cup of nonfat yogurt or milk a day. Limit alcohol to two ounces per day or less and try to stay away from caffeine, which may worsen irregular heartbeats or provoke stress.

For people who want to prevent heart disease, Ornish recommends a diet that keeps your cholesterol levels at 150 mg or less. Many people can do this by simply limiting their daily intake of butter and oils, cheese, eggs, nuts and meats, especially red meat.

The exercise factor. For the best results from Ornish's program, you also need to exercise regularly. Ornish recommends walking 30 minutes daily or one hour every other day. Walking is the exercise of choice for many people because it poses the least risk of injury.

Include warm-up and cool-down periods into your exercise time. Start your warm-up with a few gentle stretches. Begin your workout slowly and gradually work up to a faster pace in the next few minutes. To end your exercise session, slow down to your pre-workout pace for a few minutes. Finish with a few stretches.

Be aware of how you feel before, during and after exercise. If you are unusually tired after a workout, you may have pushed yourself too hard and need to cut back next time. If you feel dizzy, have irregular or rapid heartbeat or shortness of breath, see your doctor immediately.

Benefits are worth the effort. For many people, Ornish's program will mean many new changes, but the benefits are well worth the effort. And he believes that the closer you follow the program, the better you'll feel and the healthier you'll be. In one of the recent programs Ornish conducted, 82 percent of the participants experienced a significant reversal in their coronary artery disease within the first year — all without drugs or surgery.

Dr. Dean Ornish's Program for Reversing Heart Disease, Random House, New York

'Miracle drug' fights heart disease

It can prevent more than 100,000 premature deaths every year; it only costs a penny per day, and it's available at any pharmacy, grocery store or corner convenience store in America. Sound too good to be true?

Wish you had some of this 'miracle drug'?

Chances are, you do. Right in your medicine cabinet or kitchen cupboard. Just look for the bottle labeled "aspirin." Although scientists have known about some of the beneficial effects of aspirin for quite some time, recent studies have shown that simply taking one aspirin a day can save thousands of lives every year.

Prevents formation of clots. Doctors and scientists are now strongly recommending that everyone (men and women) who has experienced a heart attack, stroke, bypass surgery or angioplasty, or who has experienced angina (chest pain) or transient ischemic attacks ("mini-strokes") could benefit from taking an aspirin a day.

Aspirin helps keep the blood from getting "sticky" and forming clots that could lead to a fatal heart attack or stroke. Scientists think that baby aspirin (75 milligrams) provides as much protection as regular aspirin (325 milligrams) without some of the side effects that come with larger doses, such as upset stomach.

Most people can take a baby aspirin every day instead of taking adult doses and still experience the protective effects of aspirin. However, people who have suffered heart attacks should take a regular aspirin (325 milligrams) each day.

Should everyone take an aspirin a day? The answer is no. Right now, scientists do not recommend daily aspirin for healthy people without a history of heart problems or strokes. Scientists are not sure if the benefits of daily aspirin in healthy people outweigh the potential side effects of long-term aspirin therapy. And, until they do, they do not recommend that healthy people take aspirin on a regular basis.

Talk with your doctor about the protective effects of daily aspirin therapy. If you have any history of heart problems (angina, heart attacks) or blood vessel disease (strokes, transient ischemic attacks), you are probably the ideal candidate to receive the remarkably beneficial effects of daily aspirin therapy. A 25-percent reduction in the risk of premature death for only a penny a day is a benefit that you can't afford to live without.

Archives of Internal Medicine (154,1:37)
Medical Tribune (35,2:1)
Medical World News (35,2:25)
Science (263,5143:24)

Build a stronger heart with B vitamins

Want to reduce your risk of heart disease and stroke? An extra serving of vegetables or a daily multivitamin may be just the solution you've been searching for.

Scientists have found evidence that an increased amount of the amino acid homocysteine in your body could single-handedly increase your risk of premature heart disease.

Homocysteine is just one of the 20 amino acids your body uses to make protein. Most amino acids, including homocysteine, are obtained and properly managed through a well-balanced diet. Getting too much of the wrong foods or not enough of the right foods can lead to problems with amino acid levels. That's what appears to be the problem with homocysteine.

Scientists have discovered that people who do not get enough vitamin B6 and folic acid in their diets have high levels of homocysteine in their blood. Scientific studies on more than 1,800 volunteers have shown that high levels of homocysteine can cause premature hardening of the arteries in people under the age of 55, which can lead to heart disease and stroke.

Boost your B's to hold down homocysteine. The key to keeping your homocysteine levels in the right range and lowering your risk of heart disease seems to be as simple as increasing your intake of vitamin B6 and folic acid.

Some rich dietary sources of folic acid include liver, yeast, leafy vegetables, legumes (beans and peas) and some fruits. Some natural sources of vitamin B6 include chicken, fish, kidney, liver, pork, eggs, unmilled rice, soybeans, oats, peanuts and walnuts. Try to stay away from meat sources and eat more vegetables instead.

If you have little control over your dietary intake (lots of travel, live in retirement home, etc.), talk with your doctor about taking vitamin supplements. A daily vitamin supplement can provide you with the recommended daily allowance for folic acid, vitamin B6 and many other important dietary vitamins.

Keep exercising and eating a low-cholesterol diet to reduce your risk of heart disease. Just remember the latest piece of the puzzle — and keep those folic acid and vitamin B6 levels up to keep your risk of heart disease down.

———
Medical Tribune (34,23:17)
The Journal of the American Medical Association (270,22:2693)

These beverages heal your heart

You've probably heard about the "French paradox" — people in France have a low rate of heart disease even though they enjoy high-fat foods every day.

Researchers have speculated that one reason for the "paradox" may be the red wine the French people tend to drink with their meals. But you don't have to drink alcohol to get some of the benefits of red wine! One of the healing ingredients seems to be chemicals called "flavonoids."

Flavonoids give berries their red color and also help prevent heart disease, according to a study from the Netherlands. The flavonoids work as antioxidants to keep cholesterol from damaging your artery walls. Flavonoids may also have an anti-clotting effect similar to the effect of aspirin.

Three nonalcoholic heart-healing drinks that contain flavonoids are dark-purple grape juice, sweet cherry juice and strawberry juice. You do need to drink about three times as much grape juice as red wine to get the same amount of flavonoids.

Buy the real thing! To get the full benefits of the flavonoids in grape, cherry and strawberry juice, make sure the juice you buy is really fruit juice. Lots of enticing fruit juice products line the shelves in grocery stores, and some of them have as little as 10 percent fruit juice. In some cases, the fruit drinks are nothing but sugar water with a little fruit flavoring mixed in.

The nutrition label should list what percent of the drink is really fruit juice. If it doesn't say 100-percent fruit juice, it probably has been diluted with water and sugar. If the labels says "cocktail," "blend," "punch" or some kind of fruit "ade," that is a clue that it may not have much fruit juice. If the label

Aerobics vs. strength training:
Which exercise is heart-healthy?

For a long time, aerobic exercise has been thought to be the best exercise for avoiding heart disease. That's great for people who enjoy jazzercise, running, walking, fast-paced tennis matches or racquetball games. But what about those who like to build muscles by pumping iron?

Recent studies have shown that strength training on Nautilus equipment (including leg extensions, leg curls, overhead presses, rowing, sit-ups, etc.) has many of the same advantages as aerobic exercise for people with heart disease risk factors.

Now you weight lifters can feel good about the type of exercise you enjoy. You should always check with your doctor before beginning any exercise program, however. Lifting too much weight (especially for people with high blood pressure) or doing too many repetitions can be just as harmful as pushing yourself too far in the advanced aerobics class or trying to run a marathon after just two days of training.

Lace up your running shoes or put on your weight belt — but get out there and start an exercise program today. It really will do your heart good!

Metabolism (42,2:177)

says fruit-flavored, it may not have any fruit juice at all.

But even some 100-percent fruit juices aren't what they seem to be. Some juices, like apricot and cherry, which cost the manufacturer a lot to produce, are diluted with cheaper juices, such as grape or apple which have been stripped of color and flavor. Your tongue won't be able to tell the difference, but you might be missing some health and nutritional benefits if you don't read the label closely.

Help make your "five a day" with juice. The National Cancer Institute and the National Institutes of Health recommend five servings of fruits and vegetables a day to maintain good health. A 3/4-cup serving of 100-percent fruit juice equals one of the five servings you need. One researcher recommends drinking purple grape juice with your meals to help block the clotting effect fatty foods have on your blood.

Since the flavonoids are found in the skins of grapes, eating grapes and raisins gives you health benefits too. The flavonoids are highly concentrated in the wine and juices, but eating fruit will give you fiber as well as flavonoids.

Circulation (91,4:1182)
Nutrition Today (29,2:14)
The Journal of the American Medical Association (273,16:1249)
The Lancet (341,8843:454)

Garlic gets to the heart of good health

When it comes to good health, garlic is the herb that gets to the heart of the matter. More and more studies are shedding light on just how garlic protects the human heart. Here are five of the ways researchers believe garlic may work its wonders on one of your most vital organs:

Reduces blood cholesterol. Researchers at New York's Medical College recently reviewed five of the most scientifically sound studies on garlic and cholesterol. They found that consuming as little as half a garlic clove a day reduces cholesterol levels an average of 9 percent.

Lowers blood pressure. Scientists speculate that garlic lowers blood pressure by relaxing and opening up blood vessels. Using garlic as a salt substitute can also help lower blood pressure.

Makes blood less likely to clot. Garlic makes blood less sticky, so you are less likely to develop a blood clot when one of your blood vessels is injured. A blood clot that completely blocks off a blood vessel in your heart can lead to a heart attack.

Increases clot-dissolving activity of the blood. This helps break down any clots that develop. Clots may develop even if you eat garlic, but the herb will help to break them down.

Prevents "bad" LDL cholesterol from being oxidized. Oxidized cholesterol damages arteries.

Like many healthful foods, the benefits of eating garlic seem to add up over time. Include one to two cloves of garlic in your diet on a daily basis. Fresh garlic is probably the safest way to go.

If you're bothered by garlic's strong odor, garlic supplements may mask the odor somewhat. Dr. Varro E. Tyler, former Professor of Pharmacognosy in the School of Pharmacy and Pharmacal Sciences at Purdue University, recommended garlic supplement tablets with an enteric coating. This coating protects the garlic, preventing it from dissolving until it reaches the intestines. These supplements tend to be more odor-free and effective than other types.

The many different brands of garlic supplements available vary widely in effectiveness. Kwai is one brand that has produced positive results in several clinical trials. If you are on any anti-clotting medicines, such as aspirin or warfarin, you should talk to your doctor before adding garlic to your diet. Garlic may intensify the effects of these drugs.

Too much garlic can cause side effects, including heartburn, gas, wheezing, coughing, vomiting, diarrhea and skin rashes. If you notice any of these, reduce your garlic intake.

Regular exercise and a low-fat diet are the best ways to keep your heart healthy, but the benefits of garlic can spice up a healthy lifestyle even more.

Food Safety Notebook (4,9:85)
Food — Your Miracle Medicine: How Food Can Prevent and Cure Over 100 Symptoms and Problems, HarperCollins, New York
Heinerman's Encyclopedia of Fruits, Vegetables and Herbs, Parker Publishing, West Nyack, N.Y.
HerbalGram (30:11)
Herbal Medicine, Beaconsfield Publishers, Beaconsfield, England
Herbs, Parker Publishing, West Nyack, N.Y.
The Honest Herbal, Pharmaceutical Products Press, Binghamton, N.Y.

Monday mornings are hard on your heart

Do you already dread Monday mornings? Here's news that will really make you want to pull the covers back over your head. On Monday mornings, you have a one-third greater chance of suffering a heart attack than at any other time of the week.

Physical or mental stress on Monday mornings, changes in hormone levels, changes in behavior patterns over the weekend, and changes in the food and drink you consume on weekends all contribute to the higher rate of heart attacks. The simple shift to high gear after two days of rest also stresses your heart.

One study showed that platelets, the blood cells that cause clotting, tend to be stickier in the morning. This study also noted a general increase in blood pressure in the morning, along with a condition called silent ischemia in which blood flow to the heart is reduced.

That's enough to make even a workaholic want to stay in bed on Mondays. But don't spend your weekend updating your will or wondering who will come to your funeral.

Follow these tips, and Monday morning will be a breeze, at least for your heart.

Don't be a couch potato. The sudden change from inactivity to hard work is one of the causes of Monday morning heart attacks. You can minimize that factor by staying active on weekends. It's OK to relax, but try to relax with a game of tennis or by working in the yard.

Take it easy Monday morning. Schedule stressful meetings or heavy labor later in the day or week. Ease yourself back into the routine of work. Don't pick Monday morning to start an exercise routine.

Don't get up too quickly. Bolting out of bed, or even sitting up quickly, can stress your heart. This is especially true for people who have heart disease. So don't feel guilty about hitting that snooze alarm a couple of times on Monday.

But don't stop your morning exercise routine. You don't have to wait until afternoon or evening to exercise, even if you have heart disease. If you enjoy

Has your doctor told you ...

Your ears could warn you of heart disease

If you have a crease in one or both of your ear lobes that angles downward at 45 degrees toward your shoulder, it could be an early warning sign of heart disease.

According to a new report, Dr. William Elliot, assistant professor at the Pritzer School of Medicine, University of Chicago, studied 108 men and women for eight years. Some of them had coronary artery disease, and some had ear-lobe creases. After eight years, those people with ear-lobe creases had a significantly higher rate of death from heart disease compared with those without an ear-lobe crease.

Dr. Elliot speculates that arteries that supply blood to the heart might be similar to those that supply blood to the ear lobe. If this is true, then what happens to the heart arteries might also happen to the ear-lobe arteries at the same time. Thus, a decrease in the blood supply to the ear lobe could be a warning sign of possible heart problems. The ear-lobe crease seems to indicate such a decrease in blood supply to the ear-lobe tissue.

Although being overweight is a known risk factor for heart disease, researchers say that being fat does not influence whether people have ear creases. Both fat and thin people have them in equal numbers. Apparently, people don't usually get ear creases until they are about 50 years old.

Talk to your doctor if you have an ear-lobe crease or are concerned about heart disease.

British Heart Journal (611,4:361)
Modern Medicine (57,10:126)
Science News (139,20:319)

exercising in the morning, keep it up. The risk of having a heart attack while you're exercising moderately is very low, and the benefits of exercise far outweigh any slight risk from morning workouts.

American Heart Association news release
Atherosclerosis and Thrombosis (14,11:1746)
Circulation (90,1:87 and 90,1:121)
Science News (143,15:239)

Heartburn

A burning question ... What's causing my upset stomach?

You've done it again, haven't you? You swore to yourself after your last painful bout with heartburn that you wouldn't go overboard again by eating so much food, but you did anyway. And now you're paying the price. You reach for your favorite antacid, and you swear you'll never again eat that much at one time as long as you live.

Sound familiar? Well, if you have experienced heartburn, or some other type of upset stomach, you're not alone. Each year, over 90 million people feel those familiar burning pains that tell them they've eaten too much of the wrong thing.

Doctors use the term dyspepsia to refer to pain or discomfort in the upper abdomen. And, while heartburn is the term generally used when talking about any pain or discomfort in your gastrointestinal tract, it's not entirely accurate to blame all of your upset stomach problems on heartburn. There are other conditions that may share the blame.

Know what's causing your upset stomach. Indigestion is a familiar term used to describe that bloated, heavy feeling you get after eating too much food in a short period of time, typical for many people at holiday feasts. It's simply your stomach's way of trying to tell you to slow down, stop eating and give it a chance to digest all that food.

Heartburn occurs when the food and digestive juices in your stomach accidentally flow backward into your esophagus, the tube which connects your throat to your stomach. Doctors call this gastroesophageal reflux, and it's sometimes accompanied by involuntary belching. But whether you belch or not, you definitely feel the pain.

Although your stomach may be used to acidic digestive juices, your esophagus isn't. So when these acidic juices reach your esophagus, you could experience some discomfort and pain. And if this happens on a regular basis, you may be suffering from a condition known as gastroesophageal reflux disease, where the small valvelike opening to your stomach allows the stomach's contents to back up into your esophagus.

If the pain is lower and stays with you for a few days, however, you may be suffering from a peptic ulcer, a sore inside your stomach that keeps flaring up and causing pain over and over again. If this is the case, you need to see your doctor immediately. Many times, the stomach pain you experience can be blamed on old-fashioned heartburn or indigestion. These tips may help.

Prop up the head of your bed frame with blocks about 4 to 6 inches high. Or support your entire upper body with a foam wedge or pillows. This keeps juices flowing downward instead of upward as you sleep.

In fact, Dr. Malcolm Robinson, the medical director of the Oklahoma Foundation for Digestive Research, believes that elevating the head of your bed may be one of the most important ways to control reflux disease.

Try the "beer-belly" maneuver. If you have a lot of heartburn, you may have a hiatal hernia, a condition in which part of your stomach slides up into your chest area and causes the burning sensation of heartburn. You may be able to get relief by letting your stomach hang out for a few minutes.

Dr. Veronica D. Jenkins of Temple Hills, Md., recommends trying what she calls the "beer belly" maneuver. Stand with your feet slightly spread apart, and let your stomach relax so that it hangs over your belt. Hold this position for two or three minutes. This technique relieves heartburn by taking the pressure off your stomach contents. It may even help a hiatal hernia slide back into place.

Take your medicines with plenty of water. Don't lie down right after swallowing a pill either. Stand or sit up when taking medicines so gravity can help the pill get to your stomach. These precautions are even more important if you're taking theophylline, calcium channel blockers, progesterone, potassium chloride or nonsteroidal anti-inflammatory drugs.

Avoid stuffing yourself with a large meal. Use moderation when you eat, and you'll be thankful later. Also, don't bend over immediately after a meal.

Eat four to six small meals a day. Several small meals may sit easier on your stomach than two to three large meals.

Resist bedtime snacks, and don't lie down too soon after eating. With your body in a horizontal position, it's much easier for food to go into reverse and give you problems.

Cut down on alcohol, coffee and carbonated beverages. Coffee and drinks with caffeine tend to irritate your stomach lining.

Which beverages cause the most heartburn? Researchers at the Glaxo Institute for Digestive Health questioned 400 heartburn sufferers to find out. They asked about 17 juices or citrus drinks, 11 soft drinks, three alcoholic beverages, coffee, tea, four milk products and water.

Grapefruit juice caused more heartburn than any other juice, although orange juice and tomato-containing juices were close runners-up. The high acid level of these juices seemed to be the problem, but the low acid level of soft drinks caused trouble too. Alcohol, coffee, tea, chocolate drinks and lemonade all caused reflux. Only the fattier milks caused heartburn; skim milk seems safe.

Try getting rid of that spare tire around your midsection, and wear loose fitting clothing. Being too fat and wearing tight clothes can actually force your

Has your doctor told you ...

Tight pants pose problems

Been experiencing stomach or chest pains lately? Before you panic, check your pants. They may be too tight.

Minor abdominal or chest pain sometimes results from wearing pants which are at least 3 inches too small in the waist. People with this problem, which is called "tight pants syndrome," usually experience pain shortly after meals due to increased pressure on the abdominal area.

The name tight pants syndrome may sound amusing, but the problem itself can be serious. The abdominal pressure, if not remedied, could lead to a hiatal hernia, a condition in which part of the stomach pushes up into the chest. Hiatal hernias can cause serious heartburn when your acidic stomach contents slosh back up into your esophagus.

If you've gained a little weight, or if you've just given birth, wear loose, comfortable clothing until you can fit into your favorite clothes again.

―――
Archives of Internal Medicine (153,11:1396)
The Journal of the American Medical Association (271,20:1628)

stomach's contents up into your esophagus.

Satisfy your sweet tooth with something other than chocolate, spearmint and peppermint. They make matters worse for many heartburn sufferers. Sucking on other types of sugarless candylike lozenges during the day may relieve heartburn.

Limit the amount of acid-rich foods you eat, such as citrus fruits, fruit drinks and spicy foods. Tomato-based foods like spaghetti sauce can irritate your stomach. Onions and fatty foods contribute to heartburn too.

Drink plenty of water. This will wash any acid out of your esophagus and give your stomach a fighting chance to do its job properly.

Eat slowly. Take small bites and chew your food thoroughly.

Shed your nicotine patch at bedtime. For people trying to kick the smoking habit, that nicotine patch can cause heartburn, especially at night. The nicotine in the patch relaxes the small valve between the stomach and the lower end of the esophagus, causing burning, similar to the pain associated with heart disease. How can you avoid it? Take off your patch each night at bedtime.

Avoid straining and heavy lifting. Your abdominal muscles contract and squeeze the contents of your stomach up and out into your esophagus.

Antacids do help, but don't overdo it. The common antacids you can buy at the drugstore are usually safe and effective. You should let your doctor know how many you're taking, just in case the antacids are masking a serious stomach problem that needs to be treated.

One 69-year-old man from Scotland took 15 antacid tablets and drank three pints of milk every day to ease his upset stomach. After years of this home treatment, he felt uncoordinated, tired and unable to concentrate. He wasn't eating enough, and he had to urinate much too often.

He was admitted to the hospital, where the doctors discovered that his calcium levels were through the roof. They took him off his antacid tablet and milk regimen, and he quickly began to improve.

Antacids containing calcium are a good way to boost your calcium intake, but you have to be careful not to take too many. Taking calcium antacids for several days in a row can also cause "acid rebound," which means your stomach produces more acid than ever and makes your heartburn worse.

American Family Physician (47,6:1407)
British Journal of Clinical Practice (48,6:333)
Emergency Medicine (26,14:45)
Gastroenterology (108,1:125)
Postgraduate Medicine (95,2:88)
U.S. Pharmacist (17,10:21 and 19,2:119)

Heat Exhaustion and Heatstroke

15 ways to beat the heat

The long, hot days of summer can be more than an uncomfortable nuisance. Very hot, humid conditions can lead to serious — sometimes fatal — illnesses, such as heat exhaustion and heatstroke. But by understanding how your body handles high temperatures and taking some simple precautions, you can beat the heat whenever the mercury rises. Your body has a built-in cooling system. As the air temperature rises, the temperature of your blood also rises, and nerve impulses tell your body to sweat. It's the evaporation of that sweat that helps cool your body.

But on very hot days, you can sweat so much that your system loses too much fluid and salt. Plus, if the humidity is very high, the moisture in the air will slow

First aid for heat exhaustion

The first signs of heat exhaustion are usually fatigue, nausea, dizziness, headache and cramps in the legs, arms, back or stomach. Your skin feels pale and clammy, your pulse is fast but weak, and your breathing is fast and shallow.

Most healthy people can recover completely from heat exhaustion, but if left untreated, this illness can progress to heatstroke.

First aid for heat exhaustion should include these steps:

1) Lie down on your back in a cool place with your feet elevated about 12 inches off the ground. (If a heatstroke victim is unconscious, place him in the recovery position until he regains consciousness — that's halfway between lying on the stomach and lying on the side, with the upward-facing arm and leg slightly bent and the head turned to the side.)

2) Loosen or remove any tight clothing.

3) Drink continuous, small sips of a weak saltwater solution.

4) Sponge off with lukewarm water.

5) It's not a bad idea to get advice from a doctor even if you begin feeling better. You don't want to have a relapse.

_____

The American Medical Association Encyclopedia of Medicine, Random House, New York
The American Medical Association Family Medical Guide, Random House, New York

down the evaporation of sweat. That means your body won't be cooled as well as it should be. These conditions can lead to heat exhaustion. Or worse, your body can get so overheated that its cooling system gives out altogether, leading to life-threatening heatstroke.

These tips will help you keep your cool when the heat is on.

Stay out of the heat.

✔ Listen for the National Weather Service's heat index value in your local weather forecast. The heat index combines the air temperature and the humidity to tell you how hot it feels outside in the shade. (The value will be even higher in full sunshine!) Take extra precautions if the index is 90 degrees Fahrenheit or above and you're planning to be outdoors for a while, especially if you'll be physically active.

✔ Limit the time you spend outdoors between 10 a.m. and 6 p.m. — the hottest part of the day.

✔ Plan exercise or other vigorous activities for the coolest hours of your day.
✔ If you must be outdoors in the heat, allow yourself time to adjust. Over a period of ten to 14 days, gradually spend longer periods in the heat, taking rest periods in a cool place in between. Your body will actually adapt to the hotter environment. Most of the changes will take place in days three through five.

Give your body's cooling system a hand.
✔ Dress for the heat. Wear a single, loose-fitting layer of light-colored clothing.
✔ Wear absorbent fabrics, which allow sweat to evaporate.
✔ Wear a ventilated hat or use an umbrella to shield yourself from the sun.
✔ Take frequent cool (not cold) baths or showers.
✔ Take frequent rest breaks from your outdoor activity.

First aid for heatstroke

When a person has heatstroke, his body is overheated to a life-threatening degree. Often, heatstroke follows untreated heat exhaustion, and many of the symptoms are similar.

Look for these clues that a heat illness has progressed to this dangerous level: Sweating lessens or may even stop, the skin becomes hot, dry and flushed, and body temperature rises dramatically. Call for emergency medical care immediately. With early treatment, full recovery is common, but without treatment, the person may quickly lapse into a coma and die.

First aid for heatstroke should include these steps:

1) Move the person to the coolest place available, remove his clothing and put him in a half-sitting position, supporting his head and shoulders. (If he is unconscious, place him in the recovery position.)
2) Wrap him in a lukewarm, wet sheet, or sponge lukewarm water onto his skin. Don't sponge with cold water or blow cold air on the heatstroke victim. It's important to cool a person with heatstroke down, but causing him to shiver can be fatal.
3) Fan him with warm air to help the water evaporate from the skin and cool his body.
4) Continue applying water and fanning him until his skin feels cool.
5) If he is conscious, give him continuous, small sips of a weak saltwater solution until emergency help arrives.

British Medical Journal (309,6954:587)
The American Medical Association Encyclopedia of Medicine, Random House, New York
The American Medical Association Family Medical Guide, Random House, New York

Get plenty of water and salt.

✔ Drink at least 8 ounces of water before outdoor physical activity and keep drinking water every 15 to 20 minutes.

✔ Don't wait until you're thirsty to drink water. You'll probably need fluids long before you get thirsty. Clear or pale urine usually indicates you're getting enough fluids.

✔ Weigh yourself before and after physical activity in extreme heat. Replace lost water weight with fluids. If you lose more than 3 percent of your body weight, don't go back outside. Sit down and drink, drink, drink.

✔ After very heavy sweating, drink a weak saltwater solution (a quarter-teaspoon of salt to a pint of cold water) to replace salt lost through sweating.

✔ Eat a light diet.

✔ Cut down on tea, coffee and alcoholic beverages. They cause your body to lose fluids.

If you have a chronic health problem or are taking medicine, take extra precautions in the heat. Many drugs, such as beta blockers, decongestants, diuretics and some antidepressants, hurt your body's ability to cool itself down.

American Family Physician (50,2:389)
British Medical Journal (309,6954:587)
The American Medical Association Encyclopedia of Medicine, Random House, New York
The American Medical Association Family Medical Guide, Random House, New York

Heel Spurs

How to put your foot down on heel pain

In the course of a normal day, you're probably going to pound your heels down on the floor at least 8,000 times. And with each walking step, your feet will be hitting the ground with a pressure equal to three or four times your body weight. Running and other active sports just add to the jarring and stress. Is it any wonder your feet sometimes develop painful problems?

Foot pain arises for a variety of different reasons — ingrown toenails, corns, bunions, fallen arches, fractures, strains and ill-fitting shoes, just to name a few. But one of the most irritating — and very common — causes of foot pain is a group of problems collectively referred to as "heel spur syndrome."

Fortunately, you don't have to resort to surgery to get almost complete relief from heel spurs.

Morning heel pain points to a spur. How do you know you have heel spur syndrome? One of its most characteristic symptoms is intense pain on the bottom of your heel when you first step out of bed in the morning. After a half-hour of walking, the pain subsides, but it returns when you sit for long periods and then stand up. With heel spur syndrome, the heel can hurt even when you're walking on your toes.

Although the name implies that a spur or growth on your heel is causing the pain, that isn't necessarily the case. X-rays have shown that some people develop small, pointed growths on the heel bone, but never experience pain. Others suffer until the growth is removed.

Heel pain usually comes from inflammation of the large connective tissue that runs along the bottom of your foot. This plantar tissue connects your heel to the front of your foot. It must stretch and move as you walk. Your heel hurts when the tissue loses its flexibility or is strained or injured.

Also, when the heel bone and joints of the feet are not aligned properly to spread the pressure of walking across your foot, the plantar tissue will cause pain in your heel.

You can probably treat a heel spur yourself, but you should see your doctor in case other more serious conditions are causing your heel pain. Arthritis, nerve damage, stress fractures of the heel bone, or tissue inflammation that doesn't involve bone may need special medical attention.

To relieve heel spur syndrome, you need to protect the sore point of the heel from constant pounding. And at the same time, you need to reduce stress and inflammation of the plantar tissue.

Cushion your heel. Because age and constant pounding thins the cushion of fat on the bottom of your feet, your first step in relieving heel spur pain is as simple as adding extra cushioning in your shoes. Your cushioned footwear should support your feet properly while you walk.

➤ Wear shoes that have cushioning across the entire sole.
➤ Use donut-shaped heel inserts in your shoe to protect the sore area from impact.
➤ Wear shoes with low, but slightly raised, heels — not flat or extremely high heels.
➤ Insert arch supports in your shoes to even out the pressure on your foot.

Keep swelling down. As you improve your footwear, you also need to reduce inflammation of the tissue around your heel.

➤ Take nonsteroidal anti-inflammatory medications such as aspirin or ibuprofen.
➤ Try ice packs on the affected area.

Stretch your heel before you get out of bed. You should stretch the plantar tissue on the bottom of your feet to keep it flexible, especially in the morning.

➤ Before you walk in the morning, flex your foot up toward your head, then relax it. Do this several times.

➤ After you stand up, stand two feet from a wall and put your hands on the wall. Bend your elbows and lean into the wall. Keep your feet flat on the ground.

If you don't get relief from these techniques, ask your doctor about custom-designed orthotic inserts for your shoes, foot taping and steroid injections for your heel. With a combination of home care and prescribed treatments, most people can get rid of heel spur syndrome without resorting to painful surgery that can sometimes make the problem worse instead of better.

American Health (13,3:77)
Journal of the American Podiatric Medical Association (81,2:68)
One Hundred Orthopaedic Conditions Every Doctor Should Understand, Quality Medical Publishers, St. Louis, Mo.
The Johns Hopkins Medical Letter: Health After 50 (7,2:3)

Hemorrhoids

That little itch may be telling you something

Hemorrhoids have been the butt of jokes for years, but they are no laughing matter for the millions of people who suffer from pain, itching and bleeding in the rectal area. Hemorrhoids are very common, and those who suffer will spare no expense to find comfort. Americans spend about $200 million each year on hemorrhoid remedies which often provide no relief.

Hemorrhoids are swollen veins in or around the rectum. Doctors divide them into two categories. Internal hemorrhoids develop in the rectum. They sometimes prolapse, or hang, out of the rectum. External hemorrhoids are swollen veins around the rectum itself.

Both kinds can become itchy and painful. They can also bleed. Bleeding in the rectal area can also be a sign of more serious health problems. If you bleed from your rectum, see a doctor immediately to confirm the diagnosis of hemorrhoids. But for most cases, a trip to the doctor is unnecessary. Follow these simple tips for prevention or relief.

Change your diet. Drink more liquids and eat more fiber to help soften your stools. Hard stools can cause pressure in the rectum, aggravating the hemorrhoids.

A good level of fiber is 25 to 30 grams per day. Eat more fruit, grains and vegetables to boost your fiber. (Turn to the **Constipation** chapter for more information about the best food sources of fiber.) The regularity you gain by increasing your fiber will also help keep you from straining, which aggravates hemorrhoids. Drink six to eight glasses of fluids a day to keep your stools soft.

Sit in a warm bath. Sit in warm water for 15 minutes after bowel movements. This reduces swelling and eases spasms in the anus. Don't make the water too hot, and don't add anything like bubble bath or Epsom salts. Soaps and salts will irritate the swollen veins.

When you have to go, go. It's not always convenient to visit the restroom when nature calls. But prompt elimination will help you avoid pressure in the rectum. Also, "holding it" can lead to hard stools, which just makes matters worse.

Don't read on the throne. Just because your monthly magazine has "bathroom length" stories doesn't mean you should read it while you take care of business. Sitting on the toilet greatly increases the pressure on veins in the rectum. The longer you sit, the more your veins swell.

Avoid most over-the-counter remedies. Those expensive commercial preparations just don't work. In fact, the U.S. Food and Drug Administration recently banned the key ingredient in the most popular "hemorrhoid-reducing" ointment.

Wipe carefully. This is a touchy subject, but an important one. Toilet tissue can irritate hemorrhoids and even cause bleeding. But fecal matter left in the area after a bowel movement can be just as irritating. Gently remove the bulk of the matter with soft toilet tissue. Then wipe with a lubricated tissue, such as a baby wipe. Expensive wipes marketed just for hemorrhoid sufferers are a waste of money, as are special ointments, suppositories and pads.

Use an ice pack. Place an ice cube in a plastic bag. Use a rubber band to close the bag. A round piece of ice works better than a square one. Place the bag against your rectum. You can secure it with a feminine hygiene pad. Throw the bag away when the ice melts. The ice helps reduce swelling in the veins and helps relieve pain.

Apply a little lubricating jelly. Jelly will help hemorrhoids that hang outside the rectum. Use the nonpetroleum kind of jelly, and apply it around the rectal opening only. Don't put it inside the rectum. Gently push the protruding veins up beyond the sphincter, or valve, that holds them in place.

Should all else fail, see your doctor. Surgery, drugs and several other options can relieve hemorrhoid pain.

Emergency Medicine (25,8:19)
Medical Update (18,2:3)
Modern Medicine (58,7:56)
Postgraduate Medicine (92,2:141)

Hiccups

Home remedies for hiccups

It never fails — just when you are about to meet a new business colleague, make an important presentation, or engage in a serious conversation, you start hiccuping. It's distracting and embarrassing. And you have got to get rid of them pronto. So what do you do?

Massage your earlobes. Yes, your earlobes. Sounds crazy, but many people claim that it works. No known connection, but the hiccup control center is close by in the upper part of the spinal column in the back of your neck.

Swallow a spoonful of sugar. If an ear massage doesn't do the trick and you happen to be close to the coffee machine at the office, try swallowing a spoonful of granulated sugar. The sugar seems to trigger some kind of nerve impulse in your mouth that somehow helps to calm your spastic diaphragm (the muscle just under your lungs that is causing your hiccups). Other people report relief just from holding the sugar in their mouths until it dissolves.

Freeze them out. A doctor in Bellingham, Washington, has discovered that he can block the nerve signals that cause hiccups with a couple of ice cubes. He says to put two ice cubes on either side of your Adam's apple. If that doesn't do the trick, move the ice cubes farther out to the sides of your neck, still at the level of your Adam's apple.

Hold your breath. Hold your breath for as long as you can, and swallow each time you feel the urge to hiccup. Try this a few times, and the hiccups should go away.

Try the old paper-bag remedy. Breathe for about a minute into a paper bag gathered tightly to your lips. The buildup of carbon dioxide might shut down the hiccups. Don't try this for more than a minute at most or you may cause yourself to faint.

Drink water upside down. Get a small cup of water, bend over, hold your breath and drink the water upside down. The hiccups should be gone by the time you swallow the last gulp, stand up and let out your breath.

Chug-a-lug a glass of water quickly.

Eat some dry bread.

Swallow some crushed ice.

Squeeze your knees to your chest. Sit on the floor and pull your knees up to your chest. Wrap your arms around your knees and squeeze — this compresses your chest and forces all the air out of your lungs. Hold it for a moment, then relax. It should clear up those pesky hiccups.

Yank on your tongue. Others recommend a gentle pulling.

Tickle the top of your mouth with a cotton swab.

Gently massage your eyes through closed eyelids. Another source suggests simply putting mild pressure on your closed eyes.

Pinch your lip. Put your thumb inside your mouth between your teeth and upper lip. Pinch inward with your index finger, pressing just below the right nostril.

Gargle with some mouthwash. It helps clear up the hiccups and leaves you with fresher breath.

———
Complete Guide to Symptoms, Illness & Surgery, 2nd ed., The Body Press/Perigee Books, New York
The Lancet (338,8765:520)
The Physician and Sportsmedicine (23,5:18)
Your Good Health, Harvard University Press, Cambridge, Mass.

Hives

Take the heat out of hives

Breaking out in swollen, red, itchy welts is usually more embarrassing than dangerous. There's nothing like suddenly looking like a flashing, neon tomato for no apparent reason.

Hives are usually caused by eating or touching something you're allergic to. If you're prone to hives, you can also break out when you get hot, stressed, tense or even when you just scratch yourself.

Follow these suggestions to take the heat out of hives, but remember, your best defense for hives is to stay away from what you're allergic to.

Forego food that makes you sick! If you have food allergies, you're likely to be troubled with hives. In fact, hives and other skin problems affect 65 percent of people with food allergies. Children are particularly prone to food-allergy hives. Hives are sometimes accompanied by bloating and diarrhea, especially when you're allergic to milk or eggs.

These are the most common culprits of food-allergy hives:

> ➤ eggs
> ➤ fish
> ➤ cow's milk
> ➤ lentils
> ➤ peanuts
> ➤ peaches
> ➤ hazel nuts
> ➤ sunflower seeds

Watch out for NSAIDs. Some people may get hives when they take nonsteroidal anti-inflammatory drugs (NSAIDs) like aspirin. These drugs can make your intestines "leaky," allowing undigested food from the intestine to enter the bloodstream. This undigested food can cause hives to break out even if you aren't actually allergic to the food.

Soothe fiery skin with hot pepper cream. A cream made out of an ingredient of red peppers, capsaicin, will actually take the heat out of some cases of hives. You can buy capsaicin cream without a prescription at most pharmacies. One of the brand names is Zostrix.

Antihistamines relieve the welts. Since hives are usually an allergic reaction, antihistamines can get them under control. Many people troubled by hives take an antihistamine every day. Sleepiness is the worst side effect, but some of the newer antihistamines don't make you as sleepy as the older ones.

———
American Family Physician (45,6:2727 and 51,4:811)
U.S. Pharmacist (19,9:107)

Hypoglycemia

What to do when you get the shakes

Hypoglycemia, or low blood sugar, is a frustrating fact of life for people with diabetes. Eating too little or too late, taking too much insulin, or simply overexercising can bring it on. If hypoglycemia isn't treated quickly, you can pass out or even go into a coma.

So it's important to know these warning signs:

* shakiness
* dizziness
* sweating
* hunger
* headache
* clumsy or jerky movements

* paleness
* moodiness (crying for no reason)
* confusion
* trouble paying attention
* tingling around the mouth

Hypoglycemia often means you're at risk for diabetes, but other health problems affecting your blood-sugar control (like cancer, hepatitis or an alcohol-damaged liver) can cause it too. What if you're completely healthy and notice the symptoms of hypoglycemia? You could just be extra-sensitive to slight changes in your blood-sugar level. But to be on the safe side, have your blood sugar checked.

If you're prone to hypoglycemia, follow these steps to stop it in its tracks:

Don't switch between low-carbohydrate diets and large sugar doses. People with normal blood-sugar control can have the symptoms of hypoglycemia if they eat a large amount of simple sugar after three days on a low-carbohydrate diet. Other nutrients eaten along with the sugar can prevent a drop in blood sugar after a meal.

Don't mix caffeine with a high-carbo meal. Blood-sugar levels often drop below normal two to three hours after a high-carbohydrate meal. Add two to three cups of coffee to the big pasta dinner, and you could easily end up with a case of the shakes.

Test regularly. If you have diabetes, know what your blood sugar level should be, and test it whenever you feel any of the symptoms of hypoglycemia.

Testing involves pricking your finger and putting a drop of blood on a strip of chemically treated paper. You then match the color to a chart or feed the strip into a small meter. Once you've raised your blood sugar, wait 15 to 20 minutes and test again. If your blood sugar level is still low, or if you still feel funny, repeat the treatment.

When in doubt, treat. Taking sugar raises your blood sugar level quickly. Always keep a dose of sugar nearby, such as three glucose tablets, 1/2 cup of fruit juice, or five pieces of hard candy.

Eat regular meals and snacks. Plan your snacks to keep your blood-sugar level up between meals.

Inject glucagon, not insulin. If you pass out, you'll need immediate treatment in a hospital or an injection of glucagon. Glucagon raises blood sugar and is injected like insulin. Tell people around you how and when to inject it. People should never give you insulin when you are unconscious.

Tell others to keep their hands to themselves. Naturally, if you're unconscious, people will want to help you. But they shouldn't put their hands in your mouth or try to give you food or fluids.

Call for emergency help. Make sure that children know how and when to dial 911.

Exercise safely. Avoid alcohol and beta-blocker drugs around the time of exercise. Both promote hypoglycemia. Exercise with a buddy who knows the signs of hypoglycemia. To prevent nighttime hypoglycemia, exercise earlier in the day and, if you take insulin, reduce your evening dose after you are through exercising. You may need extra carbohydrates before you go to sleep.

Take food along for the ride. Diabetics or people prone to hypoglycemia should never drive a car when they've missed a meal or a regular snack. Carry food with you in the car in case you start getting shaky.

Ideally, you want to avoid hypoglycemia altogether. The best way to do this is by controlling diabetes and eating regularly. But just in case, always carry some form of simple sugar with you. And be sure that both you and your friends know how to respond to hypoglycemia.

Hamilton and Whitney's Nutrition Concepts and Controversies, 6th ed., West Publishing, New York
NCRR Reporter (17,4:10)
What is Hypoglycemia?, American Diabetes Association, 1660 Duke Street, Alexandria, Va. 22314

Immune System Breakdown

Supercharge your immune system

You've got a big deadline looming at work. So you get up early, gulp down a cup of coffee, and rush out the door. You snap at your coworkers as you eat a donut at your desk — funny, you can't even remember swallowing it, much less how it tasted — and wash it down with a cup of cold coffee.

About midafternoon, you're starting to drag, and your sweet tooth kicks in. So you grab a candy bar and a soda for a sugar rush, and plow back into your project. Before you know it, the other people in the department are sticking their heads in the door of your office to say good night.

When you finally shut off the computer and put away the files, it's 7 p.m. You've been at it for almost 12 hours nonstop. It's been a bear, but it's done, and now you can relax. A few days later, you wake up and your head is pounding,

A Natural Alternative

Your tongue's healing powers

Did you know your tongue contains a natural antibiotic?

Your instinct to pop a cut finger in your mouth may have a basis in scientific fact. Apparently, all the moist surfaces of your body respond to injuries by producing infection-fighting peptides. You've probably seen dogs and cats lick their own wounds. They may be doing more than cleaning them; they may be putting on some antibiotic too.

Science News (147,11:166)

your joints are stiff, and you feel like your body is made of lead. "Gee," you wonder, "where did this come from?" Nobody at the office has been sick lately.

In this hurry-up, get-it-done, push-a-little-harder world, your immune system often works overtime to keep up the pace. And just like the worker who finally collapses under a staggering workload, at some point your immune system will throw up its hands and say, "That's it! I quit!"

The problem is, just like a worker who can't do his job without the right equipment, your immune system can't do its job — fighting off infections and disease — without the right work conditions and tools.

Build on the basics. The basic supplies your immune system needs to function at peak performance are good nutrition, regular exercise, stress management techniques and sufficient sleep. And since stress makes your body burn essential nutrients faster than you normally can replace them through food, add a good multivitamin to the supply list.

Pressure kills, so destress yourself. Some people scoff at the suggestion that stress has an effect on the body. Why, a little pressure never hurt anybody!

Baloney. Pressure can kill you. Even minor irritations have some impact on your body's immune system, and the biggies — divorce, death in the family, loss of a job (or getting a new one), planning a wedding, a new baby in the house — can cut your immune system's efficiency by as much as half. A particularly cruel reality about stress is that while it increases your need for food, it cuts your body's ability to absorb the nutrients in what you're eating.

A U.S. Department of Agriculture study took a look at work-related stress and its effect on essential minerals. They examined people who had been given extra assignments and tough deadlines for a week at work. Even with adequate nutrition, the participants' blood levels of several minerals dropped by as much as a third, and their supplies of other nutrients diminished.

Stop stress with magnesium. When stress increases, it uses up the magnesium in your system. When magnesium levels go down, irritability goes up. In studies of lab animals, magnesium deficiencies made them more sensitive to noise and overcrowding. Rats with high levels of magnesium were much happier than their magnesium-deficient neighbors.

Human studies have found similar results. In fact, American College of Nutrition researchers recommend taking a magnesium supplement when stress is high. A supplement that includes chromium, copper, iron, selenium and zinc helps build your immune system's armor for fighting off attackers. Vitamins C and E and the B vitamins also play a vital part in keeping your immune system up and running under stressful conditions.

Go for complex carbos. If you get the munchies when you're stressed, stay away from the coffee, soda and candy machines. Instead, go for foods with complex carbohydrates, like whole-grain breads, pasta, cereals or bagels. If you must have coffee, don't drink it with meals. It can reduce your body's absorption of minerals, especially iron, by up to 90 percent. For every cup of coffee you drink each day, drink two glasses of water. And a fatty burger and fries? It's just what you don't need. Stress and a high-fat diet don't mix. Ask any doctor.

Stay active and fit. The effects of exercise have been studied so often that it's generally accepted as a major stress-buster. Several studies also have shown that men and women who are physically active have a much lower death rate from cancer. If you're a Type A personality (always aggressive, competitive, tense or irritable), you probably approach exercise with a lot of enthusiasm. You may

Has your doctor told you ...

Smoke signals lowered immunity

Give your children's immune systems a fighting chance — don't smoke around them. Smoking cigarettes in the house or in the car when your children are there makes their bodies less able to fight off infections and diseases.

Of course, smoking puts you at risk for infections and diseases too. When parents or day-care workers smoke, children tend to develop asthma, colds and ear infections more often.

A new study says smoking around children puts them at risk for the deadly bacterial meningitis. Protect your children by kicking your smoking habit. Or, at least, make sure your children are out of harm's way when you light up.

Journal Watch (15,8:67)

tend to overdo exercise like you overdo other things. Too much exercise, or exercising when you're sick, can weaken your immune system.

Revive while you sleep. Finally, get plenty of rest. Robert Ludlum's super-spy characters tend to say, "Sleep is a weapon." Research has shown that it's true. A recent study showed that the activity of infection-fighting cells dropped by 30 percent after just one night of insomnia. When the study's participants caught up on their sleep, the cell activity levels bounced right back.

Food and Mood: The Complete Guide to Eating Well and Feeling Your Best, Henry Holt and Co., New York
Science News (147,1:11)
The Atlanta Journal/Constitution

Vitamin C boosts body's natural immune response

When you were growing up, your mother always told you to "drink all your juice." She did it because her mother did it, and so on. Well, the logic behind that daily glass of juice was pretty good — most mothers think that getting a good daily supply of vitamin C from orange juice will help fight colds and flu.

Recently, a team of scientists from the Department of Family Resources and Human Development at Arizona State University wanted to find out just how good vitamin C was at fighting off infection.

They found that when the body is under stress (whether "normal" stress from school, work, etc., or under the stress of illnesses or other physical problems), it creates more of a chemical known as histamine. Although small amounts of excess histamine are necessary to help the body cope with the stress, too much histamine can actually be a kind of poison to the body. It can interfere with the body's natural immune responses that fight off infections and illnesses.

Scientists think that vitamin C might help get rid of the excess histamine and therefore help protect the body's natural immune defenses. The researchers from Arizona State University discovered that taking 1,000 to 2,000 milligrams of vitamin C each day can lower the amount of histamine in the blood anywhere from 20 to 40 percent.

Vitamin C may not help keep colds and flu away, but it can make colds and serious respiratory infections less severe and last a shorter time. Don't take too much vitamin C. It can also cause an irritating case of diarrhea.

Journal of the American Dietetic Association (92,8:988)
Nutrition Research Newsletter (14,1:10)

Garlic — a natural antibiotic

Garlic actually fights off some infections that modern antibiotics can't kill. In a recent study at Boston City Hospital, researchers found that an extract of fresh garlic cloves killed or slowed the growth of more than a dozen common bacteria.

If you feel like you're going to catch a cold or the flu, chow down on a clove or two of garlic. If you catch an infection in its very early stage, you may not even get sick. Raw garlic seems to fight infections better than cooked garlic, but cooked garlic is good for you too. Cooked garlic may be better at protecting against heart disease. If you're bothered by garlic's strong odor, try garlic supplement tablets with an enteric coating. This coating protects the garlic, preventing it from dissolving until it reaches the intestines.

These supplements tend to be more odor-free and effective than other types. The many different brands of garlic supplements available vary widely in effectiveness. Kwai is one brand that has produced positive results in several clinical trials.

Clear up chest congestion with garlic. Garlic can also be helpful in clearing up chest congestion that often accompanies respiratory infections. Try this chest-clearing ointment you can make yourself: Peel and mince seven garlic cloves. Put them into a pint-sized fruit jar; add enough shortening to cover the minced cloves. Place open jar into a pan of boiling water and let boil for three hours.

For extra effectiveness, add 1/8 teaspoon of eucalyptus oil to the melted shortening. Cool, cover and store. Rub ointment on the chest, stomach and back. Cover with a heavy bath towel. Garlic has been called the "jewel among vegetables." What a perfect description for an herb that can help you keep your most priceless possession, your health, in sparkling form.

Food Safety Notebook (4,9:85)
Food — Your Miracle Medicine: How Food Can Prevent and Cure Over 100 Symptoms and Problems, HarperCollins Publishers, New York
Heinerman's Encyclopedia of Fruits, Vegetables and Herbs, Parker Publishing, West Nyack, N.Y.
HerbalGram (30:11)
Herbal Medicine, Beaconsfield Publishers, Beaconsfield, England
The Honest Herbal, Pharmaceutical Products Press, Binghamton, N.Y.

Give your health a shot in the arm

You know that children need certain shots to protect them against dangerous diseases. But did you know that you could also give your health a big boost with vaccinations? Vaccines help your body's immune system do its job better. Here are some vaccines recommended by the American Academy of Family Physicians:

Influenza. Influenza, or the "flu," is very contagious and fatal for some people. Everyone 65 and older should have a flu shot once a year. The best time to get one is in the fall. A flu shot is also suggested for those with a history of heart, lung or kidney problems, diabetes, or immune system deficiencies. Spouses or close family members of people who are weak or ill should get the shot too.

If you have an allergy to eggs, be sure to let your doctor know. You have a higher risk than other people of developing severe side effects from the flu vaccine, since it's made from eggs.

Pneumococcus. A pneumococcal vaccine helps fight off pneumonia and blood infections from the pneumococcus bacteria. Generally, you only need it once, and it's recommended if you're over 65. It's a good idea to get the shot at any age if you have heart, lung or kidney problems, diabetes, cirrhosis or cancer.

Tetanus and diphtheria. Everybody needs these shots once every 10 years, and they can be taken together in one injection.

Measles, mumps and rubella. If you were born after 1956, you might need two measles shots if you get a job in the medical field. Some colleges may require you to submit records of shots before you can enroll. Women who didn't get vaccinated as a child should get the vaccine before they begin to plan a family. Pregnant women should not be vaccinated, nor should people with immune system disorders or those with severe allergies to eggs.

Hepatitis B. Hepatitis B can cause liver failure, liver cancer or death. Adults in high-risk categories, such as health care workers, people who live or work in homes for the disabled, people with more than one sexual partner, and anyone who's had a sexually transmitted disease should be vaccinated. You'll need a series of three shots.

American Family Physician (51,5:1151)

Impotence

Foods that foul up sex

If your memories of sex are as fuzzy as baseball games you played as a kid, take a good look at what you're eating. A new study found that men with high cholesterol are twice as likely to be impotent as men whose cholesterol levels are normal or low. Researchers recorded cholesterol levels of 3,250 healthy men between the ages of 25 and 83. Men with total cholesterol higher than 240 mg/dl were twice as likely to have trouble achieving or maintaining an erection than men whose cholesterol levels were below 180 mg/dl.

Men who had low levels of HDL "good" cholesterol were also twice as likely to suffer from impotence. The same high-fat diet that narrows arteries and blocks blood flow to your heart also narrows the arteries that carry blood to your penis. Blood has to be able to get to your penis in order for you to have an erection.

Don't settle for striking out. If you eat a low-fat diet and exercise regularly, you'll be batting a thousand in almost no time at all.

Medical Tribune (36,1:17)

Smoking isn't sexy

Despite what television shows and slick magazine ads might make you believe, smoking isn't sexy. If your wife swoons over sophisticated men smoking cigarettes, don't fret. Certainly don't take up smoking yourself. You don't want to develop a habit that will make your breath and your sex life stink. And that's certainly what smoking will do for you.

A recent study of 4,462 male Vietnam veterans showed that smokers have a 50-percent higher risk of impotence than nonsmokers and past smokers. Around 2 percent of nonsmokers and past smokers were impotent, and almost 4 percent of current smokers were impotent. Smoking contributes to blockages in the arteries that lead to the penis. Without adequate blood flow, your penis can't maintain an erection. The solution to this problem is simple: Don't smoke.

Medical Tribune (36,2:5)

Pelvic exercises may cure impotence

Impotence can strike any man, at anytime, at any age. But, instead of going under the surgical knife, you may be able to exercise your way back to full sexual capacity. When blood doesn't flow to the penis properly or it drains from the area prematurely, doctors often prescribe medication or surgery. But the cure can be as bad as the problem. The operation can leave the penis sore, swollen and numb for anywhere from one week to six months.

Recently, a team of Belgium urologists treated 150 men who suffered from impotence. Some men had operations and others did special pelvic muscle exercises, called Kegels. Kegels are contractions of the pelvic floor muscles — an exercise pregnant women have been doing for years to help with childbirth.

One year after treatment, 58 percent of the men who performed the Kegels were completely cured or were so satisfied with their improvement that they did not opt for surgery.

The men who had surgery had better short-term results than the men who exercised, but more of the men who had surgery had trouble with impotence returning over the long run. Some skeptical doctors say that the pelvic muscles don't have any influence on the blood flow to the penis. They say the men in the study improved because of the beneficial psychological effects of the therapy.

At any rate, if you are suffering from a mild case of impotence, then Kegels just might do the trick.

Kegel exercises:
1) Identify the pelvic muscles that need exercising. You can do this by stopping and starting the flow of urine several times when using the bathroom.
2) Tighten the muscles a little at the time. Contract muscles slowly, hold for a count of 10, and relax the muscles slowly.
3) Repeat these exercises for the anal pelvic muscles. To find these muscles, imagine you're trying to hold back a bowel movement, without tensing your legs, stomach or buttock muscles.
4) Then practice tightening all pelvic muscles together, moving from back to front.
5) Start by repeating each exercise five times three to five times a day. Gradually work up to 20 or 30 repetitions at once.

You will find that you can perform your Kegels just about anywhere or anytime. Chances are good that "pumping it up" with these pelvic exercises will have you back in top shape in no time.

British Journal of Urology (71,1:52)
Medical Tribune (34,5:19)
Obstetrics and Gynecology (81,2:283)

Incontinence

Self-help for leaky bladders

Carolyn McLain of Plantation, Florida, had a long list of things she worried about doing. Horseback riding. Skiing. Long car trips. Dancing. Running after her granddaughter. Sneezing. Coughing. Laughing. Running through the back of her mind was the question, "Am I going to wet myself?"

For years, McLain lived with incontinence, a problem that afflicts between 10 and 20 million Americans. It is much more common among women than men. Among the elderly, it's a leading cause of nursing home admissions. "It's like this plague," said McLain. "You have to think about it before you sneeze."

"The limitations are simply heart-wrenching," said Dr. Katherine Jeter, executive director of Help for Incontinent People, a national self-help organization based in Union, South Carolina. "Some women are giving up aerobics and other athletic endeavors. Some women are giving up intercourse because they leak when they have orgasm. Some grandmothers don't go visit their grandchildren, and lots of older people forego senior citizen trips because no bathroom on the bus. ... It just wrecks lives."

Get treatment. The good news is that a wide variety of treatments is available, offering a cure or significant improvement of the condition to nearly all sufferers. Still, only one in 12 sufferers seek medical help. "We're not exactly sure why that is," Jeter said. "We don't know if women internalize this is part of childbirth or getting old, or if they tried to get help and were put off by a doctor."

As with any medical condition, early treatment offers the best opportunity for cure. A medical evaluation also is important because incontinence is a symptom, not a disease. It can indicate several serious conditions, including bladder tumors and prostate cancer. It also can be a side effect of certain medications such as heart or high blood pressure medicine.

"Part of our job is to evaluate and make sure none of these problems exist," said Dr. Ronald Fauer, a Fort Lauderdale urologist. "It may not even be a urologic problem. Incontinence can be a symptom of a brain tumor or multiple sclerosis."

Know the cause. Incontinence is defined as a lack of bladder and/or bowel control. Stress incontinence is the leakage of small amounts of urine when you cough, sneeze, strain or lift, and can be caused by menopause, pregnancy, excessive weight or a pelvic injury. Urgency incontinence is an urgent need to urinate and an inability to get to a toilet in time. It can be caused by a variety of disorders, such as stroke, Alzheimer's disease or multiple sclerosis.

Overflow incontinence is the spilling over of small amounts of urine when the bladder is full. Those with overflow incontinence may not feel the urge to void, so the bladder just overflows. This happens most often as the result of a urinary blockage or nerve damage, such as spina bifida or spinal cord injury.

Self-help treatments include exercises and diet modification. "Once we get the cause sorted out, then we know how to proceed," Dr. Fauer said. "Most incontinent people don't need surgery."

Strengthen your pelvic muscles. Studies have shown that some simple exercises, known as Kegel exercises, can strengthen your pelvic muscles and get you back into your normal activities — if you do them regularly. The exercises usually are taught to women in childbirth classes and are recommended after delivery. (A great side benefit of Kegel exercises is that women have reported having stronger orgasms.) The first of the two exercises requires that you become familiar with the muscles in your pelvic area. The first group of muscles to recognize is the group located at the back of your pelvic floor.

Pretend you are trying to hold back a bowel movement by tightening the muscles around your anus. These are the muscles you want to control while doing Kegels. Do not tighten the muscles in your legs, buttocks or belly.

Has your doctor told you ...

Smoking affects your bladder

Here is yet another reason for you to put down that pack of cigarettes. Women who smoke now or have smoked in the past are at greater risk for incontinence than nonsmokers. A smoker's excessive coughing places a great amount of stress on the bladder, resulting in urine leakage. Coughing is not the only reason smokers suffer from incontinence, however. The tobacco smoke affects the bladder and urethra, and diseases associated with smoking (asthma, blood circulation diseases, etc.) affect your bladder too.

While the numbers of former smokers with incontinence were high, doctors do believe some of the bad effects of smoking can be reversed if you will put down your cigarettes today. By quitting this habit, you can lessen the severity of incontinence and get rid of some of your other problems, including smoker's cough. Kick the smoking habit and enjoy the rest of your life!

American Journal of Obstetrics and Gynecology (167,5:1213)
Geriatrics (48,5:86)

To identify the second group of muscles, found at the front of your pelvic floor, stop and start your urine flow when using the bathroom. Now that you know the proper muscles to use, you can begin doing Kegel exercises. Beginning with the back of your pelvic area and moving to the front, tighten the muscles while slowly counting to four. Then release the muscles. Repeat the exercise for about two minutes at least three times a day (approximately 100 repetitions).

You do not have to break your daily routine to do Kegels because no one needs to know you are exercising. You can perform Kegels while sitting at your desk, watching television or talking on the telephone. Do not do them while crossing your legs or moving around. You want to make sure you are using the correct muscles, so sitting or standing in one place is best.

One way to make sure you are doing these exercises correctly is to use a gizmo called weighted vaginal cones, a set of plastic-covered weights a woman inserts in her vagina one at a time. If you can hold a weight in place, you know you're doing the exercise properly.

Start and stop your urine flow. A second easy exercise for both men and women is to start and stop your urine flow about five times during each bathroom break. Do not, however, do this if you have been diagnosed with a urinary tract infection, as it can cause you some pain or discomfort. It is very important not to stop doing Kegel exercises once you regain control of your bladder. You must continue to do them if you want to maintain that control.

Schedule regular bathroom breaks. Training your bladder is another way to control incontinence. This method involves visiting the bathroom on a scheduled basis, such as once every hour, rather than waiting until you feel the urge to urinate. Your bladder can't fill up as much, thus reducing the chance of leakage. You can begin by voiding at very short intervals, then you can gradually lengthen the intervals to a maximum point that you can maintain.

Don't reduce the amount of liquids you drink. The smaller amount of urine produced may be more highly concentrated and more irritating to your bladder. That can make you go to the bathroom more often. You'll also be more likely to develop a urinary tract infection. Healthy urine is pale and yellow. Six to eight glasses of fluid a day is right for most people.

Don't eat asparagus. It can cause foul-smelling urine. Cherry juice and cranberry juice may help control odor. The most serious cause of urine odor is a urinary tract infection.

Watch out for foods that can trigger bladder control problems. These include: alcoholic beverages, soft drinks with caffeine and carbonation, milk and milk products, tea and coffee (even decaf), citrus juices and fruits, tomatoes and tomato-based products, highly spiced foods, sugar, honey, corn syrup, chocolate and artificial sweeteners. Eliminate these foods one at a time for several days to see if your bladder control improves.

Add fiber to your diet, and exercise. Constipation can affect bladder control. Bearing down to pass hard stools may injure the nerves that help control bladder filling and emptying. Added fiber and exercise help keep your bowels working well.

Women, try a tampon during exercise. Do you leak when you exercise? A third of all women do. Wearing a tampon stopped leakage for most of the aerobic exercisers in a recent study. Wet the tampon slightly to help with insertion and vaginal dryness.

Incontinence is not something to be embarrassed about, but it is something to act on right now. You do not have to accept incontinence as a "sign of growing older." You can begin your own therapy by committing to Kegel exercises every day. If you find no relief after a few months, talk with your doctor about other ways to control your bladder.

Help for Incontinent People, P.O. Box 544, Union, S.C. 29379
Medical Abstracts Newsletter (15,6:8)
The Informer: Helping People with Continence, Fall 1992, The Simon Foundation, Wilmette, Ill. 60091
The Physician and Sportsmedicine (22,5:79)

Infertility

"It's inconceivable" ... Some natural drinks delay pregnancy

Having trouble getting pregnant? So are about 15 percent of other married American women. To improve your chances of conceiving, take a look at what you're drinking.

Believe it or not, downing a few glasses of healthy milk and several cups of coffee every day might be causing your infertility, claims a team of researchers in the United States and Finland. Both caffeine and the milk sugar galactose seem to be toxic to human eggs.

Harvard Medical School and Finnish researchers recently compared data from 36 countries on rates of fertility, milk consumption, and women's ability to digest milk sugar. They reported that even a 20- to 24-year-old woman who drinks a lot of milk may have trouble getting pregnant.

Know the fertility facts. The more milk you drink, the faster your fertility will decline as you age, say the researchers. In Thailand, 98 percent of adults are "lactose intolerant," which means they can't drink milk without getting a stomachache. Obviously, dairy products aren't a big hit in Thailand. Thai women aged 35 to 39 are only 26 percent less fertile than they were at ages 25 to 29.

Compare those statistics with data from Australia and the United Kingdom, where only 5 percent of adults have trouble digesting milk sugar. Dairy products are more popular in these countries.

By the time an Australian or U.K. woman is 35 to 39 years old, she is 82 percent less likely to get pregnant than when she was 20 to 24.

All this research confirms what scientists have observed in their laboratories and doctors in their offices. First, when you feed a mouse a diet high in galactose, the mouse's fertility declines.

Second, women with a disorder called "galactosemia" (which means that their bodies can't process galactose and they have high levels of the milk sugar in their tissues) are infertile. And, five years ago, Harvard University researchers linked high intake of the milk sugar galactose to an increased risk of ovarian cancer.

But don't miss out on milk. Drinking milk seems less "natural" when you realize that most people, along with most mammals, are unable to digest milk after infancy. It's likely that no one was able to digest milk sugar after infancy until certain populations began practicing dairying a few thousand years ago.

Since the ability to digest milk sugar after infancy is an inherited trait, and a trait that makes a woman less likely to bear children, you have to wonder why it's still around.

Why are there still people who have no trouble digesting milk? The scientists have two answers. One is that milk products are much more available to people today than they have ever been in the past.

The other answer is that milk seems to most affect your fertility as you grow older, and, in the past, most women had their families when they were very young. So, what's the bottom line?

Should you cut back on the amount of milk you drink if you're interested in having a baby some day? We can't, in good conscience, recommend that step. Milk provides too many vitamins and minerals to remove it from your diet, at least until scientists study the matter further.

Cut out caffeine to increase your chances. However, there are other beverages without nutritional value that you can remove from your diet to make you more fertile — any drink containing caffeine.

Drinking caffeinated coffee, tea and soft drinks may be one reason so many women are having trouble conceiving these days, say researchers at Yale University School of Medicine and the National Cancer Institute.

Women who drink over 300 mg of caffeine (about three cups of coffee) a day have a 27 percent lower chance of conceiving in each monthly cycle. Even light caffeine drinkers have a 10 percent lower chance of getting pregnant,

Has your doctor told you ...

How often to have sex

Men with low sperm counts are often told that it's best to have sex every other day around the time of the woman's ovulation to improve the chances of pregnancy. That way, the sperm count has time to build back up before sex.

But a new study says that men with a low sperm count have as many or even more sperm in a second ejaculation that occurred one to 24 hours after the first one. The researchers concluded that sex once or twice a day at the time of ovulation will improve your odds of getting pregnant.

The best advice, though, may be not to worry about keeping track of ovulation and number of times you have sex. It's too stressful. Just try to have sex at least twice a week, and you won't miss your most fertile times.

Medical Abstracts Newsletter (14,11:5)

according to the Yale study of almost 2,000 women.

An earlier Harvard University study showed that caffeine increases your risk of disease of the fallopian tubes and endometriosis (a condition in which tissue from the uterine lining grows outside the uterus), either of which can lead to infertility.

Infertility is defined as one year of unprotected intercourse without a pregnancy. Most women who don't drink caffeinated beverages get pregnant within four and a half months. It takes an average of five and a half months for women who consume a lot of caffeine.

Help your hormones — resist coffee and tea. Other elements in coffee and tea, such as tannic acid and "phytoestrogens," (a natural substance that acts like estrogen) may be responsible for affecting your fertility, but caffeine is the most likely culprit.

Caffeine is known to affect hormones and it easily crosses cell membranes.

While giving up milk may not be a step you want to take to increase your chances of conception, avoiding coffee, tea and soft drinks containing caffeine may be a great way of helping Mother Nature along.

American Journal of Epidemiology (137,12:1353; 138,12:1082; and 139,3:282)
Medical Tribune (35,3:12)
Science News (145,11:175)

Thyroid disease can cause infertility

Thyroid hormones have a profound effect on fertility. Located in the base of your neck and shaped like a butterfly, the thyroid gland keeps your body's metabolism running smoothly. It sends out hormones to all your major organs — an important job for your complete health. That also means when things go wrong with your thyroid, many parts of your body feel the effects.

If your thyroid produces more hormones than it should, your metabolism increases. You might suffer from nervousness, bulging eyes, tremors, weight loss, and a rapid heart rate. This condition is called hyperthyroidism.

On the other hand, if your gland is not pumping out enough hormones, you could experience depression, memory loss, fatigue, high cholesterol, muscle aches, hair loss, weight gain, and constipation. This is called hypothyroidism.

A blood test can tell for sure if you have thyroid disease. Left untreated, it can lead to an increased risk for heart disease, infertility and osteoporosis.

Although seniors and adult women are especially at risk — about 20 percent of women over 60 suffer from thyroid disease — it can strike anyone. That's why the American Thyroid Association recommends all adults over 35 have a thyroid blood test every five years. You can help prevent thyroid disease with some simple changes to your diet.

First of all, without iodine, your thyroid can't make its hormones. Most Western countries add iodine to their salt to prevent just such a deficiency. However, even with the right amount of iodine, if your body isn't getting enough selenium, your thyroid can have trouble making hormones. It's fortunate many high-iodine foods, such as seafood and milk, are also good sources of selenium. In addition, vitamin A is essential for thyroid health since it helps you absorb iodine properly. Without it, you can develop a goiter even if you have safe iodine levels. Crunch on some carrots or serve up sweet potatoes, liver, apricots, or spinach. Low iron levels mean your thyroid can't function as it should. Meat is one of your best resources for iron, but you can get your iron from other foods. Vitamin C helps your body digest iron from plants. Plus, you need C anyway to make thyroxine, a thyroid hormone. Levels of zinc affect your thyroid function and oysters are a number one way to get it. If you're squeamish when it comes to shellfish, stick with lean meats, lima beans, and whole grains. A chronic deficiency of Vitamin D, "the sunshine vitamin" can bring on hyperthyroidism. For those rainy days, plan ahead by eating fortified dairy products and seafood.

Ingrown Nails, Fungus Nails, Brittle Nails

Good hygiene for healthy nails

Nails are nothing more than an attractive ending to fingers and toes — for a few lucky souls! For the rest of us, nails can be painful and troublesome. Nails can grow into the soft, surrounding skin, they can crack, split and catch on clothes, and they can be host to embarrassing fungal infections. Plus, the older you get, the harder it is to bend over and tend to toenails.

Whether you tend to your nails yourself or have someone do it for you, taking good care of your nails can keep them healthy and pain-free. Here are a few tips:

Keep your nails short and straight. Trim straight across, but never trim nails deeper than the tips of your fingers or toes.

Moisturize. Nails become more brittle as you get older. Use moisturizers on hands and feet to keep your nails from breaking, splintering and cracking.

Soak your nails. Soaking will allow them to absorb water and help them stay moisturized.

File regularly. File down any rough edges that may catch on a surface and cause your nail to tear.

Clip your nails immediately after bathing. It's much easier to clip nails when they're damp and soft.

Buff them till they shine. Instead of painting your nails, buff them with a buffing solution. Polish prevents moisture from penetrating nails, and polish removers remove cells that act as natural adhesives.

Geriatrics (49,3:21)
The Johns Hopkins Medical Letter: Health After 50 (5,8:8)

Nails give clues to your health

Your nails can also serve as a warning signal for a sick body that needs treatment:

➤ If a nail becomes thick and dull-looking, you may have a fungal infection or a more serious condition.

➤ A nail with a widening black or brown streak running up and down the nail could be a warning sign of skin cancer. A single groove running the length of one nail could be caused by a tumor at the base of the nail. If you notice a change in one or more of your nails, make sure you ask your doctor about it.

➤ You may get ridges across your nails called "Beau's" lines if you have poor eating habits and aren't getting good nutrition. Or a ridge could mean you have a bodily upset like a severe infection. Surgery can also cause a ridge, because the nail growth may be temporarily interrupted due to the anesthesia.

➤ Heart disease and diabetes can decrease blood circulation to the nails and slow down their growth. Nail surfaces may become thick, rough and yellowed.

➤ Nails don't grow as fast after age 30. But this is a natural part of the aging process.

A Natural Alternative

Polish away fungus with boric acid

Florida ranchers have an inexpensive home remedy for thick and dull-looking nails infected with a fungus. They fill a jar with water and 4 to 6 ounces of boric acid, then paint this mixture on their nails twice a day.

Only try this remedy if you have plenty of patience. It can take six months to a year to work! The ranchers keep the jar filled with water and boric acid all year long. They say the exact amount of boric acid doesn't matter, but the jar should have 1/2 to 1 inch of crystals at the bottom at all times.

American Family Physician (50,2:322)

➤ Household cleaning products and cosmetics can damage fingernails by drying them out and making them brittle.

British Medical Journal (301,658:973)
Geriatrics (49,3:21)
The Johns Hopkins Medical Letter: Health After 50 (5,8:8)

Giving the boot to ingrown nails

Here's how to keep ingrown nails from getting under your skin (and we mean that in more ways than one!)

Trim your nails straight across. Most ingrown nails come from not cutting the nails properly. You don't want the edge to curve down into the skin. This gets even more important as you get older because your nails tend to grow wider. Even better than trimming straight across: Slope down a tiny bit in the center to make a little V-shape in your nail. That will help you avoid making an upward point in the center of your nail — a definite no-no for people who tend to get ingrown nails.

Floss your toes. Wedge a piece of folded-over, unwaxed dental floss between your toenail and skin fold to help relieve the pain of an ingrown toenail.

Keep your feet as dry as possible, especially if your feet tend to be sweaty. A moist environment makes your skin softer and may allow the nail to enter your skin more easily. Use powder, and buy socks and hose made of a moisture-absorbing, natural material like cotton instead of synthetic fibers. Well-ventilated shoes will also help your feet breathe.

Stretch your skin to make room for growing nails. After a bath or shower, when your skin is moist and soft, put your thumbs along the back edges of your toenail and gently pull.

If the shoe fits, wear it! Buy shoes that fit well and aren't tight at the toes. Hose and socks shouldn't be too tight or too loose at the toes, either.

Don't try to cut away an ingrown nail. You will probably leave behind a small piece of the toenail that has already grown beneath your skin.

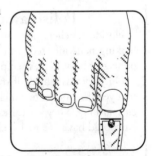

U.S. Pharmacist (19,10:20)

Trim straight across

Insomnia

Sleeping pill nightmares

Are you willing to risk violent mood swings, a crippling fall or a fatal accident for a good night's sleep? Seems like a high price to pay for something that should come naturally. But almost 20 million Americans take those risks every day.

Sleeping pills may seem like the only solution when you've spent countless nights tossing and turning. But drug-induced sleep holds many dangers for the unwary, from daytime drowsiness, dizziness and confusion to drug addiction.

Restore your body and mind. Yet few things in life are more restful, refreshing and downright luxurious than a good night's sleep.

Not only does sleep restore the body and mind in numerous ways, there is evidence that it "consolidates" learning so that you perform a newly mastered task better after having slept. No wonder Shakespeare called sleep the "chief nourisher in life's feast."

Unfortunately, if you're like 90 percent of Americans, you've had difficulty sleeping well at one time or another. Insomnia affects 20 to 40 percent of adults every year. Women and the elderly are the most frequent sufferers, but the ailment can strike anybody. You have insomnia if you (1) can't go to sleep, (2) can't stay asleep or (3) wake up far too early in the morning.

A sleep disorder unrelated to insomnia is sleep apnea. This is a blockage of breathing caused by obesity or a physical abnormality that may occur numerous times during the night. If this happens to you, you wake up (so briefly you may not be aware of it), clear your breathing and go back to sleep.

The result of constantly disrupted sleep is chronic fatigue. If you suspect you are suffering from sleep apnea, see your doctor.

Most insomnia is transient — lasting a few days — or short-term — lasting two or three weeks. About 9 percent is chronic, defined by the American Sleep Association as "poor sleep every night, most nights or several nights a month."

Some transient or short-term insomnia is perfectly natural and probably unavoidable now and then. Anxiety about a current problem, even positive emotions (for example, excitement over a coming vacation) can keep you awake.

Find out how much sleep you need. But in normal times, how much sleep should you get? It varies with the individual, but if you're getting seven or eight hours a night, you're probably all right. If you're over 60, you might need only five or six hours.

You can judge how much sleep you need by your sense of well-being. If you've had bouts of insomnia, you know how rotten you feel the next day: tired, less able to concentrate and probably irritable.

Poor sleep has other consequences as well. Lowered productivity and industrial accidents due to lack of sleep cost the United States about $64 billion per year. Drowsiness causes 200,000 to 400,000 auto accidents each year, accounting for almost half of all accident-related deaths.

Don't seek slumber through sleeping pills. How do you deal with insomnia? About 5 million to 10 million Americans take prescription medicine for it every year and roughly that many more buy over-the-counter sleeping pills.

Such medications may break the pattern of insomnia and help you sleep at first, but they can have all kinds of side effects: "hangovers," drowsiness, dizziness, uncontrollable mood swings, even diarrhea.

The prescription drugs can lead to dependence and also to "rebound insomnia," that is, after a few weeks of use their effectiveness wears off and the sleeplessness comes back worse than before. It's far better to achieve sleep in more natural ways. (Of course, if your doctor prescribes sleeping pills, you should take them.)

First, what are the causes of insomnia? There are many: use of alcohol, drugs and caffeine; low blood sugar; indigestion; lack of calcium and magnesium; anxiety; poor diet; lack of exercise; and food intolerance. In many cases, the cause is unknown. If you have a specific physical problem that may be disturbing your sleep, such as low blood sugar or food intolerance, you should work with your doctor to correct it.

Otherwise, to overcome insomnia (or better, prevent it), consider these tips.

Set your biological clock with sunlight. Whenever possible, spend at least 15 minutes in bright early-morning sunlight. Exposure to sunlight between 7 a.m. and 9 a.m. helps set your biological clock to a 24-hour light/dark cycle. It gears your body to recognize night as the time to sleep.

Drink decaf at night. Don't drink coffee, tea or anything else containing caffeine within six hours of bedtime. (Some authorities advise eliminating caffeine altogether, but we don't want to be such killjoys as to suggest that.)

Soak in a warm bath before bed. A bath will relax your muscles and soothe your nerves.

Don't let your bedroom become an office or a courtroom. The bedroom is not appropriate for work or arguing. Let it be a sleep sanctuary, so that you only associate relaxation and rest with that room.

Get vigorous exercise on a regular basis. A recent study shows that exercise may be all that older Americans need to fall asleep faster and sleep better.

Study participants, who were ages 50 to 76, had four workouts a week: two workouts of stretching, aerobics and strength training and two workouts of brisk walking.

To nap or not to nap?

If you're a longtime napper, you know the sublime delight of sneaking a snooze (although you may feel guilty about your habit). You know how an afternoon siesta restores and refreshes you and raises your energy level. And you know how deliciously pleasant it can be.

Only nap if you're a natural napper. One study showed that an afternoon nap improved moods and test scores of all who took part. However, a different study indicated that people who were normally non-nappers didn't feel better after a nap and in fact felt worse. So napping may not be for everybody.

There have been some famous partakers of the daytime snooze: Napoleon, Winston Churchill, John D. Rockefeller, Thomas Edison, Gen. Douglas MacArthur, John F. Kennedy and Bill Clinton.

Churchill was not the least bit apologetic about his habit. He called a nap "the refreshment of blessed oblivion, which, even if it lasts only 20 minutes, is sufficient to renew all vital forces."

There is some indication that daytime napping interferes with sleep at night, making it less deep.

And many authorities advise you not to nap if you are going through a period of nighttime insomnia. However, the evidence on this issue is mixed.

Snooze to reduce risk of heart disease. Americans generally look down on napping as weak or even shameful. In many parts of the world, however, such as the Mediterranean countries, South America and China, the afternoon siesta is taken as a matter of course.

It could be only coincidence that people in these napping countries have less heart disease than people in the United States.

Some people may have a biological need to nap, while others don't. So if you've been napping, keep it up. As little as 10 minutes can restore you to full power (and nobody really knows why). If you haven't been a napper, but feel a secret urge, give it a try. Midafternoon, when nearly everybody experiences a slump, may be the best time.

International Archives of Occupational and Environmental Health (61,5:341)
Psychophysiology (23,1:82)
The Complete Book of Sleep, Addison-Wesley Publishing, Reading, Mass.

The results after four months showed that the exercisers fell asleep faster and slept for an hour longer each night. Researchers aren't sure just why exercise helps so much, but they think it may be linked to stress reduction.

Go to bed at the same time every night. But only go to bed if you feel sleepy. If you don't, stay up and read or watch television till your eyelids get heavy.

Sweeten your dreams with a cup of honeyed herbal tea. Both chamomile and honey have sleep-inducing properties, so 30 or 40 minutes before bed drink a cup of chamomile tea with a spoonful of honey stirred in. (The honey also makes the tea taste better.) Other herbal teas are reputed to be relaxing. See what's available at your supermarket and health-food store.

Don't drink alcohol near bedtime. Alcohol may help you drop off, but it also may interfere with your normal sleep patterns and wake you up later.

Warm some milk. The old folk remedy, warm milk, works for some people, though scientists don't know why.

Don't look at the clock and don't keep trying. If you can't get to sleep, get up, go to another room, read, listen to music, play solitaire. Or stay in bed and concentrate on being awake. Simply opening your eyes and looking at the shadows around the room often works. This technique, crazy as it sounds, relieves your mind from the anxiety of not being able to fall asleep, and you're soon snoozing soundly.

Tell yourself it won't last. Comfort yourself with this thought: "I'm suffering now, but it won't last forever. In the next day or two, things will return to normal and I'll be sleeping peacefully again."

If these techniques don't work, and you have a stubborn case of insomnia that hangs on for weeks, better consult your doctor. But with luck and a little preparation you won't have to. Sweet dreams.

Alternative Medicine, Future Medicine Publishing, Puyallup, Wash.
FDA Consumer (28,7:14 and 23,8:13)
Food — Your Miracle Medicine, HarperCollins Publishers, New York
Journal Watch (14,5:38)
Prescription for Natural Healing, Avery Publishing, New York
The Atlanta Journal/Constitution
The Journal of the American Medical Association (269,12:1548 and 273,1:6)
U.S. Pharmacist (18,5:47)

Irregular Heartbeat

All-natural way you can stop a racing heart

How to stop a racing heart?

Soak a towel in ice water and hold the towel to your face. If you suffer from occasional heart palpitations or tachycardia, applying an ice-cold towel to your face can slow your racing heart, according to emergency room doctors.

Although tachycardia is not usually serious, it can be very uncomfortable and even scary for your heart rate to suddenly rise to 160 beats per minute. The normal heart rate for healthy adults is about 50 to 100 beats per minute.

Doctors usually treat tachycardia by massaging the arteries in the neck or putting mild pressure on the eyes. But researchers looked to trained divers to find a totally natural and more effective technique. When divers plunge into cold water, their body functions slow down automatically, in anticipation of receiving less oxygen. The same reflex takes over when you put your face into icy water, and the heart rate slows by more than 15 beats per minute.

A word of warning: Check with your doctor about the wisdom of using this cold-water technique. People who have chest pain or angina that becomes worse in cold weather should avoid this method of slowing the heart rate.

Emergency Medicine (27,3:64 and 23,21:95)

Is your hair dye causing your heart to flutter?

Trying to "wash that gray out of her hair" was almost a deadly mistake for one 59-year-old woman from California.

She had been dyeing her hair for a number of years with no problem until one day after applying the solution to her hair, her eyes began to swell, she became itchy and hoarse and began having heart palpitations.

She decided to switch to another brand of hair dye and buy an antihistamine just in case she had a reaction. As it turned out, she did have another allergic reaction, but the antihistamine did the trick and she recovered quickly.

She decided to try her old hair color one more time, and this time it really did her in. Her vision became blurred, her face and hands swelled, and she got dizzy and shaky. She couldn't breathe and fainted. Paramedics arrived and, with an injection of adrenaline, saved her life. She had a rare, yet severe, allergic reaction to a chemical in the hair dye.

Don't let an allergic reaction sneak up on you. An allergic reaction usually occurs after the first or second exposure to an allergen (the agent or substance causing the allergic reaction). However, allergic reactions may not occur until after years of exposure.

So don't dismiss any unusual symptoms you might experience just because you have used a product for several months or years. And don't be fooled into thinking you're safe just because you have used a product before. The most common allergic ingredient in hair dyes is a synthetic organic compound called p-phenylenediamine. It is found in most permanent hair colorings.

Do a patch test. If you are worried about having an allergic reaction, but would still like to color your hair, use these precautions: Do a patch test every time you use permanent coloring, wear gloves to protect your hands, avoid rubbing the dye into your scalp, and wash off any dye that touches your skin.

You can also try to avoid p-phenylenediamine. Most semi-permanent hair colors, including "cellophanes," do not contain this substance. Be sure to check the label for contents.

Caffeine and drugs can clash

People who suffer from occasional heart palpitations need to stay away from caffeine. But even more importantly, they should never mix caffeine with certain drugs.

Some drugs can slow the body's disposal of caffeine, and others stimulate the nervous system, adding to the effects of caffeine. When taking any of the following medications, you may want to skip your morning coffee or your caffeinated soft drink at lunch.

> ➤ Birth-control pills
> ➤ Ciprofloxacin (Cipro) — prescribed for bacterial infections
> ➤ Cimetidine (Tagamet) — prescribed for ulcers
> ➤ Appetite suppressants (Acutrim, Dexatrim)
> ➤ Theophylline (Slo-Phyllin, TheoDur) — prescribed for asthma
> ➤ Oral decongestants (Contac, Propagest)
> ➤ Antidepressant monoamine oxidase (MAO) inhibitors (Nardil, Parnate)

Nursing95 Drug Handbook, Springhouse, Springhouse, Pa.
Physicians' Desk Reference, Medical Economics Data Production, Montvale, N.J.

Knee Pain

Use tape for more than wrapping gifts

A simple roll of athletic adhesive tape is the latest treatment for arthritis pain in your knees. Studies have shown that pulling your kneecap to the inside of your leg with a piece of tape can lessen your discomfort and give you a safe, inexpensive way to make climbing stairs and walking a little easier.

While not a substitute for a doctor's advice or a physical therapy routine, moving the kneecap to one side can decrease leg pain for a while. According to researchers, taping, when combined with the proper exercises, is a safe method of treatment for knee pain in senior citizens as well as in young athletes.

Get your kneecap in line with tape. When your kneecap isn't aligned properly, it puts pressure on the knee and causes pain. The tape seems to relieve some of that pressure. The tape helps relieve pain so that you can exercise and build your thigh muscles. Strong thigh muscles will help hold your kneecap in place and relieve your pain permanently.

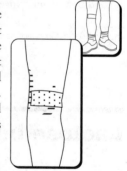

Pull tape to the inside. The proper way to tape your knee is to pull the kneecap toward the inner part of your leg. The two ends of the piece of 2-inch-wide tape should be on the outer side of your leg, not touching each other. (See illustration.) A physical therapist can give you a simple training lesson. Learning to do this yourself can help you take control of your recovery and let you get those walking shoes out of the closet and put them back on your feet.

American Family Physician (50,3:676)
British Medical Journal (308,6931:753)
Medicine and Science in Sports and Exercise (25,9:989)

Knee braces invite injury

Brace yourself for some important news: Knee braces can leave you limping!

Plenty of athletes use knee braces to reduce the chance of sustaining knee injuries. Football and field sport players (especially soccer and lacrosse) who have sustained previous injuries use them to guard against being reinjured.

But research shows that knee braces may actually put athletes at risk of further damaging not only their knees, but also their feet and ankles.

Braces cause leg fatigue. How could something used to guard against injury lead to the chance of causing injury? Researchers at universities in Sweden and California conducted extensive tests which showed that knee braces reduce muscular strength in the braced leg by as much as 35 percent, causing fatigue in a shorter time.

The result is more pressure being placed on ankle and foot muscles to compensate for tiredness in the knee, and the possibility of those lower muscle groups sustaining injury.

Researchers for both studies concluded that pressure on knee muscles caused by knee brace design doesn't allow the knee muscles to fully receive the oxygenated blood they need to stay at peak strength.

Don't wear a brace unless it's doctor-prescribed. Both studies recommended changes in knee brace design to allow better blood flow to the muscle groups above and below the knee.

But until then, you may want to avoid knee braces, whether you use them to guard against injuries or to strengthen a weak knee.

However, when the ligaments in your knee are extremely loose and your knee is so weak that it could give way easily, it is safer to wear a brace when playing a sport such as basketball or tennis. Consult your doctor about the condition of your knee.

The American Journal of Sports Medicine (22,6:830)

Lactose Intolerance

Seven stomach-soothing ideas

Milk ... it just doesn't sit right with you. A warm summer's day and your friends look forward to savoring that bowl of ice cream, but not you. After dinner the dessert tray is rolled out and your companions are tempted by that luscious cheesecake, but not you. You don't find pleasure in these foods — all you can think of is that stomach discomfort and those intestinal problems that will ruin the rest of your day.

You may be one of the many people who suffer from lactose intolerance. Lactose is the sugar found in milk and dairy products. Lactose intolerance can make you extremely uncomfortable, but it's not a disease or even a food allergy.

Lactose intolerance means that your digestive system is not producing enough

Who gets it?

Since babies and young children need milk for a large part of their nutrition, nature has seen to it that the lactose-digesting enzyme is highly active during this time of life. Lactose intolerance is rare during childhood. Most people experience a gradual decrease in enzyme function as they grow older.

Interestingly, most people with lactose intolerance are nonwhite. At least seven out of 10 blacks, Orientals and Indians suffer from lactose intolerance. That's compared with fewer than two out of 10 whites. Scientists believe that cultures which have had limited access to milk and dairy products have more trouble digesting them.

_____

Dairy Council Digest (65,2:7)
Postgraduate Medicine (95,1:113)
The Physician and Sportsmedicine (21,3:59)

of the enzyme lactase, which you need to break down milk sugar. After you eat a serving of dairy food, a large amount of undigested milk sugar moves through your digestive system, upsetting normal processes along the way.

Within a few minutes to several hours after eating the dairy product, you may feel bloating, cramping, gas, diarrhea, pain and nausea.

There are a number of easy ways to treat lactose intolerance.

Avoid milk and any foods made with milk. Be sure to read labels carefully. Look at ingredient lists for these key words: lactose, dry milk solids or whey.

Avoiding milk is the most drastic way to deal with lactose intolerance. Women in particular should take care. Limiting your intake of dairy foods can lead to a deficiency in calcium, an essential nutrient in the prevention of osteoporosis.

Nondairy creamers and soy milk products are available as dairy substitutes. Unfortunately, many of these products are high in fat or may not taste good to you. There are two more reasons why avoiding milk may be a bad idea:

1) Your lactose intolerance may just be a passing condition: a temporary reaction to a medicine, the result of an illness, or some other reason.
2) The longer you avoid dairy products, the less you'll be able to tolerate that occasional bowl of ice cream. Drinking a small amount of milk regularly may help keep your lactose-digesting bacteria strong.

A few people — about one in every 200 — are allergic to milk, and, generally, they do need to completely avoid milk. When you are allergic to milk, you get rashes, hives, wheezing, runny eyes and a stuffy nose when you drink it.

Try hard cheeses and skim-milk cheeses. Many hard cheeses (like cheddar, Swiss and Jarlsberg) and some skim-milk cheeses (like low-fat cream cheese and part-skim mozzarella) are usually low in lactose. You should try these cheeses to see if you can enjoy them.

Never drink milk or eat ice cream on an empty stomach. Products containing lactose may not bother you if you consume them along with plenty of other food.

Substitute yogurt for other dairy foods. Yogurt with live and active cultures contains helpful bacteria that digest the lactose in the yogurt for you. Be sure to check your brand for the "live and active cultures" seal.

Train yourself to tolerate dairy products. Tests conducted by nutritional scientists show that even people with severe lactose intolerance can learn to drink milk without digestive problems.

You start with a small amount of milk that doesn't hurt your stomach. Stay at that level for two to four days. Then increase your milk intake slightly and see if you remain symptom-free. If you feel no discomfort after two to four days at that new level, increase it again by a slight amount.

If you feel digestive discomfort at any time, reduce the milk you drink to the previously tolerated level and remain there for a few days. Then begin the gradual increase once again.

Try one of the lactose-reduced milks that have recently appeared on supermarket shelves. These milks have been treated so that the milk sugar has already been broken down. They usually have 70 percent less lactose than regular milk and may not upset your digestive system. Lactose-reduced cottage cheese and American cheese are also available now.

Buy lactase tablets at your drugstore. You can add the enzyme capsule directly to the dairy product and break down the milk sugar before you eat or drink it. However, this chemical process increases the amount of other sugars in the food and tends to make the food unusually sweet.

In another method, you take the tablets yourself when you eat dairy food. These pills (Dairy Ease, Lactaid, Lactrase) can be found in grocery stores and pharmacies and are very convenient to use. Just follow the directions supplied with the pills. They can reduce the symptoms of pain and bloating that many people experience.

The tablets may be too expensive to be practical for regular use, but you may want to use them when you're going out to dinner.

Dairy Council Digest (65,2:7)
Postgraduate Medicine (95,1:113)
The American Journal of Clinical Nutrition (58,6:879)
The Physician and Sportsmedicine (21,3:59)
Tuft's University Diet & Nutrition Letter (12,10: 4)

Leg Cramps and Leg Pain

Rub out the pain of leg cramps

Nestled in the warmth of your bed, cozy blankets embrace you and lull you to sleep. In the foggy moments between bliss and reality you feel enchantingly numb. Then you experience one last sensation: a searing, piercing pain in your leg — a muscle cramp, sometimes called a charley horse.

Don't panic. Everyone gets them. It's probably nothing serious. This comes as little comfort to you, sitting up in bed, excruciatingly alert, massaging your aching calf. But you're already doing the right thing.

Take hold of leg cramps. When muscle pain strikes, grab it, massage it, and use heat or ice if it helps. Stretch the muscle by standing on the affected leg and leaning forward. You also can relieve a muscle cramp by sitting on the ground, stretching your legs straight out in front of you, and gently pulling your toes and the ball of your foot toward your kneecap.

Here are some other tips to help you pull in the rein on those charley horse nightmares:

Stretch your calf muscles every day. Try this quick and easy calf stretch. With your shoes off, stand two to three feet from a wall. Place your hands on the wall and lean forward, being sure to keep your legs and back straight.

Press your heels into the floor. You should feel a pulling sensation in the back of your lower legs. Hold this position for 10 seconds; relax five seconds and do the exercise once more. Repeat exercise three times daily.

Drink at least eight glasses of water a day. You'll need to drink more if you've been physically active. Dehydration (lack of fluids) is probably the biggest contributor to muscle cramping.

Control cramps with minerals. Sometimes you may develop leg cramps because you have too little potassium, calcium or magnesium in your body.

Make sure your body has enough potassium by eating plenty of oranges and bananas. (Hint: If you don't buy bananas because they become overripe too quickly, try storing them in the refrigerator. The skins will turn black, but the fruit will stay fresh longer.) Include lots of calcium-rich foods in your diet, such as milk, yogurt, salmon, sardines, shrimp, dark-green leafy vegetables and dried peas and beans. Eat foods high in magnesium, such as almonds, cashews, apricots, whole grains, dark-green leafy vegetables and soybeans.

Expect muscle soreness. If your leg cramps occur frequently, are accompanied by other symptoms, or aren't relieved by stretching and massaging, see your doctor to make sure it isn't something more serious. But don't be alarmed if the muscle is a little sore for a few days. This is very common.

Next time you're awakened by a leg cramp, remember that you're not alone. There are plenty of us awake with you, massaging and stretching and trying to remember that great dream we were just having.

Postgraduate Medicine (96,1:155)
The Physician and Sportsmedicine (21,7:115)
U.S. Pharmacist (17,6:23)

Pain in the calf could be intermittent claudication

Do your lower leg muscles ache and cramp when you walk?

You may have "intermittent claudication." It means your heart isn't pumping enough blood to your legs, and it's a symptom of serious artery disease.

Pound the pavement for relief. Intermittent claudication can hurt so badly that the last thing you want to do is walk. But that's exactly what you need to do to get relief. You need to walk until you bring on the pain, then rest for a minute or two until the pain subsides, then start walking again. Keep this up for one hour. If you walk for one hour three times a week, you should get your leg pain under control within two or three months. If you don't do your walking exercises, you may find yourself confined to your armchair at home as your leg pain gets worse and worse.

Lifting weights won't ease the pain. Many people with intermittent claudication have weak leg muscles, so some doctors believed that strength-training would improve the condition. But when a group of people with intermittent claudication went through a 12-week strength-training regimen, their leg pain didn't improve significantly. Strength-training is good for your health, but it definitely can't replace walking as a treatment for your leg pain.

See your doctor for regular "AAA screenings." Intermittent claudication is a common sign of an "abdominal aortic aneurysm," or AAA. AAA is a weakness in the wall of the artery which supplies blood to your stomach, liver and spleen. Almost one out of every 10 men over age 65 has AAA. The worst of it is, once your weak artery ruptures, your chances of survival are low. All men over 65 should be screened for AAA every year. Start being screened at a younger age if you have a brother with AAA or if you get severe pain in your calf muscles when you walk.

Circulation (90,4;1866)
Heart and Stroke Facts and *Controlling Your Risk Factors for Heart Attack*, American Heart Association, 7272 Greenville Ave., Dallas, Texas 75231–4596
Reducing Your Risk of Skin Cancer, American Institute for Cancer Research, 1759 R Street, N.W., Washington, D.C. 20069
The Wall Street Journal
The Wellness Encyclopedia: The Comprehensive Family Resource for Safeguarding Health and Preventing Illness, Houghton Mifflin, Boston
U.S. Pharmacist (19,7:38)

Lice

When an itchy scalp means lice

It's autumn. Your kids are back at school. They're playing with other children, sharing toys and clothes. And they're coming into contact with cold germs, flu bugs and — yes — even head lice. About 10 million cases of head lice occur each year in the United States, and 75 percent of them are in children under 12. Lice infestations often occur in epidemics, especially during the back-to-school months.

Don't feel dirty — lice don't discriminate. Contrary to popular belief, lice aren't discriminating creatures. They can affect anyone, regardless of cleanliness or income. There's absolutely no truth to the myth that only "dirty" people get head lice. In fact, lice are more likely to attack clean hair than dirty hair.

Because head lice are passed from person to person by direct contact, children are at a greater risk.

They play in close contact and often share things that can pass the lice, such as combs, brushes, caps, scarves, baseball helmets, radio or computer headphones and pillows.

Conduct a head inspection. An itchy scalp is the first clue that your child may have lice. Part your child's hair, shine a bright light on her scalp, and carefully inspect her head. It's difficult to spot the lice themselves, so you may have better luck looking for their eggs, known as nits. Nits are usually found on hair near the neck, behind the ears and on the crown of the head. They appear white and look like dandruff, but, unlike dandruff, they can't be shaken off.

If your child has lice, immediately check all other family members for signs of lice. All infested family members must be treated at the same time so that the lice don't come back.

Use a fine-toothed comb and special shampoo. There *is* some good news: You'll find effective, easy remedies for lice as nearby as your corner drugstore. Here's what the experts recommend:

➤ A permethrin cream rinse is the treatment of choice for head lice. It keeps working for up to 14 days, continuing to kill any lice that hatch after you apply it.

➤ Pyrethrin shampoos are also recommended. They produce "cure rates" comparable with permethrin, but it takes a second application to get the same results.

There is only one permethrin product — Nix — but there are several pyrethrin products with well-known brand names — A-200, Tisit and RID, to name a few. These products are all available over the counter. Your pharmacist can help you determine which product is best for your needs.

Use these products exactly as directed. After rinsing out the medication, carefully comb your child's hair to make sure you remove any nits not killed by the medication. Most of these products are packaged with a fine-toothed comb. (Also pay particular attention to the package warnings. Don't use the products on children with allergies, and don't get any medication in your child's eyes.)

Stay away from old family remedies. Many old lice remedies are dangerous. Don't use gasoline, kerosene, sulfur, larkspur lotion, garden insecticides or dog lice/flea shampoos.

Delouse your house. Once you've treated your child, it's time to tend to your household. Wash and dry all washable objects that have come into contact with your child's head — this includes hats, clothes, scarves, bed linens and towels. These should be washed on the hottest cycle for at least 20 minutes.

Anything that can't be washed, like stuffed toys or coats, should be dry-cleaned or vacuumed thoroughly. Combs and brushes should be soaked in hot water (over 130 degrees Fahrenheit) for 10 minutes. Upholstered furniture and carpets must be vacuumed to remove any hairs with attached nits or lice that may have fallen out.

You don't have to treat your pets. They don't carry human lice.

Bag up all teddy bears. Lice can't live off the host for more than 48 hours, and nits hatch in eight days. So all clothing, toys (especially stuffed animals) and other items that can't be washed or dry cleaned should be placed in a plastic bag and sealed for 14 days.

Be a regular nit-picker. Inspect your child and all other family members daily for at least seven days after the lice treatment. If you see lice after seven days, try a second treatment. It's a good idea to continue frequent head checks even after your lice problem has disappeared. It's easier to get rid of lice if you catch them early.

U.S. Pharmacist (17,9:32 and 19,9:32)

Loss of Sexual Desire

Put the sizzle back in your sex life

Lost that loving feeling? Check your medicine cabinet.

Chances are, the cause of your lost sexual desire will be staring you right in the face. Both over-the-counter and prescription drugs can significantly decrease your interest in sex.

Sadly, many people don't even discuss the loss of sexual desire with their doctors. They just assume it's a natural part of growing older. The truth is, anyone taking a prescription or over-the-counter medication may be affected.

Side effects may appear after only a few weeks or develop after you've been taking a drug for years. Drugs that often inhibit sexual desire include antihistamines, antidepressants, antipsychotics, beta blockers, decongestants and tranquilizers. (See the chart on the next page for a more complete listing.)

Even if you suspect a drug of interfering with your love life, don't stop taking any medication until you talk with your doctor. Abruptly discontinuing certain medicines can be a deadly decision. Your doctor can help you safely find another alternative.

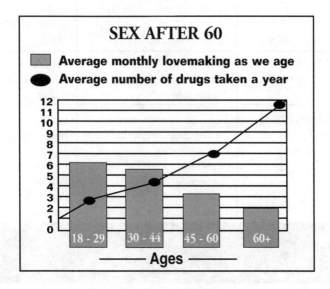

And the next time you get a new prescription, ask about the side effects it could have on your sex life.

_____

Before You Call the Doctor, Random-Ballantine, New York
National Opinion Research Center (NORC), *General Society Survey*

Prescription drugs that steal sexual desire

CATEGORY	DRUG	COMMON BRAND NAMES
ANTIHYPERTENSIVES *Used to treat high blood pressure.*	Methyldopa Propranolol hydrochloride Guanethidine monosulfate Reserpine Prazosin hydrochloride Clonidine	Aldoclor, Aldomet Inderal, Inderide Esimil, Ismelin Diupres, Hydropres Minipress, Minizide Catapres-TTS
ANTIDEPRESSANTS *Used to treat depression.*	Imipramine hydrochloride Trazodone hydrochloride Phenelzine sulfate Clomipramine hydrochloride Amoxapine Fluoxetine hydrochloride Paroxetine hydrochloride Sertraline hydrochloride Amitriptyline hydrochloride	Tofranil Desyrel Nardil Anafranil Asendin Prozac Paxil Zoloft Elavil
ANTIANXIETY *Used to treat anxiety.*	Diazepam Chlordiazepoxide Alprazolam	Valium Libritabs, Limbitrol Xanax
MISCELLANEOUS *Used to treat a variety of symptoms.*	Digoxin Disopyramide phosphate Cimetidine Acetazolamide Finasteride Nifedipine Goserelin acetate implant	Lanoxin, Lanoxicaps Norpace Tagamet Diamox Proscar Procardia Zoladex

Physicians' Desk Reference, Medical Economics Data Production Co., Montvale, N.J., 1994
PDR Guide to Drug Interactions Side Effects Indications, Medical Economics Data Production Co., Montvale, N.J., 1994

Lung Cancer

Nonsmokers' battle plan for fighting lung cancer

If you think you're not at risk for lung cancer just because you don't smoke, guess again. Up to 20 percent of the women who are diagnosed with lung cancer each year are nonsmokers.

Diets that are high in fat have long been thought to contribute to cancers of the breast, colon and prostate, as well as cause heart disease. But mounting evidence indicates that lung cancer needs to be added to the list.

A recent study has shown that women whose diets are loaded with saturated fat are five times as likely to develop lung cancer as women whose diets have relatively little fat.

A high-fat diet is one in which more than 40 percent of the calories come from fat. Health professionals recommend that no more than 30 percent of calories come from fat. Less than 10 percent of these calories should come from saturated fats. Saturated fats are found in meats, dairy products, tropical vegetable oils (such as coconut, palm and palm-kernel oil), and hydrogenated vegetable oils.

Eat more fruits and vegetables. But there is some good news in the link between your diet and your risk of lung cancer: Researchers have also discovered that eating fruits and vegetables may actually help protect you from the disease. A diet that includes plenty of fruits and vegetables may also help to prevent lung cancer in nonsmoking men. Peas and beans also appear to have a protective effect against lung cancer.

While the National Cancer Institute recommends five servings of fruits and vegetables a day for maximum health, the researchers found that eating one-and-a-half servings of fruits and vegetables each day can reduce your risk of lung cancer by 40 percent.

But, they emphasize, you need to cut the fat out of your diet at the same time. It probably won't help to eat the same high-fat diet and just include an extra serving of fruit each day. The study suggests that fruits and vegetables are more beneficial when eaten raw rather than processed or cooked. The high temperatures during cooking or processing may destroy the healthful nutrients that help protect against cancer.

Since most people fall far short of the National Cancer Institute's recommended five servings of fruits and vegetables a day, it's easy to make a simple change in your diet that could have a profound impact on your health. Choose a healthy piece of fruit for dessert next time. Your lungs may thank you for it.

Journal of the National Cancer Institute (85,23:1906)
Medical Tribune (34,8:12)
Science News (144,23:373 and 145,2:23)

A Natural Alternative

Beta-carotene and lung cancer

Beta-carotene is a vitamin that seems to be hitting the headlines regularly these days. Handfuls of scientific studies are showing how helpful beta-carotene can be in preventing the development of cancer.

But, most of the studies have been performed with volunteers who did not have major risk factors for cancer. One group of researchers wanted to know if beta-carotene would still help people who smoke and therefore have an increased risk of getting lung cancer.

The researchers from the Netherlands Organization for Applied Scientific Research Toxicology and Nutrition Institute recruited over 150 men who smoked more than 15 cigarettes per day for more than two years.

Half the men received daily 20-milligram supplements of beta-carotene, and the other half received daily placebos — sugar pills that did not contain any beta-carotene.

The volunteers were instructed to take the capsules with their evening meals: two capsules per day for the first two weeks, followed by one capsule per day for the remaining 12 weeks of the study.

The men who took beta-carotene developed stronger and more effective cancer-fighting immune cells. And that means a lower risk of developing lung cancer. The results of the study are even more exciting because most smokers have an abnormally low level of beta-carotene in their blood due to the harmful effects of cigarette smoke on some vitamins in the body.

But, even though beta-carotene can help reduce the risk of lung cancer (and some other forms of cancer too), the best way to reduce your risk of lung cancer is to quit smoking. Even large amounts of vitamins can't overcome the huge risk of smoking.

Nutrition Research Newsletter (12,4:41)
The American Journal of Clinical Nutrition (57,3:402)

Menopause Symptoms

Beyond hormone therapy: Natural alternatives for menopause

"Free at last! Free at last! Thank God Almighty, we are free at last!"

Even though menopause wasn't what Martin Luther King had in mind when he uttered those historic words, they certainly seem appropriate to women experiencing the liberation of menopause.

Finally, you're free from the worry of an unwanted pregnancy, difficult decisions concerning contraception, painful periods, PMS symptoms and a host of other uncomfortable problems that often accompany a woman's reproductive years. Children are moving out, leaving more time for you, your friends, your hobbies and your spouse. But like every great opportunity, menopause poses some special challenges.

Know the three stages of menopause. Menopause actually occurs in three stages. Premenopause begins in your early 40s. Your ovaries gradually produce less estrogen, and your periods become irregular, often alternating between light and heavy.

Actual menopause occurs when you have your last menstrual period, usually around age 52. You've reached the third and final stage, postmenopause, when you've gone for 12 full months without a period. During these transition years, many women opt for hormone replacement therapy (HRT) to help them cope with hot flashes, vaginal dryness, mood swings and insomnia.

In addition to relieving the troublesome symptoms of menopause, HRT provides protection against heart disease and osteoporosis (loss of bone mass). Other women, for health or personal reasons, seek other answers to menopause. These answers are often hard to find at your typical doctor's office.

Discover your alternatives. A 1993 Gallup poll reported that less than 2 percent of doctors consulted about menopause mentioned alternative therapies. In fact, many doctors doubt the effectiveness of such remedies.

But Dr. Susan Lark, author of *The Estrogen Decision*, believes women should be aware of all their options, including alternative therapies. Even for women who decide to have HRT, the alternative therapies Lark describes in her book can make sailing through menopause a much smoother ride.

Lark outlines a seven-step plan emphasizing diet, exercise and stress management that can help you relieve your symptoms of menopause, no matter how slight or severe.

Center your diet around beans, peas, grains, raw seeds and nuts, fruits, vegetables and fish high in Omega-3. These foods contain essential nutrients that help your body cope naturally with menopause. Some fish rich in Omega-3 are Atlantic mackerel, lake trout and bluefin tuna.

Limit caffeine, alcohol, sugar, salt, meat, fatty dairy products and saturated oils, such as coconut and palm-kernel oil. These foods will either make your menopausal symptoms worse or increase your risk of developing disorders that often occur during the postmenopausal period, including arthritis, cancer, diabetes, heart disease and stroke.

Include a daily multivitamin. The supplement should provide 100 percent of the recommended daily allowance (RDA) for most nutrients. Most vitamin packages list what percentage of the RDA the nutrients in their formula provide. Lark recommends supplements because often even a healthy diet will not include all the nutrients your body needs to completely relieve your menopausal symptoms. Keep in mind, however, that supplements won't do you much good if you don't also follow the healthy diet outlined above.

Get herbal relief. Lark suggests that herbs, when used wisely, are just a healthy addition to a nutritious diet. She has developed three different special menopause formulas, which you can purchase in an herb shop or make yourself at home by combining small amounts of the herbs listed for each formula.

Formula 1. This combination of herbs helps relieve hot flashes and vaginal dryness. Mix the following herbs together in equal amounts: black cohosh, don quai, false unicorn root, fennel, anise and blessed thistle.

Formula 2. This formula helps relieve tiredness and weakness. Mix the following herbs together in equal amounts: ginger, oat straw, ginkgo biloba and Siberian ginseng.

Formula 3. These herbs help combat anxiety, insomnia and irritability. Mix the following herbs together in equal amounts: valerian root, catnip, chamomile and hops.

Lark recommends that you add the herbs to tea or take with meals. Do not take more than one to two herbal capsules or drink more than one to two cups of herbal tea daily. Although all of these herbs are considered safe, you should stop using them if you have any symptoms that make you uncomfortable.

Be sure to let your doctor know you are using herbs. They can sometimes react with other medicines you may be taking.

Practice stress management. During menopausal years, women often find that their unstable hormones lead to more extreme responses to stress. Often the smallest incident can trigger anger, depression or tears. Stress management techniques practiced for 10 to 20 minutes a day will help you feel calmer and more in control.

Deep breathing is an especially helpful relaxation exercise that you can practice anytime, anywhere: Close your eyes and focus on moving your stomach in and out as you breathe through your nose. Breathe in and out 10 times or until you begin to feel yourself relax.

Exercise your symptoms away. Regular exercise will relieve your hot flashes, improve bladder control, help you concentrate better, think clearer and solve problems more effectively. You'll also reduce your risk of osteoporosis and heart disease. Start slowly if you haven't exercised in a while. Aim to exercise at least three times a week for 30 minutes at a time. Try to set aside a regular time to exercise. Aerobic exercise, such as walking, dancing, swimming or bicycling, is especially helpful.

Say yes to yoga. Through a series of gentle exercises and stretches, yoga restores balance to your muscles, cells and tissues, which helps your body cope with the hormone changes of menopause. Lark recommends specific yoga exercises for the different symptoms of menopause. For example, the Locust stretch helps control irregular or excessive menstrual bleeding, relieves hot flashes and

A Natural Alternative

Soybeans may be alternative therapy for menopause

When menopause steals your estrogen, replace it with plant sources. Eating plant foods with phytoestrogens can give you some of the protective benefits of estrogen. Good sources include oats, wheat, corn, apples, almonds, cashews, and peanuts.

A specific kind of phytoestrogen, called isoflavones, is found mostly in soy-based foods like soybeans, tofu, miso, and soy nuts. Asian women eat about one type of soy food every day and report very few hot flashes and mood swings during menopause. This could mean they're getting some estrogen from their diet.

Unfortunately, experts have concerns. Although some research shows soy might help your heart and prevent osteoporosis, other studies suggest it makes your brain age faster. Some health experts think the more soy you eat, the greater your risk of developing senility.

Just to be on the safe side, talk with your doctor about the pros and cons of eating soy during menopause.

Medical Tribune for the Internist and Cardiologist (36,7:11)

helps improve bladder control. You can find more information on yoga at your local library.

Try some hands-on healing. Lark suggests acupressure, an ancient Oriental therapy which involves applying finger pressure to different parts of the body to treat different ailments. She says that many women she has treated for menopause have found this technique helpful for relieving hot flashes, insomnia, mood swings and tiredness. Here's an easy acupressure technique you can try at home to relieve hot flashes and emotional tension: Sit in a chair. Press the first three fingers of your right hand on the area between your eyebrows, right at the top of your nose. Apply steady pressure for one to three minutes.

If you greet the changes of menopause with good health habits and a few simple lifestyle changes, you'll be in great shape to glide through it gracefully. You can conquer any challenge!

The Estrogen Decision, Westchester Publishing, Los Altos, Calif.

Migraines

Self-help for migraine sufferers

It's an unwelcome but familiar pattern. You feel tired all morning long, and by noon you have that sickly, nauseous feeling. Your vision starts getting blurry, or you may be seeing spots.

By now, you know what's coming. The pain and pressure begin building inside your head, and you just know you're going to spend the rest of the afternoon in bed, miserable, trying to sleep off yet another migraine headache. To make matters worse, your boss calls you a hypochondriac or blames your headache on the fact that you don't "handle" stress very well. But new research indicates that there may be more to this debilitating condition than was previously believed.

Get your brain chemicals in balance. For many years, it was believed that migraines were caused by the swelling and shrinking of tiny blood vessels in the brain. But new evidence has led researchers to conclude that migraines are probably caused by an upset in the delicate balance of two chemicals in the brain: serotonin and norepinephrine.

These chemicals, among other things, help determine your body's natural sleeping and waking patterns. Most migraines occur during times when your

What triggers a migraine?

Researchers point to many possible causes of headaches. Try reducing your exposure to the following migraine triggers in case they are at the root of your pain.

➤ Alcohol — beer, wine (especially red), liquor.

➤ Bright or flashing lights.

➤ Caffeine — chocolate, coffee, tea, colas. If you use caffeine, spread it out evenly during the day.

➤ Dairy products — milk, buttermilk, cream, ice cream and processed and aged cheeses.

➤ Emotional stress.

➤ Fruits — citrus fruits, bananas, figs, raisins, papaya, kiwi, plums and pineapples.

➤ Loud noises.

➤ Meats with nitrites and nitrates — preserved meats and deli meats.

➤ Monosodium glutamate (MSG) — a flavor enhancer.

➤ Nicotine — counteracts headache medicines.

➤ Premenstrual tension.

➤ Sulfites — found in salad bar foods, shrimp, soft drinks.

➤ Vegetables — most peas, onions, olives, pickles and sauerkraut.

➤ Yeast products — fresh breads, doughnuts, yeast extract.

American Family Physician (49,3:633)
National Headache Foundation Newsletter (87:6)
The Headache Book, Consumer Reports Books, Yonkers, New York

body is waking up. You're three times as likely to develop a headache between 6 a.m. and noon as at any other time of the day.

Migraine headaches are more common in the fall and early spring when serotonin levels, which change throughout the year, are relatively low. If these chemicals do get out of balance, it sets off a type of chain reaction in the brain which can result in nausea, vomiting and debilitating pain. This process can continue until all of the chemicals involved are used up. For some, this may be only a few hours; for others, the pain can last for days. Some medications work on your serotonin and help get your chemicals back in balance. Two of these your doctor may prescribe are sumatriptan and ergotamine.

Stop it before it starts. To win the headache battle, look for these warning signs: pressure in your temples, tightness in your neck and shoulders, and irritability. When you see these signs, take a break, relax for a while, and give your mind and body a rest.

Learn which foods trigger your migraines. Some common food triggers are alcoholic beverages (especially red wine), aged cheeses, cured meats, chocolate and beverages containing caffeine.

Go to bed and get up the same time every day. Your regular schedule must include weekends.

Don't skip meals. Make sure you eat something for each meal of the day, even if it's just a quick snack.

Exercise. As usual, try for three times a week, at least 30 minutes a session. For some migraine sufferers, exercise will stop a mild migraine even after it's begun.

Stop worrying. Don't let stress or circumstances you can't control trigger a migraine. Take time during a stressful day to relax for 20 minutes.

_____
American Family Physician (49,3:633)
National Headache Foundation Newsletter
The Headache Book, Consumer Reports Books, Yonkers, New York

The magnesium/headache connection

Researchers are now zeroing in on how pain in the head from a migraine or cluster headache could result from too little magnesium in the body.

Migraines are among the worst headaches, with excruciating, throbbing pain that can knock you out of commission for hours — even days. Equally painful cluster headaches (named for their tendency to come in "clusters" for days or even months at a time) frequently wake sufferers up in the middle of the night with stabbing pains behind or around one eye.

In one study of several hundred people, nearly half of those with migraine and cluster headaches were suspected of having a lack of active magnesium. (Some magnesium becomes attached to proteins in the body and becomes inactive; other magnesium, known as ionized magnesium, is called the active variety.)

How could too little magnesium cause headaches? Researchers are trying to figure that out, and they have uncovered an important clue — the way tiny disk-shaped blood cells called platelets behave in migraine sufferers.

Platelets produce several substances your body uses for wound healing, including the hormone serotonin. But if you suffer from migraines, platelets release more serotonin than normal. Serotonin causes blood vessels to tighten up, and researchers know migraines begin just that way — with vascular constriction. Too little magnesium in the body increases serotonin, while healthy levels of the mineral help block it. It may not be just the severe kinds of headache that are brought on by a lack of magnesium, either. One study found that people with garden variety stress and tension headaches also weren't getting enough magnesium in their diets.

The facts and stats

Over 40 million Americans suffer from migraine headaches each year.

The headaches can range in severity from a mild ache that is gone in an hour or two, to a very severe headache that occurs daily for several hours, causing nausea, vomiting, sensitivity to light and intense, stabbing pain.

Many people report "seeing things" during their headaches, such as zigzag lines, stars or other bizarre images. These visual disturbances, known as "auras," are experienced by as many as 20 percent of all migraine sufferers.

Who gets migraines? Mostly women. In fact, women make up nearly three-fourths of all migraine victims, and women between the ages of 45 and 64 are more than three times as likely to suffer from headaches as men in the same age group. Apparently, women are especially susceptible because of their bodies' delicate balance of hormones.

American Family Physician (49,3:633)
National Headache Foundation Newsletter
The Headache Book, Consumer Reports Books, Yonkers, New York

Get the Recommended Daily Allowance (RDA) for magnesium. The RDA is 420 mg for men 51 years and older and 320 mg for women 51 years and older. If you get too much magnesium, you may experience nausea, diarrhea and vomiting, have extremely low blood pressure and muscle weakness, difficulty breathing, and an irregular heartbeat. Medicines that can interact with magnesium include ketoconazole (used to treat dandruff, yeast infections and fungal infections such as athlete's foot or jock itch), mecamylamine (used to treat high blood pressure and cancer), and tetracycline (used to treat acne and infections). Don't use magnesium supplements if you are taking any of these medicines.

Give two other nutrients a try — calcium and vitamin D. The two supplements worked for four women migraine sufferers recently. Two of the women had premenstrual syndrome and migraines related to their menstrual periods. The other two women had passed menopause. The women all started with low blood levels of vitamin D. If you suspect you may have low vitamin D levels, taking a daily multivitamin that contains calcium and vitamin D may help your headaches.

Complete Guide to Vitamins, Minerals & Supplements, Fisher Books, Tucson, Ariz.
Headache (34,9:544 and 34,10:590)
National Headache Foundation Newsletter (86:14)

Morning Sickness

Suffering from morning sickness? Pass the chips!

What can you do about an unwelcome sidekick that tags along at a joyous event? As many as 50 to 90 percent of all expectant mothers face this problem — morning sickness.

It is caused by a rapid increase in hormones. For some women, morning sickness actually lasts all day long, getting worse in the evening. Some experience brief episodes of nausea and vomiting; others endure distress throughout the pregnancy. It's small comfort to hear that the condition usually ends after the first three months.

Now you can benefit from recent advances in treatment. Researchers have found that your body's own natural wisdom has triumphed over conventional medicine. Miriam Erick, R.D., an obstetrical dietitian at Brigham and Women's Hospital in Boston, works with women hospitalized for severe morning sickness.

Called hyperemesis gravidarum, the ailment causes the hospitalization of approximately 55,000 women in the United States each year. As Erick focused on these patients, she found standard dietary guidelines of no help for many.

Follow your own instincts. Erick decided to go to the source, looking for answers from the victims themselves. She found that following one's own instincts about what foods to eat worked best.

Rather than a restricted diet plan, Erick led patients down a comprehensive food list, asking them to name what they would eat if they could have anything they wanted. She reasoned that a person suffering from nausea would automatically avoid foods likely to make her feel worse and favor those she could tolerate.

Eat the flavorful foods you want. Surprisingly, the women often asked for salty, crunchy foods, such as potato chips, followed by lemonade. Sometimes they wanted a flavorful food such as spaghetti. Those choices are a far cry from typical recommendations from the American Academy of Family Practitioners: plain baked potato, white rice, dry toast, saltines, gelatin desserts, broth, nondiet ginger ale, pretzels and decaffeinated or herbal teas.

Erick appointed herself as a quick-delivery service, running to the hospital kitchen to fetch foods before they lost their appeal. And when Erick supplied the foods quickly, an important point in overcoming nausea, patients kept the meals down.

It's no wonder morning sickness has been difficult to treat since it affects each woman differently. The severity, duration and time of day nausea strikes may change with subsequent pregnancies. A woman might depend solely on cooked, hot cereals for weeks during her first pregnancy, then the next time crave strictly fruits or the spicy/salty food types. Besides listening to your own instincts, here are some additional remedies to try.

Eat smaller, more frequent meals. Eat before hunger gets a grip on you. Try persuading your husband to bring you breakfast in bed. Some women keep a stash of well-tolerated foods on a bedside table for nibbling when you wake up.

Potato chips vs. saltines

Dr. Miriam Erick was puzzled when women with morning sickness requested salty/crunchy foods and a tart beverage. How could foods that run contrary to standard advice for bland foods satisfy a queasy stomach?

To find the answer, she performed a computerized nutritional analysis comparing potato chips and lemonade to saltines and ginger ale.

The potato chips outperformed the saltines in several ways: more folic acid and vitamin C, more potassium (which you need more of when you're vomiting) and less sodium. As for the lemonade, women with morning sickness often have an excess of saliva. Swallowing this excess contributes to nausea and vomiting. The tart drink helps cut that excess saliva and tastes good after the salty chips.

Journal of the American Dietetic Association (94,2:147)

Avoid offensive, strong odors. Erick calls the heightened sense of smell during pregnancy "radar nose." Cook in a well-ventilated room, with open windows and fans if necessary. Leave off the heavy perfumes and avoid the company of those who wear it. Many women do find odorless foods best. If all else fails, consider trying processed baby foods until the nausea passes.

Change your vitamins. Talk with your doctor or other health care provider about a change in the type of vitamin you're taking. The iron in prenatal vitamins can cause problems for some women.

Take it as a good sign. According to the American Academy of Family Physicians, some doctors feel that nausea is a good sign that the placenta, the structure in the uterus that nourishes the baby, is developing well.

Monitor the advice and input you accept from family members and friends. Beware of those whose comments suggest you're imagining the nausea or, even worse, that it may indicate mixed feelings about becoming a mother. Cut them off immediately by saying you've been advised to fill your mind with only positive thoughts.

Avoid recitals of woe. If friends offer to share a successful remedy, fine. If they want to tell you how much worse they had it, forget it. Wallowing in other people's misery does nothing for your situation.

Try acupressure. In a recent study, 60 percent of those studied responded positively to acupressure treatment compared with a 30 percent positive reaction to a placebo.

An easy way to try this treatment is with acupressure wrist bands available from travel agencies, such as AAA Auto Club and boating supply stores.

Morning sickness does have two good characteristics.

First, it will pass. In the meantime, those suffering from morning sickness can best treat themselves by avoiding strong odors, eating frequent small meals and drinking plenty of liquids to avoid dehydration.

The second good point is it's not a cause for worry. Though the exact causes aren't agreed on, Erick's work points to a connection between the normal higher levels of estrogen during pregnancy and a heightened sense of smell, which can lead to nausea.

Be reassured by the vast numbers of women who have suffered through morning sickness to deliver perfectly healthy babies.

American Family Physician (48,7:1279)
Journal of the American Dietetic Association (94,2:147)
No More Morning Sickness: A Survival Guide for Pregnant Women, New American Library, New York

Neck Pain

Heading off neck pain

A pain in the neck usually comes from not keeping a straight head on your shoulders. The more you lean your head forward or sideways to work, drive, read or perhaps ride a bike, the harder your neck muscles have to work. Eventually, your tired muscles will become strained, tight and painful.

You can prevent most neck pain by keeping your head in a straight, natural position as much as possible. Neck exercises can help you get rid of a pain in the neck and will strengthen your neck — preventing strained muscles in the future.

The exercises on the following pages will help you regain mobility and strength after an injury once the severe pain has gone away.

Over-the-counter pain relievers and ice can help relieve neck pain too. Hold an ice pack over the painful area for 20 minutes. Wait two hours, then use the ice again. After a few days, when the muscle spasms in your neck have stopped,

> While lying on your back, turn your head to the left (left cheek toward the floor), until you feel a gentle stretch. Hold for 10 to 30 seconds.
> Repeat on the right side.
> Do this exercise two or three times to each side, once or twice a day. If you feel tingling or pain, stop and see a doctor.

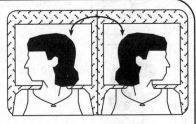

Neck exercises

> Lie on your back on the floor or on a firm mattress.
> Tilt your left ear toward your left shoulder. Tilt until you feel a gentle stretch, but no pain. Hold for 10 to 30 seconds.
> Repeat on the right side.
> Do this exercise two or three times to each side, once or twice a day. If you feel tingling in your arms or an increase in pain, stop and see a doctor.

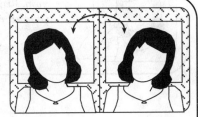

you can use a heating pad. Apply it for 20 minutes at a time two to three times a day.

You can do the previous two exercises while sitting. Your neck has to work harder while you're sitting, though. It has to hold your head up as well as turn.

If you choose to sit and exercise, make sure you don't roll your head in full circles.

Rolling your head backward strains your neck.

A collar can help when your neck pain is severe. It rests the muscles and relieves spasms. But wearing a collar too long can make your neck weak and stiff. When your pain stops, take the collar off and start the neck exercises.

> Sit and place your palm firmly against your forehead. Push your head against your hand. Hold for 10 seconds. Rest and repeat three times.

> Next, put your hand behind your head. Push your head back against your hand for 10 seconds. Repeat three times.

> Place your hand over your right ear and push. Repeat for three times, then switch to your left ear.

Nosebleeds

What to do for nosebleeds — leave the cotton in the field

Nosebleeds are messy and aggravating, but usually pretty easy to deal with. Whether your nosebleed is from the lining of your nose being too dry, nose picking or a run-in with the door frame, a few home remedies should have you fixed up and ready to go.

Leave the cotton in the field. Never, no, never use cotton to plug up a bleeding nose. Yes, it is true that the cotton fits into the nostril well and absorbs lots of blood. The trouble with cotton is that the fibers stick to the wound. And when the blood finally clots, the cotton fibers do too. Pulling out the cotton fibers usually reopens the wound and starts the bleeding again.

And even if the nose doesn't start bleeding again, many of the cotton fibers stick to the lining of the nostrils and continue to irritate the sensitive skin long after the bleeding stops.

Pack your nose with gooey gauze. Instead of cotton, use a rectangular piece of petroleum-jelly-coated gauze to pack the nose and stop the bleeding. About 10 minutes after the bleeding stops, put some water in your hands and splash your face to wet the gauze, then gently remove it from the nostril.

Pinch between your eyes. While the gauze packing is in place, pinch the fleshy part of your nose right between your eyes with your thumb and index finger. Pinch just below the bony bridge of your nose for about five to 10 minutes, and the bleeding should stop. If it hasn't stopped, try pinching for another 10 minutes or so. Think of the inside of your nose as two pliable plates that you want to press closely together tightly enough to restrict breathing through your nose.

Don't lean your head back. Most people lean their heads way back when their nose bleeds. Instead, sit upright, with just a little upward tilt on your head.

Ice it. Also try placing an ice pack on your nose to help reduce the bleeding and relieve any stinging you might feel.

Leave it alone. After your nose stops bleeding, try to avoid any trauma (hitting or picking your nose) for about a week to make sure the bleeding site heals properly.

Lubricate dry membranes. An ounce of prevention is worth a pound of cure, so try this tip for preventing the nosebleeds you get from breathing dry winter air. Put a small dab of petroleum jelly in each nasal passage and rub in gently. Lubricate the dividing wall in your nose especially well. This will moisturize your nasal membranes and keep the crusty scabs out of the inside of your nose. You can also squirt a solution of sterile water and salt up your nose to keep your nostrils moist.

Take a look at your alcohol consumption. Studies have shown that many people who are regular drinkers have more nosebleeds. Researchers think it's because of alcohol's effects on the body. It can dilate blood vessels and decrease the ability of platelets to form clots, both of which can lead to nosebleeds. But an occasional alcoholic beverage shouldn't increase your risk.

If you have problems with frequent nosebleeds or a nosebleed that just won't stop bleeding, see your doctor. That could signal underlying problems, such as vitamin deficiencies, nasal tumors or bleeding disorders.

Consumer Reports on Health (7,1:6)
Emergency Medicine (24,6:26)
Medical Tribune for the Internist and Cardiologist (35,19:14)

Obsessive-Compulsive Disorder

When order becomes a disorder

You may have an unusually strong need for order and cleanliness in your life. For example, after supper you insist that every plate, glass and utensil be thoroughly rinsed and put in the dishwasher before anybody watches TV.

You may keep all the books in your bookcase in alphabetical order by author. You may insist on a precise arrangement of clothes in your closet.

OK, you're a little fussy. In fact, you may be a perfectionist.

There is an illness, however, related to orderliness and cleanliness known as obsessive-compulsive disorder (OCD). But people who suffer from it exhibit bizarre behavior far beyond keeping things neat and clean.

Understand obsessions and compulsions. An obsession consists of frightening and insistent thoughts, such as fear that something horrible will happen or bizarre sexual fantasies. (One OCD sufferer's wife had trouble getting the laundry done because her husband kept opening the washing machine to make sure the cat wasn't inside.)

A compulsion consists of repetitive acts, such as counting one's steps or repeating the same words or washing the same foot over and over. Obsessions and compulsions go together.

The obsessive fears lead to anxiety, and the anxiety is relieved by the compulsive actions. So in a way, it makes sense that compulsions naturally follow obsessions.

Know when your need for order is out of control. OCD seems to be related to a need for orderliness and perfectionism. Consider the case of an eight-year-old girl who was taking riding lessons. She was told by her mother that she was a "beautiful rider" and a "good rider."

The child became quite upset and demanded to know which she was, a "beautiful" or a "good" rider. Her next symptom was a compulsion to place her doll in a certain exact spot on her bed. Her condition worsened and eventually she was diagnosed as having OCD.

A law student had no time to study because of his compulsive need to constantly dust and vacuum whenever he was in his apartment. He tried staying in a motel, but the manager threw him out after the student showered for 12 continuous hours.

The poor fellow finally took to sleeping on park benches — anything to stay out of the apartment where his obsessive-compulsive disorder drove him to clean endlessly.

Just because you like to keep things neat and orderly or you double-check doors or stove burners doesn't mean you have OCD.

But if your neat habits or your tendency to check things begins to take more than an hour a day or if it interferes with your normal daily routine, you should talk with your doctor.

Don't get sucked in by profit-seekers. Drugs such as Luvox, Prozac and Anafranil can help some people with OCD. OCD seems to have a biochemical basis, according to researchers.

However, two drug companies, Solvay and Upjohn, have launched a publicity blitz to make OCD famous — and to sell products. These companies produce Luvox.

The drug companies do admit they want to make a profit. But they insist that they also want to make the disease better known and prompt people who

Common compulsions

These are some of the most common obsessive-compulsive behaviors:

Cleanliness. A woman who saw cockroaches one day in a supermarket went home and washed her groceries. For the next 14 years, after every trip to the grocery store, she followed the same routine. Another woman spent 16 hours a day cleaning her house and wouldn't let her husband go upstairs until he had showered downstairs.

Checking. Some people are obsessed with making sure the stove is off and the doors and windows are locked. These people say that if they didn't have to go to work, they would check these things all day long.

Fear of violence (by oneself or others). A person afraid of his own violence might constantly wonder if he stabbed his mother.

Counting. One man repeated everything four times. Every morning he would turn the bedroom light on and off four times, brush his teeth four times, take four showers, etc.

Rituals. A boy would avoid stepping on cracks when he walked to school. If he stepped on one, even at the school entrance, he would go all the way home and start over. A young woman driving through Europe decided that if she broke any self-imposed rules, such as showing anger, she had to go back to her starting point, a Spanish village. She repeatedly got as far as Germany and Scandinavia, but returned to the village 200 times.

FDA Consumer (26,4:6)
Health (8,5:78)
The Boy Who Couldn't Stop Washing, E.P. Dutton, New York

think they have OCD to seek treatment.

There is a danger, though, that perfectly normal people who are exposed to sensational news coverage about OCD will begin to worry that they have this disorder and may even take medicines they don't need.

Get your hands dirty. Several natural methods have helped some people with OCD. One is behavioral therapy. It calls for you to write down all of your symptoms and face them honestly. Then you must take action against them. For instance, if you are a compulsive hand washer, dirty your hands. Then look at them and don't wash them for a specified time.

Get it out of your system. Another behavioral method is to deliberately perform your compulsive acts until you can't stand it anymore. For example, if you check the stove burners 25 times, force yourself to check them 200 times. When you are thoroughly sick of doing it, you may gain some insight into your behavior.

Involve your family. Along with behavioral therapy goes family therapy. In this approach, family members offer understanding, but they stop supporting the sufferer in the obsessive-compulsive behavior patterns.

OCD is more widespread than people once thought. Most sufferers keep their condition secret out of shame. But more and more people are coming forward. Estimates of the number of people with OCD in the United States range from 4 million to 5 million.

It strikes men and women and all ethnic groups equally. It can start at any age, including early childhood, but age 18 to 20 is the most common time.

If you think you or a family member has OCD, consult your doctor. For the names and addresses of behavioral therapists in your area, contact the Association for Advancement of Behavior Therapy, 305 7th Avenue, 16th Floor, New York, NY 10001 or call 212-647-1890.

Before making an appointment, make sure the therapist has worked with obsessive-compulsives. And for additional information, call the Obsessive-Compulsive Foundation at 203-315-2190.

American Family Physician (49,5:1129 and 49,5:1142)
American Journal of Psychiatry (150,3:460)
Bioscience (42,6:257)
FDA Consumer (26,4:6)
Health (8,5:78)
Parents (68,10:237)
The Boy Who Couldn't Stop Washing, E.P. Dutton, New York
The Good News About Panic, Anxiety & Phobias, Villard Books, New York
The Journal of the American Board of Family Practice (6,5:507)
The Wall Street Journal

Osteoporosis

Building stronger bones

For Aunt Eve's dowager's hump, Mrs. Zinn's broken hip, and Grandmother's cracked wrist from her fall on the doorstep — osteoporosis, the "brittle bone disease," is responsible.

Osteoporosis causes your bones to lose calcium and other minerals very slowly, over many years. The bones aren't diseased or abnormal in any way. They're just not as dense as they were when you were younger.

These thin, weak bones are easily broken, especially in the spine, wrist or hip. Although there's no cure for osteoporosis once you have it, you can easily prevent the disease.

Even though osteoporosis isn't usually detected until much later in life, it actually begins in your earlier years when your body is building up its bone mass. In fact, about 45 percent of your bone mass is formed while you're a teen-ager.

But don't worry if your teen-age years are just a distant memory. It's never too late to start taking care of your bones and begin the healthy habits that will keep them strong for the rest of your life.

Exercise. Whether it's walking, running, lifting weights or doing yardwork, regular weight-bearing exercise is essential throughout your life to keep your bones healthy and strong. Most doctors recommend that you exercise regularly three to five times a week for about half an hour at a time.

Get plenty of calcium. The bones are always at work, busily laying down, releasing and replacing their storehouses of calcium, adjusting to your body's needs. Most of the time, your bones do a pretty good job of maintaining the correct amount of calcium, replacing any that gets used up.

But after age 35 in women, and a little older in men, your bones don't replace the lost calcium as well as they used to. That's when osteoporosis sets in. Good sources of calcium include low-fat and nonfat dairy products and dark-green, leafy vegetables, such as broccoli and kale. Keep reading for more information on a calcium-rich diet.

Quit smoking. Smoking lowers women's estrogen levels and reduces the ability to absorb calcium, in both ways contributing to weaker bones.

Avoid heavy drinking. Heavy drinking is defined as more than two drinks a day. Alcohol affects your bones' ability to grow and function properly, and it reduces your absorption of calcium.

Consider estrogen replacement. If you're a woman over the age of 50, ask your doctor about estrogen replacement therapy. Estrogen helps keep your bones strong.

Fall-proof your home. Falls can result in hip fractures, and they usually happen in the "safety" of your own home. See the *Falling Accidents* chapter for tips on staying firmly on your feet.

———
American Family Physician (50,6:1193)
Annals of Internal Medicine (25,4:413)
The Physician and Sportsmedicine (21,2:56 and 22,1:71)

Build bones with calcium

If you're not getting enough calcium, your bones may be at the breaking point. Literally. You need calcium to build a strong skeleton. Without it, bones

---

Gray hair means weaker bones?

Researchers have linked prematurely gray hair and osteoporosis. Premature graying means that more than half of your hair is gray before age 40. The researchers speculate that the genes that determine premature graying may be linked to the genes responsible for bone mass.

Of course, there are several other well-known risk factors for osteoporosis.

Age. The main contributor is age. The disease is usually diagnosed in people over the age of 60.

Gender. Unfortunately, your gender is the next most important factor in determining how likely you are to develop osteoporosis. Women are eight times as likely to be affected by the disease as men. Women, on the average, are born with less bone mass than men. Then, to make matters worse, menopause causes a woman's natural supply of estrogen to decrease, so she loses bone mass faster than a man.

Nutrition. Third, nutrition plays a vital role in keeping your bones healthy. Doctors recommend getting most of these essential building blocks from the foods you eat instead of supplements.

Exercise. Fourth, the amount that you exercise is directly related to bone mass and density. A regular exercise program increases the stress you put on your bones. They respond to this mechanical stress by becoming stronger and more dense.

———
American Family Physician (50,6:1193)
Annals of Internal Medicine (25,4:413)
The Physician and Sportsmedicine (21,2:56 and 22,1:71)

weaken and break easily.

But if you're like many Americans, your diet may be low in calcium. Half the adults in the United States don't get enough calcium each day, a big reason for the rise in bone disease in recent years. In fact, not getting enough calcium could land you in the emergency room with broken bones from simple things, like bending down too quickly or even being hugged.

Bone up on your calcium intake. The best calcium sources are dairy products and green, leafy vegetables. Most adults require about 1,000 milligrams of calcium each day. That may sound like a lot, but you can be halfway there before dinner if you eat properly. Have an 8-ounce glass of milk with breakfast and two cups of cottage cheese or a cup of yogurt with lunch. That gives you nearly 600 milligrams.

Have one or two cups of greens or broccoli with dinner, and you've given your body the daily calcium it needs. Even splurging on ice cream can be rewarding: Less than two cups for dessert provides you with about 300 more milligrams.

Don't overdose on calcium. If your diet is healthy, you probably don't need calcium supplements. More than 2,000 milligrams a day is too much. Going over that once in a while is OK, but it may cause other problems over a long period.

Pay close attention to your children's calcium intake. Kids need calcium too. Bones grow the fastest from childhood through the mid-20s, and children need enough calcium to keep pace with that growth.

Without it, your children's skeletons won't form properly, and they may have bone disease once they become adults. This bone disease often occurs after it's too late to build up bone mass. If your children are between 1 and 10 they need about 800 milligrams of calcium a day. Infants require between 400 and 600 milligrams a day.

Meet the new requirements. The National Institutes of Health has recently suggested that the current recommended daily allowances for calcium are too low. They suggest the following Adequate Intakes:

Age	Calcium
9 - 18	1,300 mg
19 - 30	1,000 mg
31 - 50	1,000 mg
over 50	1,200 mg

Don't like milk? Try vegetables and seafood. Milk and dairy products remain the best sources of calcium, but if you have trouble digesting milk that doesn't do you much good.

To make up for that, take extra helpings of vegetables like kale, turnip greens, collard greens and mustard greens during dinner.

Consider other excellent calcium sources like clams, oysters and shrimp, or try snacking on canned sardines or salmon, including the bones.

Calcium supplements are also available at most grocery stores and come in liquid, tablet or chewable forms. While these may help if you can't have dairy products, avoid them if you can get calcium naturally. Some of these supplements contain lead.

To equal the calcium in one cup of milk (291 mg), you'd need to eat:

> 2 cups of broccoli
> 1 cup of collards, turnip, kale or mustard greens
> 2 cups of cottage cheese
> 1 ounce of Swiss cheese
> 4 ounces of salmon, with bones and oil
> 5 cups of green beans

Don't worry about your kidneys. Kidney stones contain calcium, and many doctors were concerned that recommending calcium supplements for osteoporosis would cause a kidney stone epidemic. But a new study says if you need to take calcium supplements, don't worry about your kidneys.

The women in the study who took calcium citrate for six months didn't have an increased risk of the painful and dangerous stones.

The Journal of Optimal Nutrition (3,1:32)
Medical Tribune for the Internist & Cardiologist (35,13:5)
National Institutes of Health news release
Science News (145,25:390)
The American Journal of Clinical Nutrition (60,4:592)
The Real Vitamin and Mineral Book: Going Beyond the RDA for Optimum Health, Avery Publishing, Garden City Park, N.Y.

Making the most of your calcium intake

You may be taking in plenty of calcium, but is it doing your body any good? Counting milligrams toward your daily allowance means little if your body isn't absorbing the calcium you eat and drink.

Getting your body to absorb more calcium is a function of two old reliables — eating right and exercising regularly.

Get more calcium by eating less protein. Many Americans don't get enough calcium because they eat a diet high in protein. Too much protein interferes with your body's ability to use calcium and causes bone loss.

High-protein foods dump fatty acids into the blood. Since your body produces acid naturally, this extra acid increases blood toxicity and puts a strain on your kidneys. Your body's first instinct is to correct this by "robbing" the skeleton of calcium, which is then lost through your urine.

Eating less protein reverses this trend, and helps your body keep the calcium you take in.

Eat fortified foods to enhance calcium absorption. Certain calcium sources are more easily absorbed by your body than others.

Fortified orange juice and yogurt are excellent sources that your body absorbs better than calcium supplements or antacids.

In other words, a supplement or an antacid tablet may provide the same amount of calcium that a glass of orange juice provides. But your body doesn't absorb all the calcium in the supplement or antacid. You get more calcium benefits from the orange juice or yogurt.

Get your calcium at mealtime. Researchers learned in a recent study that your body absorbs more calcium when you take it in at mealtime than when you take it without other food.

Getting your calcium with meals is not only smart, it's easy to do. The best calcium sources are dairy products, fortified orange juice, and green, leafy vegetables — foods we should eat at breakfast and dinner anyway.

If you decide to take calcium supplements, it's best to do so with meals. That seems to increase their effectiveness.

Put the fizz of bicarbs in your life. Some researchers say you can absorb calcium better by taking a daily dose of potassium bicarbonate.

That's because potassium bicarbonate may also lower acid levels in the blood, meaning you lose less calcium in your urine. Since your body doesn't need to compensate for extra acid, more calcium is put to use building bone and slowing bone loss.

Other experts say these preliminary findings are not conclusive and more study is needed to see what long-term effects, if any, you gain from taking potassium bicarbonate daily.

Remember your potassium and vitamin D. Potassium and vitamin D both work to regulate acid levels in your blood.

This affects how much calcium your body soaks up and puts to use building strong bones. Potassium, vitamin D and calcium work together, so make sure you get plenty of each.

Having an 8-ounce glass of orange juice provides about two percent of the daily requirement of calcium and gives you 430 milligrams of potassium.

Sunlight helps your body produce vitamin D. If you don't get out of the house much or if you suffer indoors through long winters, you may need extra vitamin D.

Experts recommend 10 to 15 mcg of vitamin D daily for seniors.

Don't forget to exercise. Doing all the right things with your diet may not help if you don't exercise regularly.

The way your body uses calcium is affected by the amount of exercise you get. Regular exercise helps your body absorb calcium and increase bone mass, the best way to guard against bone disease.

Medical Tribune for the Internist & Cardiologist (35,14:18)
Nutrition Research (11,9:961)
The American Journal of Clinical Nutrition (49,2:372 and 58,3:398)
The American Journal of Medicine (94,6:646)
The Journal of Optimal Nutrition (3,1:32)
The New England Journal of Medicine (330,25:1776)
The Real Vitamin and Mineral Book: Going Beyond the RDA for Optimum Health, Avery Publishing, Garden City Park, N.Y.

Has your doctor told you ...

Drinking coffee may weaken your bones

Drinking coffee can weaken your bones if you don't regularly drink milk too. Researchers at the University of California in San Diego studied the coffee-drinking habits of 980 women between the ages of 50 and 98.

The women who drank more than two cups of caffeinated coffee per day without also regularly drinking milk had weaker spinal and hip bones than the average woman.

Women who drank just one cup of coffee a day had no increased risk of bone loss. Researchers aren't sure what effect, if any, decaffeinated coffee has on bone loss. If you're a caffeinated coffee lover, make sure you drink at least a glass of milk a day to offset any possible risk of bone loss.

The Journal of the American Medical Association (271,4:280)

Ovarian and Cervical Cancers

Daily dose of B vitamin essential for women at risk

If you are one of the women who has a low level of folic acid, a B vitamin, in your body, you may have a higher-than-normal risk for cervical cancer.

Low levels of folic acid may cause body tissue to become more vulnerable to cancer-causing substances, according to researchers. Women with little folic acid in their systems are more likely to have "precancerous cervical changes."

Women who smoke and those who are taking oral contraceptives could be at greater risk for cervical cancer if they also have low levels of folic acid in their bodies. Women who have had numerous sexual partners and a low folic acid level may also be at higher risk for cervical cancer.

Correct folic acid deficiency with diet and supplements. Folic acid deficiency can be detected with a simple blood test and can be corrected by adding broccoli, spinach, collards, citrus fruits, beans and whole-grain breads and cereals to your diet. Vitamin supplements should not take the place of these healthy foods, but you may need them to add folic acid to your system if you do not eat a well-balanced diet every day.

Other foods may soon be fortified with folic acid to make sure people with different tastes in foods get an ample supply of the vitamin. While whole-grain foods, spinach and broccoli will help keep you healthy, nothing can take the place of regular checkups. Pap smears are still one of the best ways to detect cervical cancer early. A good diet is just another weapon against a very serious illness. After your next visit to the doctor, stop by the grocery store on your way home and pick up some fresh fruits and vegetables for dinner. What can it hurt?

FDA Consumer (28,4:11)
Journal of the National Cancer Institute (85,11:875)
Medical Abstracts Newsletter (12,3:3)
Stay Healthy
The Journal of the American Medical Association (267,4:528)
The Wall Street Journal

Five a day keeps ovarian cancer away

Good news for women! You can lower your risk of ovarian cancer 37 percent just by eating two servings of vegetables a day. Researchers believe that diet is linked to 35 percent of all cancer deaths. By eating plenty of fruits and vegetables and lowering your fat intake, you can slash your risk of many kinds of cancer in half.

Eat at least five servings of fruits and vegetables a day. You may think you eat your five servings, but are you sure? A recent study commissioned by the United Fresh Fruit and Vegetable Association found that people overestimated the amount of fruits and vegetables they ate by a whopping 33 percent.

The study examined menu diaries kept by 2,000 households across the nation. Study participants believed that they ate an average of nearly five servings of fruits and vegetables a day. After keeping menu diaries, the people in the study discovered they were eating 13 percent fewer vegetables and 56 percent fewer servings of fruits than they thought.

On the other hand, consumers greatly underestimated the amount of fats, oils and sweets consumed. People reported they ate just two servings of these products a day when in reality they actually consumed about four servings per day — nearly twice as much as they thought.

Keep a food diary. If you aren't sure you're getting enough fruits and vegetables in your diet, keep a food diary for a day. The National Cancer Institute recommends a minimum of three vegetables and two fruits every day. You'll get the best cancer protection from eating different-colored vegetables every day — orange carrots, green brussels sprouts, yellow corn, red tomatoes, etc. The different colors mean different health benefits. Green leafy plants, for

A Natural Alternative

Take five!

If you have trouble finding ways to squeeze in five fruits and vegetables a day, try these suggestions from the National Cancer Institute:

➤ Keep a bowl of fruit on your desk or dining room table for a quick, easy snack anytime.

➤ Pour 100 percent fruit juice into an ice tray. Freeze. Add toothpicks and enjoy your homemade frozen fruit pops.

➤ Keep fresh fruits and vegetables on the top shelf of your refrigerator instead of the crisper. The easier they are to see, the more likely you are to eat them.

➤ Substitute finely minced vegetables with low-fat ricotta cheese for meat in your favorite lasagna recipe.

➤ Marinate a variety of sliced vegetables in low-fat Italian dressing and use with turkey or low-fat cheese in a pita bread sandwich.

5 A Day, National Cancer Institute, 9000 Rockville Pike, Bethesda, Md. 20205

instance, are full of lutein, a very powerful antioxidant. Be sure to track your fat intake too. You may be eating more than you think. A low-fat diet that includes plenty of fruits and vegetables will also help you shed unwanted pounds. Now, that's a deal that's hard to beat.

Everything Doesn't Cause Cancer, American Institute for Cancer Research, 1759 R Street, N.W., Washington, D.C. 20069
United Fresh Fruit and Vegetable Association, 727 North Washington Street, Alexandria, Va. 22314

Panic Attacks

Don't panic

You're stopped in traffic, waiting for the light to change. Without warning, your hands start to sweat and your heart beats faster. It feels like someone's got their hands around your throat, and a wave of nausea comes over you. Your fingers clamp down like a hawk's talons on the steering wheel, and you fight the overwhelming urge to throw open the car door and run away. There's screaming in your ears.

Then you realize the noise is the sound of horns blaring in the line of traffic behind you. You look up at a green light and an empty lane in front of you. Shaken and embarrassed, you drive on to your destination.

You've just had a panic attack.

Stop the attacks before they escalate to panic disorder. Panic attacks and anxiety disorders are among the most common problems treated by mental health professionals. Statistically, about one in every 10 people has had a panic attack. When panic attacks or the fear of having them becomes so frequent or severe that it affects a person's ability to function, it's diagnosed as a panic disorder. Between 4 and 6 percent of the general population suffer from panic disorder.

"It's common to have a panic attack when you're under tremendous stress," said Dr. Cynthia Last, director of the Anxiety Treatment Center at Nova Southeastern University in Davie, Florida. "It's the fear about the attacks that tends to make them keep coming, so it's kind of a vicious circle."

Blame it on your parents, or on circumstance. Basically, a panic attack is one reaction a person's body can have to stress, and there is a strong genetic link, Last said. You also can have a panic attack as a result of other mental health problems, such as post-traumatic stress disorder, obsessive-compulsive disorder or a phobia. "Any major life change, good or bad, can bring on an attack," she said. "There seems to be a link between hormonal and endocrinologic changes too. We see panic in women who have had babies or are going through menopause."

Panic attacks come in two varieties — the kind that is linked to the circumstance, like the person who has a panic attack every time he gets in an elevator or flies on an airplane, and the kind that seems to come out of the blue and is unrelated to the immediate situation. It can take some time to figure out what triggers the second kind, but it's linked to something stressful, Last said.

Know the symptoms. Mental health diagnostic criteria list the following symptoms of a panic attack: shortness of breath or smothering sensations; dizziness, unsteady feelings or faintness; choking; palpitations or increased heart rate; trembling or shaking; sweating; nausea or abdominal distress; depersonalization or derealization; numbness or tingling; flushes or chills; chest pain or discomfort; fear of dying; and fear of going crazy or of doing something uncontrolled during an attack.

Panic disorder usually first appears in a person's late 20s, and it's equally common in men and women. When panic disorder is accompanied by agoraphobia (fear of open spaces), it's about twice as common in women as in men.

"It's definitely a treatable disorder," said Dr. Thomas Mellman, director of the anxiety disorder and post-traumatic stress disorders program at the University of Miami. "Treatment can be several things. Sometimes it's a relatively straightforward debriefing.

For others, it's just the passage of time or supportive interaction with others. Those all can help. But like any other problem, the longer it's established the more difficult it is to intervene."

Exercise, cut out caffeine, and face the music. You can do several things to help reduce the chance of a panic attack. Doctors often recommend cutting back or cutting out caffeine and starting an exercise program. Also, try not to avoid situations that bring on panic attacks.

Learn relaxation techniques. Relaxation techniques similar to those taught in prepared childbirth classes are very helpful. They include muscle relaxation, controlled breathing and imagery, plus thinking thoughts like, "The feeling is uncomfortable, but it's not dangerous" and "I've had these feelings before and I know they will pass."

Think yourself out of a panic attack. Handle a panic attack with these four steps:

➤ Stay where you are. It may be tough, but try. It's very important to stay and face the situation.

➤ Breathe slowly and try to relax. Start at your head and work your way

down through each part of the body, tensing and relaxing muscles.
➤ Visualize a pleasant experience or place.
➤ Think to yourself that the feeling is uncomfortable, but it's not dangerous and it will pass.

_____
Dr. Cynthia Last, director, Anxiety Treatment Center at Nova Southeastern University, Davie, Fla.
Dr. Thomas Mellman, director of the anxiety disorders and post-traumatic stress disorders program at the University of Miami, Fla.

Poison Ivy and Poison Oak

Put the scratch on the itchy rash

If you don't know what poison ivy and poison oak look like, don't plan a long hike in the deep woods without first getting a little coaching on the subject. And beware, these plants can grow in urban areas as well, even in your backyard.

Poison Ivy

Both types of plants have three leaves on each stem. Poison ivy is the most common, and it has green leaves and white flowers in the spring. In the fall, its leaves turn red and it has yellow berries. Poison ivy is a shrub or vine that can either be trailing or free-standing. In the Western United States, poison oak can grow 15 feet or higher and look like a vine or a shrub. In the East, it is a low shrub. A related plant is poison sumac, which has smaller leaves but usually more than three on a stem. It grows mainly in Eastern wetlands.

Poison Oak

An oil called urushiol is what gets on your skin when you touch the poison plants. At first, you may just see red scratch marks. Generally, these appear in streaks or lines. It takes about nine to 14 days for the redness and itching to start, but you may see clear blisters within as few as four days.

You can spread the oil to your eyes and ears if you rub those areas immediately after touching the plants. Never been infected by poison ivy or oak? Don't assume that you are immune to them. You should still take all possible means of prevention.

Keep your skin under wraps. Wearing protective clothing in the woods is always a good idea. The less skin exposed, the better you'll be protected.

Wipe it down every 30 minutes. If you do come in contact with one of the plants, you can reduce your chances of a severe infection by washing the area immediately. Always carry premoistened towelettes in your hiking gear, and wipe your skin every half hour or so. Wiping can help remove the oil from your hands and exposed skin, but only if you do it within 10 minutes to a half hour after being exposed to the oil. If you take pets along, wipe them off too.

Poison Sumac

Load up the laundry. When you return home, don't throw the clothes you wore back in the closet or drawer. The oil can spread easily. Handle your clothes carefully and wash them immediately. Wipe off your hiking gear too.

Hands off! Once you see the scratch marks, it's too late to wash off the oil. At this point, scrubbing will only make things worse. Do your best not to scratch the itchy rash. That could cause additional infection. Expect to put up with the irritation for several days to three weeks. Generally, rashes from poison ivy or oak go away without leaving scars.

Find itch relief at your drugstore. Cool baths and washcloths can relieve itching, especially when combined with products you can get from your pharmacy. To relieve itching and protect your skin, look for products with these ingredients:

allantoin	petrolatum
aluminum hydroxide gel	shark liver oil
calamine	sodium bicarbonate
cocoa butter	white petrolatum
colloidal oatmeal	zinc acetate
dimethicone	zinc carbonate
glycerin	zinc oxide
kaolin	

When the pain and itching get serious, you may want to try anti-inflammatories or pain relievers, including local anesthetics and antihistamines. Look for:

benzocaine	camphor
lidocaine	camphorated metacresol
dydonine	menthol
benzyl alcohol	hydrocortisone
pramoxine	phenol
dibucaine	phenolate sodium
diphenhydramine	resorcinol
juniper tar	

Most of these products should not be used more than seven days. If you have a particularly severe case of poison ivy, you will need oral steroid medication prescribed by your doctor.

Get rid of the stuff. If you should find poison ivy in your yard, take care to cover your body completely and wear disposable gloves if you want to pull it up. Wrap it carefully in plastic and put it in the trash, and dispose of your gloves and clothes along with it. Never burn poison ivy. The oil can get in your lungs, as well as your neighbors', through the smoke. It may be best just to spray it with an herbicide on site.

Medical Update (18,2:4)
The Physician and Sportsmedicine (22,7:23)
U.S. Pharmacist (19,6:40,99)

Potbelly

Beat the potbelly blahs

If you're tired of people teasing you about your "Buddha" belly or asking when the baby's due and you're not even pregnant, take heart.

Here are five ways you can avoid the potbelly blahs.

Don't eat a lot of calories at once, especially in the evening. Too much food in your stomach puts pressure on your stomach muscles and pushes them out.

When you eat a lot and then go to bed, your abdominal muscles relax, making it easy for the food to exert pressure on your tummy muscles. Do this enough times and you're likely to be the not-so-proud owner of a perfect potbelly.

Suck it in. This advice is especially important for regular runners, who tend not to hold their stomachs in when they run, particularly when they get tired.

All the jiggling and bouncing that your stomach does when you run weakens your abdominal muscles. Consciously trying to hold your stomach in while you run will help it stay strong. Some runners also find that standing up straight instead of slightly slouching as they run makes holding in the stomach easier.

Don't forget to stretch your hamstrings (muscles on the backs of your thighs) after you run. Tight hamstrings can cause you to develop a slight swayback and make your potbelly all the more noticeable.

Try this easy hamstring stretch: Sit on the floor. Extend your left leg straight in front of you. Place your right foot against the inside of your left knee.

Place both hands on the lower front part of your left leg. Lean forward until you feel the muscles stretch in your left thigh. Hold for 30 seconds. Switch legs, then repeat the exercise.

Exercise your stomach muscles regularly. Stomach exercises improve posture and help prevent your stomach from sticking out.

Sit-ups and pelvic tilts provide great toning for the stomach. Sit-ups exercise the upper abdominals while the pelvic tilt tones the lower abs.

Sit-ups: Lie down on the floor with your arms folded across your chest. Bend your knees, keeping feet and back pressed to the floor.

Lift only your head and shoulders off the floor. Be careful not to raise all the way up. You won't do your abdominals any good, and you're likely to hurt your back. Repeat exercise 10 times.

Pelvic tilt

Pelvic tilt: Lie on your back with your knees bent and your hands at your sides. Put a folded towel under your head and a rolled up towel under your neck. Inhale. Press your back to the floor and pull in your stomach. Hold position for 10 to 20 seconds. Exhale. Slowly repeat exercise 10 times.

Keep your lower back strong to help hold your stomach in. The cat stretch and the pseudo swim are two easy exercises that will help keep your back strong.

Cat stretch: Get on your hands and knees on the floor. Keep your back straight. Arch your back. Hold for two seconds. Return to starting position and repeat exercise 10 times.

Pseudo swim: Lie face down on the floor. Place a plump pillow under your

Pseudo swim

stomach and hips. Raise your right arm and your left leg at the same time until you feel the muscles in your lower back and buttocks tighten. Hold two seconds. Repeat with your left arm and right leg. Do exercise 10 times.

Try to work at least 30 minutes of strength-training exercises like the ones described above into your routine three or four times a week. Push-ups and pull-ups are also good exercise choices.

And fear no more. With a few simple changes, you should easily be able to prevent your stomach from being the target of a lot of "pot" shots.

The Journal of the American Medical Association (273,6:503)
The Physician and Sportsmedicine (20,12:141; 21,2:177; and 21,3:187)

Premenstrual Syndrome

Breaking the PMS cycle

One of the moms at the dance studio told us that the calendar in her kitchen — the one where the whole family jots down their activities — has one week marked off in big, red letters that say "PMS."

"Everybody knows that's the week you leave Mommy alone," she said.

Long thought to be just in women's minds, doctors now understand what women have known for — well, forever. Premenstrual syndrome is real. Its symptoms are many, and its impact can be crippling. In fact, PMS has been used successfully as a legal defense in the United States, Canada, Great Britain and France, where it is recognized as a form of insanity.

The medical literature on menstrual disorders goes all the way back to Hippocrates. The term "hysteria" was used to describe menstrual dysfunction, thought to be due to the uterus wandering through a woman's body and causing trouble wherever it lodged.

In the figurative sense, that's not too far off base. Researchers have documented more than 150 symptoms, running from dizziness and migraines to forgetfulness and suicidal tendencies. It's been estimated that 70 to 90 percent of women of reproductive age have some symptoms associated with their periods, and 40 percent of them have true PMS to some degree. About one in 10 have symptoms severe enough to disrupt their normal routines.

On the brighter side, one researcher found that 66 percent of women reported at least one positive premenstrual symptom, such as more energy, increased creativity, a greater tendency to get things done, or a higher sex drive.

A disorder that affects both the body and the emotions, PMS can respond to a variety of treatments. Many women find a large measure of relief in education, emotional support and reassurance.

The knowledge that PMS is a disorder of their reproductive endocrine system, instead of a psychological problem, gives women a sense of control. Stress management classes and PMS support groups can be helpful. There's no cure for PMS, but it can be managed. Here are some suggestions to help control the symptoms:

Get plenty of sleep. PMS sufferers sometimes experience what's called an altered circadian rhythm, leading to insomnia and other sleep disturbances. Try to go to bed and get up at about the same time every day.

Exercise. Women who exercise regularly tend to have fewer PMS symptoms. Exercise also cuts down on fluid retention. Try adding 30 minutes a day to your workout the week before your period starts. (This should also help you get to sleep more easily.)

Watch what you eat and drink. Stick to a low-fat, low-salt diet, and stay away from caffeine, which is a stimulant and can increase tension, irritability and sleeplessness. Alcohol and recreational drugs can also make you more emotionally unstable.

Try a vitamin supplement with calcium, magnesium and vitamin B6. Doctors aren't sure why, but 1 mg of calcium a day has reportedly reduced both the physical and emotional symptoms of PMS, including depression, irritability, headache, mood swings, back pain and bloating. You can also drink an extra glass of milk if you don't want to take a calcium supplement. Magnesium and B6 have been shown to help with reducing water retention and fatigue, as well as the emotional symptoms.

Don't get married. Or plan any other major stressful event for the time of the month when your PMS symptoms are at their height. If there's one benefit of PMS, it's that you know when it's going to hit and can plan around it.

A Natural Alternative

Can magnesium help PMS?

Although a man can suffer the effects of premenstrual syndrome indirectly when the woman in his life has PMS symptoms, it takes a female to really understand how aggravating a bloated stomach, tender breasts and unexplainable mood swings can be.

Looking for help? Improving your nutrition — especially your intake of magnesium — could alleviate, or at least reduce, your monthly problems.

Some researchers have linked low levels of magnesium with premenstrual symptoms; others believe a magnesium deficiency, combined with a lack of B vitamins, zinc and linoleic acid (a natural substance found in many vegetable oils), leads to PMS.

How can magnesium calm PMS symptoms? Nutrition scientists haven't pinned down all the answers yet. But they do know the mineral interacts with the female hormone estrogen, as well as catecholamines — hormone-like substances that are linked to anxiety and a "flight or fight" response to stress.

A magnesium dose of 360 mg per day worked to improve the mood and reduce water retention in one group of women studied.

Relax. Deep breathing, yoga and visualization are all relaxation techniques. They're used frequently by people who experience panic attacks, spastic colons and other stress-related disorders, as well as by women in labor.

Select a quiet, private place for a time out, where you can calm yourself, and put on some soothing music. Breathe in slowly through your nose, hold your breath for a few seconds, and breathe out slowly through your mouth. Think of a relaxing place and picture it in your mind.

Educate the people in your life. Women with PMS do not suffer alone. The disorder has helped to ruin some people's personal lives and careers. In varying degrees, your family, friends and co-workers need to know what's happening. The mom who marks it on the calendar helps herself and her family.

American Family Physician (50,6:1309)

Prostate Cancer

Prostate cancer protection from the foods you eat

You don't have to rely on good luck to avoid prostate cancer. You can control a major risk factor — what you eat. Prostate cancer, like breast and colon cancers, is partly caused by eating too much fat and too little fiber. In fact, up to one-third of all cancer deaths each year are caused by poor dietary habits.

In countries where people eat a lot of meat and fats, there are many more cases of prostate cancer than in other countries. In a Harvard University study, men who ate beef, lamb and pork nearly every day suffered from the worst complications of prostate cancer 2 1/2 times more often than men who ate meat as little as once a month.

Here's what you can do to control your chances of getting prostate cancer. The basic rule is this: Fat promotes cancer; fiber protects against it.

Most days, try to eat only 15 percent of your daily calories in fat. If you are like most Americans, you may eat 37 percent of your diet in the form of fats. Some dietary fats are more dangerous than others. The most harmful fats are contained in meats, eggs, cheese, cream, hydrogenated vegetable oils, butter, mayonnaise, salad dressings and many baked goods.

Poultry fat, on the other hand, has not been linked to prostate cancer. Omega-3 fatty acids from fish oils seem to suppress tumor growth. To reduce the amount of fat you eat to 15 percent of your daily calories, you will need to read package labels and keep track of the grams of fat you consume.

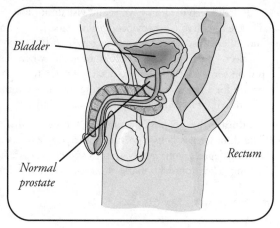

Bladder

Normal prostate

Rectum

The amount of fat you can eat depends on the daily calories you need to stay at a healthy weight. A gram of fat contains about 9 calories. This means that you can eat:

> 28 grams for a 1,700 calorie diet.
> 34 grams for a 2,000 calorie diet.
> 37 grams for a 2,200 calorie diet.
> 42 grams for a 2,500 calorie diet.

Be sure that your diet is rich in fiber. Enjoy whole-grain breads and at least five servings of fruits and vegetables every day.

High-fiber vegetables include broccoli, cabbage, brussels sprouts, and legumes such as dried beans, lentils, peas and lima beans. Eat fresh vegetables raw, steamed or microwaved. Boiling leaches away up to half the beneficial nutrients. Fresh and dried fruits, such as raisins and dates, are good sources of fiber. For maximum benefit, leave the skins on fresh fruits.

Eat less, if you are overweight. Obese men have up to 44 percent more deaths from cancer than men at their normal weights.

Feast on seafood, lean meats and rich grain products to ensure that you are eating enough selenium. Selenium is a powerful anti-cancer mineral. One of the best sources of selenium is Brazil nuts. You may want to eat three to six Brazil nuts a day to increase your body's selenium content. Brazil nuts are high in fat, though, so be careful. Large amounts of selenium are toxic. Don't overdo it on the nuts, especially if you are taking a multivitamin that contains selenium.

Add soy products to your diet. Soy products are a rich source of chemical agents that suppress tumor growth. Tofu, a soy product, is available in many supermarkets. It can be scrambled like eggs and used in many stir-fry recipes, in lasagna or chili. You can use soft tofu in salad dressings, dips and milkshakes.

You can make a half-and-half mixture of soy milk and regular milk for your

Understanding prostate cancer

Chances are, if you're a man, by the time you're 80 years old, you will develop the beginnings of prostate cancer. Prostate cancer develops in 40 percent of men over age 50 and up to 70 percent of men over 80.

But you certainly don't have to die from it. You can catch it early with the proper tests. Plus, a low-fat, high-fiber diet reduces the risk that microscopic prostate cancers will spread and become life-threatening.

The prostate is a walnut-sized gland located above the rectum, between the bladder and the penis. The prostate produces semen, the fluid that carries sperm. Since the prostate wraps around the tube that carries urine to the penis, it may block the flow of urine, causing pain and discomfort, if it becomes enlarged.

There are several causes of inflammation and swelling. Prostatitis occurs mainly in younger men and does not lead to cancer. In middle-aged and older men, the prostate may enlarge and require treatment to relieve discomfort. Some of the symptoms are like those for cancer.

Indications of cancer are difficulty urinating, pain or burning during urination or ejaculation, and blood in your urine or semen. By the time you notice the symptoms, the cancer may be too far along to be cured. Early diagnosis includes rectal examinations and use of ultrasound.

Diet, Nutrition, and Prostate Cancer, American Institute for Cancer Research, 1759 R Street, N.W., Washington, D.C. 20069
Pharmacy Times (59,12:29)
The Johns Hopkins White Papers, Prostate Disorders, The Johns Hopkins Medical Institutions, Baltimore, Md.

breakfast cereal, pudding, cream soups and sauces. Try adding miso (another soy food) to soup, or grill sliced tempeh and vegetables for a healthy soy meal.

Include foods that contain the antioxidant vitamins A, C, E and beta-carotene in your diet. Antioxidants sweep up unstable oxygen molecules, called free radicals, that promote cancer. Antioxidants can be harmful if they are taken as megasupplements, so get them by eating a variety of fresh foods.

Good sources of vitamin A are deep-green and yellow vegetables and fruits, including broccoli, winter squash, apricots, peaches and cantaloupe.

Citrus fruits are rich in vitamin C, including oranges, grapefruit, berries and melons. Vegetable sources include cabbage and cauliflower. Sources rich in both vitamins A and C are brussels sprouts, leafy greens, spinach, tomatoes, sweet green and red peppers, and sweet potatoes. Whole-grain cereals and dark-green vegetables contain vitamin E, as do wheat germ, nuts, vegetable oil and margarine.

Get out in the sun to stimulate production of vitamin D. Men who live in the cold northern latitudes are at greater risk of prostate cancer. They may not be soaking in enough sunlight, researchers say. Sunlight helps your body produce vitamin D, and vitamin D seems to slow prostate tumor growth. Studies show that men with prostate cancer often have low levels of vitamin D in their bodies.

Cut back on foods preserved with nitrites, such as some luncheon meats, as well as salty, pickled, smoked and barbecued foods. Charcoal grilling and smoking foods produces chemicals similar to those in cigarette smoke. The charcoal-grilled and smoked food absorbs these chemicals.

Don't expose yourself to cadmium. This means putting out your cigarette — forever. Cadmium also is found in chewing tobacco. Cadmium is an occupational hazard for welders, people who work in the manufacture of alkaline batteries, or people who work around electroplating. All these activities slightly increase your risk of prostate cancer. Cadmium from your diet is not linked with prostate cancer.

Finally, change your habits slowly, over time. Read package labels carefully and become aware of what you are eating. You don't have to be lucky to avoid prostate cancer, but you must make healthful eating a part of your everyday routines.

Diet, Nutrition, and Prostate Cancer, American Institute for Cancer Research, 1759 R Street, N.W., Washington, D.C. 20069
Medical Tribune (34,3:13)
Medical Tribune for the Family Physician (35,18:19)
Medical Tribune for the Internist and Cardiologist (34,22:8)
Nutrition and Cancer (22,1:1)
Nutrition Research Newsletter (12,11/12:117)
Pharmacy Times (59,12:29)
The Johns Hopkins Medical Letter: Health After 50 (4,3:4)
The Johns Hopkins White Papers, Prostate Disorders, The Johns Hopkins Medical Institutions, Baltimore, Md.

3 tests to save a man from cancer

Men, don't learn the importance of regular health checkups the hard way — after disaster strikes.

Have regular screening tests now for prostate cancer and testicular cancer. You may save a lot of pain, disability and heartache later.

Prostate Cancer. Prostate cancer, while it progresses, causes no symptoms and no pain. The cancer has spread to the lymph nodes and the bones by the time it's diagnosed in half the men who have it. At this point, it's incurable.

The tests you need to stop it in time:

A **digital rectal exam** every year for all men older than 50. The test may not be comfortable, but it's cheap and quick.

A **prostate specific antigen (PSA) test** every year for men 50 and up. Men in their 40s should also have a PSA test every year if they are at high risk of prostate cancer. Risk factors are a high-fat diet, a family history of prostate cancer, prior sexually transmitted disease, and occupational exposure to cadmium.

The PSA test has come under fire recently for not being sensitive enough. Up to now, any man with a PSA over 4.0 was supposedly at risk.

Some older men were being frightened by high PSA levels when they didn't actually have prostate cancer.

So the American Prostate Society came up with new guidelines for PSA values by age.

African American Men		Caucasian Men	
Age	Normal PSA	Age	Normal PSA
40-50	0 to 2.0	40-50	0 to 2.5
51-60	0 to 4.0	51-60	0 to 3.5
61-70	0 to 4.5	61-70	0 to 4.5
over 70	0 to 5.5	over 70	0 to 6.5

In the future, the PSA value may also be compared with another value called alpha-1-antichymotripsin or ACT. The PSA to ACT ratio may be able to tell doctors even more about a man's risk for prostate cancer.

According to researchers, this ratio needs to be studied further to see if it can be effective in helping to screen men for prostate cancer.

A Natural Alternative

Exercise sends prostate cancer running

You're wise if you're looking for ways to protect your prostate. Prostate cancer is all too common. You may think living a healthy lifestyle — eating nutritious meals and staying active — will head off heart disease, but your chances of getting cancer are up to your genes and your lucky stars.

But that's not completely true. Exercising regularly really can reduce your risk of prostate cancer. So can burning extra calories in your everyday activities, such as climbing stairs and walking.

A researcher at Harvard University looked at over 20,000 Harvard graduates and compared men who exercised with men who were inactive. Prostate cancer was extremely rare (only one case) in the 365 men who burned over 4,000 calories a week. There were 38 cases of prostate cancer in the 1,869 men who burned fewer than 1,000 calories a week.

You don't have to be a math whiz to figure out what the Harvard researchers concluded. The numbers indicate that if you're staying active, you're doing your prostate a favor.

American Journal of Epidemiology (135,2:169)

Testicular Cancer. More young men have this disease than any other. It's an easily curable cancer if you detect it early, but, like prostate cancer, it's diagnosed too late half the time.

Most women know the importance of regular self-exams to catch breast cancer early, but many men have never given a thought to self-exams for testicular cancer. All men older than 20 should give themselves a **testicular self-exam** once a month.

Testicular self-exam

➤ Make sure you are relaxed — lying in bed after a warm shower is best.

➤ Gently roll each testicle between your thumb, index and middle fingers.

➤ Cover the entire area, including the ropelike part called the epididymis.

➤ Feel for lumps, swelling and changes in size, shape or consistency.

A testicle that hasn't descended properly may be a risk factor for testicular cancer. If one testicle seems small or absent, have your doctor check it.

If you notice anything unusual during your monthly exam or have a dull ache in your groin and lower stomach area, make an appointment with your doctor.

Medical Tribune (36,1:16)
U.S. Pharmacist (19,7:38)
The Wellness Encyclopedia: The Comprehensive Family Resource for Safeguarding Health and Preventing Illness, Houghton Mifflin, Boston

---

Psoriasis

Relief for scaly, red skin

Off with the old. On with the new. Every day your body has to shed an incredible amount of old, dead surface skin tissue just to make room for new cells that are constantly pushing their way out from deeper skin layers.

It's a change most people don't even notice if their bodies are functioning normally — meaning the old cells drop off at the same rate as the new tissue arrives.

However, for some people, that balanced rate of skin replacement goes haywire. New cells develop much faster than the old are shed, And the result is itchy, red, scaly patches of thickened skin — the most common sign of psoriasis. An estimated 50 million people worldwide suffer with psoriasis. It attacks men and women of all ages equally, although it often starts during adolescence or in late middle age or older.

It can appear without warning, stay centralized in one area, or spread. And it can go into remission for no apparent reason. It just never totally goes away. At one time, few treatments brought relief from this incurable disease.

When the condition became very severe, people with psoriasis often stopped working and socializing, suffering both economic and emotional consequences.

But now, thanks to intense research and a better understanding of psoriasis, its victims have a variety of treatment options to help reduce the symptoms and sometimes put the disease in remission.

Get it diagnosed. Since there are other skin problems that may look like psoriasis, first get your condition diagnosed by a specialist. Psoriasis also comes in several forms, and you need to identify the type you have before starting treatment.

While the majority of psoriasis sufferers have plaque psoriasis, about 15 percent are diagnosed with arthritic psoriasis that attacks skeletal joints.

A possible genetic or immune system disorder may contribute to psoriasis. No one knows for sure. But researchers do know that common plaque psoriasis develops when the production of skin cells speeds up to almost seven times the normal rate and the shedding process can't keep up. Treatment focuses on removing the buildup of skin cells and slowing the rate of new skin growth.

Although psoriasis is triggered by internal, biological mechanisms, you can help prevent flare-ups.

Lay off the booze. Several studies reveal that alcohol triggers psoriasis flare-ups.

If you smoke, quit. Smoking may account for one-quarter of all cases of a certain type of psoriasis, one study suggests.

If you're overweight, try to lose a few pounds. Maintaining a normal weight should improve your psoriasis.

Get your skin in shape. Exercise is one of the greatest natural healers, even for psoriasis. Skin, like all the other body organs, will be healthier if you exercise and eat a healthy diet. Good nutrition and exercise habits will keep your immune system functioning well too.

Keep your skin moist and supple. Buy a humidifier for your home. Your skin won't get so dry if the air is moist. Stay away from harsh soaps; cleaners; and long, hot baths. A warm bath with an oatmeal bath product will help heal your skin. Water- or oil-based moisturizers will soften your skin and help control flaking and bleeding. Use moisturizers with alpha hydroxy skin exfoliants. Find a concentration that doesn't burn.

Ask your doctor about your medications. Some medicines, such as steroids, certain heart regulators, lithium and blood pressure medications, aggravate psoriasis.

Buy soft clothes. You don't want to chafe your skin with rough clothing.

Keep your hands off. Don't scratch or pick at affected areas.

Get over-the-counter relief. Two psoriasis healers you can buy without a prescription are topical corticosteroid creams and coal tar preparations. You can buy coal tar soaps, shampoos and ointments. Make sure you follow the manufacturer's directions carefully. You don't want to make your problem worse instead of better.

Try mineral baths. Some people believe in the healing powers of natural mineral waters, such as Soap Lake in Washington state and the Dead Sea between Israel and Jordan.

Have fun in the sun. Sunbathing may help, but be careful. You certainly don't want to burn your skin.

British Medical Journal (308,2:428)
Cutis (53,1:21)
Journal of the American Academy of Dermatologists (28,4:632)
Pharmacy News, National Psoriasis Foundation (5,1:8)
The Johns Hopkins Medical Letter: Health After 50 (5,11:6)
The New England Journal of Medicine (322,9:581 and 322,16:1449)

Raynaud's Syndrome

15 warming techniques for cold fingers and toes

When Jana Smiley bought a brand-new refrigerator to replace the ancient appliance she'd had for 20 years, her top priority was an ice dispenser.

You see, she has Raynaud's syndrome, and she'd spent a lifetime slipping on mittens to fill her glass with ice cubes or dump the cubes from their trays.

If you have Raynaud's (pronounced Ray-nose), you know the symptoms — your fingers (or toes, nose or ears) first turn white when exposed to the cold. That's when the blood supply is cut off. Then they turn blue and numb because they are starved for oxygen. Then finally they grow red and painful as the blood comes flowing back.

Cold isn't the only thing that brings on the symptoms; vibration can have the same painful effect. Mowing the lawn or typing a report can turn your fingers red, white and blue too.

You may be surprised to know that at least 5 percent of American adults, mostly women, have the condition. There's no cure for Raynaud's syndrome. The worst case scenario is amputation of fingers or toes because of ulcers or gangrene, but that's extremely rare. Most attacks can be warded off simply by keeping warm, especially your hands and feet.

Dress in layers. Wear woolen socks and mittens, plus a hat, when you go out. When it's chilly, keep your wrists and neck covered even indoors.

You may want to stay warm with chemical hand-warmers, available in most sporting goods or camping supply stores. Slip them in your pockets or shoes. Or try reflective insoles.

Take mittens or gloves to the supermarket. You can slip them on before reaching for a carton of milk or frozen vegetables.

Embark on a home cold patrol. Don't forget the simple remedies that can make your own home more comfortable for you.

➤ Keep a pot holder or oven mitt beside the refrigerator.
➤ Rinse food and dishes in lukewarm water instead of cold.
➤ Use stemware or insulated picnic tumblers. (Or, if you're away from home, put your glass in a foam rubber holder, or wrap several napkins around it.)
➤ Cover your cold metal doorknobs and keys with rubber caps.

Warm your engines. Start the engine and turn on the car heater for 10 minutes before driving in the cold. Cover the steering wheel with sheepskin or insulated leather. If the seat is plastic or leather, sit on a fabric cushion.

Pick your cold medicines carefully. You should avoid over-the-counter cold remedies and diet pills that contain the drug phenylpropanolamine.

Think your fingers warm. Some people have actually learned to raise their fingers' temperature just by concentrating on it. One reason this technique may work is that the act of concentrating itself can help you relax. Stress can trigger Raynaud's. Any relaxation technique you enjoy, such as deep breathing or imagining the sights and sounds of a deserted beach, may help you conquer the cold.

Condition yourself to the cold. You can help your body adapt to colder temperatures. Every other day, spend some time outdoors in cool weather or in a cool room. Try for 10 minutes at a time, several times a day. After three to four weeks of this treatment, you should have a more comfortable winter.

Don't smoke. Need another reason to quit? The nicotine in cigarettes is a big contributor to Raynaud's.

Prepare your resume! Since vibration can bring on attacks, the condition is common for typists, musicians, meat cutters and those who use vibrating tools such as jack hammers and chain saws. Normally, an attack won't end until the offending activity is stopped, so it could require retraining for a different job.

Mention it during your yearly checkup. Raynaud's can occur by itself, or as a symptom of another health problem. It's best to have it checked by your doctor to rule out such diseases as lupus, scleroderma and rheumatoid arthritis.

Nurse Practitioner (18,3:18)
The New York Times

Shingles

How to douse the flames when chickenpox virus strikes back

If you've suffered from chickenpox, you probably remember the fever and the intense itching, and a parent swabbing your body with calamine lotion. And do you remember someone telling you that you won't have to worry about chickenpox any more, since you can only catch it once?

While it's true that most people who have had chickenpox won't break out in that itchy rash again, the virus that causes chickenpox can lie dormant in your nerves for years until something triggers it to become active again. The result is far more serious than a little fever and itching. When the virus becomes active again, the illness is known as shingles. About one in five people who have had chickenpox will develop shingles. You're at risk if you're over 50 or if your immune system is down because of an illness, recent surgery or stress.

Watch out for signs of shingles. If you've had chickenpox, look out for these warning signs:

➤ A line of pain, itching or burning on one side of your body. Because the virus lives in nerves, the pain follows the line of a nerve. These symptoms may begin as much as two weeks before any blisters form.

➤ Small blisters rising in a line on one side of your body when you know you didn't burn yourself. The fluid in the blisters is usually clear for the first couple of days, then it turns cloudy. Eventually the blisters will crust over and heal, though pain may continue.

➤ Fever and fatigue.

Don't neglect this medical emergency. If you have the symptoms of shingles, you should see a doctor immediately. If not treated quickly, shingles can do permanent damage to your nerves and cause intense pain that may never go away. It can cause permanent scarring, and it may even damage your eyes.

The receptionist who schedules the doctor's appointments may have no idea that your blisters need immediate treatment. Don't let her put off your appointment for later in the week. Several prescription drugs can fight the virus that causes shingles, but you must start taking the drugs within 72 hours after the blisters form to get the best results. While shingles is not an illness you can care for with home remedies alone, you can relieve your pain while you wait for the antiviral drugs to run their course.

Mix crushed aspirin with body lotion for a pain-relieving cream. Crush one 325-milligram aspirin tablet and mix with two tablespoons of lotion, like Vaseline Intensive Care. Rub it on the affected area three or four times a day. The skin absorbs the aspirin quickly, so you won't have to wait long for relief. Applying the lotion may be quite painful, but the relief will be worth the wait.

Get pepper cream relief. You may feel like a fire is blazing on your skin, so the last thing you would want to do is rub chili peppers on the shingles.

But once the blisters have healed, a nonprescription cream called Zostrix may work wonders to relieve your pain. The active ingredient in this skin cream, capsaicin, comes from red chili peppers.

Capsaicin works by deadening nerves in the area you rub it on. It may cause a slight burning or tingling when you first use it. Many pharmacies keep Zostrix behind the counter, so you may have to ask for it. Make sure you see capsaicin in the list of ingredients. Don't be confused by drugs which have similar names, like capsicum or capsicum oleoresin.

Cool off with a compress. Compresses made of towels moistened with water can help relieve the pain.

Keep infection away with antibiotic cream. Rub-on antibiotic creams, available at your local pharmacy, can help prevent blisters from becoming infected.

Get some rest. You may want to stay in bed at first. Stretching skin that's blistered, even with the smallest movements, can cause intense pain.

Don't spread the virus. Keep in mind that if you have shingles, you can spread the virus to others and cause chickenpox. You should be especially careful around small children who have not had chickenpox.

The good news is that, like chickenpox, you should only get shingles once. And if you can keep your immune system strong with a healthy diet and exercise, you may never get shingles at all.

Emergency Medicine (21,3:35)
Medical Tribune (31,2:9)
Medical Tribune for the Family Physician (35,19:2)
U.S. Pharmacist (18,8:20)

Shinsplints

Keeping shinsplints at bay

Once you've made the decision to start exercising regularly, you don't need any barriers to stand in your way. You don't need your friends to encourage you to stay at home and chat, you don't need an impossible work schedule that leaves you no time for exercise, and you certainly don't need shinsplints.

Shinsplints can stop a successful exercise program in its tracks. The pain in the front of your lower leg can keep you from exercising, or even working, for several days, or longer if you don't treat it correctly.

Ease into exercise. You should never have a problem with shinsplints if you begin an exercise program slowly and carefully. Shinsplints are usually caused when you overuse and strain the muscles of your lower legs.

Be nice to yourself — don't do too much too soon. Even when your muscles are in good condition, you can overdo the exercise and end up with shinsplints.

Step out in style with shiny new shoes. Worn-out shoes are a common shinsplint culprit. Some people who run regularly believe the shock-absorbing power of running shoes wears out by about 300 miles.

Don't work out on hard surfaces. You should always do aerobics on a floor with a little give to it. Cement floors are too hard. And don't run on asphalt if you can avoid it.

Fix flat feet. Fallen arches can cause shinsplints. If you have flat feet, you may need shoe inserts to get your legs correctly balanced.

Never push through the pain. If you start to feel pain in your lower legs while you are exercising, stop! If you keep going, you'll probably make the injury worse.

For the next three days, ice the area for 15 minutes twice a day. If the pain doesn't go away, apply moist heat for the next week. A hot shower or bath, along with gentle massage for five to 10 minutes, can help ease shinsplints.

When the shinsplints go away, you can begin exercise again. Start with half the workout you were doing before the shinsplints. Work up to your normal level over the next week or so.

Be sure to apply ice to the injured shin after you exercise, at least until the 10th day after the injury. (If you still have pain after 10 days, you should see a doctor.)

Stretch and strengthen. Lack of flexibility causes many cases of shinsplints. Stretching should be a part of every workout.

Stretching and strengthening exercises will also help heal your injury once you have shinsplints. Begin the exercises the third day after the injury.

Calf muscle stretch.

➤ Lean against a wall with your arms outstretched at shoulder height.

➤ Place one foot forward, keeping your back leg straight with the heel down.

➤ Bend your front knee and push into the wall.

This should not cause pain, but you should feel tightness in the back of your calf. Hold the position for 10 seconds, then repeat with the other leg forward. Stretch each leg five to 10 times. Repeat two or three times a day.

Lower calf muscle and Achilles tendon stretch.

➤ Start in the same position as previous stretch (one foot forward).

➤ Bend both knees and keep your heels on the floor.

You should feel tightness in the sides of your calf, but this should not be painful. Hold the position for 10 seconds, then stretch with the other leg forward. Stretch each leg five to 10 times. Repeat two or three times a day.

Calf raises (for strength).

➤ Stand straight, holding onto something that will support you, like a table or chairback.

➤ Rise up on your toes for five seconds.

Repeat 10 times, two or three times a day. If you don't feel pain, work your way up to 30 calf raises at a time.

As an alternative, you may want to ride a stationary bike for five to 10 minutes a day. Set the tension at low to medium. Work your way up to 20 minutes a day. Or try running in a pool to strengthen your calves.

The Physician and Sportsmedicine (22,4:31)

Shoulder Pain

Shrugging off a sore shoulder

Tom Cox, a construction superintendent for Habitat for Humanity, traces his shoulder pain to the day he hoisted a heavy bundle of roofing shingles. He knew right away that he'd done something wrong, but he didn't give it much thought. That was two years ago. Now he feels a dull pain in his shoulder almost every day. "It feels like a knife in my shoulder," he says.

Cox's story is not unusual. The shoulder ranks right after the knee as the most common painful joint. Most people hurt their shoulders by using them more than they normally do, or they injure it like Tom Cox did, in one specific incident.

Whatever the cause of your shoulder pain, there are ways to ease it. First, remember the old joke, "Doctor, it hurts when I do this"? Well, you have to try to stop doing what hurts. You can't quit using or exercising your arm, but you don't want to do anything that is painful. You should also put ice packs on your shoulder for 20 minutes three or four times a day.

Finally, you need to do these stretching and strengthening exercises (only if they don't cause pain). Do the exercises twice a day. For the exercises without other instructions, start with three sets of 10 repetitions and work your way up to three sets of 20.

Draw circles in the air. While standing, lean over and look at the floor. Let the arm with the sore shoulder hang straight down. You may want to hold a pocketbook or other light object in your hand. Now let your arm swing in circles for about a minute. Start with small circles, and then swing in wider ones.

Stretch with a broomstick. Lie on your back and hold a broomstick in both hands. Use your uninjured arm to pull your injured arm through a complete range of motion. Continue for three to five minutes.

Pull your arm across your chest. Grasp the bent elbow of your sore arm with your other hand. Gently pull the sore arm by the elbow across your chest until you feel a stretch in your shoulder muscles. If it hurts, don't pull the arm so far across your chest. Hold for 10 seconds. Repeat three times.

Run your fingers up the wall. Stand near a wall and walk your fingers up and down the wall. When your shoulder starts hurting, don't go any higher and hold for 10 seconds. Repeat three times. You can do this both facing the wall and with your side toward the wall.

Give yourself a pat on the back. Reach one palm over your shoulder to pat your back and place the back of your other hand on your lower back. Slide your hands toward each other, trying to touch your fingertips. Hold for 10 seconds. Alternate arms.

Get ready for a soup-can workout. For these exercises, use either hand weights or a 15- or 16-ounce can of soup. If you do have weights, start with a low weight and increase the weight as you become comfortable. Don't use weights heavier than 5 pounds.

➤ Lie on your back with your elbows on the floor touching your sides. Put your hands in the air like you're holding a steering wheel. With a weight in your hand, lower your forearm to the side, then raise it.

➤ Lie on your side with your top elbow tucked into your waist. With a weight in your hand, lower your forearm across your stomach, then raise your forearm into the air. Keep your elbow at your side.

➤ Standing with your arms hanging loosely, lift your arm out to the side — 90 degrees from your body. Hold it there, then lift above your head (unless it hurts). Pause, then lower your arm. Next, turn your palms backward with your thumbs pointed down, and lift your arms to the side.

Build your strength with an exercise band and a handy doorknob. You will need an inexpensive 3-foot exercise band (about $3). Start by standing right next to the door and move away as you grow stronger.

Has your doctor told you ...

How to get a good night's rest with a dislocated shoulder

If you've dislocated your shoulder and have to wear an immobilizer to bed, chances are you're not getting a good night's sleep. And for good reason ... they're extremely uncomfortable to sleep in.

For the sake of a good night's sleep, many people risk another painful dislocation by removing their immobilizer. But an alternative may be hanging in your bedroom closet — your T-shirt.

A relatively tight T-shirt, worn with the injured arm folded against your body instead of through the sleeve, will prevent another dislocation that often occurs during sleep.

Emergency Medicine (26,2:79)

➤ Loop the exercise band around the doorknob of a closed door. Stand with your side to the door and hold the band as if you were going to open the door with it. Your arm should be at a 90-degree angle. Pull the band toward you, then all the way across your stomach.

➤ This time, hold the band with your other hand — the one that is farthest from the door. Again your arm should be at a 90-degree angle. Pull the band across your stomach, then swing your arm (elbow bent) out to the side.

➤ You don't need the doorknob for this exercise. Just put the exercise band under one foot. With your arm straight and your thumb pointed down, pull the band up and out in front of you until your arm is at shoulder level. Then lower and repeat.

American Family Physician (51,7:1677)

Sinusitis

Tricks to treating sinus problems

Hammers pounding anvils, a tightening noose, huge lightening bolts, a gripping vise — props like these fill the television-commercial studios when advertisers want to show the miseries of sinus trouble.

In addition to the *"Tension ... pressure ... pain!"* celebrated by pain-reliever advertisers, sinus congestion can have other unpleasant effects. Difficulty breathing through the nose can cause you to lose sleep, or at least to snore. Postnasal drip trickling down your throat can cause nausea. Worse, sinuses clogged for a long time seem to invite infection.

More than 31 million people in the United States suffer from sinus complaints, making over 16 million visits a year to their doctors. Many others resign themselves to daily discomfort. What can they do about it?

The sinuses that cause all this trouble are hollowed-out places in the bones around your nose. A layer of mucus lines the nose and the sinuses. The mucus filters the air we breathe, trapping smoke or other irritants before they can pollute the lungs.

However, the sinuses can't always handle the volume of mucus some people produce, particularly those susceptible to allergies. When excessive irritants or a common cold causes you to produce too much mucus, the sinuses can be overwhelmed. You feel growing pressure, pain and swelling in your face.

Has your doctor told you ...

The signs of a sinus infection

If you have two or more of the following symptoms, you may need antibiotics to cure infected sinuses.

➤ Pain and pressure in your face, especially over the sinuses.
➤ Stuffy nose.
➤ Pain in your upper teeth.
➤ Pain and pressure around your eyes.
➤ Creamy yellow or greenish colored discharge from your nose.
➤ Little relief from decongestants and antihistamines.

Postgraduate Medicine (91,5:281)

Overflow from the sinuses may cause sniffles, or it may clog the nose as solidly as an icy Hudson Bay in February. Some people don't produce too much mucus, but their sinuses can't handle the mucus flow because they aren't shaped properly. Other people have growths in their sinuses called polyps that get in the way of mucus flow.

Sinusitis can cause pain in other areas that share a common nerve. For example, pressure in a sinus beneath the eye might send throbs of pain down the cheek toward the mouth, producing a kind of toothache. The eyes may also feel irritated from pressure in a sinus.

Sinusitis may go away in time. Otherwise, at best it produces discomfort, at worst, serious medical consequences. If your sinusitis isn't too severe, you can treat yourself with some home remedies and over-the-counter medicines.

Drink lots of fluids. Drinking fluids will moisten and thin your mucus and help your sinuses drain.

Vaporize your air. Vaporizers will help your sinuses drain too. Try adding menthol or eucalyptus preparations to the water.

Chew horseradish root or slurp soups made with garlic. Any hot and spicy herb or food will help open your nasal passages.

Sleep with your head up. Put blocks under the head of your bed or use pillows to keep your head elevated. This will help keep mucus from draining back into your sinuses. You don't want the mucus to sit in your sinuses and become infected.

Find out what's triggering your allergies. Allergies may be at the root of your nasal and sinus inflammation, especially if you also have itchy eyes. You may be able to get rid of your sinusitis by getting your allergies under control. See the *Hay Fever* chapter for more information.

Get over-the-counter relief. You should be able to get relief from some type of over-the-counter drug. *Antihistamines* block the effect of histamines on your nose. The histamines in your body trigger allergic reactions. While antihistamines reduce itching and sneezing, they may not work well for swelling sinuses and a dripping or stuffy nose.

They may produce dry mouth, dizziness, drowsiness and other side effects.

Decongestants may be taken by mouth or as nasal sprays or drops. They reduce the swelling that clogs your airways.Nasal sprays or nose drops work quickly, can last up to 12 hours, and are quite safe to use for up to three days. If you use them for longer than three days, though, you risk a rebound effect harder to remedy than the original stuffiness.

Nervousness, irritability and insomnia are potential side effects. People with high blood pressure, heart disease, diabetes or hyperthyroidism should not use nasal decongestants without the advice of their doctors. The longer your sinusitis lasts, the less effective over-the-counter drugs become. You may develop a drug tolerance to the nasal decongestants and antihistamines. Simply switching products with different ingredients from time to time may work, but you may have chronic sinusitis that needs more aggressive treatments.

You may need antibiotics. Have you cancelled plans because of your sinusitis? Do you have to take naps or miss work regularly? Do over-the-counter drugs do little for you? Do you have frequent colds or stubborn earaches?

You may have a sinus infection that needs antibiotic treatment. Clogged nasal passages and filled sinuses become infected easily. Because of their closeness to such sensitive areas as the eye muscles and the brain, infected sinuses can have serious consequences. Antibiotics are used to kill the bacteria that cause infection. If antibiotic therapy fails, surgery may be necessary.

Know when you need surgery. Very few cases of sinusitis require surgical treatment. Yet when sinus trouble never ends, you may need surgery, not just to relieve discomfort but to protect against serious consequences. Polyps or cysts that hold mucus may grow in your sinuses, and they can be cancerous or simply grow too large.

One procedure called irrigation works by blasting encrusted matter out of the sinuses with a stream of warm salt water, the way you might clean the backyard grill with a garden hose. You can have surgery to reshape the sinuses and nasal passages to allow proper drainage.

A deviated septum (an off-center wall down the middle of the nose) may be straightened to allow proper air passage or pierced to create alternative airways.

Bloated tissue blocking passages can be removed. In some cases, sinus walls may be removed without harm.

Laser surgery is used to clear blocked sinuses when possible. In simple cases, you can have outpatient laser surgery. You don't even need bandages or wadding in the nose afterward.

Properly performed, sinus surgery has a very high success rate, freeing many people from daily miseries and allowing them to breathe properly for the first time in years.

With so many medical tools at hand, there seems no reason now for anyone to be resigned to a lifetime of sinus discomfort. Moreover, clogged sinuses invite infection that can become quite dangerous, so don't tolerate it too long. A lifetime of discomfort isn't inevitable if you take sinus trouble seriously.

FDA Consumer (26,8:20)

Skin Cancer

Tans are out of fashion

"Slip on a shirt. Slop on some sunscreen. Slap on a hat."

With skin cancer on the rise, you'd be well-advised to follow this sensible slogan Australians have adopted to check their skyrocketing skin cancer rate.

Even if you follow this advice, you should still think twice about how long you stay out in the sun. Each time you expose yourself unprotected to the sun, you raise your risk of developing skin cancer. A history of sunburns or even just one massive sunburn can increase your risk.

Winter sun can be just as damaging as summer sun. Ultraviolet A rays, which cause your skin to age, stay constant throughout the year. Ultraviolet B rays, which cause sunburn and tanning, are most intense during the summer. Both types cause cancer.

Baby your baby's skin. Protecting your children from the damaging effects of the sun is especially important. Use a sunscreen with a Sun Protection Factor (SPF) of at least 15.

Most pediatricians say you shouldn't worry about sunscreen for babies younger than six months because you shouldn't have them out in the sun long enough to need it. Babies this age have not completely developed their ability to sweat, so they can't cool down their own bodies. They can easily get heat exhaustion, which can develop into heatstroke and be fatal.

Also, babies are more likely to become sunburned because they have very little melanin, a skin pigment which absorbs ultraviolet rays.

Don't be fooled by sunscreens. Sunscreens can protect you. However, they may also lull you into a false sense of security. You seem to be suffering no ill effects from the sun, so you stay out longer.

That extra sun exposure, even with sunscreen protection, may put you at a greater risk for skin cancer, speculate researchers at the M.D. Anderson Cancer Center in Houston, Texas.

Steer clear of tanning beds. You may have heard that tanning beds are safer

A Natural Alternative

Secret weapon battles skin cancer

Think you're safe from skin cancer because you faithfully wear a hat and slop on sunscreen?

Not as safe as you could be.

Your latest defense against skin cancer seems to be the cure-all for everything that ails people these days — a low-fat diet. Researchers at the Baylor College of Medicine in Houston found that people who eat low-fat diets develop fewer solar keratoses, those scaly, reddish patches on the skin that often precede skin cancer.

Doctors looked at 76 people who had previously been diagnosed with skin cancer. Half of the people were told to remain on their usual diets, which, like the typical American diet, were about 40 percent fat. The other half were told to follow a diet of 20 percent fat or less.

At the end of the two-year study, the people following their usual diets had an average of 10 more precancerous skin growths, while the people following low-fat diets averaged only three new growths.

While studies linking low-fat diets to reduced risks of skin cancer are still in the early stages, many earlier studies have already found low-fat diets to protect against cancers of the breast, colon, ovary and prostate. So start your low-fat diet today. Protection against skin cancer is just another benefit added to an already long list.

And don't forget your hat and sunscreen!

Mayo Clinic Family Health Book, William Morrow and Company, New York
Medical Tribune for the Family Physician (35,10:3)
The New England Journal of Medicine (330,18:1272)

than sunbathing, but don't believe it. Visit a tanning bed 20 times a year for most of your life, and you'll double your risk of skin cancer.

You may also want to steer clear of tanning beds for cosmetic reasons. The beds give off mostly Ultraviolet A rays and a few Ultraviolet B rays. Exposure to too much Ultraviolet A can cause wrinkles, old-looking skin and an uneven tan. You may also develop freckles, blisters and have more fragile skin.

Some advertisers claim that tanning beds can bolster your immune system. Actually tanning beds depress your immunity and can even speed up the development of viruses.

Binge bathing, or recreational tanning, is the most damaging type of sun exposure. Dermatologists warn that "there is no such thing as a safe tan."

If you want to save your skin and maybe even your life, remember that "pale is in, tan is out."

AAP News (9,11:2)
British Medical Journal (6918,307:1508)
Medical World News (33,2:19)
The Wall Street Journal

Choosing a sunscreen

Here are a few tips to help you choose a sunscreen to shield you from the sun's harmful rays:

➤ Look for a sunscreen labeled "broad spectrum," which means that it protects against both Ultraviolet A (UVA) and Ultraviolet B (UVB) rays. Sometimes a sunscreen may simply say "protects against UVA and UVB."

➤ Check the Sun Protection Factor (SPF) number on the label. The higher the number, the greater the protection the sunscreen offers against burns. The lighter your skin and the longer you plan to be in the sun, the more protection you need.

➤ Look for a sunscreen that provides protection when you perspire or swim. Water-resistant sunscreens provide in-the-water protection for as long as 40 minutes of swimming. Waterproof sunscreens provide in-the-water

Soothing a sunburn

Mix a 3 ounce bottle of Mennen's Afta aftershave with a 1 ounce tube of .5 percent hydrocortisone cream. Apply to sunburned areas. Repeat after 30 minutes. Treatment is very effective and will also prevent blistering.

Aspirin and soaking in a tub of cool water can ease the pain too.

British Medical Journal (309,6954:587)
The Physician and Sportsmedicine (21,3:30)

protection for as long as 80 minutes.

➤ Sunscreens that contain PABA or PABA derivatives often provide the most long-lasting protection. You should put these on when your skin is wet. They become most effective one hour after application.

➤ Since the lower lip is a common site for skin cancer, you may want to pick up some lip balm that contains sunscreen. A lip balm with sunscreen can also protect against cold sores, which may be triggered by ultraviolet radiation.

_____
Cutis (50,3:190)

Skin self-exam

When performing a skin exam, don't forget to check the palms of your hands, the soles of your feet and your scalp. Always be alert for:

✔ Any change in a mole's appearance.

✔ Any sore that doesn't heal.

✔ Any rough, pinkish-gray bumps.

✔ A mole or bump that is scaly, lumpy, crusty, oozing or bleeding.

✔ Pain, itchiness, tenderness or changes in sensation in a mole or growth.

✔ Swelling, redness or spread of color into the skin near a mole or growth.

✔ Raising of part of mole that used to be flat.

Men at high risk

A construction worker who's shed his hot shirt, a farmer with ears burnt permanently red, a golfer with scaly, pink arms — many men have jobs and hobbies that put them at high risk for skin cancer.

Caring for your skin is not a sign of unmanly vanity. About 8,500 Americans will die of skin cancer this year. Men who work outdoors, especially fair-skinned ones, must protect themselves by wearing a sunscreen of at least 15 SPF every day. If you've had many tans and sunburns in the past, you should have your skin examined by a doctor once a year. Nearly all skin cancers can be cured if found early enough. Most precancerous growths can be removed right in the doctor's office. Also, do a quick and easy skin exam at home every month.

If you notice anything unusual, see your doctor immediately.

_____
Reducing Your Risk of Skin Cancer, American Institute for Cancer Research, 1759 R Street, N.W., Washington, D.C. 20069

Smell and Taste Loss

Rediscover tasty meals and fragrant roses

Your senses of smell and taste are closely connected. When your sense of smell isn't up to par, chances are, your sense of taste isn't either. Here are a few ways to get your nose and your taste buds back in working order.

Don't get hooked on nose sprays or drops. Not only can allergies, a cold, the flu or a chronic sinus infection interfere with your sense of smell, but so can the sprays or drops you use to relieve your stuffy nose. Never use nasal sprays or drops for more than three days in a row. You'll get rebound congestion, and you won't be able to get relief except by using more of the medicine. Your sense of smell will probably suffer.

Sniff out cigarette smoke and avoid it. Exposure to cigarette smoke can dull your smelling sense.

Boost your smelling power with a multivitamin. Sometimes a vitamin or mineral deficiency can affect your sense of smell. You may want to try taking a multivitamin for a while to see if your sense of smell improves. Make sure the multivitamin includes zinc, a mineral closely connected with your sense of smell.

Get a whiff of spicy cooking. As you age, you will lose some of your smell and taste abilities. If your loss of smell is due to aging, you can perk up your sense of smell and turn up your taste buds by adding extra seasonings to your food. Good choices include:

➤ allspice	➤ oregano
➤ basil	➤ paprika
➤ cinnamon	➤ pepper (black and red)
➤ dill	➤ soy sauce
➤ fennel	➤ thyme
➤ garlic	➤ vanilla extract
➤ ginger	➤ vinegar
➤ lemon	➤ Worcestershire sauce
➤ onion	

See your doctor if your loss of sense of smell persists for longer than two weeks. A malfunctioning nose sometimes signals a more serious disorder.

Before You Call the Doctor, Random House, New York
Cecil Textbook of Medicine, Harcourt Brace Jovanovich, Philadelphia

Snakebites

What you should know about snakebites

Snakebite! A movie scene from the old westerns flashes through your mind. Your partner pulls out his Bowie knife, cuts the wound and sucks out the venom. Then he pours whiskey on the wound and gives you a swig. Right? ... No! ... This Hollywood scene actually portrays all the wrong things to do if you are bitten by a poisonous snake. Here's what you need to know about snakes:

Don't get bitten in the first place. Snakebite season falls between April and October when snakes are most active. Stay away from areas that have tall grass and weeds. Keep hedges trimmed and brush cleared.

Avoid weedy vacant lots. When you must travel through these areas poke the grass ahead of you with a long walking stick to scare any snakes. Be careful when working around firewood and brush piles. Protect yourself by wearing loose, long pants, high boots and work gloves.

Learn which snakes are venomous villains. Even if you don't get a chance to stare a snake between the eyes before you're bitten, you'll need to check him out after you're bitten to see if he's poisonous. Two families of poisonous snakes are native to the United States: the pit vipers (cottonmouths, copperheads and rattlesnakes) and the coral snakes. Look for these features: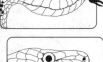

Slit-like pupil. The pit vipers have a slit-like pupil in their eyes, like cats.

Nonpoisonous snakes have round pupils, like people.

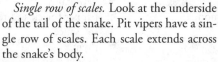

Single row of scales. Look at the underside of the tail of the snake. Pit vipers have a single row of scales. Each scale extends across the snake's body.

Nonpoisonous snakes have a double row of scales — each scale extends only halfway across the tail.

Rattles. Most, but not all, rattlesnakes have rattles.

Yellow, red and black bands. The poisonous coral snakes are small with black faces and bands of yellow, red and black circling their bodies.

Know the signs of poisoning. A bite from a poisonous snake doesn't necessarily mean you're poisoned. Snakes don't release venom every time they bite.

Has your doctor told you ...

What not to do for a snakebite

It's important to know what not to do when bitten by a snake.

➤ You should never cut the wound or try to suck the venom out of the bite.

➤ You should not give anything to eat or drink, especially alcohol, to a snakebite victim. Alcohol increases blood flow and will speed the spread of venom.

➤ Do not put ice on the bite.

American Family Physician (50,1:123)

The reaction to pit viper venom is unmistakable. You will feel severe pain and burning at the bite, and it may redden, swell and even bleed. You may then experience nausea, bleeding, itchy eyes, drooping eyelids, drowsiness, muscle weakness, shakes and a metallic taste in your mouth. The more venom you receive, the stronger your symptoms will be. The only symptom you are likely to feel immediately after a coral snake's bite is a mild burning sensation at the bite itself.

Reaction to the venom will only be noticeable several hours after the bite. The symptoms include nausea, weakness, double vision, tearing, sensitivity to light and muscle paralysis. Poisonous snakebites are especially dangerous to children. Because they are small, children are more sensitive to venom.

Tie a band above the bite. If you are bitten by a poisonous snake, it's important that you stay calm, lie still and keep the bite below heart level to slow the spread of venom. If the bite is on an arm or leg, use a splint to keep the limb still. If it's going to be more than an hour before you can get to a medical center, you may carefully use a constriction band to help reduce blood flow from the bite and slow the spread of venom. You have to get the band in place within five minutes for it to help.

Place the band several inches away from the bite and towards the heart. Be sure that the band is not too tight. Always keep the band loose enough so that you can easily slip a little finger under it. Every 10 minutes, loosen the band slightly so that blood is not cut off completely and to adjust for any swelling. Once you apply the band, do not remove it completely until you are in the emergency room.

Treat all snakebites as a medical emergency. You should go to the nearest hospital immediately after a bite. You may need treatment with antivenin.

Snoring

How to fight snoring

Before you give up the fight against snoring, make sure you've taken the following steps:

Lose weight. Carrying extra pounds causes soft tissue to accumulate in your throat. The tissue blocks your air passages and leads to snoring.

Avoid alcohol and tranquilizers. Anything that works as a sedative, like alcohol or even most antihistamines, causes your tissues to relax and can contribute to snoring.

Stop smoking. Smokers tend to snore.

Don't sleep on your back. To prompt you to roll over on your side or stomach, sew a tennis ball into the back of your pajama top.

Prop up the head of your bed. You may be able to breathe a little easier with your head elevated. Propping up the whole upper part of your bed works better than adding extra pillows. Pillows can cause you to bend your neck, which closes the airways more and makes snoring worse.

British Medical Journal (300,6739:1557)
Emergency Medicine (24,6:83)
FDA Consumer (26,5:33)

Put a 'Band-Aid' on your nose

If you snore because your nose is stuffy or obstructed, you may get some relief from the new "nose springs" you can find at the drugstore.

The small adhesive strips work like a spring to pull your nostrils open a bit.

The springy strips give you more room in your nasal airways and make breathing through your nose a little easier. That could help you close your mouth at night and possibly prevent your snores.

Breathe Right package insert

Sore Throat

Betony soothes sore throat

Used by Caesar Augustus' personal physician to treat no less than 47 different ailments, the herb betony has a long and illustrious history. A perennial with pink or purplish flowers, betony grows up to three feet tall and would be a beautiful border herb in your own home herb garden. However, you can also buy betony in health food stores as dried leaves or a liquid extract.

Betony

Soothe with a natural astringent. Betony contains about 15 percent tannin, which is an astringent. Tannin contracts body tissue and blood vessels, checking the flow of blood and causing blood vessels to shrink. It is this astringent quality which soothes irritations of the throat, mouth and gums.

Make an herb tea. To soothe a sore throat or mouth, place two heaping teaspoons of dried betony or eight to 12 drops of betony extract into a cup and add boiling water. If you use the dried herb to prepare your tea, you must strain it before drinking. You can either drink the tea or let it cool and use as a gargle. Don't drink more than three cups of betony tea a day because you may irritate your stomach.

Treat your aching head and get some rest. In earlier times, betony was widely used to treat insomnia, nervous headaches and migraines. Even betony's name reflects its reputation for relieving headaches. The Celtic word for betony, Betonic, which comes from *ben* meaning head and *ton* meaning good, refers to the centuries old practice of using betony to treat headaches.

In fact, early medical texts describe the ability of betony to relieve headaches as miraculous. While scientists have not previously been able to understand how betony could ease headaches, a recent Russian study found that betony contains glycosides that appear to lower blood pressure. These glycosides may explain betony's supposed effectiveness in treating headaches and insomnia.

While you've got no guarantee that betony will cure your insomnia or halt your headaches, it will soothe a scratchy throat. So the next time you're suffering from a sore throat, seek relief and comfort in a steaming hot cup of betony tea before bed. You may even sleep better.

Miracle Medicine Herbs, Parker Publishing, W. Nyack, N.Y.
The Honest Herbal, The Haworth Press, Binghamton, N.Y.

Stomach Cancer

Hot peppers may damage your belly

Attention, all people who like their meals hot and spicy: Now there's another reason besides heartburn for those chili peppers in your favorite Mexican dishes to keep you up at night. Chili peppers may cause stomach cancer, Mexican researchers claim. You knew the peppers felt as if they were eating away at your stomach lining, but you didn't know they really could be damaging it.

Don't get burned, researchers warn. When animal studies indicated that chili peppers might cause cancer, scientists headed for Mexico City to find out if it was true for humans too. After all, Mexicans eat an average of one chili pepper a day. The scientists knew that about 10 percent of all cancer deaths in Mexico were stomach cancer deaths. They didn't know whether there was any link between eating hot peppers every day and stomach cancer. The scientists surveyed hundreds of people with and without stomach cancer and asked whether or not they ate chili peppers or chili sauces with their meals.

They concluded that the people who said they ate the most chili peppers had a 17-fold greater risk of stomach cancer compared with people who said they didn't eat chili peppers. The people who enjoyed the feeling of "getting burned" by the spicy peppers were more likely to get stomach cancer too.

A Natural Alternative

Garlic protects the stomach

Some good-tasting foods are actually good for you! Garlic is a basic ingredient in some of our favorite dishes and is an important medicinal herb.

Large-scale studies conducted in China and Italy revealed that people who eat large amounts of garlic or other members of the garlic family, such as onions, chives, leeks and shallots, have a reduced risk of stomach cancer. Garlic may also provide protection against cancers of the colon, breast, skin and bladder. The herb seems to work by stimulating the immune system and keeping cancer cells from growing.It doesn't matter whether you eat the garlic or take it in tablet form; both will give about the same amount of protection.

Food, Nutrition and Health (18,7:5)

All in all, 76 percent of stomach cancer cases in Mexico City can be attributed to eating chili peppers, the scientists said.

Rub it on, but don't eat it. The ingredient in chili peppers that may cause cancer is capsaicin. Capsaicin is also the ingredient that makes the chili peppers hot. The word may be familiar to you. In a cream form, capsaicin works wonders to relieve arthritis pain, the itching of psoriasis (a common skin disorder), and pain from shingles and diabetic neuropathy. Capsaicin seems to be safe and effective as a cream to rub on your skin, but some alternative-medicine doctors are even recommending that you take cayenne pepper capsules. They say the capsules will prevent heart disease, give you energy and keep you alert.

Beware of cayenne capsules. Until scientists learn more about the possible chili pepper-stomach cancer link, taking cayenne capsules is not a good idea.

You should probably even cut back on the amount of chili peppers you eat if Mexican fare is a daily habit for you.

Don't feel that you have to give up chili peppers altogether. The Mexico City study was done in the "real world" instead of a laboratory, so it's far from error-free. Even though animal studies seem to show a link between capsaicin and cancer, more human scientific studies need to be done before we condemn chili peppers as cancer causers.

American Journal of Epidemiology (139,3:263)
U.S. Pharmacist (18,8:20)

How to lower your stomach cancer risk

Fortunately for our neighbors to the south, Mexicans have a relatively low rate of stomach cancer even though they eat large amounts of chili peppers. Why?

Probably because they have so many healthy dietary habits. They tend to avoid many stomach cancer risk factors. They don't eat many processed meats or salted, smoked and pickled foods, and they eat plenty of fruits, vegetables and beans. A diet that combines a lack of important nutrients with too many irritants, such as salt, predisposes you to stomach cancer.

To lower your risk of stomach cancer, follow these healthy habits:

Eat hearty helpings of fruits, vegetables, and fiber-rich breads and cereals. Raw tomatoes work especially well to prevent stomach cancer, a large Italian study has shown.

Avoid salty and pickled foods. Some of the worst offenders are processed and smoked meats and dried, salted and smoked fish.

Stay away from alcohol. Or drink it in moderation only. Alcohol is hard on your stomach.

Don't smoke cigarettes. As you already know, smoking increases your risk of

A Natural Alternative

Another stomach-friendly spice

If you're a big fan of hot curried dishes, here's another good reason to stop by your favorite Indian restaurant once in a while. Turmeric, the herb that gives curry powder its yellow tint, may help fight cancer.

In recent studies, turmeric was shown to stop the growth of certain types of stomach and skin tumors caused by common chemicals found in smog. Diets containing 2 percent turmeric and 5 percent turmeric both were shown to be effective against stomach and skin tumors in mice. An ingredient in turmeric, called curcumin, is the compound that suppressed the tumors, scientists say.

Newer studies indicate that turmeric's disease-fighting properties stem from its ability to destroy bacteria. In one laboratory study, very low concentrations of curcumin destroyed bacteria, such as *Salmonella*, within 15 minutes when light and oxygen were present.

In fighting cancer, turmeric appears to act in the same way as antioxidant vitamins, such as vitamins C and E. The curcumin soaks up damaging free radicals, those cancer-causing elements that are produced in the body by various chemicals. It appears that the curcumin in turmeric works even faster than antioxidant vitamins in attacking free radicals. So the next time you're in the mood for curried chicken or vegetables, go ahead and indulge!

Journal of the American College of Nutrition (12,2:203)
Medical Tribune for the Family Physician (35,7:12)

all kinds of cancer.

Get rid of troublesome bacteria. If you're troubled with ulcers or stomach problems, ask your doctor to check you for an infection caused by the *Helicobacter pylori* bacteria. About one of every three Americans is infected with *H. pylori,* and the infection may put you at risk for stomach cancer. It can be treated with antibiotics and Pepto-Bismol.

American Journal of Epidemiology (139,3:263 and 139,5:466)
Nutrition Research Newsletter (13,11/12:127)

Stomach Upsets

Bran gets the boot for irritable bowel syndrome

If you've had to deal with a case of irritable bowel syndrome (IBS), also known as spastic colon, you've probably followed the advice of doctors and nutritionists who told you to include plenty of bran in your diet.

And like most people who followed that recommendation, you've probably also had to deal with a new set of problems: painful stomach cramps and a more irritated bowel than ever. If you've been wondering whether boosting your intake of dietary fiber was worth it, you're not alone. New research shows that it's time to rethink the use of bran to treat IBS.

Don't eat bran for IBS. A study of 100 people with IBS by researchers at England's University Hospital of South Manchester confirms what many IBS sufferers have known for a long time. Eating more bran makes IBS worse, not better. Fifty-five of those involved in the study reported that increased bran in their diets made them feel worse, while only 10 said they found it helpful for their condition. And researchers said their study points to the likelihood that too much bran in the diet may actually worsen some people's mild cases of IBS, creating full-fledged spastic colon conditions.

Stick with fresh fruits and veggies. The good news is that the study uncovered evidence that other kinds of dietary fiber produce better results with far less chance of abdominal pain and bowel disturbance. Researchers said that people with IBS should stick with other forms of dietary fiber, such as fresh fruits and vegetables. However, the study also specifically identified citrus fruits as having the same results as bran and suggested avoiding citrus in favor of other fiber sources.

Get sold on psyllium. Researchers also said they were told by some study participants that psyllium, found in many fiber supplements (such as Metamucil), produced good results for them. Experiment to see if psyllium works for you.

The study did note that bran can benefit those whose IBS is linked to constipation. But it strongly urged people with chronic, long-term IBS to avoid bran as a frequent part of their diet.

American Family Physician (50,5:1072)
Journal Watch (14,3:20)
The Atlanta Journal/Constitution
The Lancet (344,8914:3,39)

Chamomile — cure for upset tummies

Named herb of the year by Germany in 1987, chamomile lays powerful claims to cure-all of the century.

Actually, chamomile's claim to fame goes back much further than this century. The Egyptians worshipped chamomile above all other herbs for its healing properties, and the Greeks used it to treat fevers and menstrual cramps.

Today, we use this versatile herb to relieve a number of disorders, including stomach upsets. Chamomile works to stop stomach cramps and put the brakes on intestinal gas. If you have an upset stomach, drink a cup of chamomile tea between meals and before going to bed.

Don't worry — German or Roman will do. The most common form of chamomile sold in the United States is German chamomile (*Matricaria chamomilla*). Rarely, you may see Roman or English chamomile (*Anthemis nobilis*). Although the healing abilities of German chamomile have been the most tested, Roman chamomile contains similar, though not necessarily identical, active ingredients. The FDA considers both German and Roman chamomile safe for human consumption.

Buy whole flower heads. When buying chamomile, your best bet is to purchase whole flower heads. Avoid products that have lots of stems mixed in with the heads. You may also want to avoid powdered chamomile because the quality is difficult even for experts to determine.

In addition, be wary of chamomile oils. Only buy these oils from companies that have excellent reputations for quality products. In 1987, three-quarters of the commercial chamomile oil products were diluted with other compounds.

Grow your own sweet-smelling herb. If you prefer to grow your own, chamomile will make a sweet-smelling addition to your herb garden. Select a sunny area with well-drained soil. Sow the herb in spring. Plant German chamomile 9 inches apart; plant Roman chamomile 6 inches apart. Divide in either spring or fall. Pick flowers that are fully open. The yellow center of the flower contains the active ingredients.

Think twice if you have allergies. If you're allergic to ragweed, asters or chrysanthemums, you're more likely to be allergic to chamomile and may want to think twice about using it. People who are allergic to chamomile may experience itching, develop a skin rash or, in rare cases, have severe breathing problems.

However, very few people are allergic to the herb. Between 1887 and 1992, only 50 allergic reactions to chamomile were reported worldwide.

Only five of those reactions were to German chamomile, the herb most commonly used in the United States. Generally, chamomile is a safe and easy way to relieve what ails you.

Two more precautions: Don't use chamomile at the same time that you're taking prescription drugs because chamomile can interfere with the absorption of some medicines.

And don't overdo it — large quantities of chamomile can cause vomiting.

———
Herbs, The Reader's Digest Association, Pleasantville, N.Y.
Herbs of Choice: The Therapeutic Use of Phytomedicinals, The Haworth Press, Binghamton, N.Y.
Herbal Medicine, Beaconsfield Publishers, Beaconsfield, England
The Honest Herbal, The Haworth Press, Binghamton, N.Y.
The Lawrence Review of Natural Products, Facts and Comparisons, St. Louis, Mo.

Stress

How to relax

Steel will snap from it. A pressure cooker will blow its lid. But stress, pressure, tension is a fact of everyday life for most of us. It puts us at increased risk for heart attack, stroke, insomnia, backache, headache, irritable bowel syndrome, sports injuries and infertility. Stress can trigger such serious ailments as Graves disease and fibromyalgia. Stress even makes us more susceptible to the common cold.

With your health at stake, relieving stress is essential. There are many practical steps you can take to get rid of stress — and most of them won't cost you a dime.

First, what is stress? Medical researchers say stress is a physiological response to situations, most of which are beyond our control to change. The "flight-or-fight" mechanism works overtime, pumping body chemicals into the bloodstream that we need to rev our system when we're running for our lives. Nowadays, when the need to run for our lives is rare, these substances can have harmful effects when triggered because our lives are simply running us.

It's important to remember that stress is a physiological response. It is not all in your head. You owe it to yourself to take the time to use stress-reducing techniques on a daily basis. Pick several techniques so that you have a wide range of coping skills to use at home, work and other places.

Our 12 keys to stress reduction open the door to a more relaxing life. They contain dozens of helpful hints. Choose those best suited for you.

Breathe deeply. Relax your muscles, expanding your stomach and chest. Exhale slowly. Repeat several times.

➤ Follow your breath as it flows in and out. Do not try to control it. This is a good way to relax in the midst of any activity. This technique allows you to find a breathing pattern that is natural and relaxing to you.

➤ Use this yoga technique: Inhale slowing, counting to eight. Exhale through your mouth, even more slowly, counting to sixteen. Make a sighing sound as you exhale, and feel tension dissolve. Repeat 10 times.

Exercise regularly. Aerobic exercise, such as walking and swimming, produces brain chemicals that uplift your mood and mental well-being. Exercise also improves sleep and gives you time to think and focus on other things. Beware of compulsive exercise, however.

➤ Yoga is an age-old system for stretching and strengthening the muscles. Take a class or learn at home with a good book or video.

➤ Neck and shoulder exercises are useful for the desk-bound and arthritis sufferers.

Neck roll: Look to the right, then roll your head forward, as if you're trying to touch your chin to your chest. Keep rolling until you're looking over your left shoulder. Repeat in the other direction.

Shoulder lift: Relieve tension in the neck by lifting the shoulders toward the ears, then dropping them as low as they will go. Repeat 10 times.

Eat healthy foods. You should never skip meals. Take time out for lunch no matter how busy you are.

➤ Carry nutritious snacks to the office, or even the shopping mall. A nutritionally balanced diet is important. For example, researchers have found that even small deficiencies of thiamin, a B-complex vitamin, can cause anxiety symptoms. Pantothenic acid, another B-complex vitamin, is critical during times of stress.

➤ Avoid caffeine, alcohol, and large amounts of sweets, which can aggravate symptoms of stress.

Don't let others get you down. Choose positive friends who are not worriers. Friends who constantly put you down or talk gloomily about life will increase your anxiety.

➤ Ask a good friend to help you talk out a problem and get it off your chest. A long-distance call to an old pal can be great therapy.

➤ Forgive others instead of holding grudges. Relax your standards — for yourself and others. Perfectionism is not the way to happiness. Become more flexible.

➤ Communicate clearly with your co-workers and boss. Ask questions. Repeat instructions that you are given. Clarifying directions at the start of a project can save hours later straightening out misunderstandings.

➤ Be truthful with others. Lies and deception lead to stress that always takes its toll.

Be optimistic. Count your blessings, especially when everything seems to go wrong. Believe that most people are doing the best that they can.

➤ Don't blow problems out of proportion. Live by a philosophy of life that whittles problems down to size. The maxim, "Live one day at a time," has helped millions.

Plan your time wisely. And realistically. For example, don't schedule back-to-back meetings with tight travel time. Remember to leave room for unanticipated events — both negative and positive. Be flexible about rearranging your agenda.

➤ Get up 15 minutes early in the morning. Allow an extra 15 minutes to get to all appointments.

➤ Avoid procrastination. Whatever needs doing, do it now. Schedule unpleasant tasks early so that you won't have to worry about them for the rest of the day.

➤ Keep an appointment book. Don't rely on your memory.

➤ Do one thing at a time. Focus your attention on the person talking to you or the job at hand, instead of worrying about other things. This also

What's causing your stress?

A stressful day for one person may be a walk in the park for another. What sets you off?

➤ **A slow buildup of everyday annoyances**: a dead car battery, traffic jam, buttons that pop off your clothes as you are going to an important meeting. It's the little things that get under some people's skin.

➤ **A tight schedule and seemingly insurmountable problems**: bills to pay, a boss to please, a colicky baby to pacify. Juggling many roles is a main cause of stress.

➤ **Positive and negative life changes**, from the joy of a wedding to the loss of a spouse; from the exhilaration of a job promotion to sadness at moving away from old friends.

➤ **Inner conflict.** Anger with your boss actually may be old anger against a parent bubbling to the surface. If you can recognize a pattern from the past, this can be an instant stress reliever. Take time, even just 30 seconds, and write down your feelings.

44 Easy Ways to Relieve Stress, Arborvitae Publications, Ann Arbor, Mich.

reduces mistakes — which lead to more anxiety.

➤ Be prepared to wait. Carry a book to read in case of delays.

➤ Say "no" to requests that stretch you to the limits.

➤ Delegate. You don't have to do it all yourself. Break a job into separate tasks, and assign them to people with the appropriate skills. Then leave them alone to do their work.

Prevent problems before they occur. This takes some planning.

➤ If you're flying to another city for an important meeting, carry your presentation materials and dress suit on board the plane. Baggage does get lost.

➤ Buy gas for the car before the tank is empty. Get regular oil changes and checkups.

➤ Keep food staples on hand so you can fix a fast meal without going to the store.

➤ Keep food, toilet paper and toiletries on hand so you never run out. The same goes for postage stamps, paper and envelopes.

➤ Keep duplicate keys for home, car and office in secure locations.

Retreat to recharge your spirit. Schedule private time every day: You deserve it. Unplug the telephone and enjoy a quiet evening alone or with your family, or even 15 uninterrupted minutes in the shower or bathtub.

You may want to spend a few minutes writing your feelings out in a journal. It can help you find a new perspective and relieve hidden conflicts.

Here are more spirit rechargers:

➤ Wear earplugs for instant peace anytime, anyplace.

➤ Learn a meditation technique. Two methods: Observe your thoughts as they pass through your mind. Or, repeat a word or phrase with an uplifting meaning.

➤ Practice progressive relaxation for 20 minutes twice a day to relieve high blood pressure and other physiological responses to stress. Tighten and release each muscle group in turn, starting with the soles of the feet and slowly working up to the scalp.

➤ Plan a weekend activity that is a change of pace. If your week is heavily scheduled, relax and enjoy noncompetitive activities. If you are never able to finish anything during the week, choose a project that you can complete in a few hours on Saturday or Sunday.

➤ Take time out for a diversion in the middle of your workday. When the pressures of completing a project are too great, your productivity can drop. Take a walk or stop for lunch.

Savor life's little delights. Give yourself some physical pleasure to help your stress slip away:

➤ Treat yourself to a professional massage, or trade massages with a loved one.

➤ Give yourself permission to enjoy a movie, watch a sports event, listen to music or read a book.

➤ Savor a soothing cup of chamomile herb tea with a dollop of honey. Chamomile has long been used to relieve nervous tension.

➤ Plan a day of beauty with a friend. Do each other's hair, or paint your nails and chat.

➤ Create a simple steam facial at home by boiling water. Remove the pan from the stove. Cover your head with a large towel so that it creates a tent over the pot. Steam your face for five or 10 minutes. Add aromatic herbs to the water for a sensual touch.

➤ Focus completely on any of the senses — hearing, seeing, eating or body movements — for a few minutes. Even washing your hands can become a sensual experience.

Use visualization and affirmation techniques. You can inoculate yourself against a situation you fear by going over the event in your mind. Imagine the scene in vivid detail and picture the best possible outcome.

➤ You can also shrink an imagined fear down to size by picturing the worst possible results. Imagine describing this worst case to your best friend the next day and the sympathy you receive. Imagine telling a group of friends the next month, who share their similar experiences. Finally, imagine joking about your unpleasant experience with a complete stranger a year later. If you carry this exercise through to the end, your stress will become something to laugh about.

➤ Replace negative self-talk with affirmations. The chatterbox in your mind is filled with gloom: You're too fat … you're too old … you'll never amount to anything. Like the little engine that could, nourish your mind with a constant stream of "I know I can."

Get enough sleep. Determine how much sleep you require for optimum performance. Sleep deprivation aggravates the body's responses to stress. Consider setting an alarm clock to remind yourself that it is time to go to bed.

Strive for your dreams. Plan ahead to meet your most cherished goals in life.

➤ Time management experts emphasize the importance of writing down your important goals.

Perfectionists

Aim for excellence, not perfection. Perfectionists are 75 percent more likely to get sick than other people.

Send your brain to the beach

Need a mini-vacation? Right now? We've got just the ticket for you. It's called visualization. You can relieve stress by retreating to a favorite place that exists in your imagination. Be prepared to spend 10 minutes to a half hour of time in a quiet room without any interruptions.

Lie down, or sit in a comfortable chair with both feet touching the floor and your hands lying lightly in your lap. Shut your eyes. Allow your breath to become quiet and peaceful. If you have time, start with a progressive relaxation exercise.

Now, imagine an outdoor scene. Do you love the fresh mountain air? Feel it caress your face. Smell the heady fragrances of wild herbs, and see the bright colors of wildflowers blooming on the hillside.

Do you prefer the ocean? Retreat to a peaceful beach, with white sand sparkling in the sunshine. Look at sea oats waving on the dunes in a slight breeze. Feel the heat on your skin. Where does your skin end and the invigorating sunlight begin? Hear the soothing sound of the ocean rolling in, one wave followed by another in a steady rhythm.

Imagine the scene in vivid detail. Attend to each of your senses and imagine what you would be seeing, feeling, smelling, hearing and tasting in this environment. Become aware of the landscape. You may imagine other people around you. Pretend you are an artist or a great detective and take note of every little thing about them.

Pay attention to your body. How are you positioned? What are you doing with your arms and your legs? Become aware of a deep feeling of relaxation spreading through all your muscles, bones and organs. Feel the rhythm of your breathing.

Enjoy your mini-vacation until you feel refreshed and reinvigorated. The physiological responses that we call stress are actually reduced as your muscles relax, your breathing becomes slow and regular, and your brain wave patterns change. After you have practiced this scene several times, you will be able to recall it in the middle of any stressful activity for relief from tension.

44 Easy Ways to Relieve Stress, Arborvitae Publications, Ann Arbor, Mich.
Creative Visualization, Whatever Publishing, Berkeley, Calif.

➤ Break big projects down into a series of small steps that you can work on every day. Want to change jobs? Make one phone call contact today. Is writing a book your dream? Commit to writing one page a day.

Knowing that you are striving toward your dreams relieves frustrations that mount when you feel stuck in a rut of endless responsibilities that seem to lead nowhere.

If you will use these 12 keys to stress relief, you can become a happier, healthier person, a more efficient worker, and a better friend to others. Keep a notebook as new ideas come to you through your reading and your own creativity. The most important key is your decision to take time for yourself and to simplify your life whenever possible.

44 Easy Ways to Relieve Stress, Arborvitae Publications, Ann Arbor, Mich.
Diet and Nutrition: A Holistic Approach, Himalayan Institute, Honesdale, Pa.
Herbs & Things: Jeanne Rose's Herbal, Grosset & Dunlap-Workman, New York
How to Be an Effective Speaker, NTC Publishing, Chicago
How to Get Control of Your Time and Your Life, Signet-New American, New York
52 Proven Stress Reducers, National Headache Foundation, 5252 N. Western Ave., Chicago, Ill. 60625
Science News (144,25/26:404)
The Physician and Sportsmedicine (22,7:66)

Stroke

Surviving a stroke

Surviving a stroke — the third leading cause of death in the United States — means knowing the warning signs. Be ready to call 911 or get to an emergency room if you experience any of these symptoms:

➤ A sudden weakness or numbness of the face, arm or leg on one side of your body.

➤ Sudden dimness or loss of vision, particularly in one eye.

➤ Loss of speech, or trouble talking or understanding speech.

➤ Sudden severe headache.

➤ Unexplained dizziness, unsteadiness or sudden falls.

These symptoms could mean that a stroke is on the way. Don't delay in getting help.

Strokes: A Guide for the Family, American Heart Association, 7272 Greenville Ave., Dallas, Texas 75231

When beauty salon shampoos turn deadly

Anyone who's ever suffered through the agony of a bad shampoo job at a beauty salon knows how miserable this experience can be. Fortunately, for most people the discomfort usually stops as soon as they sit upright.

But medical researchers are now warning that for certain high-risk individuals, a painful salon shampoo can be more than just a painful ordeal. It can bring on a life-threatening condition known as "beauty parlor stroke."

If you're an adult with an arthritic neck, high blood pressure or high cholesterol, keeping your neck tilted backwards at a sharp angle for long periods may be enough to seriously restrict blood flow to your brain and trigger a stroke.

Studies of older women who suffered strokes during shampooing indicate all the victims developed at least one of the classic symptoms of stroke, including dizziness, severe headache, nausea, vomiting, weakness on one side of the face and slurred speech. In some instances the disabilities were permanent.

Ask for an extra-gentle shampoo. For years, there's been a suspicion in the medical community that beauty salon clients were being injured by this traumatic manipulation of the neck and head. Now, doctors are strongly urging both customers and beauticians to take some common-sense precautions to avoid this potentially serious condition.

✘ Don't arch the neck backwards more than 15 degrees.
✘ Don't allow the head to tilt back for long periods of time.
✘ Don't twist or turn the head and neck while it is extended backward.

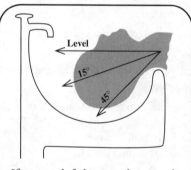

If your neck feels strained, your stylist may be pushing your neck back more than 15 degrees. Speak up and let her know you're uncomfortable.

Get to the doctor right away. If dizziness, headache or any signs of physical discomfort occur, see a doctor immediately. You significantly reduce your risk of permanent side effects if you receive treatment within the first six hours after experiencing symptoms. Your chance of having a stroke is greater if you smoke, take birth control pills, have diabetes, a damaged heart valve, clogged arteries or high blood pressure, or have recently had a heart attack.

Stroke is the third leading cause of death and the first leading cause of disability.

If you think you may be at risk for a beauty salon stroke, talk to your hairstylist about alternative ways of washing your hair. You may even want to wash it yourself in the shower before you go to the beauty salon.

Solving a medical mystery: The false stroke and the missing mineral

Some of the most baffling mysteries don't involve murder and mayhem — they involve health. Take the case of a high school football team that suddenly fell ill with strange and frightening symptoms.

Here's what happened: Young athletes, ages 15 through 18, practiced hard under the blazing south Florida sun. They ran, tackled, threw the football — and worked up a sweat. Some of the boys began to get leg cramps.

Their coach knew that calcium can be lost through perspiration. So, he reasoned, dosing the team with lots of calcium might relieve their muscle pains.

His good intentions almost proved fatal. Soon after taking calcium-rich pills, eight of the players showed all the signs of a stroke. They couldn't walk straight. They slurred their words, gasped for breath, then collapsed in convulsions. Thirteen other boys suffered weakness, headaches, blurred vision, nausea and muscle twitches.

Eventually, all the youngsters recovered. But what caused the bizarre symptoms in the first place? To find out, the Federal Food and Drug Administration (FDA) launched an investigation worthy of Sherlock Holmes. Food poisoning from a fast-food restaurant popular with the teen-agers was quickly ruled out. Were the vitamins tainted with poison or toxins? Tests revealed the answer was no.

Magnesium RDA
Men over 50 — 420 milligrams
Women over 50— 320 milligrams

Determined to solve the mystery, the researchers focused on a possible clue: The boys' symptoms were almost identical to those of grass tetany (GT), an animal disease that afflicts magnesium-deficient cows and horses. GT causes seizures and even death when the animals graze on calcium-rich spring grass.

Did the stricken youngsters lack enough magnesium in their diets? And, like animals with GT, did ingesting a whopping dose of calcium make that deficiency worse? FDA investigators studied the boys' eating habits and discovered that, like many teen-agers, the kids seemed to live off junk food. They seldom consumed nuts, cereals, dairy products and other magnesium-rich foods.

Like animals with GT, the FDA team concluded, it was only when the boys took in an excessive amount of calcium that their magnesium deficiency worsened to the point that serious symptoms developed. Here's why: Parathyroid glands, a group of cells located in your neck, produce hormones that keep blood calcium levels within a healthy range and help bones absorb the mineral.

However, overloading the body with a huge dose of calcium can throw this internal balancing act off — sending blood calcium levels up and magnesium

> ## Magnesium-rich foods
> Nuts
> Whole-grain cereals
> Peas and beans
> Green vegetables
> Bananas

levels down. It's not only youngsters who need to be aware of the danger of magnesium deficiencies and the role excess calcium can play in bringing on frightening, even life-threatening symptoms.

In one dramatic case, an elderly widow became confused, slurred her speech and could barely walk. Was it Alzheimer's disease? A stroke? Worried friends rushed her to a hospital where doctors discovered the 74-year-old woman was taking a calcium supplement, but no magnesium, and eating a nutritionally poor diet.

Tests showed her magnesium levels were dangerously low. Treated with magnesium injections, and later with supplements, the 74-year-old made a miraculous

A Natural Alternative

'Good fats' prevent strokes

You've probably heard that some fats are healthier than others. What you may not know is that some fats even reduce your risk of stroke. You can find some of the stroke-fighting fats in walnuts, soybean oil and canola oil.

Walnuts, soybean oil and canola oil contain alpha-linolenic acid. The more of this acid men have in their blood, the lower their stroke risk, according to a recent study at the University of California, San Francisco.

Researchers don't know exactly how alpha-linolenic acid works to prevent stroke, but they do know that omega-3 fatty acids come from alpha-linolenic acids. Omega-3 fatty acids keep blood clots from forming, so alpha-linolenic acids probably do too.

We've heard lots of good news lately about another fat — stearic acid. Stearic acid is the fat found in chocolate and juicy steaks. Several studies have shown that moderate amounts of stearic acid don't seem to raise your cholesterol. Some studies even show that it doesn't raise your stroke risk. Unfortunately, this new study said that the more stearic acid you have in your blood, the higher your risk of stroke. So the jury is still out on chocolate and steaks, but you can definitely reduce your stroke risk with a handful of walnuts or a tablespoonful of soybean or canola oil daily.

total recovery. While both the football players and the elderly woman suffered from too much calcium and not enough magnesium, that doesn't mean calcium is a villain. In fact, it is essential to good health and strong bones.

But the cases described above underscore the importance of a balanced, nutritious diet — and the wisdom in avoiding large doses of any supplement without your doctor's supervision.

Archives of Internal Medicine (151,3:593)

Stuttering

How to communicate with a person who stutters

Imagine this: You're trying to communicate with someone, but you keep tripping up on your words. To make matters worse, the person you're talking to keeps interrupting and trying to finish your sentences for you.

The frustration is all too familiar to people who stutter. Stuttering is not a nervous or personality disorder, but it can affect your personality and happiness if you aren't able to control it.

Get professional help. Getting help from a speech therapist as soon as possible is critical for children who stutter. Don't just assume a child will outgrow the problem. Testing can help determine whether she's likely to outgrow it or not.

Speak slowly. You can help a child who stutters by making a conscious effort to speak more slowly. Also, try to use words a child can easily imitate.

Be patient, and be a good listener. Don't interrupt or complete sentences for someone who stutters.

Don't be patronizing. Never say things like "slow down" or "relax."

Try not to seem uncomfortable. Don't look away when someone who stutters is talking to you. If you have questions about stuttering, politely ask them.

Don't pretend to understand. If you don't understand what the person has said, ask him to repeat it.

Incidentally, few people appreciate being labeled for a behavior. "Person who stutters" is a more considerate term than "stutterer."

Canadian Medical Association Journal (150,5:754)

TMJ

Turn off TMJ headache pain

At age 40, Angela Clark began waking up in the morning with terrible headaches. "I felt like someone slammed my head against the wall during the night," Angela remembers.

She tried aspirin; she visited her doctor. No one had any answers, and nothing relieved her throbbing pain.

Finally, her dentist told her that she had temporomandibular joint syndrome, commonly called TMJ. Basically, while Angela slept, she clenched her teeth together with a powerful force. She had no idea she did it, and she didn't know how to stop.

Teeth grinding and clenching are common causes of TMJ, a joint disorder of the jaw that often leads to severe headaches.

Some doctors estimate that up to 96 percent of adults and 15 percent of children have "bruxism," the official name for tooth grinding or clenching, at some point in their lives.

One common cause of TMJ is upper and lower teeth that don't fit together perfectly. Most people's teeth don't fit well, but Angela's square jaw and even teeth matched like a dentist's dream.

For her, that perfect fit just meant it was easier to bite down hard.

Teeth grinding can lead to other problems besides TMJ, such as mouth infections, worn-down teeth and sore necks and backs. Older people may develop painful arthritis in the overused jaw joint.

Bruxism is a problem that is difficult to cure, but there are some ways you can help yourself quit this harmful habit.

Think calm. Many people grind their teeth unconsciously in response to stress. On the surface, Angela Clark seemed to be handling problems at work and home well, but her inner tension was revealing itself while she slept.

Anything you can do to make your life less stressful will probably help you quit grinding your teeth. Give yourself an hour to relax before bedtime. You may want to seek counseling if you feel stressful circumstances are out of your control.

Examine your psyche. Bruxism may be a subconscious outlet for anxiety or anger. If you are very achievement-oriented and compulsively punctual, you're more likely to grind your teeth. Even a stressful event late in life, such as the loss of a spouse, can trigger bruxism.

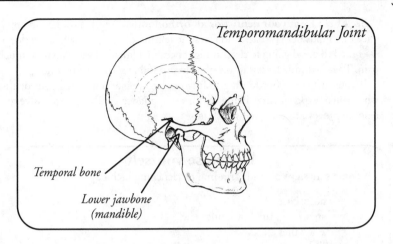

Temporomandibular Joint

Temporal bone

*Lower jawbone
(mandible)*

Ask your sleeping partner to wake you up. Sleeping partners don't have to grit their teeth and bear it when they hear you grinding your teeth. Waking you up will help you break the habit. (Don't ask your partner to describe what your tooth grinding sounds like. Doctors say the noise is almost impossible to make consciously.)

Close your lips, hold your teeth apart and relax your jaw. Do this 50 times a day. When you are comfortable with this exercise, picture yourself sleeping with your mouth in this relaxed position.

Clench your teeth for five seconds, then relax your jaw for five seconds. Do this exercise five times in a row, six times a day, for two weeks.

Change your sleeping position. Lying on your back with a pillow under your neck and knees may help relax your lower jaw. If you must sleep on your side, try piling pillows so that they support your shoulder and arm as well as your head. That position should take some of the strain off your neck and pressure off your teeth.

Create a stress-free home environment for child tooth grinders. Have a relaxed and enjoyable bedtime ritual. Talk about what happened during the day, especially about anything that may have scared or worried your child.

Get rid of allergy triggers. People with allergies, especially children, have a tendency to grind their teeth. It somehow helps relieve itching, sneezing and coughing. See the *Hay Fever* chapter for hints on how to control your allergies.

Be nice to your jaw. If your tooth grinding is causing your jaw to ache, try eating soft foods for a while, take aspirin or ibuprofen, and hold a heating pad to your jaw. Stop chewing gum, and avoid hard, chewy foods like caramels, tough meats, raw carrots and celery. Don't open your mouth too wide when you yawn either.

Seek help from your dentist or an orthodontist. Angela now has an appliance that holds her jaw back and eases the tension on her joint while she sleeps.

"I used to dread going to sleep at night because I knew I'd wake up in so much pain. That just added stress to my already stressful life. I'm past that now."

If you can't treat your tooth grinding or clenching at home, tell your dentist what you're experiencing. Being fit for an appliance can be an expensive and lengthy process, but it's well worth it.

Diagnose yourself

Some sure signs of teeth grinding or clenching include:

➤ headaches
➤ an aching, tired or tender jaw
➤ a jaw that clicks
➤ sharp pain when you yawn, talk or chew
➤ pain in your neck or shoulders or near your ears
➤ sensitive teeth

That toothache you think you have may just be a symptom of bruxism. Angela Clark's dentist gave her an appliance to wear that held her jaw open at night. Her headaches went away, and she eventually quit wearing the device. About a year later, she went back to the dentist, sure she had a bad tooth. "You'd think I would have known," Angela says wryly.

TMJ is easy to mistake for a simple earache too. Before you go to the ear specialist, put your little finger into your ear canal with the fingernail facing toward the back. Open and close your jaw. You will easily be able to feel the movement of your temporomandibular joint. If this causes you a lot of discomfort, you may have TMJ.

American Family Physician (49,7:1617)
Pain and the TMJ, American Academy of Otolaryngology, Alexandria, Va. 22312

Tooth Decay and Knocked-Out Teeth

Cavity crunchers: Foods that fight tooth decay

If strong, healthy teeth — and fewer dental bills — are important to you and your family, then the latest dental studies should really have you smiling.

Researchers have recently discovered a whole new group of cavity-fighting products. They're inexpensive, tasty and easy to use. And you'll find them at the grocery store — in the dairy case.

That's right! According to recent tests, certain dairy foods help slow cavity formation, replace calcium in enamel and, in some cases, relieve dental problems caused by a lack of saliva.

Have some milk and cheese. So if you find you can't brush after a meal — just follow it up with a glass of skim milk or a chunk of low-fat cheddar.

These dairy products can help protect against cavity-causing acids that attack your teeth.

Whenever you eat or drink carbohydrate-rich foods, such as breads and cakes, small particles get left behind on your teeth and gums.

And if those particles aren't removed, they'll eventually turn into the acids that cause tooth decay.

Soft, chewy foods and sticky liquids containing a lot of sugar and starch can really cause problems. Given enough time, the bacteria in your mouth will convert a cookie crumb or the residue of a soft drink into a massive dose of tooth-decaying acid.

Tests show that milk or cheese, eaten just before or after meals, can neutralize the effects of organic acids in several ways. As soon as they enter your mouth, these milk products help stimulate saliva production. And you need saliva. It's your body's best natural defense against decay.

Get a natural rinse with every swallow. Saliva acts as a mouthwash, rinsing away food particles every time you swallow. The chemicals in saliva also shield teeth and gums from acid corrosion.

And finally, after the acid attack is over, saliva helps replace important minerals that were stripped away from tooth enamel. Milk, yogurt and certain cheeses, such as mozzarella, Swiss, Edam, Monterey Jack, Gouda, cream cheese, processed American cheese and cheese spreads, also contain many of the same cavity-fighting chemicals as saliva. And that's good news for anyone who suffers from "dry mouth."

Dry mouth occurs when the body is unable to produce enough saliva — and it can be a serious problem. Many people, including a lot of older adults, develop dry mouth as a reaction to medications they are taking. Whatever its cause, reduced saliva flow can make you especially susceptible to gum infections and cavities. Fortunately, the ingredients in milk and many cheeses may provide dry mouth sufferers with some of the benefits of saliva — protection from acid buildup and replacement of calcium in tooth enamel.

Keep sugars from turning into acid. Finally, many cheeses and milks do more than just protect and harden teeth. Several experiments show that these dairy foods can actually interfere with the production of acid. Certain cheeses, eaten before or after a sugary snack, help keep sugars from turning into acid. Brushing, flossing and professional care will always be your best defense in the war on cavities.

But for a little extra protection against tooth decay, try a remedy that's easy and tasty — have a piece of cheese or a glass of milk.

Dairy Council Digest (65,1:1)
Nutrition News (56,1:1)
U.S. Pharmacist (19,5:16)

Saving a knocked-out tooth

You may not be a boxer or a hockey player. But you might lose a tooth in an accident some day — over two million teeth are knocked out each year in the United States. Your chances of keeping the tooth are best if you can get to a dentist within 30 minutes. In the real world, that isn't always possible.

Here's what to do if it happens to you.

Put the tooth back where it belongs. No matter where you are, you can greatly increase the odds of success by transporting your tooth to the dentist in the most logical place — its own socket. Grasp it by the crown (never touch the roots), rinse it off with water or salt water, and gently put it back in the socket.

Since living cells and tiny, fragile ligament shreds cling to the root, don't scrub or dry the tooth. Hold the tooth in the socket. If it won't stay in place, just hold it inside your mouth. When a young child knocks out his tooth, a parent should store the tooth in his own mouth.

Transport tooth in Hank's solution or milk. If putting the tooth in your mouth disturbs you, or if the tooth has fallen out and is dirty, there are other options you can try.

➤ Best option: Carry the tooth to the dentist in Hank's solution, which you can buy in the "Save-a-Tooth" kit. This liquid, which helps to restore tissue fibers, can preserve a tooth for several days, if necessary. It might be a good idea to keep some on hand, especially if you or your children play sports.

➤ Good option: Transport the tooth in cold milk. Milk's chemical makeup helps preserve the tooth, and the cool temperature will retard the growth of bacteria.

Leave baby teeth alone. "Baby" (primary) teeth should never be reimplanted. To do so can cause uneven bone growth and facial deformity. A temporary "tooth" can fill the gap if looks are a concern.

Generally, your chances of keeping a knocked-out tooth fall by about 1 percent per minute, starting the instant the tooth leaves the socket. So don't delay — this is one "knockout" where the outcome is very much up to you!

Emergency Medicine (25,15:27)

Ulcers

New ulcer cure works four times out of five

Got a stomach that's plagued by ulcers? More likely than not your doctor will treat it by prescribing a drug like Tagamet or Zantac or a foul-tasting antacid to stop the flow of acid in your stomach. If this doesn't work, your doctor may want you to have an operation to remove a large part of your stomach.

Even if these drugs help and you don't have to have an operation, your doctor may not tell you that you'll probably have to take stomach-acid reducers for the rest of your life. These drugs often reduce symptoms of chronic stomachache and ulcers without curing them.

Plus, a lifetime of taking these drugs can cost you a lot of money.

Get the permanent cure. Now there's a way to actually cure your ulcer instead of treating the symptoms for life. In the early 1980s, an Australian scientist began to believe that most ulcers are caused by a type of bacteria in your stomach, called *Helicobacter pylori*.

The medical world has been slow to accept the fact that most ulcers are caused by bacteria, but now the National Institutes of Health has even put out a recommendation about *H. pylori*. The NIH says if you have an ulcer and you are infected with the bacteria, you need to be treated for it. A simple, cheap treatment will kill these bacteria and cure your ulcer.

Give your ulcer a triple punch. All you need is a two-week treatment with two antibiotics and bismuth subsalicylate, better known as Pepto-Bismol. Doctors using the triple therapy of Pepto-Bismol and the antibiotics metronidazole (Flagyl) and tetracycline are reporting a 90-percent cure rate for their patients with ulcers. Recently, a group of researchers found they could heal most ulcers with just one week of antibiotic/bismuth therapy.

Pepto-Bismol, which you can buy without a doctor's prescription, may be all you need to cure simple indigestion. But for ulcers, Pepto-Bismol works best when taken briefly with two prescription antibiotics. Therefore, you'll need to get the cooperation of your doctor.

Test your blood for *H. pylori* antibodies. What if your doctor is skeptical and doesn't believe that something as simple and easy to cure as a bacterial infection could be the cause of a problem that has baffled doctors for decades? The solution is simple. Ask your doctor about taking a blood test, designed specifically to test for the *Helicobacter pylori* bacteria. New blood tests for *H. pylori* are very accurate and very inexpensive.

Once the presence of *Helicobacter pylori* is verified, your doctor can feel comfortable about prescribing the antibiotics which will clear up the illness, usually in two weeks or less, for good.

The American Journal of Medicine (97,3:265)
The New England Journal of Medicine (332,3:139)

Vision Loss

Leafy greens protect baby blues

Remember when you'd ask your mom why you had to eat your spinach?

"Because it's good for you," she'd say.

Well, as usual, mother knows best. Spinach and other leafy greens may help prevent age-related macular degeneration (AMD), the leading cause of vision loss in people over age 50. AMD is simply the deterioration of the part of the eye concerned with central vision, called the macula. The macula is located in the back center part of the eye and is actually part of the retina.

Here's how a healthy retina works

➤ The retina, made up of light receptors, gathers light.
➤ These receptors change light into electrical signals.
➤ The optic nerve carries these signals to the brain.
➤ The brain translates the signals into images.
➤ We see!

The macula contains the highest concentration of light receptors, and it enables us to see what is in front of us. If the macula can't do its job, peripheral vision remains intact, but central vision pays the price.

Two types of AMD can develop when the workings of the macula are thrown out of kilter. The more common, less serious form is known as "dry" AMD. It occurs when macular tissues begin to waste away. The more serious "wet" AMD occurs when tiny blood vessels begin to sprout under the macula.

By leaking blood, these blood vessels distort vision. Even though only 10 percent of AMD is "wet," 90 percent of all blindness results from it. Although researchers generally agree that AMD results from a nutritional imbalance, they haven't pinned down a more exact cause. What's more, AMD is irreversible. Because AMD often affects only one eye, many people don't realize they have it until their vision is significantly impaired.

Keep an eye out for symptoms. The good news is that if you detect AMD early, you can save your eyesight. Blurred vision and visual distortions (seeing straight lines as curved lines) are warning signs of AMD. If you experience these symptoms or if you need more light to read or your eyes take a long time to adjust to darkness, see your eye doctor.

But the most telltale sign is one or more spots in the center of the field of vision that move as your eyes move. These spots, called Drusen, are the built-up excretions of troubled retina cells. Your ophthalmologist can detect them during a routine eye exam. They look like slightly raised yellow/white dots.

Send spinach to the rescue. Now for the light at the end of the tunnel: Eat a lot of spinach! Spinach contains carotenoids, special nutrients which may prevent or slow the onset of AMD. Most of us have heard about the carotenoid beta carotene, which protects us from other ailments. But two different carotenoids, lutein and zeaxanthin, can help you avoid AMD.

In fact, studies show that if you eat lots of foods rich in lutein and zeaxanthin, you dramatically lower your chance of developing advanced AMD. Collards and spinach have the highest levels of lutein and zeaxanthin. But other green leafy vegetables, like kale, mustard and turnip greens, are also great sources of these carotenoids.

Pamper your precious vision. You can do other things to reduce your risk of AMD. Quit smoking, stay out of the brightest sun of the day, control your blood pressure, and have an ophthalmologist examine your eyes yearly once you turn 40. Perhaps the most important thing you can do is feature fruits and vegetables in your diet. Be sure to include lots of greens, especially those rich in carotenoids.

You will reduce your risk of macular degeneration (and heart disease). And you'll make your mom happy!

Science (146,20:310)
Senior Patient (2,9:39)
The Atlanta Journal/Constitution

Test your vision

The most simple way to test your vision for macular degeneration is to use the Amsler grid, found on page 345.

Hold the grid in front of you at a comfortable reading distance, about 12 inches away from your eyes.

Place one hand over one eye and look at the dot in the center of the grid. Now try the other eye. Do any lines look broken, distorted or wavy?

If they do, contact your ophthalmologist immediately.

Cover one eye while you check the other. Covering one eye is important because one good eye may compensate for an eye that's becoming damaged. Macular degeneration often affects only one eye.

Keep your grid in a conspicuous place, so you'll be reminded to check your vision daily. "Wet" AMD can progressively worsen in just a matter of days. And there is only a short time during which treatment may help.

This is why it's so important to check your vision daily and to contact your ophthalmologist immediately if your vision seems blurry or distorted.

Remember — the quicker you catch AMD, the better your chances of successful treatment.

Senior Patient (2,9:39)

Amsler grid

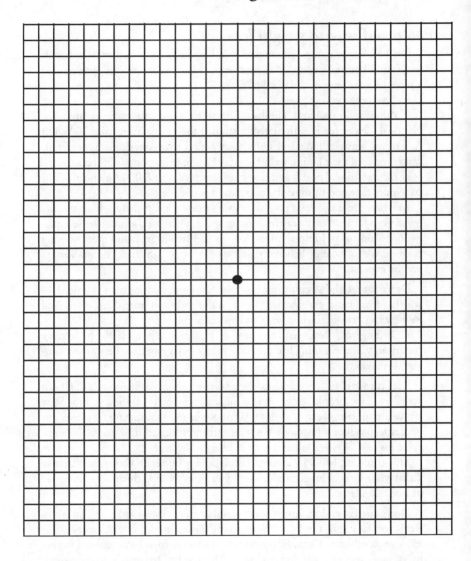

Weight Problems

Foolproof way to weight loss

Unlike a few years ago, you now live on low-fat foods — lots of baked potatoes (but no butter!), pasta, fruit, veggies and fat-free cookies. You even refused a piece of your own birthday cake.

So how come you've gained 10 pounds?

If this scenario sounds familiar, you aren't alone. Researchers from the National Center for Health Statistics studied the eating habits of 8,260 adult Americans between 1988 and 1991. They found that Americans have significantly reduced their fat intake but still packed on extra pounds in recent years.

In fact, a national health and nutrition survey of over 8,000 American adults concludes that one-third of the population is overweight.

So where are those extra pounds coming from? Unfortunately, it's not some mysterious fat-producing ray from outer space. There's a common-sense explanation: Many of us jumped on the low-fat diet bandwagon and quit counting calories. We mistakenly believed that if it's low-fat, it can't make us fat. Wrong, say the experts.

Don't forget about counting calories. Eat more calories than you need — whether from fat or carbohydrates — and the body will store them as fat. And eating excess calories is just what Americans are doing.

According to a National Institutes of Health study, by 1990 the average American was consuming hundreds more calories a day than he was consuming 10 years ago.

Eat fat to feel full. Some researchers believe eating small amounts of fat can actually keep people from overindulging on total calories. Ohio State University nutrition scientist John Allred points out that dietary fat causes our bodies to produce a hormone that tells our intestines to slow down the emptying process. We feel full and are less likely to overeat.

This could explain why adding a little peanut butter to your rice cake may satisfy your hunger longer and prevent you from wolfing down the whole bag of rice cakes later.

Don't cut fat and maintain your weight. Here's more surprising fat news: Reducing fat might not be as "heart-smart" as it sounds. Tufts University scientists recently put 11 middle-aged men and women volunteers on a variety of average, reduced and low-fat diets. The results? Extremely low-fat diets, which provided only 15 percent of fat from calories (a diet so strict it's almost impossible in real-life situations) did have a positive effect on blood cholesterol and triglyceride levels. But a reduced-fat diet, a more realistic way of eating, only affected those levels if accompanied by weight loss.

In fact, the investigators concluded, cutting fat without losing weight actually increased triglyceride levels and decreased high density lipoproteins (HDLs) — the "good" cholesterol that helps protect against heart disease.

Eat fat for a healthier body. So while excess fat isn't healthy, fat isn't a dirty word. Without some fat in our diets, our bodies couldn't make nerve cells and hormones or absorb the fat soluble vitamins (including A, D, E and K).

Certain fats, like olive oil and the omega-3 fatty acids found in salmon, may help prevent heart disease. And most people say a little fat simply makes food taste, look and smell more appetizing.

Determine your ideal weight. Just how much fat — and how many calories — should you eat to reach and maintain a healthy weight?

Since one answer won't work for everybody, you'll have to do a little figuring to find out how much fat and how many calories you can have. First, you need to determine your ideal weight.

Dr. Richard Freeman, vice-chairman of medicine at the University of Wisconsin in Madison, has developed a simple formula.

Calculate your calorie needs. Once you've determined your ideal weight, you can easily calculate how many calories you need each day. To get an accurate estimate, you need to take into account how active you are.

➤ If you are totally inactive and usually get no exercise, multiply your ideal weight by 11.
➤ If you get regular exercise two to three times a week, multiply your ideal weight by 13.
➤ If you get regular exercise four to five times a week, multiply your ideal weight by 15.
➤ If you get regular exercise six to seven times a week, multiply your ideal weight by 18.

On average, healthy adult men need between 2,000 and 3,900 calories a day and women need 1,200 to 3,000.

Figure your fat grams. Now that you know how many calories you need each day, you can easily figure out how much fat you can eat. Nutrition experts say that you should limit your daily fat calories to about 30 percent of your total calories. If you want to lose weight or if you have a history of heart disease or cancer, you should limit your daily fat intake to 20 percent of your total calories.

For example, if you're a 5-foot-4-inch woman with a medium frame, your ideal weight would be 120 pounds. If you're trying to lose weight, you'll want

The weight 'calculator'

Dr. Freeman's formula for figuring your ideal weight has two steps. First you figure your ideal weight based on your height, then you adjust that number to match your frame size. Don't consider the number you come up with to be carved in stone. You may weigh a little more or less depending on your age and activity level.

Women:

The ideal weight for a woman who is exactly 5 feet tall is 100 pounds. For every additional inch above 5 feet, add five pounds. If you are shorter than 5 feet tall, subtract five pounds for every inch you measure below 5 feet.

Next, you must determine whether you have a small, medium or large frame. Using a measuring tape, measure your wrist.

If your wrist measures exactly 6 inches, you have a medium frame and the weight number that you calculated earlier does not need to be adjusted.

If your wrist measures less than 6 inches, subtract 10 percent from your ideal weight.

If your wrist measures more than 6 inches, add 10 percent to your ideal weight.

Men:

The ideal weight for a man who is exactly 5 feet tall is 106 pounds. For every additional inch above 5 feet, add six pounds.

To determine whether you have a small, medium or large frame, measure your wrist.

If your wrist measures exactly 7 inches, you have a medium frame, and you do not need to adjust your ideal weight.

If your wrist is smaller than 7 inches, you have a small frame and should subtract 10 percent from your ideal weight.

If your wrist is larger than 7 inches, you have a large frame and should add 10 percent to your ideal weight.

Here's an example: If you're a 5-foot-11-inch man, your ideal weight would be 172 pounds. 106 + (11x6) = 172. If you have a large frame, you should add 10 percent to 172 to determine your adjusted ideal weight. Ten percent of 172 is a little over 17 pounds. Add that to your ideal weight of 172 for an adjusted ideal weight of 189 pounds.

Choices for a Healthy Heart, Workman Publishing, New York

to keep your fat calories down to about 20 percent. If you exercise two to three times a week, you would multiply your ideal weight by the number that matches your activity level, which in this case would be 13. Now you know that the total calories you need each day are 1,560.

Take 20 percent of 1,560 (1,560 multiplied by .20) to figure how many fat calories you can have, and you get 312. If you translate fat calories into fat grams, it will be very helpful when you're checking food labels. Simply divide your fat calories by 9 (the number of calories that one gram of fat contains). You could eat approximately 35 grams of fat a day.

If your ideal weight and your present weight don't match up, you'll have to adjust your total calorie consumption. In order to lose one pound, you'll have to eliminate 3,500 calories.

Lose a pound a week with the 500-calorie solution. You can easily lose a pound a week just by cutting 500 calories a day out of your diet. You can burn 250 of those calories with about 30 minutes of aerobic exercise, such as bicycling, dancing or walking. To get rid of the other 250, look for high-calorie foods you can easily eliminate from your diet, like mayonnaise, doughnuts and alcoholic drinks.

Keep track of your daily calories for a couple of days. This will help give you a better idea of where you can cut calories you don't really want or need.

You also want to make sure you don't let your calorie intake fall too low. Less than 1,200 calories for men and 900 for women can cause the metabolic rate to drop and make losing weight even harder. Consult your doctor before making any drastic changes in your diet. And remember, there's no magic way, including a low-fat diet, to lose weight.

But if you take a healthy, nutritious, calorie and fat-sensible approach, you can reach your goals — and still indulge in a piece of birthday cake once in a while!

Atherosclerosis and Thrombosis (14,11:1751)
Choices for a Healthy Heart, Workman Publishing, New York
Controlling Your Fat Tooth, Workman Publishing, New York
Healthy Weight Journal (9,3:45 and 8,5:86)
Journal of the American Dietetic Association (95,4:417)
Science News (146,4:53 and 146,13:195)
The Physician and Sportsmedicine (23,3:15)

Slim down your favorite recipes with fruit purees

The latest stand-in for butter or margarine is prune puree. Cooks from all over are creating culinary magic with this versatile fat buster.

Just mix up your favorite brownie, cake, cookie or bread recipe and substitute prune puree for the exact amount of butter, shortening or oil the recipe recommends.

Recipe for homemade 'lite' cheddar

Don't want to give up your favorite high-fat cheese? Make a low-fat version by zapping it in the microwave for a minute or two. Any oil you can pour off will significantly reduce the cheese's fat content. This method works well for fajitas, cheese sandwiches or cheese toppings on casseroles.

Nutrition Action Healthletter (20,3:13)

Consider that one cup of prune puree has 407 calories and one gram of fat, while one cup of butter has 1,600 calories and 182 grams of fat and one cup of oil has 1,944 calories and 218 grams of fat. Now you can begin to understand why bakers are so excited about prunes.

Prunes contain large amounts of pectin which helps hold in the air bubbles that make baked goods rise. Prunes also contain fairly large amounts of sorbitol, a sugar alcohol, which helps keep baked goods moist and gives them the flaky, tender taste of shortening or butter. To make enough prune puree for several recipes, mix one pound of dried, pitted prunes with one cup of hot tap water and puree in food processor. Keep your prune puree in a covered jar in the refrigerator.

For more information on cooking with prunes, send a stamped, self-addressed envelope to Prune the Fat, P.O. Box 10157, Pleasanton, CA 94588-0157. Applesauce and apricot purees are also good substitutes for butter and margarine in baked goods recipes. In some cases, you may only be able to replace three-quarters of the butter or margarine. Experiment to see which substitution works best for you.

The only drawback to using applesauce and apricots as fat substitutes is that these baked goods tend to become soggy and moldy within a day or two.

When baking with fat substitutes, use cake flour instead of all-purpose flour. This will help keep your baked goods tender. Also, be careful not to overbake fat-reduced recipes, which dry out more quickly than traditional variations that call for butter or oil.

ESHA Research Issues (8,4:5)

When you should exercise to burn the most calories

Very overweight people who are exercising to burn calories would get the most benefits from exercising after eating a meal. Your body has to work harder to digest food when you exercise on a full stomach. You use more calories during and just after exercising on a full stomach than during and just after exercising on an empty stomach.

On the other hand, don't despair if you prefer to exercise before you eat. Intense exercise will suppress your appetite for at least a half-hour. Your body doesn't want to be digesting food when it's still cooling down from a workout.

If you just need to lose a few pounds, waiting until after exercising to eat has its advantages.

➤ You burn extra calories for at least an hour and sometimes several hours after exercising. This is called "afterburn" or "excess postexercise oxygen consumption." (People who are obese don't get the same "afterburn" benefits as people who are not obese.)

➤ For about two hours after you exercise, your tired muscles need glycogen — their energy source. Carbohydrates and even candy bars eaten after exercising will be more easily converted to glycogen instead of being stored as fat.

➤ If you exercise vigorously, eating first will usually give you a stomachache. You'll probably find that you need an empty stomach to jog or do a hard workout.

The Physician and Sportsmedicine (21,11:89 and 23,4:16)

Easy 'OJ diet' might help you lose weight

The "OJ diet" has nothing to do with one of the great murder trials of the century. "OJ" just stands for "orange juice," and you've got the whole diet right in your supermarket produce section or chilled juice case.

When you should never eat

Don't eat while watching television. The average person eats eight times more food watching prime time TV than any other time.

A good time to eat the majority of your calories is in the morning. Adults who eat breakfast every day tend to weigh less and have lower cholesterol levels. The body's ability to burn calories is greater in the morning than in the afternoon or evening. People who skip breakfast tend to eat more high-fat snacks too.

Dairy Council Digest (64,2:7)
Food, Nutrition and Health (17,4:1)

It's simple: Scientists have discovered that water mixed with fructose suppresses your appetite better than glucose with water or even diet drinks. Fructose is the kind of sugar found in fruits.

Suppress your appetite naturally. Drink a glass of fructose-rich orange juice a half-hour to one hour before a meal, the investigators suggest. You'll eat fewer calories during the next meal and still feel comfortably full, indicates a Yale University researcher.

The diet drink, glucose-water and fructose-rich fruit juice all seem to work as appetite suppressants. It's just that fructose works better than sugar-water, and the glucose-water works better than drinks flavored with the low-calorie sweetener aspartame. Plain water was least effective of the four.

In the Yale study, overweight men who drank fructose-rich orange juice ate nearly 300 fewer calories at lunch. Overweight women consumed an average of 431 fewer midday calories. Their intakes were compared with similarly over-weight men and women who drank plain water before lunch.

Even when the participants switched fruit drinks, the results were the same. The people drinking the fructose-sweetened lemonade mixture ate fewer calories than those drinking the other lemonade-flavored mixtures.

Lose over 10 pounds a year. But what about the calories in the fructose drink itself? You might well ask. Since the fructose drink was about 200 calories, the net calorie suppression was about 100 to 230 calories per meal. That still puts the orange juice diet ahead of its glucose, aspartame and plain-water competition.

If only for one meal a day, that still adds up to a savings of 700 calories a week or 36,400 calories a year, certainly enough to make a difference over the long run. Long-term, slow weight loss is the healthiest form of weight loss for most people. The diet benefit, however, doesn't carry over to soft drinks sweetened with high-fructose corn syrup.

People who drank a lot of aspartame-sweetened diet drinks reduced their intake of calories from sugar more than those who gulped regular, high-fructose soda pop, says a report three months later in the same journal.

_____

The American Journal of Clinical Nutrition (51,3:428 and 51,6:963)

Yeast Infections

10 steps to keep the yeast away

Have you experienced the symptoms before — the annoying vaginal itch and thick, milky discharge? Was that first attack irritating, maybe even frightening? If you've suffered through just one "yeast" infection, you certainly don't want to go through it again.

But don't despair. While there is no permanent cure, there is good news. Here are the basic facts:

First-timers, see a doctor. You may have heard that itching and discharge signal the start of infection. But did you know that some women also experience soreness or rashes in the vaginal area, even pain during urination or intercourse? And did you know that other, more serious conditions, like sexually transmitted diseases, can have some of the same symptoms?

Don't make the mistake of self-diagnosis when those first symptoms appear. You could be headed for trouble if you're treating the wrong disease.

See your doctor. Remember, it often takes laboratory tests to know for sure.

Understand your risk. What are your chances for a yeast infection? To get some idea of what puts you at risk, you need to understand how and why a very small "yeast" can become so much trouble. At any given time, different areas of your body may be harboring colonies of *Candida*, the tiny fungus cells responsible for yeast infections.

Usually, that's no problem. When you're healthy, your body's various defense systems are quite capable of handling these little organisms. But when your immune system is weakened, fungus cells can quickly launch an invasion, especially in the genital tract, where there's plenty of warmth and moisture.

Stress, both mental and physical, hormonal changes from pregnancy or birth control, diabetes, common viruses and HIV are just a few conditions that can put your immune system "out-of-order."

Even the medication you took to cure another infection may be a problem. Some antibiotics are so strong they destroy both "good" and "bad" bacteria in your body. And you need those good bacteria. They're the first line of defense against fungal growth.

Keep your "cool." Sometimes you can't avoid the problems that leave your immune system vulnerable to infection. But you certainly don't need to make it easier for yeast to take hold. A yeast cell in your vaginal tract will thrive with extra heat and moisture. And unless you take a few precautions, you could be providing a very "warm welcome" for the next fungal invasion.

Blow it dry. Keep the area around your thighs and crotch as dry as possible. Take extra time to towel off after a shower, especially in the summer. You may want to use your blow dryer on a low setting to help dry your genital area after you bathe or shower. Change out of that damp bathing suit as soon as possible too. If you don't, you are inviting trouble.

Dress loose and cool. Try to avoid fabrics that keep moisture trapped against your skin. Summer or winter, the right clothes can make a healthy difference. First, wear cotton panties.

Second, don't wear pantyhose or tight clothes every day. Synthetic fibers in panty hose and underwear, even the heavy fibers in very tight-fitting jeans, won't draw dampness away from your body. Loose, cool and dry — that's the prescription for smart dressing.

Wipe from front to back. Wiping front to back when you use the toilet will help keep the bacteria in your rectum away from your vagina.

Don't douche. And don't use feminine hygiene sprays, deodorant sanitary pads or tampons, bubble bath, or colored or perfumed toilet paper. All of these products can change the acidic environment in your vagina, and that allows the yeast to grow.

Eat yogurt to ward off bacteria. Wouldn't it be great if you could just take a "spoonful of medicine" to stop yeast growth before the infection ever got started?

Unfortunately, experiments taking this approach have had limited success.

However, some studies suggest that eating live bacteria found in yogurt might ward off fungal growth.

Buy an over-the-counter anti-fungal medicine. But for now, your best answer is medication that you apply after the symptoms appear. Inexpensive, nonprescription anti-fungal drugs usually destroy most yeast cells in just a few days. To make sure the infection is really cleared up, you should use the full supply of medicated inserts or suppositories as directed.

And always heed the manufacturer's warnings — if the symptoms don't improve within three days, see your doctor. Don't let the problem drag on.

It could be a lot more serious than a yeast infection.

_____
American Family Physician (51,7:1723)
FDA Consumer (27,10:10)
Medical Tribune (33,6:25)

Index

A

A&D Ointment, 45
Abdominal aortic aneurysm, 254
Accutane, 6
ACE inhibitors, 60
Acetaminophen, 101
  for arthritis, 13
  for headaches, 197-198
Acid rebound, 215
Acne, oatmeal bath for, 159
Acupressure, 264
  for morning sickness, 270
Acupuncture, 102
Agoraphobia, 286
Alcohol
  colds and, 105-106
  conditions caused or worsened by
    altitude sickness, 4
    asthma, 27
    bad breath, 40
    breast cancer, 63
    cataracts, 89
    colon cancer, 113
    diabetes, 13
    enlarged prostate, 165
    frostbite, 185
    gout, 16
    hangover, 190-191
    heartburn, 213
    insomnia, 246
    nosebleeds, 273
    osteoporosis, 277
    psoriasis, 299
    snoring, 318
    stomach cancer, 321
Allergies, 26, 191-196
  Beano and, 188
  food. *See* Food allergies
  hair dyes and, 247-248
  hives from, 223-224

latex, 176
  tooth grinding and, 337
Aloe vera, 119-120, 160
Altitude sickness, 4-5
Aluminum
  Alzheimer's disease, 6-8
  antacids containing, 8
Alzheimer's disease, 5-8
  aluminum, 6-8
  aspirin for, 7
  dialysis and, 7
  zinc and, 5-7
AMD (age-related macular degeneration), 342-344
Amsler grid, 344-345
Anemia, 171
  caffeine and, 74
  folic acid and, 14
  hair loss and, 189
Angina, 9-10
  body suit for, 10
  tachycardia and, 247
Ankle sprain, 11-12
Antacids, 215, 341
  aluminum in, 8
Antibiotic(s)
  acne treated by, 3
  blisters treated by, 44
  creams, 121, 123
    for shingles, 303
  sinus infections treated by, 310
  ulcers cured by, 342
  yeast infections and, 353
Antihistamines, 196, 310
  hives relieved by, 224
Antioxidants, 207
  prostate cancer and, 295
Antiperspirants
  aluminum in, 8

and salt substitutes, 55
Potassium bicarbonate, 281
Potbelly, 289-290
Powder, to prevent blisters, 45
Pregnancy
 caffeine and, 74, 77-78
 conditions associated with
  back pain, 39
  blood clots, 48
  carpal tunnel syndrome, 83
  high blood pressure, 54
  incontinence, 233-236
  morning sickness, 268-270
 electric blankets and, 239-240
 hair loss after, 189
 infertility and, 237-240
 salt intake and, 55
 vaccinations when planning, 231
Pritikin program, 50
Prostate
 cancer of, 293-298
 enlarged, 165-166
Prostatitis, 295
Protein, 130
 calcium and, 280-281
Prozac, 275-276
Prune puree, 349-350
Psoriasis, 124, 298-300
Psychiatric problems, OCD, 274-276
Psyllium, 94-95, 115, 323
Pulmonary embolism, 47-49
Purees, fruit, 349-350
Purines, 16

R

Range-of-motion exercises, for
 arthritis, 22
Rash
 from arnica, 15-16
 from loofah sponge, 159-160
 from poison ivy and oak, 288
 from whirlpool folliculitis, 161
Raynaud's syndrome, 185, 300-302
Rebound effect, from painkillers,
101,198
Rectum, bleeding from, 220-221
Red wine fatigue, 173
Reflux, gastroesophageal, 212-215
Relaxation techniques, 286-287, 293,
325-326, 328, 330
 for Raynaud's syndrome, 301
Repetitive motion injuries, 83
Retina, 342-343
Rheumatoid arthritis, 17, 19
Rockerboard, for ankle sprains, 12
Roughage. See Fiber
Rubella shot, 231
Ruptured disk, 33-34

S

SAD (Seasonal Affective Disorder),
.128
Sage, 82
Saliva
 cavities and, 339-340
 dry mouth and, 155-156
Salmonella, 178
 arthritis and, 18
Salt
 and asthma, 27
 and carpal tunnel syndrome, 84
 and high blood pressure, 52-54
 and Meniere's disease, 152
 and sweating, 218
Salt resistance, 56
Salt sensitivity, 54-55
Saturated fat, 91, 99-100
 diabetes and, 138
Scarring, 119, 221
Sciatica, 39
Scrapes, 120-122
Seafood, asthma and, 27
Selenium, 66-67, 294
Senility, 180-181. See also Alzheimer's
 disease
Serotonin, 129-130
 migraines and, 264-267
Sexual activity
 drugs that affect, 257-258